Sociology and Critical Inquiry
The Work, Tradition, and Purpose

ADVISING EDITOR IN SOCIOLOGY
Charles M. Bonjean
University of Texas–Austin

Sociology and Critical Inquiry
The Work, Tradition, and Purpose

John Walton

Department of Sociology
University of California–Davis

The Dorsey Press
Chicago, Illinois 60604

Cover photo by David Robbins. "Along the Waterfront." Records of the
Works Projects Administration, National Archives (69-ANP-13-P759-70)

ISBN 0-256-03409-5
Library of Congress Catalog Card No. 85–72697

Printed in the United States of America

1 2 3 4 5 6 7 8 9 0 ML 3 2 1 0 9 8 7 6

A number of long quotations appear in the book with the kind permission of
the publishers: Chapter 2, page 46, from *The Grapes of Wrath*, by John
Steinbeck. Copyright 1939, renewed © 1967 by John Steinbeck. Reprinted by
permission of Viking Penguin, Inc.

Chapter 3, pages 84–85. Copyright 1982, Los Angeles Times. Reprinted
by permission.

Chapter 7, pages 267–68 and 269–70, from *The Sovereign State of ITT*, by
Anthony Sampson. Copyright © 1980 by Stein & Day. Pages 273–301 and
305–306, copyright © 1984 by The New York Times Company. Reprinted by
permission. Page 288, copyright © 1979 by *The Wall Street Journal*.

Prologue

In the pages that follow I attempt something unusual by way of an introduction to sociology. I try to present the method and a strong dose of the substance of modern sociology in a manner that is both accessible to the general reader and faithful to the discipline. I want to portray the best work of professional sociologists and carry it forward to matters of public concern, rather than tone it down for indifferent consumption. That is possible, I believe, for two reasons.

First, sociology is a lively subject that engages people of diverse occupations and avocations. It enjoys the distinction among academic disciplines of addressing matters that involve a broad public similarly devoted to understanding pieces of the social order. Sociologists and journalists conduct surveys or opinion polls trying to fathom public moods. Sociologists and lawyers study the development and application of laws. There is a sociology of medicine, welfare, occupations, art, and many more. Sociologists theorize about the roots of social order and conflict, as do others who reflect on, say, the causes of crime or family dissolution. Indeed, many sociological explanations bear a close resemblance to lay theories and vice versa. Many of sociology's central problems coincide with important dilemmas of public policy and social ethics.

Second, sociology is intrinsically lively. Its investigative methods have the intrigue of detective stories. Its results turn up bracing refutations of common assumptions. Its diagnoses have been incorporated into public policies on social welfare and reform. We all experience society and share in the perplexities of how to explain it. We can see our collective selves in social research about the changing structure of social classes, jobs, leisure, or cities and suburbs.

This book is written for people who are curious about explanations for social phenomena. I address students and the more elusive educated public who come to sociology out of their own curiosity. I hope to reach that audience without condescending or holding back important ideas because they defy oversimplification. Yet I have written this book for newcomers to sociology, avoiding jargon and the professional idiom in favor of clear language and fertile examples.

This is a book with a purpose. The phrase "critical inquiry" in the title means that the book takes a critical stance on sociology and society. I am critical of social inequality meted out along lines of social class, race, gender, and prestige. Similarly, I criticize varieties of sociology that ignore inequality by celebrating a vaguely alternative "value integration" or justify it according to some "function" it presumably performs in society. More importantly, critical sociology differs from a descriptive, applied, or theoretical sociology by going to the roots of historical and contemporary social practices. Critical sociology is not always grim. It also looks for alternatives to pernicious social practices, particularly those alternatives fashioned in the struggles of classes and communities.

Each succeeding chapter develops this central idea from a different point of view. I begin with a description and set of illustrations about how sociologists actually do their work—what the sociological method means in practice and the unity of this method across a range of techniques appropriate to different research problems. The second chapter is a concise history of sociology, suggesting that the discipline enjoys a classical tradition and a distinctive perspective on the world. Sociology is not a new science. The classical tradition began with the inheritors of the French Revolution, was perfected in different ways by Karl Marx and Max Weber, refashioned for North American use by Thorstein Veblen and C. Wright Mills, and is alive in sociological practice today. The subseqent chapters clarify this perspective by applying it to specific topics. Chapters 3 and 4 develop the crucial concepts of social class and status group—the fundamental dimensions of social organization and inequality. Here, as in most of the chapters, the concepts and explanations are developed in close connection with historical and contemporary society. Chapter 5 adds a third key element too often ignored in sociological analysis; namely, the state, which mediates political struggles over class and status, assuming some autonomy in the process. Chapters 6 and 7 chart a course of social change from rural to urban life and describe how today's urban societies are increasingly ensnared in a world system that affects the individual's daily life. Finally, Chapter 8 explains how efforts to control society are implemented along lines of privilege, how those efforts change, and how people resist or rebel against them.

This book began as an effort to convey a sense of the sociological craft to a wide audience. That proved more demanding and time-consuming than I had anticipated. In the process of revising the original manuscript I received helpful criticism from my colleague Gary Hamilton and the reviewers for The Dorsey Press who commented on draft chapters: Beverly Burris, Shelley Coverman, Peter Heller, Vincent Jeffries, and George Kilpatrick. I am especially grateful to Edwin Lemert, who shared his demurs with my critical treatment of the North American Sociology that he has done so much to help build. I appreciate his friendship and example. As consulting editor for The Dorsey Press, Charles Bonjean has been unfailingly supportive and generous with his advice.

Contents

List of Tables

List of Figures

1

Sociological Work

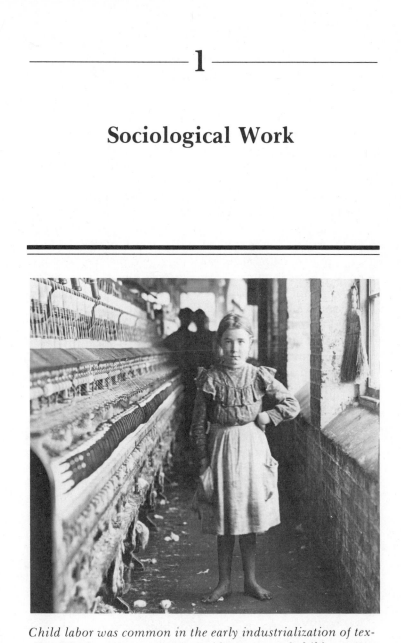

*Child labor was common in the early industrialization of tex-
tiles. The low wages factories paid women and children offset
the costs of expensive new machines and kept profits high.
(Culver Pictures, Inc.)*

PART I
ESSENTIALS OF THE CRAFT

Sociology is many things: a body of knowledge about society to those who study it, a discipline for those who follow it, a practice for those who apply it, a plan for social reorganization for those who revere it, and a pretentious restatement of common sense to those who criticize it. For those who do it, sociology is a type of work, a craft like many others. The best introduction to what sociology is, and how each of these descriptions fits into a general appreciation, begins with a look at how sociologists go about their work—the methods and products of their craft.

A common criticism of sociology, one that reveals much about public perceptions and professional aims, is that sociology is just common sense—conventional wisdom in pedantic guise. Long ago an ingenious rebuttal was provided by Paul Lazarsfeld, late of Columbia University and a pioneer in the work of its Bureau of Applied Social Research. The bureau was the first important university social research center in the United States and it carried out a number of path-breaking studies of voting, mass communication, and opinion formation beginning in the 1940s. Under the direction of Samuel Stouffer and Lazarsfeld, this research was largely responsible for the development of public-opinion polling, now a major industry and a source of political influence in its own right.

Lazarsfeld was a German immigrant who joined the Information and Education Branch of the Army of the United States, also headed by Stouffer during World War II. With a team of social scientists, they conducted an enormous study of morale and adjustment in the armed services which was published in four volumes under the title, *The American Soldier: Studies in Social Psychology in World War II* (1949–50). The study typified what has been criticized as a social science boondoggle; an expensive and long-term binge of fact-gathering by a team of so-called experts whose end result was just common sense. Lazarsfeld's response to the criticism began by openly acknowledging that sociology does sometimes produce findings that sound like common sense, and he went on to list some results, followed by the conventional reasoning that would have led one to expect them:

1. Better educated men showed more psychoneurotic symptoms than those with less education. (The mental instability of the intellectual as compared to the more impassive man-in-the-street has often been commented on.)

2. Men from rural backgrounds were usually in better spirits during their army life than soldiers from city backgrounds. (After all, they are more accustomed to hardships.)

3. Southern soldiers were better able to stand the climate in the hot South Sea Islands than Northern soldiers. (Of course, Southerners were more accustomed to hot weather.)

4. White privates were more eager to become noncoms than Negroes. (The lack of ambition among Negroes is almost proverbial.)

5. Southern Negroes preferred Southern to Northern white officers. (Isn't it well known that Southern whites have a more fatherly attitude toward their "darkies"?)

6. As long as the fighting continued, men were more eager to return to the States than they were after the German surrender. (You cannot blame people for not wanting to get killed.) (Paul F. Lazarsfeld, "The American Soldier: An Expository Review," pp. 379–80).

Behind this list lurks the question, "Was it worth all the time, effort, and money to produce such commonplace results?" or, "Didn't we know all this before the experts went out and rediscovered it?" Lazarsfeld, expecting that kind of reaction, had a surprise in store. "Every one of these statements is the direct opposite of what was actually found" (p. 380). For example, the better-educated soldiers showed *fewer* signs of neurosis than the less-educated, blacks were *more* eager for promotion than whites, soldiers were more anxious to go home *after* the fighting was over than while it was going on, and so forth.

The real point of the demonstration, however, is not that the true results just mentioned are great discoveries either. Assuming that we are not being fooled this time, a commonsense rationale can be as easily adduced for each true result. Educated people, one might speculate, are better able to cope with frustration and less likely to become neurotic owing to their experience in dealing with difficult new situations and their knowledge of bureaucratic procedures. An urban background, including exposure to a variety of social groups, might be better preparation for military life than a quiet rural upbringing. Blacks would take to the less discriminatory armed forces setting and strive for advancement more than in civilian life where they knew opportunities would be denied them. Lazarsfeld's point, then, is that after-the-fact common sense is capable of explaining or providing a rationale for almost anything, but before the facts are known, common sense supports all manner of contradictory conjecture. Common sense, as Bertrand Russell observed, is vague, cocksure, and often wrong.

CONCEPTS AND DISCOVERY

In the interest of uncovering something fundamental about sociological method, this material can be profitably pursued beyond Lazarsfeld's moving demonstration. For just as Lazarsfeld demolished one myth about sociology, he helped to build another.

Lazarsfeld belonged to a generation of sociologists who fancied themselves hard-headed scientists whose primary job was the discovery of social facts. As an inveterate methodologist, Lazarsfeld was convinced that research provided the bricks out of which sociological theory is constructed. The first order of sociological work, accordingly, is the discovery of those facts. Many like-minded sociological positivists believe that the discipline will not achieve its scientific potential until a solid inventory of fact is created to provide the elements from which any generalization may be cautiously assembled and evaluated.

It is no surprise that popular conceptions of sociology have assimilated this view, and having heard that sociologists are in the business of discovering unknown facts about society, respond with understandable criticism when elaborate studies turn up nothing new. The trouble is that this simple (empiricist) view of the sociological enterprise is mistaken in the first place. Sociological reasoning and research are not matters of discovering the unknown or of fabricating theoretical chimneys from factual bricks. Rather, sociology is a matter of making interpretive sense of facts, new and old. Sociological work involves essentially producing ideas.

Facts to Concepts

The results of *The American Soldier* (Lazarsfeld, 1949) are a case in point. Following the publication of the volumes, Lazarsfeld's colleagues at Columbia, especially Robert Merton and Alice

Rossi, began to reflect on the more general meaning of these facts. They were drawn to the study's repeated demonstration that the amount of deprivation soldiers felt for having been inducted into the Army (as most were) depended upon their social status and whom they compared themselves to. Older and married men, for example, felt more resentment about their induction than the younger and unmarried. The reason was that the older and married soldiers knew more people who had been granted deferments and compared themselves to those exempted from service. Similarly, soldiers who remained in the States felt less deprivation than those sent overseas, who, in turn, considered themselves better off than overseas combat soldiers. Black soldiers stationed in the South felt themselves much better off than the black civilians who lived in the South. In short, deprivation was a relative matter, depending on individual comparisons with "like-statused" people (other married men, other blacks, and so forth).

This was well understood by the authors of *The American Soldier* who used the term *relative deprivation* to explain many of their results. But Merton and Rossi were more ambitious: "By provisionally generalizing these concepts, we may be in a position to explore the wider implications of the materials for social theory" (p. 226). The first step toward generalizing these results consisted of replacing relative deprivation with a broader concept (a shorthand summary for a large number of similar observations). The concept "reference group" was chosen for several reasons. Merton and Rossi noted that relative deprivation was a rather narrow psychological notion referring mainly to the individual and not really exploring the question, relative to whom is deprivation felt? other than the blanket allusion to others of like status. In a meticulous review of the original study, they discovered that individual soldiers compared themselves and their social status (for example, their education or marital status) with a variety of social groups, some of which they held membership in (other married men) and others in which they placed themselves vicariously (Southern black civilians), all for the purpose of deciding how well-off they were relative to others. Deprivation, therefore, depended upon which of many possible groups individuals turned to as reference points or relevant standards of comparison.

The more general question was not so much that soldiers felt deprivation, but how much they felt as a function of which reference groups they selected as most pertinent to their circumstance (itself a composite of their social status and present situation). The reference group provided a *sociological construct* with more explanatory potential than the psychological idea of relative deprivation because it captured the many kinds of comparisons that soldiers actually made and linked individual judgments to the social context.

In the end, Merton and Rossi rest their claim for the superiority of reference group theory on its ability to explain the results of *The American Soldier* (which its authors attributed to relative deprivation) and, also to explain some of the authors' results that contradicted their own explanation. Among several illustrations of the latter, Merton and Rossi review the data on those soldiers ready to get into an actual battle zone. People facing the prospect of combat were divided into three categories: new units of green troops, combat veterans, and green replacement troops integrated into experienced units. On the original authors' presumption of like-statused comparisons, all of the green troops (whether in their own new units or in ones that integrated green and experienced troops) would be expected to show a similar enthusiasm or reluctance to enter combat.

In fact, however, 45 percent of the green troops in new units wanted to get into combat, while only 15 percent of the weary veterans and 28 percent of the green replacement troops were so disposed. The replacement troops, therefore, resembled less the similar status (green) group than they did their new associates, the veterans (measured by the 28 percent figure). In other words, the green replacement troops fell between the other two groups, but closer to the seasoned veterans. The idea of relative deprivation alone does not explain this. According to that reasoning, all of the green troops (whether in their own units or as replacements in experienced units) should have had the same feelings about entering combat. Merton and Rossi concluded that a more general theory of reference groups explained the difference on the premise that "insofar as subordinate or prospective group members are motivated to affiliate themselves with a group, they will tend to assimilate the sentiments and conform with the values of the authoritative and prestigeful stratum of that group" (p. 254).

So stated, the principle is intended to apply to a wide variety of situations; to constitute, therefore, a non-common sense generalization that can be drawn from the original study. In a less wordy rendition, Merton and Rossi are saying that newcomers assume the attitudes of prestigious group members rather than those of persons in the same objective circumstance. Returning to the matter of common sense, does the new proposition say anything that we did not already know? I think it does. Illustratively, none of us would be surprised by a pronouncement from public school officials to the effect that black children are pessimistic about the value of education for their occupational futures, a "fact" justifying special programs in the schools to encourage optimism in black children. But suppose, as Merton and Rossi imply, that black children in integrated schools turn out to be nearly as optimistic as all the other children and that pessimism is less a matter of being black than of attending segregated schools. The second "fact" (which we have reason to believe is true) would be revealing by the standards of common sense and, just as important, would carry very different policy implications for programs of educational reform.

Discovery to Invention

The larger point in this discussion of reference groups is that the distinctive sociological contribution comes not with the uncovering of certain facts (a valuable task that journalists, pollsters, and others do very well), but with tracing the implications of facts to a new and fruitful interpretive idea. If there is a discovery involved in this, it is the discovery of a new idea. The reference group is one such idea, and one that has come in for much debate and critical research, which is appropriate if it is doing its job. The essential work of sociology, far from simply discovering facts or coining terms, lies in the invention of concepts and in reasoning and conducting research about their implications. The point is gracefully stated by Howard S. Becker (1982):

> I think it generally true that sociology does not discover what no one ever knew before, in this differing from the natural sciences. Rather, good social science produces a deeper understanding of things that many people are already pretty much aware of...[the virtue of any analysis] does not come from the discovery of any hitherto unknown facts or relations. Instead, it comes from system-

atically exploring the implications of [a] concept. (Howard S. Becker, *Art Worlds*, p. x)

Strictly speaking, then, sociology does not "discover what no one ever knew before," but sometimes it does, in a weaker sense of discovery, produce unexpected results. It uncovers certain facts whose charm is mainly in the refutation of complacent common sense. Debunking myths is a useful result of social research. Sociology also reveals relationships that no one had thought much about previously. Both sources of revelation account for some of the adventure in doing and reading about social research. Research may also produce expected results, which is reassuring once we have become skeptical about common sense. At its characteristic best, however, sociology fashions concepts that organize all these facts and generate from them implications which, in sometimes quite unexpected ways, produce new explanations of social phenomena. Sociologists do not haphazardly blunder into great finds or pile up pure facts until the pile sprouts the flower of an idea. On the contrary, they labor over closely focused problems and search for that just-right concept that will catch the essence of a process and at the same time suggest a set of implications about its operation. This is the fundamental objective of sociological inquiry and the goal that research methods must serve if they are to be anything other than technical exercises. In place of fact-gathering or discovery, Arthur L. Stinchcombe (1968) has provided a more appropriate phrase and image for sociological work. Sociological accounts of the world, "theory" in a practical sense, "ought to create the *capacity to invent explanations*" (p. 3).

METHOD

Beyond inventing concepts and explanations for social phenomena, sociologists spend a good deal of their time determining whether those are true. Ideally, the sociological method generates or assembles factual evidence in a purposeful manner; it evaluates concepts, follows implications from the arena of reasoning to results, and then tests the explanations. When such conceptual tools are not yet available, social research may perforce undertake exploratory missions with the aim of finding evidence that will inform new concepts. In any case, method involves a series of logical and procedural steps that link concepts and explanations to facts. Method is a bridge between the two realms of reasoned interpretation and fact.

Technique and Method

There is an important difference between method in this sense and research procedures or techniques. There is also a regrettable, even misleading, tendency to equate the sociological method with a series of techniques—an unfortunate habit in textbooks and specialized writing to separate methodology from other (substantive) sociological work and to treat method exclusively as a statistical or technical problem. In a proper sense, however, there is one *sociological method* and a number of useful techniques or research strategies which, in a given study, appropriately implement that method. Some of these strategies are illustrated in the sections that follow and need only be characterized here.

The *sample survey* is the most conventional research strategy and involves obtaining responses to a standard questionnaire from a systematically chosen sample of people representing some population. In situations where greater intimacy or flexibility are desired, researchers employing *participant observation* enter social group settings, thoroughly recording events and conversations in their own research journals. Sociologists do research with previously, perhaps officially, collected information such as the census of population using *archival* sources; and they move into the recesses or archives, into museums, records, and diaries, to do *historical* research.

The practical strategies of sociological method are as varied as its problems and imagination. Another source of the adventure in research lies in inventing ways to get at recalcitrant information. Some sociologists put college sophomores through laboratory experiments while others interview heads of state; some live in urban ghettos and others at the computer center. In any case, the value of the research strategy depends on whether its evidence informatively and critically addresses the concepts and explanations invented in sociological work. A good bridge is firmly anchored on two sides of some otherwise unnavigable expanse and good method insures brisk traffic between explanations and evidence.

In general, then, there is only one sociological method, although there are many strategies for implementing that method. The philosopher Abraham Kaplan (1964) has done us a service by distinguishing among different meanings of methodology. One of those is "technique" in the sense of the social survey or statistical procedure just mentioned. Another Kaplan calls "honorifics" or statements about what constitutes *the* scientific method. Third, "methods" per se are more precisely construed as:

> Logical or philosophical principles sufficiently specific to relate especially to science as distinguished from other human enterprises and interests... such procedures as forming concepts and hypotheses, making observations and measurements, performing experiments, building models and theories, providing explanations, and making predictions. (Abraham Kaplan, *The Conduct of Inquiry*, p. 23)

Methodology unavoidably involves all these things, but a practical emphasis on the last enables appreciation of method as a general way of proceeding with social science research that distinguishes it from other kinds of inquiry and provides a standard for evaluating the fruits of that inquiry. "In sum," Kaplan says with refreshing clarity, "the aim of methodology is to help us understand, in the broadest possible terms, not the products of scientific inquiry, but the process itself" (p. 23).

Why Questions

The sociological method is, first, a general process of inquiry, rather than an ensemble of techniques, parochial loyalties, or honorific pieties about science. The process conforms to scientific tenets in the sense that it invents concepts and hypotheses, refines and tests these, and aims at more general explanations and theories. Focusing only on this aspect, however, can turn methodology into a rather dreary topic, which is unfortunate since the core problem of method—how to find and substantiate the answer to a problem—suggests some excitement. A second and distinctive thing about sociological method, the point at which it becomes exciting, is that it begins with genuine puzzlement about what is happening or has happened in society—

with a why question or problem-consciousness. In *The American Soldier*, the investigators (and their official sponsors) wanted to know why there were problems of morale in the armed services. Merton and Rossi wanted to know why soldiers evaluated their situation in ways not anticipated by the notion of relative deprivation, and whether the general idea of reference groups would fit a variety of situations.

This goes back to the question of fact-gathering and the difference between sociological research and other useful forms of inquiry. Undisciplined research seldom has an explicit why question in mind before setting about its work and the result is bad if it does not find one as it goes along. The work may be aimlessly descriptive or abstractly speculative without such a question, just as it may be polemical and self-serving if the question *and* the answer are selected prior to the research—the latter by no means a rare occurrence. The German sociologist Ralf Dahrendorf (1958) developed this contrast 25 years ago in words that have lost none of their bite:

> "The Social Structure of a Hospital," "The Role of the Professional Football Player," and "Family Relations in a New York Suburb..."'chosen because nobody has studied them before or for some other random reason, are not problems. What I mean is that at the outset of every scientific investigation there has to be a fact or set of facts that is puzzling to the investigator: children of businessmen prefer professional to business occupations; workers in the automobile industry of Detroit go on strike; there is a higher incidence of suicides among upwardly mobile persons than among others; Socialist parties in predominantly Catholic countries of Europe seem unable to get more than 30 per cent of the popular vote [then]; Hungarian people revolt against the Communist regime. There is no need to enumerate more of such facts; what matters is that every one of them invites the question "Why?," and it is this question, after all, which has always inspired that noble human activity in which we are engaged—science. (Ralf Dahrendorf, "Out of Utopia: Toward a Reorientation of Sociological Analysis," p. 123)

Dahrendorf makes two observations that effectively summarize this discussion of method. First, sociology begins its effort to interpret and explain social life with "the simple impulse of curiosity, the desire to solve riddles of experience, the concern with problems" (p. 123). Second, once that curiosity is formulated in researchable (why) questions, the issues of method present themselves in a manageable form: "Problems require explanation; explanations require assumptions or models and hypotheses derived from such models; hypotheses, which are always, by implication, predictions as well as explanatory propositions, require testing by further facts; testing often generates new problems" (p. 124). In short, sociology will go a long distance toward its substantive and scientific goals by becoming more problem-conscious.

SOCIOLOGICAL PROBLEMS

Dahrendorf is right, but that leaves us with the question, perhaps the real question of method, namely, how sociology generates a fertile problem-consciousness—where do the why questions come from? I suspect that there are many answers and none that is fully satisfying, since sociology, like any other creative activity, has many intuitive wellsprings. Nevertheless, we can make a lot of headway by showing some important ways in which problem-consciousness arises. It comes from at least three sources: (1) the work of our predecessors, (2) reflection on our own social lives, and (3) important events that surround us in society.

In the last category, for example, a rich source is provided by the cultural and political worlds that are full of purported explanations for daily events; explanations, ironically, that are often drawn from antiquated or misunderstood social science. Unemployment, we are told, is high because people do not want to work or prefer receiving welfare benefits for not working; people riot in the cities because they are outside the mainstream of organized society; revolution brews in Central America because of communist subversion; children do not perform well in school because educational fundamentals are ignored. Although we do not customarily think of it this way, and it may glorify ordinary prejudice, there is a sense in which all of these answers are also popular theories of social behavior. Moreover, they are sometimes consequential theories to the extent that they inform public policy (for example, to eradicate unemployment by cutting off welfare benefits or to snuff out revolution by military containment of subversion). As theories, they invite problem-conscious evaluation.

Theoretical Problems

Some illustrations will help clarify these three sources of problem consciousness, showing at the same time their interconnection. Among our sociological predecessors, none is better known or more controversial than Karl Marx. Marx, as we shall see later in this chapter and the next, endeavored to explain the process of capitalist development and, particularly, what it meant for people engaged in various branches of economic production. One of his central hypotheses was that the growth of capitalism destroys small business and the independent crafts and professions (the petty bourgeois stratum), turning those occupations into wage labor (or proletarians). This experience of degradation, Marx inferred, would help to generate a revolutionary mood (or class consciousness) in the new working class. C. Wright Mills (1951) explored this question in his book *White Collar*, and documented Marx's prediction insofar as the destruction of the old middle classes was concerned. On the other hand, Mills found that far from sinking into the working class, members of the former craft and professional occupations were reabsorbed into a decidedly unrevolutionary new middle class of white-collar, salaried employees in large public and private bureaucracies. Mills regretted this development and chided the new white-collar workers in his own inimitably trenchant style:

> They are worried and distrustful but, like so many others, they have no targets on which to focus their worry and distrust. They may be politically irritable, but they have no political passion. They are a chorus, too afraid to grumble, too hysterical in their applause. They are rearguarders. In the short run, they will follow the panicky ways of prestige; in the longer run, they will follow the ways of power, for, in the end, prestige is determined by power. In the meantime, on the political market-place of American society, the new middle classes are up for sale; whoever seems respectable enough, strong enough, can probably have them. So far, nobody has made a serious bid. (C. Wright Mills, *White Collar: The American Middle Classes*, pp. 353–54)

Mills pruned one theory and advanced another that still has a decided critical appeal. As a Texas-born populist, Mills revered the ethic of Jacksonian democracy and smalltown society which seemed to him lost in modern bureaucratic society—and he clearly mixed his personal values with his research interests.

Yet, the research was inspired by an earlier theory and questions about the accuracy of its predictions.

Problems of Experience

Personal experience, the second source of sociological questions, carries as many pitfalls as insights. A valuable record of the tension involved in this kind of research is Tamotsu Shibutani's (1978) book *The Derelicts of Company K*. Shibutani is a Japanese-American sociologist who was interned in a U.S. concentration camp at the beginning of World War II, but later allowed to enter the Army with a great many of his fellows. Most Nisei fighting units distinguished themselves in the European theater and thereby successfully overcame discriminatory challenges to their loyalty. Company K, Shibutani's outfit, was different; in the author's words, they were "fuck-ups." Shibutani's personal and research question was, "Why the radical deviation of this group from the general pattern set by other Nisei soldiers?" (p. 3). But his answer was exceptionally difficult to ponder and write about.

Although he was trained as a sociologist and diligently recorded his field notes beginning with his internment, Shibutani was also a Japanese-American with normal sensitivities, the scars of prejudice, and an understandable reluctance to write about his personal and group humiliation.

> Because of deep emotional involvement in the events, the intensity of which I could not appreciate at the time, I was unable to understand many things that now appear obvious. (Tamotsu Shibutani, *The Derelicts of Company K: A Sociological Study of Demoralization*, pp. x–xi)

Of course, Shibutani did write the story of Company K, explaining why it became demoralized. The outfit was segregated within the armed forces and suffered inept Caucasian leadership. Although initially promised jobs as linguists, they were later shifted into the lower status of reserve combat troops. Discrimination affected their promotional opportunities. All of these unhappy experiences were endured by members of a primary (face-to-face) group which, as American citizens in the first place, held firmly to the norms of fair play. "Thus, pain and inconvenience in themselves do not arouse resentment. Men become indignant when they believe that they are being deprived of something that is rightfully theirs" (p. 421). Yet, it took the passage of 30 years before Shibutani could write this about the events he suffered through as he researched.

Shibutani was able to write an extraordinary sociological account of his experience because, with the lapse of time, he could get outside himself; because he came to understand that experience in terms of a general issue—the question of why groups become demoralized. Unfortunately, the difference is lost in the pseudosociology of "me" or popular works that focus on self-experience as the ultimate source of authority on subjects such as racism, sex, or politics. The writer Tom Wolfe (1979) commented on this vaunted importance of self in recent years calling it "a truly aristocratic luxury: the habit of putting oneself on stage, analyzing one's conduct, one's *relationships*, one's hang-ups, one's personality, precisely the way noblemen did it during the age of chivalry.... Me... became something all the world analyzed, agonized over, drew conclusions from, or, in any event, took seriously" (Tom Wolfe, "The Sexed-Up, Doped-Up, Hedonistic Heaven of the Boom-Boom '70s," p. 114). But me is not a sociological problem. Personal experience sometimes brings people to social research and it always affects our understanding. Alone, however, it does not translate concern into useful research—which is the job of method.

Event Problems

The third source of sociological questions, events surrounding us in everyday life, is especially rich when those events come packaged in popular theories. These are expressed everywhere, in newspapers, television, as public deliberations, official judgments, and so forth. Broken homes produce juvenile delinquents. Television makes kids violent or nuclear war scares them. Some of these ideas influence society and deserve evaluation of just how true they are.

A dramatic instance was provided by the Los Angeles-Watts riot of August 1965. Watts was far from the first race riot or massive civil disorder in U.S. history, but it was, perhaps, the most noteworthy in a series that occurred in the late 1960s: it was the most destructive to that date; it inaugurated a new type of public disorder in which issues of civil rights were intertwined with ordinary mayhem in the eyes of participants and observers; it happened in Los Angeles where no one expected it, given a less discernible ghetto, few slums or tenements, and more homeownership by contrast to older cities of the East and Midwest; and it prompted the first in a new series of quasi-social science, riot-commission studies.

Beginning with the mishandled arrest of a black youth by white police officers, and police brutality in the eyes of a crowd that gathered at the tense encounter, the disturbance raged for the next six days over the 46-square-mile area of South Central Los Angeles. When it was over, 10,000 people had joined in rebellion, 34 were killed (3 white law enforcement officers and 31 black residents), more than 1,000 injured, 4,000 arrested, and some 40 million dollars worth of property damaged in the looting and burning of 600 buildings and stores. One week after order had been restored, the McCone Commission (1965) was empaneled to unearth the causes of riot and provide, in the short 100 days allotted for its inquiry, a "deep and probing" analysis of what troubled Los Angeles.

The McCone Commission found three basic causes for the riot: unemployment and idleness, low cultural and educational levels among black youth, and poor police-community relations. In each case, this conventional diagnosis, with much liberal hand-wringing, laid the blame on the black community. The absence of employment opportunity in South Los Angeles was noted forthrightly, but little attention was given to why this was the case (as, for example, in the facts of urban disinvestment or discriminatory hiring). The report emphasized problems of black youth on the unexamined assumption that most rioters were young. Educationally, young people were seen as caught in a "dull devastating spiral of failure" (p. 6A)—ill-prepared for school in the first place, leading to poor performance and a high dropout rate. The matter of police-community relations was treated obliquely, indeed delicately, by a recitation of those purported characteristics of the black community that made it difficult to police (such as the assumed high number of recent migrants from the South with unrealistic expectations about California living).

In sum, the report leaned on what Anthony Oberschall, a sociologist who lived in Los Angeles, called the "criminal riff-raff theory" of civil disorder. Oberschall (1968) demonstrated this interpretation in the report and then asked, Is it true? Are there facts that allow for testing the theory or inventing a better one?

One striking fact was that the McCone Commission, with all its experts and $250,000 to support its research, had never asked itself Oberschall's questions. The commission used some capable sociologists as consultants, including Edward Ransford, Melvin Seeman, and Robert Blauner (who later wrote a scathing analysis of its "Whitewash over Watts"), but, as Blauner noted, the report was mute on the question of who participated in the riot and why. Oberschall did the sensible thing; he went to the record of police arrests of participants in the riot. The facts exploded the riff-raff theory. Arrested riot participants were not seasoned criminals or the dregs of society. Seventy-five percent had lived in Los Angeles for more than five years, refuting the recent-migrant assumption. Their average educational level matched the population of South Los Angeles as a whole. They were not especially young; 41 percent were between 25 and 39 years of age, and another 17 percent were over 40, meaning that 58 percent were far from teenaged gangsters. And they were representative of the area-wide lower-class background, not scum. From all this Oberschall concluded:

> What strikes one is the extent to which the riot drew participants from all social strata within the predominantly lower-class Negro area in which it took place. The riot cannot be attributed to the lawless and rootless minority which inhabits the ghetto, though, no doubt, these were active as well. The riot is best seen as a large scale collective action, with a wide, representative base in the lower-class Negro communities....(Anthony Oberschall, "The Los Angeles Riot of August 1965," p. 329)

Contrary to the official commission's judgment, Oberschall showed that Watts was a rebellion and that people rebelled (as Shibutani had learned) because the conditions they lived with came to outrage their sense of justice. People do not engage in massive civil disorder mainly, in Edward Banfield's (1968) calloused phrase, "for fun and profit" (p. 185). The rebellion in Watts came from the grass roots and attacked particular representations of perceived injustice: policemen and their patrol cars and the stores of exploitative white merchants. Violence was the expression of a desperate insistence on simple civil rights. It had little to do with the malintegration of these citizens into U.S. urban culture. On the contrary, it was energized by that culture—the civil rights movement and the esteem attached to social mobility.

The fact that the riot commission failed to see these truths merely reflects the public mood of denial, scapegoating, and resentment. It was more convenient, even reassuring, to locate the problem within the black community itself. The fresh sociological analyses that exposed this prejudice were no doubt motivated by individually held values of equality and a passion for debunking, but their analytic cunning followed from a simple question—why?

Radical Sociology

There is no way to completely eliminate the kinds of myths perpetuated, among other sources, by public agencies and the mass media. They can, however, be minimized and rooted out in two ways: (1) through the imperfect process of self-correcting tests and reformulations, and (2) by radical reconceptualization of a problem and its causes—much as Oberschall reversed the question of riot causation by shifting it from deficiencies within the black community to the reasons for rebellion against the larger society. The first tack is imperfect, slow, and sometimes the source of new myths. The second is bold and often unpopular. For all its methodological blunders, the commission report and the prejudices behind it had a stronger impression on public policy than the work of a few critical sociologists.

All of this means that research is a social activity and a political reality. Sociology does not lack public recognition or political relevance. On the contrary, the fact that riot commissions and other deep-and-probing official studies of social problems posture at sociology's diagnostic authority is an ironic compliment to the discipline. If anything menaces sociology's independent, demythologizing role, it is an easy familiarity with conventional ideas and the blandishments of power. Sociologists need to strain in a critical direction simply to ensure evenhandedness. That is, radical sociology, in the sense of going to the root of a problem (like radical surgery), is often the best sociology and the surest method for demythologizing our understanding of society. Howard Becker and Irving Louis Horowitz (1972) have argued, convincingly in my judgment, that good and radical sociology are highly coincident, though not identical:

> Good sociology is sociological work that produces meaningful descriptions of organizations and events, valid explanations of how they come about and persist, and realistic proposals for their improvement or removal. [Radical sociology shares the values of equality and individual freedom with radical politics.] Radical sociology also rests on a desire to change society in a way that will increase equality and maximize freedom, and it makes a distinctive contribution to the struggle for change. On the one hand, it provides the knowledge of how society operates, on the basis of which a radical critique of inequality and lack of freedom can be made. On the other hand, it provides the basis for implementing radical goals, constructing blueprints for freer, more egalitarian social arrangements. ...(Howard S. Becker and Irving Louis Horowitz, "Radical Politics and Sociological Research: Observations on Methodology and Ideology," pp. 50 and 52–53)

The three previous examples of good sociology show the varied sources of research questions. They also make a single point. Good research and method derive from good why questions, irrespective of their source, and good questions assume a radical stance by asking for explanations of the origins, persistence, and change of social arrangements. In moving from such questions to the many inventive strategies for doing research work, there is one general method that is the sociological method. Having stated that case, it remains to support it with a closer look at social research.

PART II
STRATEGIES AND METHOD

EXEMPLARS OF SOCIOLOGICAL METHOD

Method comes alive in practice as sociologists go about their work. The preceding points are illustrated here in a series of research biographies about important and engaging exemplars of sociological work. The following set of studies spans 19th-century classical and recent work, a variety of methodological strategies and substantive problems, and what will appear as some unlikely bedfellows. This is deliberate, as we shall see in the end.

Marx on Profit and Labor-Time

A good place to begin is with the work of Karl Marx since it shows the continuities between classical and recent work, demonstrating at the same time that the classical sociologists were not just speculators, but energetic fact-mongers. Throughout his 50 years of research and writing, Marx pursued one master question: What are the laws of socio-economic, and particularly of capitalist, development? He wisely refined this with a series of more limited questions that would yield to conceptual and factual answers: What is the source of value in the production process; where does the capitalist's profit come from; and what share of all this does the worker receive?

Marx rested his interpretation of capitalist development on the concept of surplus value, the result of a process in which workers are exploited by factory owners who pay workers less than the full value of their labor. The new concept reversed earlier accounts of where value came from, explanations by the bourgeois political economists who held that the value of a commodity, say a pair of shoes, was somehow in the shoes themselves, or in the process whereby the shoes were exchanged for money. These were not explanations at all, but pure mysticism, according to Marx. What sense did it make to say that there is value in a pair of shoes—how did it get in there? If one follows the career of the shoes, it is clear that they have a use value for their buyers and an exchange value for their sellers, but neither of these explains how value is created in the first place or where the capitalist seller's profit comes from. The key for Marx was that the origin of value could be found only in the process of production and, specifically, in the amount of labor-time required to produce the shoes (since the additional requirements for production such as equipment and raw material came either free from nature or from past labor).

This, it should be stressed, is Marx's conceptual premise, advanced for the purpose of making other facts intelligible, and not itself a factual assertion. The utility of the concept and the basis for its factual evaluation come with its ability to explain the origin of profit. Profit is now understood concretely as the amount of unpaid labor that the worker involuntarily donates to the capitalist—the difference between the amount of labor-time embodied in the commodity and the value at which the capitalist exchanges it. Where else, Marx asks rhetorically, could value come from? The essential source of profit for the capitalist, whose livelihood depends upon being as competitive or more so than the next capitalist, lies in extorting from the worker more value in labor-time than is returned in the purchasing power of wages—or simply to get more unpaid labor-time from the worker.

The capitalist can generate profit in a variety of ways such as speeding up work in order to get more produced for the same time and wage, lowering wages for the same amount of time and work, mechanizing production in order to get more produced with the same or a lesser amount of labor (and even with higher wages, provided that the additional value of the wages did not exceed that of the additional commodities produced), or simply extending the length of the working day at the same wage.

Marx researched the operation of all these mechanisms in the English industrial setting. Moreover, as a sociologist rather than an abstract economic theorist, he researched the social and political conditions through which the drive for profit operated. His analysis of "the working day" (Chapter 10 of *Capital*, Vol. 1) is a fine example of how his invented explanation and its implications make sense of a complex history: "Nothing characterizes the spirit of capital better than the history of English factory legislation from 1833 to 1864" (p. 390).

Marx traced this history beginning with the first "Statute of Labourers" enacted in 1349 after the great plague as a means of attracting scarce workers and holding down their wages. By the early 19th century, the length of the working day had extended well beyond the initial 12-hour "natural day" for adult males to 15 hours (5:30 AM to 8:30 PM) for all workers, including women and children. The lives of the factory workers were full of drudgery, bleak, and cut short by disease and hazardous conditions. Hardship and a growing working-class culture produced a political movement dedicated to a new Peoples' Charter and a Ten Hours Bill.

Here the story becomes intriguing. The workers mounted their struggle for 10 hours against the factory owners and sought the support of Parliament for passage of the bill. Parliament at the time was still dominated by aristocrats and landowners, with whom the industrialists were struggling for repeal of the Corn Laws and other protective tariffs. The industrialists wanted free trade and, particularly, elimination of duties on grains imported into the country from Europe (which protected English agricultural interests), since that would result in cheaper food for workers and less pressure for wage increases.

Marx saw the situation as rife with *inter*class conflicts (between workers and industrial owners) and *intra*class conflicts (between industrialists and landowners). In the maneuvering that followed, the industrialists were most clever, taking advantage of the situation in an unexpected way:

> The spokesmen and political leaders of the manufacturing class ordered a change in attitude and in language towards the workers. They had started their campaign to repeal the Corn Laws, and they needed the workers to help them to victory! They promised, therefore, not only that the loaf of bread would be twice its size, but also that the Ten Hours Bill would be enacted in the free trade millennium. (Karl Marx, *Capital*, Vol. 1, p. 393)

The new class alliance worked. Factory owners and workers joined forces and the Corn Laws were repealed along with duties on cotton and other raw materials. The new Factory Act of 1847, which promised a reduction of the legal working day, came as a concession to the working class for their support—helped along by revengeful landowning interests in Parliament that still smarted over their defeat by the industrialists. However, as soon as the industrialists had what they wanted, they began to sabotage the new Factory Act by reducing wages. Thus, although the workers now had the 10-hour day, it netted them much less money and they were required to return to the longer day for the same wage.

The manufacturers claimed in Parliament and the press that workers voluntarily took on additional hours. This falsehood was exposed by the factory inspectors, for whom Marx had great respect. Marx cited the work of one Leonard Horner, an aggressive inspector and investigator who helped interview 10,270 workers in 181 factories showing that 70 percent preferred the 10-hour day even for some loss in wages, if they had a choice in the matter, which they did not. Nevertheless, with all their maneuvers and power, the industrialists were still having trouble nullifying the Ten Hours Bill. Providence intervened on their behalf. In June 1848, a revolution in France sent shock waves through Europe and across the channel:

> Insurrection in Paris and its bloody suppression united, in England as on the Continent, all factions of the ruling class, landlords and capitalists, stock-exchange sharks and small-time shopkeepers, Protectionists and Free Traders, government and opposition, priests and free-thinkers, young whores and old nuns, under the common slogan of the salvation of property, religion, the family, and society. Everywhere the working class was outlawed.... The manufacturers no longer needed to restrain themselves. They broke into open revolt, not only against the Ten Hours Act, but against all the legislation since 1833 that aimed at restricting to some extent the "free" exploitation of labour-power. (Karl Marx, *Capital*, Vol. 1, pp. 397–98)

Through political power, guile, and luck, the industrial-owner class won this engagement in the class struggle and went on to enhance its profits by re-extending the working day and adding new forms of exploitation. In effect, while they were engaged in a parliamentary struggle with the land-owning aristocrats, they made a temporary political alliance with the working class based on a promise of better working conditions. Once the industrialists had beaten the old aristocrats, they took back the concessions to labor and added new methods for extracting more labor time at no additional cost to their profit margins. On the contrary, industry emerged from the struggles richer and more powerful politically.

Marx's research method involved two key features. First, it was the concept of surplus value that got to the heart of the welter of events by showing the connection between profit and labor—just as it helped to explain later why the extended day could be profitably abandoned with further mechanization. Second, Marx unraveled the intricate ways in which the drive for surplus value worked itself out through meticulous research. Studying in the British Museum, he pored over hundreds of volumes of *Reports of the Inspectors of Factories*, parliamentary inquiries by the *Children's Employment Commission*, the *Factories Inquiry Commission*, and the vast *Parliamentary Papers*. The amount of factual evidence that he synthesized is amazing, although it is also true that his own preference was for research with historical and archival documents. For original data, he relied mainly on the reports of factory inspectors, although in 1880 he did draft an enormous, 100-item questionnaire for distribution among French workers. Evidently, very few of the 25,000 printed questionnaires were ever completed, and it is no wonder. Inspection of the questionnaire, reprinted by Tom Bottomore and Maximilien Rubel (1956), shows that it would have required an inordinate amount of time and sophistication to fill out. Marx was no pollster, but he was an exceptional researcher.

Durkheim on Suicide

Émile Durkheim was a French academic who, like Marx, studied the great transformation from feudal to industrial society. Durkheim's research in the late 19th century began with questions and operative concepts much different from those of Marx. The Frenchman wanted to know why late-19th-century society was disintegrating and what could be done about it. The concept he developed to summarize the disjunction between past and potential future forms of social solidarity was *anomie*—the absence of normative regulation or binding commitments to a stable moral order. The consequences of anomie included class struggle and inequality. But Durkheim (1951), in a book originally published in 1897, wanted to show how a uniquely sociological method could explain pathological behavior. The book was entitled *Suicide: A Study in Sociology*.

The choice of suicide as a problem to be explained sociologically was strategic. What could be a more individual and appropriately psychological question than why people take their own lives? What could sociology—the study of social facts that are exterior and constraining to the individual according to Durkheim—explain about the ultimate act of self-renunciation? Naturally, Durkheim had an answer. Whatever the individual factors in suicide might be, they scarcely exhausted the problem, since they could not explain variations in the social suicide rate across time in a single society or across societies and social groups at a given time. "At each moment of its history, therefore, each society has a definite aptitude for suicide" (p. 48).

As Durkheim began to analyze the European data on suicide rates, he became convinced that psychological, geographic, and other nonsocial factors explained very little. There was, for example, no systematic difference in the suicide rates of the sane versus the insane, no unique connection with alcoholism, no greater incidence in the gloomy climes of Northern Europe than in the sunny South, no differences by race and national character. Indeed, as Durkheim tracked down some fairly preposterous theories about the effects of climate and season, the only regularities he found were higher rates of suicide in daytime, summer, and in cities—all of which he interpreted as occasions of more intense social activity. This was a clue.

Having excluded many false leads, the question narrowed to which social groups might have especially high (or low) suicide rates and, if those could be found, what would explain the differences? Now a wealth of meaty results began to appear. Suicide rates were higher for Protestants than for Catholics, although Catholics, in turn, had a higher rate than Jews. They were highest for single people, next for widowed and divorced, less for married, and least for the married with children. Rates rose positively with education; they were higher among members of the army than for civilians; males were four times more likely to kill themselves than females; and the urban exceeded the rural rate. Durkheim identifies many more correlations and examines them in detail looking for some underlying coherence. Making sense of the results requires attention to the overall pattern. Illustratively, one could make a good deal of the differences in religion by searching for theological injunctions against suicide, but if religion were the principal factor preventing or disposing to suicide, why would education or military status, neither of which is highly correlated with religion, also show patterned differences?

As Durkheim reflected on the question of a pattern, he reasoned that there was a common denominator in all these statuses. Being Protestant, single, and educated, for example, all involved greater individualism (or egoism); Protestants enjoyed greater freedom from religious dogma and greater latitude of individual interpretation; single people had fewer responsibilities to a family; educated persons were more accustomed to think for themselves, and so on. Jews, married persons with children, and the less educated were all less individualistic and more bound to social responsibilities or group expectations. In short, and this should come as no surprise, suicide rose as normative regulation declined. Suicide was a positive function of anomie—just as Durkheim had suspected or hypothesized.

At this point, one might conjecture that Durkheim had been engaged in an elaborate demonstration of what he already knew or wanted to prove. In a way that is true. He certainly had an inkling that the moral disintegration he had worried about all his life was connected with the kind of social pathology represented by suicide. But here is where the unexpected came in, owing to the implications of the invented explanation. That is, if suicide varies with anomie, there should be other sorts of anomic circumstances that bear a relationship to suicide.

Durkheim reasoned this way and checked out the implied expectations. Periods of economic collapse, depression and recession, for example, all clearly disrupt the normative order of society and should produce a higher suicide rate, according to the argument. Durkheim then discovered that the suicide rate does indeed rise with downturns in the business cycle. Common sense, one cries. People jump out of skyscrapers or into the moats of French chateaux during depressions. That is figuratively true, also. But Durkheim is ahead of us. He reasoned that periods of rapid economic prosperity should also disrupt the normative order and he went on to show, quite contrary to common sense, that the suicide rate rises during economic boom times.

What would common sense say about periods of political upheaval? What should happen to the suicide rate during wars, revolutions, or electoral crises? Conventional thinking might predict a higher suicide rate as in the case of economic crises. That would be wrong. Durkheim, focusing conceptually on anomie rather than the unexamined effects of social crisis, reasoned that war and revolution would reassert the moral order, call for greater social regulation, and thereby lower the suicide rate. His prediction was borne out by the evidence on suicide during political upheavals throughout Europe.

The concluding chapter of *Suicide* is entitled "Practical Consequences," and it asks, in effect, what is the remedy. The simplistic social engineering answer might be that suicide is correlated with high education, Protestantism, and being single. To solve it, you give people less education, convert them to Catholicism, or better yet to Judaism, and marry them off—or, failing these, you live with it. That is nonsense to Durkheim who, as a radical sociologist in every sense of the word, went to the root of the problem and proposed a solution based on social reorganization.

Religion, education, and the rest were different symptoms of the anomie that had overtaken society with the atrophy of institutions. "Thus, the only remedy for the ill is to restore enough consistency to social groups for them to obtain a firmer grip on the individual, and for him to feel himself bound to them" (p. 373). But what groups? is the next question. Durkheim argues that they should not be the traditional religious, political, or family groups, or the far-removed state. They should be decentralized groups that have an organic connection to modern life: "The only decentralization which would make possible the multiplication of the centers of community life without weakening national unity is what might be called *occupational decentralization*" (p. 390). So, Durkheim's most rigorous quantitative study and the one classic that continues, properly if exclusively, to be read as a primer in sociological method, came home to his reform passion.

Lipset, Trow, and Coleman on Union Democracy

Occupations have been the focus of some fascinating sociological research. For many years at the University of Chicago, Everett Hughes encouraged his students to go into the community and learn how people do their work. Monographs resulted on such diverse jobs as taxi drivers, funeral directors, and dance musicians. The occupational association that interested Durkheim has attracted modern researchers, although few of them were inspired by Durkheim's theory or method. The new issues that concerned researchers by mid-20th century are reflected in the study of *Union Democracy* by Seymour Martin Lipset, Martin Trow, and James Coleman (1956). Lipset, who initiated the collaborative project, has written its research biography in a way that reveals much about the personal and situational influences on sociological work.

Lipset began graduate school in 1943 at Columbia University, studying with Merton and Lazarsfeld. His interest in the International Typographic Union (ITU) started with his father who was a printer and took him to union meetings. Later, as a graduate student, Lipset decided to write about the union because it had a unique, internal, two-party democratic system. It might have been an illustration of Durkheim's decentralized occupational association, but Lipset was viewing it in a different light appropriate to his own circumstance. As a youth, he had participated in socialist politics, but like so many of the young U.S. intellectuals of the 1930s and 1940s, Lipset (1964) had become skeptical about the fate of democracy:

> The experience of the left and labor movements in various countries indicated that the building of a large socialist or labor movement, or even its coming to power, was not sufficient to democratize a society. In the Soviet Union, a supposed Marxist revolution has resulted in the creation of a new, even more exploitative, form of class rule than existed in capitalist countries. The social-democratic parties and trade-unions in other countries seemed to exhibit more concern with organizational stability and survival than with the need to advance radical solutions to social problems.... The question was why. (Seymour Martin Lipset, "The Biography of a Research Project: Union Democracy," pp. 112–13)

Lipset found the best available answer to that question in the book *Political Parties* by Robert Michels (1959), which proposed that combative organizations such as unions and parties followed an "iron law of oligarchy" that eschewed internal democracy for the sake of doing battle with industry and the state. But the ITU belied that law, providing a fertile exception to the undemocratic process in most large organizations. Lipset's question could now be refined and focused on an explanation for the uniqueness of the ITU. What was different about printers?

The answer to this question was a long time in coming. Lipset drew on his personal knowledge, study of the union's history, particularly the development of its two-party system, and interviews with members of the New York locals. With a proper question in mind, the clues began to appear in certain extraordinary features of the printer's trade. On the job, they took a good deal of pride in their work and thought of themselves, if not as middle class, then certainly as a highly skilled pinnacle of the working class. Off the job, they engaged in a variety of leisure activities with one another: social clubs, veterans' organizations, athletic teams. This made further sense because the printing trade was relatively homogeneous (status distinctions between printers were small) and it involved odd working hours. The leisure-time activities of printers took place when most people were working, meaning that printers spent most of their time together. From this kind of theoretical reflection and factual material, Lipset reached his conceptual invention: the printers had an "occupational community" rooted in the conditions of their work that maintained democratic practices in their union.

Just as Durkheim had a pretty good idea of the consequences of anomie before he collected his data on suicide rates, Lipset had discovered the occupational community before he, Trow, and Coleman (1964) conducted the survey research on union members that makes up the bulk of *Union Democracy*. Indeed, it was this refined understanding of the union that made an informative social survey possible:

> The methodological innovations evidenced in our sample design did not stem from any special concern with creative methodology. Rather, it and the questions reflected the fact that the survey was planned to test a highly complex analytic model; it was a sophisticated survey design precisely because years of prior investigation of the attributes of a complex system had preceded it. Having the hypotheses formulated well in advance meant that the methodology almost created itself. (Seymour Martin Lipset, "The Biography of a Research Project: Union Democracy," p. 125)

The parallel with Durkheim's research style goes further. Lipset's critics could ask what was the use of the elaborate survey (in three stages, including a sample of 434 regular members selected by the size of shop they worked in, a subsample of union stewards, and another of leaders of the internal political parties) given what he knew before getting to this phase of the research. Was this just quantitative window-dressing? Lipset notes that the question challenges the principal assumptions on which most sociologists work. His answer was that not only did the invented explanation about democracy in the union need to be evaluated, but many of its implications had to be followed through to issues that the researchers did not presume to know beforehand.

The survey research supported the explanation, but it added many new and unanticipated insights: the size of the union shop had a lot to do with a flourishing democracy, since small shops were unable to support two-party differences as amicably as large shops; special hiring practices encouraged the occupational community even before printers became regular union members; the structural effect of shop size revealed and helped explain why only the larger locals had a competitive party system; yet at the individual level, political participation was explained by the extent to which printers had working-class reference groups.

Having shown why democratic unionism survives in this atypical setting, the book concludes on a pessimistic note. The implications for organizational democracy are sobering precisely because the conditions that supported it in the ITU, the pride and skill of the craft, are being destroyed by industrial rationalization, business unionism, and technological advances in printing. The tendency toward oligarchy that Michels described was more grimly prophetic than Durkheim's occupational associations. In their conclusion, Lipset, Trow, and Coleman (1964) anguish over the fact that their research:

> Does not offer many positive suggestions for those who would seek consciously to manipulate the structure of such organizations so as to make the institutionalization of democratic procedures within them more probable...[but they also caution vaguely that it] would be foolhardy to reject the possibility that major changes in the social structure will increase the potential for democracy within the labor movement. (Seymour Martin Lipset et al., *Union Democracy: The Internal Politics of the International Typographic Union,* pp. 404–6)

Although they provide no hint about what those changes might be, their honest confrontation of unhappy facts is laudable. If nothing else, it would suggest that we need to look elsewhere for the conditions under which communities struggle for autonomy and moral order.

Suttles on the Slum and Kornblum on the Community

Looking elsewhere for the answer to a question frequently involves adopting different research methods that gain access to other social worlds. Questions about the viability of community life as a haven of sociability denied in the workplace have led some researchers into urban neighborhoods as observers and participants in a special kind of social order. This method, pioneered by the early North American sociologists, had fallen into disuse in urban studies until the late 1960s, when Gerald Suttles (1968) published *The Social Order of the Slum*. By becoming a sociological resident of Chicago's multi-ethnic West Side community, Suttles discovered a moral order that Durkheim would have missed by looking for it in industry and one that Lipset correctly saw vanishing from mechanized occupations. Suttles asked why the moral order persisted in the inner city, which other sociologists had called a hotbed of social pathology and disorganization.

His answer required, first, that he characterize the kind of order that did exist. In the slum, a provincial morality thrived that was "not so much the heart-felt sentiments of people as a set of defensive guarantees demanded by various minority group members" (p. 4). Slumdwellers have the same desire for security and self-respect as members of the larger society, although they live in a more dangerous and economically precarious environment. Consequently, their moral order is different, but not independent of the larger society. Lacking conventional bases for mutual trust, slum dwellers restrict their social relations to close associates and inquire closely into the personal character of people outside those provincial circles. As a result,

> The major lineaments of the area's internal structure are such commonplace distinctions as age, sex, territoriality, ethnicity, and personal identity. Some ethnic customs have been preserved, and numerous localisms have been developed. Many of the residents are

so thoroughly acquainted with one another that only personalistic standards are relevant. Frequently the residents emphasize these structural components to the exclusion of educational, legal, and occupational considerations. Taken out of context, many of the social arrangements of the...area may seem an illusory denial of the beliefs and values of the wider society. Seen in more holistic terms, the residents are bent on ordering local relations where the beliefs and evaluations of the wider society do not provide adequate guidelines for conduct. (Gerald D. Suttles, *The Social Order of the Slum: Ethnicity and Territory in the Inner City*, pp. 3–4)

Suttles's neighborhood formed an intricate patchwork of territories, usually divided by such physical barriers as an expressway or railroad tracks, within which Italians, Puerto Ricans, blacks, Mexicans, and Southern whites tended to segregate themselves and organize their interaction on the basis of personal characteristics and trust. There were definite patterns to all this which Suttles called "ordered segmentation." Among the implications of ordered segmentation was "a standardized routine for managing safe social relations [and] a sequential order in which these groups can combine" (pp. 225, 231). Territoriality is the primary basis of affiliation, followed by ethnicity, age, and sex differentiation. Across ethnic groups, blacks and Italians are most divided. Mexicans often maintain cordial relations with Italians, although they also have ties to blacks that they do not jeopardize. Against outside threats, all the groups may unite, but for the most part they are badly divided.

The implications of the ordered segmentation in urban communities for industry and politics have been developed by William Kornblum (1974), a student of Suttles, who observed and participated in Chicago's South Side steel-mill communities. Kornblum's book on *Blue Collar Community* implicitly returns to the questions of Durkheim and Lipset by examining how industry, neighborhood, and union politics interact. Kornblum discovered the same segmented ethnic neighborhoods that existed in the slum. Working in one of the steel mills, however, he also learned that ward politics carry over into union politics, that interethnic cooperation is promoted in the factory-union setting, and that those arrangements are carried back to the community.

The industrial union helped to democratize community politics and vice versa. Local Mexican-Americans, long-time steelworkers, found a respected place in ward politics. The

Chicago-Gary District of the United Steelworkers of America elected a progressive and independent slate of officers in a rare demonstration of union democracy. Kornblum also puts to rest the myth of the working-class redneck or bigoted white ethnic. Although prejudice exists in most places, it is no more common among steelworkers than in middle-class occupations and communities:

> The conflict, the violence, and the lingering hatreds which may persist after generations of ecological invasion are only one side of the picture. The negotiations of new alliances and constituencies in which racial and ethnic cleavages are played down and blend into a more unifying working-class culture is the other side. (William Kornblum, *Blue Collar Community*, p. 215)

The point here is not that Lipset was wrong in concluding that union democracy was in serious peril or that Durkheim was wrong to look for social order in professional associations that presumably superseded Kornblum's kind of neighborhood community. Rather, the point is that questions once posed and examined lead to new ones. Kornblum knew what the previous questions were, but he asked them in a new way. Instead of focusing on the decline of democracy in the union or on the organization of community in isolation, he asked how factory and neighborhood interpenetrate in the experienced world of workers and residents. Employing a different concept, in the blue-collar community Kornblum found a kind of social organization that other experts would have said was long gone.

Goffman on Asylums

The social order that Durkheim saw changing with industrialization and Suttles found thriving in the slum, Erving Goffman discovered in the unlikely confines of a mental hospital. This is not surprising since Goffman (1961) chose to examine the society of mental patients from the standpoint of the inmates themselves, rather than through the eyes of their psychiatrists and custodians. His book *Asylums* poses a question about mental illness that departs radically from conventional views by proposing to study "the moral career" of a mental patient.

Goffman chose the career concept precisely because of its two-sidedness, its capacity to integrate matters internal to the individual with the public aspect of life. The moral career allows study of the individual in a social setting by linking public and private sides of the person in ways that are lost in psychological studies—particularly those that assume that individuals suffer diseases of the mind. Goffman believed that more could be learned about mental illness through an institutional approach to the self. In order to follow the career of mental patients, Goffman got as close to them as he could by working in a minor staff position at a large public hospital (he ruled out actually becoming a patient as too restrictive of his freedom to study the institution). Once Goffman had entered this unique but sensible world, he found he was "participating in a community not significantly different from any other" (p. 130).

The unique question in this study was what are the effects on a person of being treated as a mental patient? Goffman noted that people get to the mental hospital for all sorts of reasons in addition to their mental condition. Hospitals admit people who certainly appear crazy, but they admit others who seem quite normal. Psychiatry, an unreliable science at best, cannot yet distinguish between the more and the less sick. What really distinguishes arriving mental patients from the general public is less a common condition than the fact that the individual "somehow gets caught up in the heavy machinery of mental-hospital servicing." In Edwin Lemert's (1967) phrase, patients are less victims of some reliably diagnosed disease than of "career contingencies," such as the energy with which their relatives pursue their commitment. "But once started on the way, they are confronted by some importantly similar circumstances and respond to these in some importantly similar ways" (Goffman, p. 129). That is, the career of a mental patient begins, and this has relatively uniform effects on individuals apart from their mental condition on entering the hospital.

Much of Goffman's fascinating book describes a socialization process in which people learn to behave as mental patients. On admission, they are alienated from friends and from the conspiring hospital staff. They undergo a degradation ceremony in which their possessions, clothes, and other symbols of self are taken away. Staff supervision robs them of freedom, invades their personal space, and conveys a judgment of incompetence. The hospital's ward system manipulates small privileges in a way that constrains the person to accept official views of his or her craziness. The main thing that the person learns is how to make out under these circumstances by ingenuously playing the system; by learning "to practice before all groups the amoral acts of shamelessness" (p. 169).

But mental patients are not crazy in the specific sense that they submit to all of this compliantly. Playing the system creates an "underlife of a public institution," all those adjustments and subversions by which people maintain some privacy, sense of efficacy, and self-respect. They break the rules in small ways: smuggle liquor into the hospital, pursue romantic liaisons with other patients or community volunteers, ridicule therapy sessions, keep stashes of personal or illicit possessions, find safe and unsupervised places to meet, and develop an underground system of communication. Thus, rebellion in all these ways is actually what is taught in the mental hospital. Unwittingly, the staff denies the patient many of the perquisites of self-respect which are then regained in subversive underlife activities.

The important implication of this moral conflict is that the subversion of institutional rules is caused by other rules. In their hospital career, patients are deprived of many features of their selves. To the extent that they grudgingly cooperate with this process, the patients enable the institution to perform its official functions (conducting the therapy sessions or therapeutic dances). But in exchange for patient cooperation, the staff lays itself open to reciprocal demands; it bargains cooperation for illicit privileges such as reduced supervision or a blind eye to contraband. As a result, the institutional system corrupts itself and the self that results from all this is an institutional product.

> Each moral career, and behind this, each self, occurs within the confines of an institutional system, whether a social establishment such as a mental hospital or a complex of personal and professional relationships. The self, then, can be seen as something that resides in the arrangements prevailing in a social system for its members. The self in this sense is not a property of the person to whom it is attributed, but dwells rather in the pattern of social control that is exerted in connection with the person by himself and those around him. This special kind of institutional arrangement does not so much support the self as constitute it. (Erving Goffman, *Asylums: Essays on the Social Situation of Mental Patients and Other Inmates*, p. 168)

With his concepts of moral career and the institutional self, Goffman takes us a long way toward a new way of understanding, and perhaps even dealing with, mental illness. Goffman's work is read and used by people interested in reforming psychiatric treatment and by advocates of deinstitutionalization, or the elimination of hospitals and reformatories in preference to community-based treatment.

Goffman reflected on what his research implied for other kinds of institutions. Mental hospitals resemble in some respects other institutions where people live, work, and pass their leisure all in the same place. He called these total institutions and cited other examples such as the military, prisons, boarding schools, and monasteries. Now, if this much is valid, Goffman reasoned, then the institutional self produced in those institutions should bear essential similarities to the moral career of the mental patient. A good deal of evidence supports his inference. Army recruits begin their military careers with degradation ceremonies in boot camp. Novitiate monks are stripped of their personal possessions along with their mortal corruptions. Prisons generate an underlife of illicit activities, a special argot, and open rebellion. The total institution is another conceptual invention that leads research to unexpected factual results.

Piven and Cloward on the Poor

The last example demonstrates some of the same research issues treated previously, but in historical work taking us back to Marx's method and the beginning of this excursion. In *Regulating the Poor*, Francis Fox Piven and Richard Cloward (1971) deal with the background and contemporary controversy of public welfare. Their opening paragraph clearly states a why question: "We seek to explain why relief arrangements exist, and why—from time to time—the relief rolls precipitously expand or contract" (p. xiii). Noting that welfare systems of one kind or another have existed since the beginnings of industrial capitalism, Piven and Cloward reformulate the question in a strategic manner to read, "What functions does relief-giving serve for the larger economic and political order?" (p. xiii).

The last question assumes that public welfare is something more than a beneficent means of responding to the needs of poor people. That assumption is supported by the facts that public welfare appears in history at a particular time independent of prior need and the amounts in which it is doled out subsequently vary independent of the level of poverty. Therefore, other factors must intervene between need and relief giving; and their identification should help to identify the true functions of welfare. Piven and Cloward have radically shifted the conventional or commonsense perspective. They propose that an explanation for the creation of welfare and for its varying generosity lies in the functions that welfare performs for the economy—not in any intention to alleviate poverty.

Public relief appears in Western history coincident with the beginnings of capitalism in the 16th century. It becomes a public (as opposed to church) activity in response to the problem of unemployment, particularly the process in which people are displaced from agricultural occupations and crafts with modernization and industrialization. Yet it was not the level of unemployment per se that prompted relief, but the civil disorders and protest movements that displaced people undertook to redress their condition. In other words, the function of relief was to control civil disorder, to dampen, perhaps buy off, protest against the economic system—a system that was producing poverty for some as others profited. Welfare was mainly a political gambit, an instrument used to control protest and promote stability.

When the strategy succeeded and civil order was restored, the next step was to insist that relief recipients work for their dole in some way. The first institutions designed for that purpose were the poorhouses (or workhouses) and the apprentice systems that used pauper children as unpaid labor in manufacturing—practices that the novels of Charles Dickens repeatedly criticized. New functions came into play as relief publicly subsidized work for private manufacturers or channeled labor directly into the private market. When this stage had run its course and protest had subsided, relief rolls were reduced in order to force people into whatever low-wage work existed. During these periods, the welfare system was not dismantled since it served an additional function.

> Once an economic convulsion subsides and civil order is restored, relief systems are not ordinarily abandoned. The rolls are reduced, to be sure, but the shell of the system usually remains, ostensibly to provide aid to the aged, the insane, the disabled, and such other

unfortunates as may be without economic utility. However, the manner in which these "impotents" have been treated, in the United States and elsewhere, suggests a purpose different from remediation of their destitution. For these residual persons have been universally degraded for lacking economic value. (Francis Fox Piven and Richard A. Cloward, *Regulating the Poor: The Functions of Public Welfare*, p. 33)

Piven and Cloward found these cycles and functions in the history of European capitalist expansion and went on to assess how the explanation fit the United States, particularly the origins of public welfare in the 1930s and subsequent policies of "workfare" or enforced low-wage work combined with reductions of the rolls. The pattern fits, making a good deal of sense of welfare politics and the policies that shift from one administration to another—the efforts first to appeal to poor voters with new welfare programs, and next to business with reduced rolls and more available cheap labor.

Finally, Piven and Cloward take their concept to a higher level by asking what are the implications of the fact that public welfare is used for the political reintegration of disaffected groups? Their answer shows a fascinating similarity to Goffman's treatment of mental patients. Political reintegration invests certain rights in welfare recipients. Eligibility rights, for example, come with official programs and recipients have organized political protests around their perceived welfare rights—a political movement, incidentally, in which Piven and Cloward took an active part.

Since so many fewer people actually collect relief than are eligible, a movement that enrolled as many as possible could put enormous pressure on the system, conceivably helping to bring about real reforms in the economy: "in the absence of fundamental economic reforms, therefore, *we take the position that the explosion of the rolls is the true relief reform*, that it should be defended and expanded" (p. 348). The irony is that a program whose function was to control disorder and protest, ended up creating a protest movement by investing its clients with the right to petition for eligibility under circumstances that helped mobilize people. Like Marx, Piven and Cloward carried their radical sociology into politics. Yet, in a more general way, each of the examples shows that good research is radical in the sense that it challenges accepted views, goes to the root of a problem, and suggests alternative forms of social organization.

THE SOCIOLOGICAL METHOD

Interpretation of the six studies unabashedly joins Marx and Goffman, or Durkheim and Piven and Cloward, since they are all skillfully engaged in a similar enterprise. If the six research projects were classified by the usual categories of method, two would be considered historical research (Marx and Piven and Cloward), two participant observation (Suttles and Goffman), and two survey or quantitative work (Lipset and Durkheim). That classification would miss the more interesting similarities, which also seem to capture the purpose and flavor of the work.

Let us recall the similarities that run through all these exemplars.

1. Each began with a clear question and important problem: Why does the suicide rate vary with social factors? Why does democracy survive in one exceptional union?
2. Each investigator invented an explanation for the problem and summarized that in a key concept (surplus value, ordered segmentation, the functions of welfare).
3. Each study pursued a radical approach by challenging conventional ideas, reversing the usual assumptions, and going to the root of the question rather than treating its superficial correlates.
4. Each study employed multiple research strategies in complementary ways. Marx consulted the surveys by factory inspectors; Lipset engaged in years of historical work before his survey; Goffman participated in the mental hospital routines and then read widely in the organization of other total institutions; Suttles interviewed neighborhood boys and presented his results in tables; Piven and Cloward participated in the Welfare Rights Movement.
5. Finally, each study is explicitly or implicitly critical and thereby sympathetic to social reconstruction—the investigators had clear value commitments. Marx and Durkheim are explicit about the social reconstruction they propose. Lipset is concerned about the fate of organizational democracy. Goffman is bothered by the amoral experiences of a mental

patient's career. Piven and Cloward advocate the rights of the poor. And Suttles is concerned for the lives of slumdwellers. These investigators vary in the extent to which they carry the lessons of their research into social action, a choice they have every right to make. All, however, are concerned about social ills and the practical applications of their work.

Sociological work at its best involves inventing explanations for important problems and finding out whether they are true. Concepts summarize observations of social life in distinctive ways and they embody implications about other things that should be observed if the concepts are fertile. The sociological method, subsuming a variety of techniques, is a process of investigating whether explanations and implications fit the known facts and generate new ones. This is the purpose and the beauty of method; what makes it at once inseparable from theory and a challenge to imaginative detectives in search of critical facts. When methodology is lifted out of the sociological craft and turned into a specialized technique, both theory and method suffer—the first because it cannot move into the world of experience and the second because it wanders there aimlessly.

The work that sociologists do testifies to the unity of the sociological method; inquisitive and radical work which, in the end, is useful because it convinces us that we now understand something that was once baffling. Edmund Wilson's (1983) description of the passion that drives writers to reinterpret their times applies as well to sociologists.

> With each such victory of the human intellect, whether in history, in philosophy, or in poetry, we experience a deep satisfaction: we have been cured of some ache of disorder, relieved of some oppressive burden of uncomprehended events. (Edmund Wilson, "The Historical Interpretation of Literature," p. 353)

SELECTED BIBLIOGRAPHY

BANFIELD, EDWARD C. (1968). *The Unheavenly City: The Nature and Future of Our Urban Crisis*. Boston: Little, Brown.

BECKER, HOWARD S. (1982). *Art Worlds*. Berkeley: University of California Press.

BECKER, HOWARD S., & HOROWITZ, IRVING LOUIS. (1972, July). Radical Politics and Sociological Research: Observations on Methodology and Ideology. *American Journal of Sociology, 78,* 48–66.

BLAUNER, ROBERT (1966 March/April) "Whitewash over Watts." *Trans-action*, 3:3–9, 54.

BOTTOMORE, T. B., & RUBEL, MAXIMILIEN (1956). *Karl Marx: Selected Writings in Sociology and Social Philosophy.* New York: McGraw-Hill.

DAHRENDORF, RALF (1958, September). "Out of Utopia: Toward a Reorientation of Sociological Analysis." *American Journal of Sociology, 64,* 115–27.

DURKHEIM, ÉMILE (1951). *Suicide: A Study in Sociology* (John A. Spaulding & George Simpson, Trans.). New York: Free Press. (Original work published in 1897.)

GOFFMAN, ERVING (1961). *Asylums: Essays on the Social Situation of Mental Patients and Other Inmates.* Garden City, NY: Anchor Books.

KAPLAN, ABRAHAM (1964). *The Conduct of Inquiry: Methodology for Behavioral Science.* San Francisco: Chandler Publishing.

KORNBLUM, WILLIAM (1974). *Blue Collar Community.* Chicago: University of Chicago Press.

LAZARSFELD, PAUL F. (1949, Fall). "The American Soldier: An Expository Review." *Public Opinion Quarterly, 13* (3), 378–80.

LEMERT, EDWIN (1967). *Human Deviance, Social Problems, and Social Control.* Englewood Cliffs, NJ: Prentice-Hall.

LIPSET, SEYMOUR MARTIN (1964). "The Biography of a Research Project: Union Democracy." In Phillip E. Hammond (Ed.), *Sociologists at Work: The Craft of Social Research* (pp. 111–39). Garden City, NY: Anchor Books.

LIPSET, SEYMOUR MARTIN, TROW, MARTIN A., & COLEMAN, JAMES A. (1956). *Union Democracy: The Internal Politics of the International Typographical Union.* New York: Free Press.

MARX, KARL (1977). *Capital,* Vol. 1 (Ben Fowkes, Trans.). New York: Vintage Books. (Original work published in 1867.)

McCONE COMMISSION REPORT (1965). *A Report by the Governor's Commission on the Los Angeles Riots.* Los Angeles: Kimtex Corporation.

MERTON, ROBERT (1957). "Contributions to the Theory of Reference Group Behavior," in collaboration with Alice S. Rossi, pp. 225–80 in *Social Theory and Social Structure* (rev. ed.). New York: Free Press.

MICHELS, ROBERT (1959). *Political Parties: A Sociological Study of the Oligarchical Tendencies of Modern Democracies.* New York: Dover (First published in 1915).

MILLS, C. WRIGHT (1951). *White Collar: The American Middle Classes*. New York: Oxford University Press.

OBERSCHALL, ANTHONY (1968, Winter). "The Los Angeles Riot of August 1965." *Social Problems, 15*, 322–41.

PIVEN, FRANCIS FOX & CLOWARD, RICHARD A. (1971). *Regulating the Poor: The Functions of Public Welfare*. New York: Vintage Books.

SHIBUTANI, TAMOTSU (1978). *The Derelicts of Company K: A Sociological Study of Demoralization*. Berkeley: University of California Press.

STINCHCOMBE, ARTHUR L. (1968). *Constructing Social Theories*. New York: Harcourt Brace Jovanovich.

SUTTLES, GERALD (1968). *The Social Order of the Slum: Ethnicity and Territory in the Inner City*. Chicago: University of Chicago Press.

WILSON, EDMUND (1983). "The Historical Interpretation of Literature." In Lewis M. Dabney (Ed.), *The Portable Edmund Wilson* (pp. 338–53). New York: Penguin Books. (Original work published in 1940.)

WOLFE, TOM (1979, December). "The Sexed-Up, Doped-Up, Hedonistic Heaven of the Boom-Boom '70s," *Life*, 103–12.

2

The Sociological Tradition

Thorstein Veblen was the first major North American social theorist but found it difficult to hold academic posts. As John Dos Passos said, "there seemed no place for a masterless man." (Painting by Edwin Burrage Child, with permission of Culver Pictures, Inc.)

PART I
CLASSICS

Sociology excites a unique set of reactions—it bores some and frightens others. Doubtless it kindles additional moods, including the passion of a few, but the extraordinary thing about sociology is that it can be regarded as both trivial and threatening. This anomaly suggests, at least to a sociologist, that there is more here than meets the eye.

Consider the following loosely connected facts. Before a national television audience in the United States, the eminent, and now retired, journalist Eric Sevareid once referred to sociology as slow journalism. Yet only a few years before, in 1967, the Greek military junta abolished the teaching of sociology as a menace to the right-wing Heleno-Christian Revolution. Socialist revolutions have also found reason to outlaw sociology. It virtually disappeared from the Soviet Union under Stalin and was banned for a time after 1952 in China, in both cases, owing to its contaminating influence on the "science" of Marxism-Leninism. Despite these credentials, such exponents of plain speaking as journalist Edwin Newman (1974) grumble, "A large part of social science practice consists of taking clear ideas and making them opaque" (p. 174). Beginning in the 1920s, however, Mussolini's government purged Italian universities of sociologists whose criticism of fascism was all too clear. How is it that the same subject can arouse fears of subversion and state repression in some settings and a smug indifference in others?

An appreciation of the nature of sociology, as well as of these diverse perceptions, requires some description of the discipline's special perspective and history. That is the purpose of this chapter.

Beginning on a necessarily formal note, sociology is defined as the study of group life and those aspects of individual lives that are affected by social interaction.

The *sociological perspective* differs from the way we view the world as individuals; differs in ways that require us to step outside, but never abandon, personal experience and gain a new vantage on the world. The reason for doing so is simple: There are many features of social life that cannot be explained otherwise. This principle was demonstrated in the chapter on method. Individuals understand suicide, for example, as a consequence of mental depression, personal or financial loss, or insanity. But none of these explains the social suicide rate, something that Durkheim (1960) could explain by the unseen, but nevertheless potent, disruption of rules governing social life (anomie). Similarly, individuals know when they belong to a democratic union, although they may not comprehend the collective fact of an occupational community that lies behind their personal experience. Sociology explores the determinants of individual and collective behavior that are not given in personal experience, but fashioned in the broader arena of social interaction. Once these social influences are revealed, they make intuitive sense; they explain something that we did not know before and would not have discovered by searching the contents of individual experience. The question, therefore, is how one gains this perspective.

SOCIOLOGICAL IMAGINATION

C. Wright Mills (1959) called it the "sociological imagination" and suggested that the perspective provides a means for people to interpret their lives and social circumstances:

> [It] is a quality of mind that will help them to use information and to develop reason in order to achieve lucid summations of what is going on in the world and what may be happening within themselves.... The sociological imagination enables us to grasp history and biography and the relations between the two within society. (C. Wright Mills, *The Sociological Imagination*, pp. 5 and 7)

The sociological perspective is acquired, in the first instance, by asking particular sorts of questions about social life. Illustratively, sociologists do not ask, "What makes people do this or that?" (which implies that people have individualized dispositions or motives that explain whatever they do); sociologists ask instead, "Why does one group of people do this or that in a different way from, or more often than another group?" (this implies social causes of varied group actions). There are many other forms in which proper sociological questions can be asked, but the key is that they address the characteristics of groups and categories of people, that is, *interactive* groups such as families, clubs, and organizations and distinctive *categories* of unrelated persons such as occupations and social classes. Moreover, the sociological perspective assumes that the answers lie in social, as opposed to exclusively psychological or economic, influences. Sociology has no quarrel with the other social sciences. Indeed, it often combines with those in complex explanations. It simply insists that much of social life has its own explanations that cannot be reduced to the more elementary compounds from psychology, biology, or some other science.

In the opening line of *The Sociological Imagination*, Mills observed that nowadays people "often feel that their private lives are a series of traps" (p. 3), that they have little control over the forces that shape their lives. Sociologists beginning with Marx have referred to this feeling as alienation or the individual's sense of separation and estrangement from useful work, other people, and from the self. The sociological perspective should allow people to understand this mood (an aspect of biography) by relating it to historical and social forces that close in on the individual.

One of the most poignant statements of the alienated mood comes from John Steinbeck's (1939) novel *The Grapes of Wrath*. During the Great Depression of the 1930s, an exchange takes place between a tenant farmer who is being evicted from his land and a tractor driver in the employ of the new corporate owners. The farmer begins speaking of his house that is about to fall under the tractor's blade:

> "I built it with my hands...it's mine. I built it. You dump it down—I'll pot you like a rabbit."
>
> "It's not me. There's nothing I can do. And look—suppose you kill me? They'll just hang you, but long before you're hung there'll be another guy on the tractor, and he'll bump the house down. You're not killing the right guy."
>
> "That's so," the tenant said. "Who gave you the orders? I'll go after him. He's the one to kill."
>
> "You're wrong. He got his orders from the bank. The bank told him, clear those people out or it's your job."
>
> "Well, there's a president of the bank. There's a board of directors. I'll fill up the magazine of the rifle and go into the bank."
>
> The driver said, "Fellow was telling me the bank get orders from the East. The orders were, 'Make the land show profit or we'll close you up.'"

"But where does it stop? Who can we shoot? I don't aim to starve to death before I kill the man that's starving me."

"I don't know. Maybe there's nobody to shoot. Maybe the thing isn't men at all. Maybe like you said, property's doing it. Anyway I told you my orders."

"I got to figure," the tenant said. "We all got to figure. There's some way to stop this. It's not like lightning or earthquakes. We've got a bad thing made by men, and by God that's something we can change." (John Steinbeck, *The Grapes of Wrath*, p. 40)

There are several ways to understand this scene, different explanations of the tenant farmer's frustration and anger. One might say that the tenant has a violent personality, another that he is economically motivated. The sociological perspective would recognize, first, that the actors in this drama represent broader social categories: hundreds of thousands of tenants who lost their land and livelihood, thousands of tractor drivers who were among the fortunate minority that still had jobs, and hundreds of bankers who foreclosed on their neighbors, perhaps reluctantly, on "orders from the East." Why did the tenants want to shoot someone and the tractor drivers counsel restraint? Probably because the tenant farmers felt moral outrage based on the social values of the American West ("I built it with my own hands"), because they faced an unprecedented situation with no established avenue of redress ("There's some way to stop this") and, perhaps, because the hard and solitary lives of tenant farmers did not generate politically organized communities that might have found a way to resist ("We all got to figure"). The tractor drivers, on the other hand, came from the same social class backgrounds, but they had the desperately needed jobs and they understood the connection between the evictions and the changing economy ("property's doing it... the bank get orders from the East... Make the land show a profit or we'll close you up.").

In fact, the tenant farmers neither shot anyone nor organized politically to save their farms and way of life. Instead they migrated in response to the destruction of former lives by the combined forces of drought and corporate capital (the banks and Eastern owners). And they migrated as social groups. As Steinbeck's extraordinary novel shows, they took to the highways in caravans of families and friends, followed the routes that social networks informed them led to safe passage and California jobs, and helped one another along the way through socially innovated means of mutual support. The migration followed social patterns that reflected their origins in regions of high tenancy, drought, and, in troubled times, a certain cultural solidarity among these Okies.

History and Biography

In the 50 years since this fictional incident, the tenants' dawning sense of alienation has diffused to the rest of society. It has become an accepted part of the human condition, only temporarily escaped in leisure, fantasy, mood-altering substances, other-worldly visions, or acts of rebellion. It may be alleviated, too, in efficacious action or satisfying work, but the difficulty is that that alternative is also harder to find. In 1981, Chicago autoworkers took sledgehammers to an imported Japanese car for the benefit of photographers and policymakers, but their action failed to restore their jobs or halt the steady decline in manufacturing employment. As in the case of the tenant farmer, they failed to find an appropriate or responsible agent on whom their troubles could be pinned. Action to ameliorate social problems is ever more elusive. Does sociology speak to such issues?

Today's alienation is expressed in a set of questions that wants a sociological answer: Why is unemployment so high in societies that we are told enjoy prosperity? Will technology eliminate all forms of satisfying work and turn the next generation into computer technicians? Why has the civil rights revolution passed with little change in the income inequality of minorities? Why do problems of crime and drug abuse seem ever on the increase? Why are fundamentalist religions and outer-space movies so popular? Why are developed nations involved in new wars despite the once-vivid lessons of the old? Where are we headed and what can we do about it?

The sociological perspective is uniquely suited to answer these kinds of questions. It begins by establishing the social facts at issue (rates of unemployment by social category, net effects of technological displacement, actual rates of and participants in crime and drug abuse). Next, it invents and tries out alternative explanations (whether sloth, production methods, or prejudice account for categorical differences in employment and income).

Finding the best available explanation, it pushes ahead asking what are the implications for related problems and solutions.

When sociology begins to answer these questions, it may also become useful, nettlesome, threatening—in short, controversial. An explanation that helps the tenant to understand may bore the tractor driver and threaten the banker. Sociology is as much a part of the world as the conflicts it examines. Its perspective is necessarily critical to the extent that it finds causes for consequential social change. The best way to describe the perspective, and to discover much of the substance of sociology, is to review the work of the people who developed it. Similarly, an appreciation of that work depends on understanding the times of the early sociologists and the parts they took in events of their times.

THE CLASSICAL TRADITION

Sociology is not a young science, contrary to some opinion and misguided apologies for the state of its knowledge. It originated in the 19th century at a time when many of the modern sciences and humanities appeared. It was a product of the same milieu that produced these disciplines and, until the turn of the 20th century, was part of a unified tradition of inquiry that embraced philosophy, law, economics, history, anthropology, and many aspects of the natural sciences. Yet among these pursuits, sociology was always a prodigal child of the "great transformation"—the historical epoch that fashioned the modern world from feudalism to industrial capitalism and set in motion the institutions of urbanism, bureaucracy, political revolution, and the nation state. Sociology's prodigal bent derives from its critical concern over where those changes were leading society. This was the dominant theme that created sociology and preoccupied

The Beginnings

Sociology was made possible by the French Revolution. The capture of the Bastille on July 14, 1789, and the Women's March on Versailles introduced a new principle into history by demanding political action to redress mass poverty. The authority of king and church that once justified social inequality was challenged by the philosophical notion of the general will come to life among people convinced that their suffering was no longer inevitable. Public opinion became a legitimate method for expressing these social concerns. But the nascent forces of democracy did not at once take institutional shape. The revolution first produced a Reign of Terror that also justified itself in appeals to the will of the people and later a self-proclaimed emperor, Napoleon. As the political revolution faltered, the Industrial Revolution in England and France gathered momentum mixing new ingredients with social unrest.

Comte Henri de Saint-Simon (1760–1825) was a product of his age and prophet of a new society. As an aristocratic youth, he fought with the French Royalists against the North American revolutionaries, although his sentiments lay with neither side. Later he renounced his title, made and lost a fortune speculating in estates confiscated by the French government, and was imprisoned under the Reign of Terror. But he earned a new title: the founder of sociology. Saint-Simon's passion was social reconstruction. He was an eccentric and, in Edmund Wilson's (1940) words, "a dilettante on an enormous scale, made restless by an all-trying curiosity" (p. 81). He studied physics, mathematics, and philosophy, spent his money on dissipation and travel, "and was able to investigate poverty at first hand."

Saint-Simon's genius was to see what conventional thinkers could not: that society, no less than nature, was governed by scientific laws whose mastery could produce social institutions for the benefit of humanity. History, he surmised, alternated between periods of equilibrium and breakdown. The revolution was a breakdown setting the stage for a new equilibrium based not on the discredited formulas of politics, but on the new and scientifically organized industrial system. Political schemes and unrealistic notions of equality (alongside the facts of corruption and inequality) would be replaced by artists and scientists, at the behest of public subscription, in a hierarchy of merit. The aim of industry would be provision for human needs and fulfillment. On his deathbed, Saint-Simon remarked, "All of my life may be summed up in one idea: to guarantee to all men the free development of their faculties" (Wilson, p. 85). His hope was that the new order would be installed, though not governed, by the party of workers.

The title "founder of sociology" is a somewhat mythical and not altogether enviable status. Saint-Simon had his own mentors in the science of history and he was followed by others who claimed parentage of sociology. Auguste Comte, who studied and then repudiated Saint-Simon, first used the term and popularized the notion of a "positive science of sociology." But it was Saint-Simon who first combined 18th-century inklings of a social science with an analysis that laid bare the workings of postrevolutionary industrial society in the 19th century. Next to that achievement, Comte's hierarchy of the sciences, which placed sociology at the pinnacle (and Comte, the father, at the head of the new intellectual priesthood), all seemed a bit rarified and derivative. Unlike Saint-Simon, Comte's twin ambitions were to create a new science of society and an elite of social experts, not a radically reorganized industrial society based on individual merit.

The modern U.S. sociologist Alvin Gouldner (1970) has shown there were two roads from Saint-Simon. The first road taken by Comte and the academic sociologists led into the university and mitigated commitments to social reconstruction as the price of state support—a price that Comte and his followers were eager to pay. The second road taken by the early socialists, Karl Marx among them, and by reformers of various political leanings, led into politics, the new labor movement, and social action. Since the latter tendency is more consistent with Saint-Simon, academic sociologists have preferred to recognize Comte as their disciplinary progenitor. Gouldner (1962) notes wryly that "if sociologists acknowledge descent from Saint-Simon rather than Comte they are not only acquiring a father, but a blacksheep brother, socialism" (p. 12).

Whatever these preferences for a founder, it remains true that many contributed to the discipline born in response to the trauma of political and industrial revolution. With these origins, sociology has always had a dual nature: as a disciplined method and corpus of study and as a purposeful activity in society— analysis and action. The manner in which this dual nature is balanced by individual practitioners varies, but the tension between the two is always present.

As sociology evolved from the mid-19th to the early 20th century, that tension was healthy, cross-fertile, and more often embraced than shunned. Characteristically, works that came to comprise the classical tradition set forth broad interpretations of historical trends and the main drift of modern society. As C. Wright Mills (1960) said of the classical sociologists, "their intellectual problems [were] relevant to the public issues of their times, and to the private troubles of individual men and women" (p. 4).

Marx

Karl Marx (1818–83) is the preeminent social and political thinker of the 19th century and he personifies the classical tradition. Marx and his lifelong collaborator, Friedrich Engels, invented a social theory so compelling for their own times, and so provocative for the future, that all subsequent work in the classical mode must first come to terms with it.

Marx was born in Trier located in the western German Rhineland then under French Napoleonic rule. He came from a middle-class family, growing up in prosperity and his mother's devotion to Judaism, albeit in an atmosphere of discrimination against Germans and Jews. Marx was a precocious and idealistic youth, but not a distinguished student. In 1835, he entered the University of Bonn with no clear purpose beyond the harmless rebellion that he enjoyed in tavern society and a Poet's Club (which the police considered subversive). He made the dean's list for dueling and "nocturnal drunkenness and riot." His father's concern over these exploits led him to move on to the more studious climate of the University of Berlin where he intended to study law. At Berlin from 1835–41, Marx was now attracted to the intellectual rebellion brewing in philosophy, completing a thesis on the subject of materialism in early Greek thought.

From adolescence, Marx had courted Jenny von Westphalen, a neighbor in Trier whose father had introduced the young suitor to the politics of Saint-Simon. After the university, Marx hoped to obtain a position teaching philosophy, but the radical ideas of his Berlin training were already unpopular with school officials. So Marx began a career in journalism writing for the *Rhineland Times*, a newspaper financed by liberal industrialists of the region who encouraged his maturing criticism of the

Prussian state. Marx proved a witty, relentlessly logical, and devastatingly critical writer. He contributed pieces on Prussian censorship, the oppression of peasants, orthodox religion, and the crisis in the wine industry. Although he was soon promoted to editor and circulation advanced briskly, the paper became embroiled in controversy with a conservative competitor, was accused of communist leanings, and forcibly closed by the state in 1843. At the time Marx knew nothing about communism, but decided to read about it. As the suppression of critical thought grew in Germany, he married Jenny and went into exile in Paris.

Paris was a magical world for the 25-year-old journalist, a world teeming with political exiles from all of Europe, French revolutionaries, Saint-Simonians, and partisans of varied socialist sects, all of them writing and endeavoring to organize the working class. Marx began a new journal, contributed to others, and above all sought to square his philosophical education with the currents of French political thought and society. He knew little about economics and was introduced to its mysteries through an article by Engels on the British political economists. Immediately Marx began corresponding with the fellow Rhinelander who was already a published critic of the conditions of the English working class—an odd position since Engels was also the manager of his family's textile manufacturing firm. They soon met in Paris and began a thoroughly mutual collaboration that outlived Marx by 12 years until Engels's death in 1895. Marx possessed a flashing intelligence and an iron determination to revolutionize social thought. But the partnership was greatly enhanced by Engels's splendid talents as a writer, observer, investigator, linguist, historian, genial human being, a practical businessman who knew industry at first hand and, not least, by an income that helped support the Marx family in frequent hard times.

These were the decisive years for Marx. In 1844 he drafted the *Economic and Philosophical Manuscripts* and, with Engels, completed *The German Ideology* in 1846—although neither work was published for some time to come. In germ, these writings embodied the social theory that Marx and Engels would elaborate and change over the next 50 years. They claimed to turn on its head an earlier philosophy that believed ideals governed history. On the contrary, they said, ideals and social relations arose from the material conditions of production. A new materialist conception of history was fashioned for an eventful future. In Paris, Marx embarked on a life of socioeconomic study and political action that never wavered. He decided to change the world.

Marx and Engels built a bridge from the uncertain beginnings of sociology to the 20th century. They studied Saint-Simon and agreed that industry, or more properly capitalism, was the driving force in contemporary society. They agreed that a science of society was both possible and essential for getting to the roots of social ills—but a science of true socialism as distinct from the variety of utopian, ethical, feudal, petty bourgeois, and other naively reformist socialisms. True socialism relied on a materialist understanding of historical development, on an appreciation of the fact that social relations were most effectively shaped by the conditions of production that, in turn, generated antagonistic classes such as the owners of industry, workers, landlords, and peasants.

The key for Marx and Engels, what distinguished them from the crowd of social reformers, was the premise that labor produced everything of value in society apart from nature's endowments and, under the conditions of capitalist production, labor was exploited—meaning that it received less than the value of what it created (as we saw in Chapter 1 with the concept of surplus value). The bulk of the value produced went to the capitalist for reinvestment or for the capitalist's own consumption and wealth. This implied two new and radical interpretations of social conditions: one, that poverty, inequality, inhuman factory conditions, and hunger were direct consequences of competitive capitalism; and two, that only revolutionary action by the working class would change matters.

In 1848, a series of short-lived revolutions spread across every major European country. Anticipating these events, Marx and Engels prepared a pamphlet for working-class audiences entitled *Manifesto of the Communist Party* (1959) which they hoped would influence the direction of events. No communist party existed at the time and another purpose of the tract was to coalesce various socialist factions in a new party founded upon the insights and proposed strategies of Marx and Engels. Its famous closing line implored, "Workingmen of all countries, unite!" By this time, Marx had been expelled from Paris for his subversive writing and he traveled often to London from his new residence in Brussels. Engels introduced him to working class activists in England (many of them also German exiles) who made up the League of the Just. That organization, a small band by all accounts, changed its name to the Communist League and sponsored the *Manifesto* as its program. The document's publication attracted no attention and Marx's followers had little influence in the broad socialist movement.

The results of 1848 were nil. Revolutionary governments in Europe were quickly replaced and reform movements dealt a serious setback. Marx and Engels would not return to political activism until the more successful organization of the International Working Men's Association (the First International) in 1864. In the meantime, urged on by expulsion from both Paris and Brussels, Marx settled in London and began his encyclopedic studies in the British Museum that would result in his magnum opus, *Capital*.

Durkheim

Sociology was slow in gaining recognition. During the first 50 years since the term's invention in the 1830s, it had actually fallen into disuse in France and was a mere novelty in England and the United States. The survival and growth of the discipline owed much to Émile Durkheim (1858–1917) who decided that the "barbarous neologism" was nevertheless useful for identifying a distinctive and sound method of social study. Yet Durkheim also understood that the new science lacked a persuasive conceptual or practical justification. The indifferent fortunes of sociology over the previous half century, by the time Durkheim's first writings appeared, would not be reversed until the discipline distinguished itself from history and philosophy by proving that it had practical uses.

Émile Durkheim came from the Lorraine region of eastern France. His birthplace in Épinal lay just 100 miles south of Trier where Marx was born 40 years earlier. Durkheim came from a family of modest means and orthodox Judaism. At the age of 18, he went to Paris to study philosophy and impressed his teachers as serious to a fault. After completing his first course of study in 1882, Durkheim taught in provincial schools for five years while preparing a doctoral thesis, *The Division of Labor in Society*. Published later as a book that would become a classic, the thesis helped him land a faculty position at the University of Bordeaux in 1887. In French academic circles, Durkheim's views were controversial, accounting for the fact that he remained in the provincial university for 15 years before the call came from the Sorbonne in Paris—even then the post was on the faculty of education and he waited a few more years for a chair in sociology.

In today's language, Durkheim was an inveterate academic. Politically he favored a French Republic in preference to an imperial monarchy, a secular state in opposition to the strong Catholic right, and he espoused progressive social reforms. But he was aloof from practical politics, cleaving to his belief that reform must be based on the most thoughtful and detached analysis. This is far from saying that Durkheim was indifferent to practical action. He simply wanted to place it on a solid foundation. In the preface to the *Division of Labor* (1960) he wrote, "We would judge our researches to have no worth at all if they were to have only a speculative interest. If we separate carefully the theoretical from the practical problems, it is not to neglect that latter; but, on the contrary, to be in a better position to solve them" (p. 33). Durkheim was not a socialist. He doubted the wisdom of its revolutionary wing, despairing the bitter harvest of the French Revolution, and he had no taste for agitation. But he shared the aims of socialist reform and tried to promote those in his own way.

In Durkheim's lifetime, France suffered chronic crises that added urgency to the need for reform. His youth coincided with the national humiliation of the Franco-Prussian War (1870–71) and the aborted rebellion of the Paris Commune (1871) that ended in the bloody repression of urban revolutionaries by other French forces. Reflecting on these events in his thesis a decade later, Durkheim concluded that Saint-Simon was right about the deterioration of French society. But sociology had to prove itself with a practical solution for the crisis.

Saint-Simon correctly identified industrialism as the watershed of modern society, the source of social tensions arising from the gap between old customs and modern practices. New institutions were needed that would promote the kind of social solidarity consistent with industrialism. Durkheim believed that, in the absence of new moral rules, social anarchy would prevail in the form of class war and overproduction, much as Marx had described. Practical reforms could produce the needed solidarity.

For example, class conflict and exploitation stemmed from accumulated privilege (wealth and power) passed along generationally through the institution of inheritance. This inequality invalidated truly free contracts, such as between workers and owners, since the respective parties were not free and independent. One had an enormous unearned advantage over the other, meaning that the free and contractual rules that were supposed to govern industrial society according to its own principles were contradicted in practice. The institution of inheritance was wholly incompatible with individual liberty and opportunity, moral principles appropriate for industrial society. Accordingly, the abolition of inheritance would eliminate a major impediment to social reorganization.

The problem was what to put in place of the exhausted morals and institutions. Durkheim's inspiration on that score is the centerpiece of all his work, running through the thesis to his posthumously published lectures, *Professional Ethics and Civic Morals* (1958). The idea is close to what is called economic democracy today. By the late 19th century, Durkheim concluded, the expansion of industry and government had weakened all those "intermediate powers" or "secondary groups" between the family and the state that integrate people into society (civic organizations and voluntary associations). The idea was not new to Durkheim and had been used by Alexis de Tocqueville (1959) in his classic *Democracy in America*. A decline in associational group life and regulative communities was the source of the social crisis. It fostered the moral confusion which he called anomie and was related to various social ills including the suicide rate. A new basis for group life was required that would capture and express the potential solidarity of an interdependent industrial society.

The concrete answer that Durkheim proposed was the professional or occupational association as a new focus of group life and as a substitute basis for political representation, superseding the geographical districts that now lacked a common interest or moral integration of citizens. Noteworthy in Durkheim's plan, beyond its continuing appeal to reformers, is a close affinity to Saint-Simon's proposal for a new form of government consistent with the "positive industrial order." Moreover, by returning to the founder, Durkheim developed a synthesis of Comte and Marx. And he accomplished this by keeping his promise of a practical sociology, since a revitalized sociology was uniquely able to investigate the causes of anomie and evaluate alternative cures. Durkheim was fond of the medical analogy in which sociology diagnosed social ills and prescribed more healthy measures. At bottom, it was elegantly simple: egoism was the bane of modern society and its amelioration depended upon new corporate groups promoting social organization by virtue of their organic connection to the real conditions of contemporary life.

Weber

While Durkheim pioneered a sociological renaissance in France, the intellectual world in Germany discouraged such innovation. Universities in the newly united country shared with the state a contentious and conservative bearing, as well as a phobia for socialism and anything associated with their own expatriate Marx. Yet this milieu produced Max Weber (1864–1920), a man whose stamp on the social sciences is still unequalled.

Weber was raised in Berlin, the son of a prosperous lawyer and National-Liberal Party member of Parliament. His father was something of a Prussian autocrat and young Max developed a close attachment to his mother, a cultured woman with humanitarian interests. He began university at Heidelberg in 1882 as a student of law, but approached that field, as he would everything in life, from a catholic viewpoint that embraced history, economics, philosophy, and a new sociology of his own creation. His dissertation on the history of medieval business organization (1889) and a second work on Roman agrarian history led him to the University of Berlin as an instructor in law. From 1893–97 he held his first and last regular academic position as professor of economics at the University of Freiberg.

Weber's early years were crowded with professional and civic activity. He held lectures and seminars for 19 hours a week, participated in state examinations of lawyers, consulted with government agencies, wrote prodigiously, and conducted research whose results he tried to impress on policymakers. Given his own brooding temperament and poor medical history, the load proved crushing. In the fall of 1897 he suffered a breakdown that prevented work for the next four years. For the rest of his life he held only part-time and visiting, if celebrated, posts, although an inheritance (one Durkheim might have exempted) allowed him to live as a private scholar and political actor. By this time, Weber had achieved some fame and never wanted for offers as a lecturer or public servant. Despite the complexity of his lectures, which are still studied with profit, Weber was a platform attraction, packing halls with students and professors, civil servants, business people, and politicians.

Following his early studies on legal history, Weber accepted the request of a scholarly reform group to analyze parts of a large social survey dealing with German agrarian society. He relished the assignment, and the manner in which he worked his way from the gritty questionnaires to a critical examination of social classes and the state exhibited his energy, values, and extraordinary insight.

Weber's specific task was to analyze data on agricultural production in eastern Germany, the social base of the Prussian state and province of the large landowners or Junkers. The immediate problem that concerned his reformist sponsors was the migration of German farmworkers to western regions of the country and their replacement by Polish and Russian day-laborers of a decidedly lower cultural level. From the standpoint of liberal reformers, the social problem was defined by several aspects: conditions of labor were declining in the East as immigrant workers were paid less and lost an attachment to the land, productivity was low, German society was being degraded by the infusion of foreign workers and the displacement of a stalwart peasantry from the East to the industrial regions of the West. In the process of exploiting the new labor force, the Junker estates were neglecting the agricultural modernization necessary for Germany to maintain its position in the world market of agricultural commodities.

Most of these facts were familiar to public officials and the sponsors of the research, but Weber surprised everyone in his summary of a 900-page report that he offered in a speech to the reform society's convention in 1893. His analysis laid bare the agrarian problem, explored its roots in the transformation of the state and economy, and ended with some unsettling political implications. Every political ox was gored and no facile remedies were baited for the reformers. In the first place, Weber blamed neither the migrating German farmworkers, who sought a life free of the drudgery and paternalism of the old estates, nor the large landowners whose aristocratic society and economic base had enabled political unification of the country. True, the Junkers were now becoming an outmoded, even parasitic class, but in the face of the capitalist transformation of the economy that had overtaken them, they were obeying a certain perverse rationality. As a nationalist, Weber despaired of both developments, although he saw more virtue in the motives of the migrating workers.

The real problem lay in a new alignment of social classes and the state. German unification had benefited the urban and industrial classes of the West to the disadvantage of the Junkers who were forced to buy nationally manufactured goods at high prices without compensating stimulants to productive agriculture. Meanwhile, the state was building a new coalition that amalgamated large landowners and the rising industrial capitalists. One of the ways this was done involved granting land trusts that allowed acreage to be taken out of production and rented to reactionary Junkers and status-climbing industrialists who mimicked the style of the old aristocracy. The state assisted in the formation of a group of "satiated capitalists" for reasons of its own political support, thereby defying agricultural modernization and corrupting the civil service.

In this work that did so much to establish Weber's reputation as a researcher and political critic, the style is very close to Marx's historical writing. That was no accident. Throughout his life, Weber pursued a spirited dialogue with Marxist thought. In the 1890s, his emphasis was on the incompleteness of one-sided materialistic explanations. Weber agreed that economic considerations were potent forces for social change, always present, but seldom the singular causes of social behavior. One must also appreciate the role of ideas that sometimes operates in conjunction with material forces and at other times with a power of their own. The blend and sequence of these complementary influences were more subtle than Marxists allowed. For example, the German farmworkers who migrated to industry certainly wanted to improve their economic condition, but they were also emboldened by the prospect of greater individual freedom. Weber's insight was the importance of the values that individuals acquired in group settings and how they could be fitted into an analysis that also counted the role of social structure without trivializing either or reducing one to the other.

Ten years later, in his best-known book *The Protestant Ethic and the Spirit of Capitalism* (first published in German during 1904–05), Weber (1958) elaborated another instance of the point. Why, he asked, did capitalism flourish in Western Europe rather than in the Far East which had comparable material and technological endowments? His answer was that religion, especially Calvinism, inspired an ethic that motivated the aggressive pursuit of gain, not for its own sake, but for what it proved in this life about one's place in the next. The rich and pious of this world were God's elect, according to the ethic of the early capitalist entrepreneurs. Ideas not only coincided with the material conditions of capitalism (the resources, technology, and communications), but had a prior and autonomous causal effect.

At other times, particularly in Weber's later years, his interpretation of history emphasized institutional structures with scant reference to subjective meanings. His analysis of political change, for example, developed in acknowledged harmony with Marx, and it seems that Weber's aim was to generalize historical materialism from economic to all-social change.

Two years before his death, in a lecture, "Politics as Vocation," he says that the modern state grows through the expropriation of all private holders of power: "The whole process is a complete parallel to the development of the capitalist enterprise through gradual expropriation of the independent producers" (p. 82). In politics, the pervasive consequence that overshadows class struggle is the growth of rational bureaucracy—a society reorganized according to mechanical, depersonalized, and oppressive routine. Although, with characteristic irony, Weber also notes the efficiency and democratizing consequences of bureaucracy, he feared the eventual merger of the state and economy in bureaucratic capitalism. In this, he not only extended Marx, but showed his gift for prophecy.

It would be wrong, however, to fix Weber's methodological and political beliefs in any general or timeless mold. He had less interest in, and many more reservations about, creating a theoretical system than did Marx or Durkheim. His political positions changed, appropriately, with the circumstances that occasioned them and the channels through which they might have some effect. In later life, particularly during World War I when he served as an administrator of hospitals, he became more embittered and critical of the German state. Yet, as a consultant to the Armistice Commission at Versailles, he foresaw the dangers of a punitive peace—the terms of German surrender that subsequent historians would adduce as the first cause of the next world war. Above all, Weber's gift was for intricate and deep inquiry, realism leavened with irony, keen insight held to strict confines, and originality.

The Classical Tradition

The *classical tradition* is a way of thinking and a responsibility for acting. It was built through the efforts of a great many men and women (including among the latter Harriet Martineau, Beatrice Potter Webb, and Rosa Luxemburg). Marx, Durkheim, and Weber describe its outlines, but scarcely exhaust its contents. The classical tradition means engagement with the pain, misery, and confusion, as much as with the achievements of the spirit that exist in society. It assesses the character of a social order, asks how it originated, where it is going, and where it could go with the contribution of a clear and humane vision. It participates by connecting social issues and individual lives with sociological imagination.

The exemplary classical sociologists differed in their politics and participatory styles: from Marx, the intellectual worker and political activist, to Durkheim, the academic and social planner; from Weber, the nationalist and respected critic, to Marx the exile and revolutionary; from Durkheim's faith in an organic corporate society to Weber's premonition of bureaucratic state domination. Underlying these differences, however, was a common purpose to beneficially reorganize the prevailing order and participate in its reform.

The classical sociologists spoke to the people. Each would have had something to say to Steinbeck's tenant farmer or today's autoworker: Marx about exploitation by a ruling class of industrial capitalists (the ones to overthrow if not shoot) and the power of organized workers; Weber about the participation of the state in such injustices and the opportunities presented by its vulnerability; Durkheim about a new social solidarity and non-revolutionary politics of occupational groups close to the peoples' interest. The compassionate alternatives are revolution, political reform, and economic democracy—a list that pretty well encompasses our repertoire 100 years later.

PART II
TRANSITION

As the classical tradition flowed out from continental Europe, it followed unanticipated channels, nourishing open fields of revolution in one direction and fenced academic gardens in another. Marxism traveled east to Russia, assisting in the movement to overthrow Tsarist absolutism that had been brewing throughout the late 19th century. Marx saw these developments in his own lifetime, although the first Russian Revolution came 22 years after his death and the Bolshevik victory 34 years later. The first translation of *Capital* was into Russian and this, coupled with a favorable reception of socialism among reformers, led Marx to learn the language and study the Russian system of land tenure. As a result, Marx amended his theory of revolution in the industrial countries and allowed for revolutionary transformation in the less developed societies.

Although Marx and Engels were now living in England, their revolutionary politics had a limited effect on British socialists and the larger labor movement. The influence of Marxism was not negligible, only indirect. Revolutionaries of the Socialist League, led by the writer and designer William Morris, knew Marx's writing and consulted with Engels on strategy. But English socialists, such as the playwright George Bernard Shaw, mixed the ideas of Marx with the left wing of the Labor Party in their reformist brew.

The classical tradition itself began to fragment in the early 20th century owing to a growing rift between the socialists and reformers and the first academic sociologists. Durkheim had a major influence in England, but mainly among anthropologists studying primitive societies throughout the Empire. British sociology came under the sway of Leonard Hobhouse (1864–1929) who, despite his own reform work in journalism and trade unionism, disputed the socialists and moved steadily toward the abstractions of social psychology and philosophy. Symptomatic of the split, Hobhouse devoted his energies to a new sociological society and the general principles of the unifying science. A breach opened between academic sociologists of the Hobhouse stripe and research-minded reformers such as

Charles Booth (1970) and Beatrice Potter who worked together on the monumental 17-volume study of *Life and Labor of the People of London*. The classical tradition began to divide with reformers enjoying a public reception and academics the fruits of scientific status.

THE DEVELOPMENT OF SOCIOLOGY IN NORTH AMERICA

The beginnings of sociology in the United States were tentative and deferential. There was no mad Count to propose a reorganization of the industrial system. Indeed, there were no counts, and industry was not yet a system in the 1870s. More important, there was no indigenous tradition of social philosophy to draw upon and only a selective understanding or tolerance for European thought. The first North American sociologists were impatient with the speculative fancies of European intellectuals, some of whom appeared decadent or politically unsavory.

In the early years, the main foreign writers to have a measurable impact on the North Americans were Comte (now seen as the father) and the Englishman Herbert Spencer (1820–1903), a self-educated engineer, self-styled moral philosopher, and devotee of evolutionary theory. Spencer developed an elaborate, and certainly speculative, scheme for understanding society much as a biological organism; a creature that evolved, differentiated over time, adapted, and generally edged up the scale of social evolution from simple to modern society. Spencer owed a great deal to Comte and Charles Darwin, although, in the case of the latter, Spencer claimed that the influence was mutual. Spencer reminded everyone that he coined the phrase "survival of the fittest."

In London's Highgate Cemetery, the modest headstone of Spencer stands opposite Marx's tomb and gigantic bust. These two are closer in death than ever in life. Spencer had no use for what he saw as unscientific polemics and he passed that judgment on to his North American readers. The value of Spencer's work is still argued (Mills saw merit in it), but his impact in the United States was forceful and ironic—Spencer's was the theory that the early social scientists read and disagreed with the most.

The Pioneers

Sociology in the United States was begun by two men, contemporaries vigorously opposed on the implications they drew from Spencer: Lester Frank Ward (1841-1913) and William Graham Sumner (1840–1910). Both agreed that a proper sociology would have to be scientific, by which they meant not a historical science after the Europeans, but one that was naturalistic and evolutionary. Great appeal lay in the idea that society evolved along the lines of the biological organism and, therefore, invited the same sort of scientific analysis.

Sumner was a professor at Yale University and offered the first social science courses in the United States beginning in the 1870s. Although he differed with Spencer on many points concerning the determinacy of social evolution, Sumner was attracted by the conservative political implications of evolutionary theory. He felt that society evolved progressively, though not mechanically, from adaptive folkways to higher mores in a fashion that was best left alone. Certainly governments and reformers should not dabble in such verities. Sumner was considered stuffy by his more liberal colleagues.

North American sociology, like populism, was more at home in the Midwest and Lester Ward was closer to the mood of the new discipline. Born in Joliet, Illinois, his youth was spent on the prairies of Iowa where he acquired a love of nature. The family moved again to Pennsylvania where Lester taught school and attended Susquehanna Collegiate Institute with the hope of studying law. Lincoln's call for Pennsylvania volunteers ended that plan. Private Ward marched off to Virginia where he was wounded by Stonewall Jackson's troops and pensioned out of the Civil War.

Ward settled in Washington, D.C., and sought the fruits of his war effort in a government job. He obtained a post in the Treasury Department and slowly, with the help of a college degree from night school, moved up the bureaucratic ladder, eventually finding a home in the Geological Survey. Ward married Lizzie Vought in 1863 and together they mingled in civic circles of Washington dedicated to temperance, woman's suffrage, and abolition of capital punishment. The short-lived National Liberal Reform League was born in their living room in 1869 and Ward edited its paper, *The Iconoclast*, contributing articles that praised Lincoln and attacked religious hypocrisy. An unpublished essay on "Washington City" smacked of Mark Twain's criticism of official corruption in *The Gilded Age*.

Critical as he was on some subjects, Ward remained an optimist, reformer, and ambitious public servant. He completed a law degree, also in night school, but became so absorbed in his work that neither the practice of law nor his reform activities could compete with his growing interest in biology, botany, and paleobotany. Ward became an authority in the latter field; a scientist of international repute.

Ward's sociological and reform interests, which had been shelved while he pursued his science, revived in later life. He read and enjoyed Comte's *Positive Philosophy* (1853), where he came across the term "sociology," reporting later, "I fell in love with it." Indeed, Ward decided to retitle one of his manuscripts on social evolution *Dynamic Sociology*, which was published as a book in 1883 at his own expense. In detached and technical terms, Ward assailed Spencer's (and, later, Sumner's) "gospel of inaction" and mechanistic views of social evolution that ignored the self-conscious and purposeful capacity of societies to improve themselves through law and education. In practical terms, he found their science amateurish and their politics fatalistic.

After a slow start, *Dynamic Sociology* (1883) became a standard college text and the first exposure to sociology for the next generation. In the years that followed, Ward wrote more sociology and enjoyed a growing reputation as a bona fide scientist of a new sort. He joined the American Economic Association, helped some of its breakaway members found the American Sociological Society in 1905, and was chosen its first president, much to his own surprise. In the same year, at the age of 65, he retired from the Geological Survey and accepted his first academic position at Brown University. But his liberal views, unorthodox course on "A Survey of All Knowledge," lady admirers (attracted by his advocacy of women's rights), and his geological hikes in the Rhode Island countryside, all convinced his colleagues to respectfully conclude that "Ward was not of the academic type."

The Academicians

It is odd that Ward, who had no training in sociology or philosophy and only stumbled across a few of the European masters midway through his most influential book, nevertheless became the magnet that drew the next generation of career sociologists to the field: people like Franklin Giddings (1855–1931), Albion W. Small (1854–1926), Charles Horton Cooley (1864–1926), and Edward A. Ross (1866–1951). This second generation of U.S. sociologists was drawn to the idea of a true science of society and led the movement for its professionalization and institutionalization as an academic discipline in U.S. universities.

They had much in common; like Ward they were aspiring professionals from middle-class and mostly rural backgrounds who wanted to build a respectable science under themselves. In the United States, this meant borrowing the naturalistic premises of the physical sciences, yet mixing those with a malleable interpretation of evolution. As Small said, Ward saved them all from Spencer's misconstrued evolutionism. But they also considered historical science a contradiction in terms. Social science had to be built up from biological and psychological processes. They were forthright social psychologists, as Edward A. Ross exemplified when he insisted that sociology and history had to be separated in order to reduce the unit of analysis—and thereby avoid the sins of the speculative Europeans.

They were also progressives in U.S. politics, a happy combination since the root of progressivism was in the idea that society had to be reorganized and managed along scientific lines. They believed, with Ward and against the classical English liberals, that government needed to play an active regulatory role in society to prevent the abuses of unchecked competition. Scientific direction of society was the highest achievement of a purposive evolutionary process. Teddy Roosevelt, symbol of Progressivism, wrote a preface to Ross's popular book *Sin and Society* (1907), and Franklin Giddings at Columbia University was a close adviser to the president.

Among the first professional sociologists, Edward Ross is colorful and exemplifies a collective paradox. Ross was another prairie populist first exposed to the discipline through *Dynamic Sociology*. He sought out Ward, married his niece, and came to call Uncle Lester "my master." Ross was the equal of his master as a social critic and reformer. In the 1890s he taught at Stanford University while writing and keeping a frantic schedule of public lectures to labor, church, women's, and reform groups.

He supported the Democratic-Populist presidential candidacy of William Jennings Bryan in 1896 and spoke on monetary reform (free silver), a hot, anticapital issue in the campaign. This and his support for the socialist labor leader Eugene Debs in the 1894 Pullman Strike antagonized his employer, the widowed railroad heiress, Mrs. Leland Stanford. Ross bowed to Mrs. Stanford's discipline, but continued speaking. His next target was the employment of immigrant Japanese labor on the West Coast which Ross felt depressed the standard of living of domestic workers. Since the railroad was the chief employer of immigrant Japanese, Mrs. Stanford took this as another indiscretion and fired him. But Ross stuck to his convictions and moved on to better jobs at Nebraska and Wisconsin, where he defended the right of the anarchist Emma Goldman to speak on campus.

Ross traveled all over the world; to Europe before graduate school and later to China (1910), South America (1913), Portuguese Africa (1924), India (1925), and South Africa (1929). To help finance the trips, he usually contracted to write a series of magazine articles and later combined these in a book on the customs, people, and politics of the countries. His most engaging trips were to Mexico in 1922 (followed by the book *The Social Revolution in Mexico*) and to Russia at the height of the revolution in 1917 (*Russia in Upheaval* and *The Russian Soviet Republic*). Each book was a quick study and without historical perspective, a quality Ross ruled out of his sociology sometime back. He tended to treat social events through the individual people he met along the way.

The gregarious Ross liked these people, but the unfortunate result for his analyses was that revolution was attributed to misunderstandings among well-intentioned actors. The Mexican dictator Porfirio Diaz "had the good of Mexico at heart" and Alexander Kerensky, the head of Russia's provisional government, made "an honest effort to enforce the law." But Ross had the gumption to get out of his professorial armchair and confront history in the making. With the U.S. journalist John Reed, whose book *Ten Days That Shook the World* far outsold his own *Russia in Upheaval*, Ross mixed with the revolutionary crowds in Petrograd, attended Bolshevik committee meetings, and interviewed the revolutionary party's secretary, Leon

Trotsky—judging him far too theoretical to succeed with the Russian workers. Few North American sociologists were so intrepid or sought as he did firsthand knowledge of contemporary cultures and politics.

The irony in all this is that very little of Ross's personal knowledge of progressivism, culture, or revolution showed up in his social theory, except anecdotally. His formal sociology was so psychological and abstract that it defied use in the study of the concrete social activities he had observed so widely. In this he did not differ greatly from others such as Small and Giddings who served up theories that were virtually without content. The mature years of these sociologists, from 1880 to 1930, saw the most turbulent and metamorphic changes in U.S. history. They witnessed the creation of industry and empire, the great immigrations, populism and agrarian protest, a colonial war in the Philippines, forcible repression of socialism, and militant unionism at home. None of this was treated in the pioneering North America sociology. This contrasts dramatically with the classical tradition, with Weber's penetrating analyses of agrarian problems and German social structure or Marx's detailed examination of the British factory system. Academic sociology was fashioning its own tradition which, for good or ill, departed from the classical tradition.

Sociology in the United States assumed a unique form; a compound of affinities which, nevertheless, carried its own contradictions. It emulated science, particularly as that was understood through borrowings from biology and evolution. It stressed pragmatism in both the mundane and philosophical sense of a problem-solving approach to knowledge. It melded these doctrines with a commitment to social welfare and reform. And, last, it hitched all of these aims to professional ambition; the understandable, even creditable, wish to make sociology a key part of the organizational society that was taking shape in the early decades of 20th-century progressivism. The rub, however, was that winning professional recognition did not always square with the spirit of social criticism. As sociology found a place inside the universities and councils of power, it also risked drifting into a self-serving insularity. Conversely, some of those engaged in social criticism and reform-inspired research felt themselves marginal in professional circles. Sociology grew with conflicting aims.

Organization

The emphasis on professionalization is reflected in efforts to create an organization that would promote and monopolize the new science. At the American Sociological Society's meeting in 1909, it was decided that there should be a standard sociology curriculum developed for the universities:

> In taking rank as a science and in attaining to that dignity and respect which the importance of the subject and the wide interest in it demand, it seems... desirable that sociology should standardize its fundamental courses in the same way that the fundamental courses of other sciences are standardized. For illustration, when a student takes Chemistry 1, Physics 1, Biology 1, Economics 1, or Law 1, such course stands for a definite subject matter. (*Footnotes*, March 1980, pp. 1 and 6)

In 1920, the need for research money was addressed:

> We must also interest rich men in providing money for the prosecution of research until we have shown niggardly boards and legislatures the importance of finding out the facts bearing on social theory and social policy. (*Footnotes*, March 1980, p. 6)

Having laid a plan to monopolize control of a standard course of instruction and to find patrons, the last step in professionalization, which dawned on the (renamed) American Sociological Association (ASA) in 1936, was to make itself necessary:

> To get sociological training and field experience recognized as a qualification or substitute qualification for certain Federal and state civil service positions.... To study ways of getting the graduate training program in sociology to meet the need for equipping students for technical positions in Federal bureaus and administrations in state and local agencies.... To move wisely and expediently against the practice of hiring persons without any graduate training as teachers of sociology in American universities and colleges. (*Footnotes*, 1980, p. 4)

A new organizational society was emerging from progressivism and, rather than analyzing or fearing the bureaucratic state, as Weber had done, many North American sociologists wanted in on it.

Sociology in the Cities

There were as many others with a wholly different emphasis on the special U.S. problems of urbanization, race, and industrial concentration; topics for which the European tradition was not always a reliable guide. W. I. Thomas (1863–1947) taught at the University of Chicago and (with Florian Znaniecki) studied the city's Polish immigrant population in the early 1900s—their problems of adjustment, occupational lives, patterns of mutual assistance, and neighborhood associations. These were the same workers, streets, and factories that Upton Sinclair illuminated for a shocked and fascinated public in his novel *The Jungle*. The five-volume study of Thomas and Znaniecki, *The Polish Peasant in Europe and America*, is more accurate, equally good reading, and a sociological landmark that rivaled the new social realism in literature.

Thomas was born in rural Virginia and raised in Knoxville, Tennessee. He had been a professor of English at Oberlin College before his interest in comparative literature led him to study the social origins of various cultural groups, including Eastern European peasants. Reflecting on this period, Thomas (1973) said, "My interests...were in marginal fields and not sociology as it was taught at the time" (p. 249). As a result of his writing on folk psychology, Thomas received a letter from Booker T. Washington in 1910 inviting him to a conference on the American Negro and providing an appreciative criticism of his work. When Thomas arrived at the Tuskegee Institute for the conference, he discovered that his fan and correspondent was not Washington at all but Robert Park. Their meeting began a long friendship and collaboration which developed into a new "Chicago School" of social research.

Robert Park (1864–1944) was from Red Wing, Minnesota, a newspaper reporter by trade, and a self-described intellectual vagabond. He attended the University of Michigan and earned a Ph.D. in Germany. Between those engagements he worked for the *Minneapolis Journal*.

The yellow journals went in for reform, and I became a reformer.... The city editor... discovered that I would stay on a story
longer than anyone else, so he set me to work hunting down gambling
houses and opium dens. This was the beginning of my interest in
sociology, although at the time I did not know the word. (Robert E.
Park, "Life History," p. 254)

Park practiced what he called scientific reporting and when
he learned that it was close to the new methods of inquiry being
developed in the social sciences, he returned to graduate school
to study the newspaper. This was the way he got into sociology.
In 1906, Park worked for the Congo Reform Association and
wrote an important magazine exposé on Belgium's exploitation
of the African colony. Booker T. Washington then hired him as
a public relations officer for the Tuskegee Institute, and through
this association Park acquired an intimate knowledge of the
condition of Southern blacks. He was the only prominent white
sociologist in those years to take an interest in the U.S. race
problem. Park's black friend, W.E.B. Du Bois (1868–1963), was
a Ph.D. from Harvard University and, for a time, professor of
sociology at Atlanta University. Du Bois was ahead of his time;
he wrote books on black history and culture such as *John Brown*
and *The Souls of Black Folk*. Du Bois was forced out of the
Atlanta post for criticizing the moderate racial views of Washington, but he went on to head the first militant black political
(Niagara) movement and the N.A.A.C.P. which he helped establish in 1910. Thomas, Park, and Du Bois began a new sociology
focused on urban and ethnic problems that contrasted sharply
with the orientation of many of their academic colleagues—one
stressing social reform and the other social science professionalism.

Veblen

There was one bright example of the classical tradition among
U.S. social scientists. Thorstein Veblen (1857–1929) was a trained
philosopher, self-educated economist, and self-made sociologist.
Veblen was the leading theoretician of industrial society, social
critic, and academic celebrity of his day. He was reclusive and,
by the standards of polite society, a strange man.

Veblen came from a Norwegian immigrant family that settled in Minnesota. In 1884, he completed a Ph.D. at Yale University, where Sumner's evolutionary sociology attracted him despite their opposing political views. Veblen found no jobs open to an offbeat philosopher and returned to the family farm to read economics for the next seven years. Later he found, and lost, university positions at Cornell, Chicago, Stanford, Missouri, and the New School for Social Research. After the example of Ross, Veblen was fired from Stanford, less for radical political views, which he had, than for living like a bohemian in a rustic cabin with a woman student. Asked whether his dismissal was political, Veblen replied, "The president does not approve of my domestic arrangements, and for that matter neither do I."

Veblen's books attracted a vast academic and public audience from the beginning with *The Theory of the Leisure Class* (1899). Deadly serious and tendentiously written, his work nevertheless caught the imagination with its garrulous criticism of the public's conspicuous consumption, pecuniary emulation, and the force and fraud of corporate monopolies built on intangible wealth. Veblen resembled his sociological contemporaries in the strong evolutionary and social psychological aspect to his work, but these were anthropologically and historically anchored. He believed that humans possessed an instinct of workmanship which expressed itself in useful labor, material progress, and self-realization. Social evolution, however, leads to a struggle between instincts and their contamination through conquest, ownership, and the imposition of leisure classes living off productive craftsworkers. Corruption follows once social honor is attached to possessions rather than useful labor. In modern society, business is honored instead of engineering and consumption instead of production.

These ideas, fully developed in *The Instinct of Workmanship and the State of the Industrial Arts* (1914) which Veblen considered his best book, are highly reminiscent of Marx. Veblen knew Marx in depth and wrote critical articles on technical features of the theory. He was the only U.S. scholar intellectually prepared to challenge Marxist theory on its own ground. He agreed that productive labor was the source of value, but considered Marx's theory prescientific for its failure to follow evolutionary principles. Moreover, he had little faith in social reformers. Effective social change would come from productive people—engineers and workers. His criticism of Marx, however, paled in contrast to his views on the academic establishment. In his critical book on U.S. education, *The Higher Learning in America: A Memorandum on the Conduct of Universities by Business Men* (1918), Veblen chided the professors as "captains of erudition" who liked attending "gatherings of the well-to-do for convivial deliberation on the state of mankind at large."

The writer John Dos Passos (1969) portrays some of the major figures of the early 20th century in his remarkable trilogy *U.S.A.* Veblen is included because:

> he established a new diagram for a society dominated by
> monopoly capital,
> etched in irony
> the sabotage of production by business,
> the sabotage of life by the blind need for money profits,
> pointed out the alternatives: a warlike society strangled by the
> bureaucracies of the monopolies forced by the law of diminishing
> returns to grind down more and more the common man for profits,
> or a new matter-of-fact commonsense society dominated by the
> needs of the men and women who did the work and the incredibly
> vast possibilities for peace and plenty offered by the progress of
> technology. (John Dos Passos, *The Big Money*, p. 119)

Academics and Progressives

The formative period of North American sociology from 1880–1930 was defined by an uneasy alliance between an academic sociology that stressed scientific professionalism and a progressive sociology that advocated applied science in the service of reform. Sometimes these emphases came together as in the "Chicago School" of urban sociology. The Chicago sociologists (including Thomas, Park, Small, and later Louis Wirth) assisted Jane Addams's settlement work and Hull House devoted to rescuing homeless young people and poor families. The influential philosopher John Dewey was a trustee of Hull House, a natural place for him to practice his pragmatism that so impressed sociology (in part through another Chicago philosopher, George Herbert Mead). While Dewey and the sociologists saw Hull House as a vehicle for reform and for their own research and education, Veblen, who was at Chicago around the turn of the century, considered "the 'solicitude' of settlements ...in part directed to enhance the industrial efficiency of the poor."

At other times, the two tendencies diverged widely, particularly as academic sociology devoted most of its effort to laying the scientific foundations of the discipline, rather than researching social problems. For every fresh study like *The Polish Peasant* (1918–1920) there were a dozen treatises on the "Principles of" (Giddings), "Foundations of" (Ross), "General" (Small), and "Pure" (Ward) sociology. Doubtless, any new discipline needs to define its philosophical and methodological principles. The distinctive thing about the new North American sociology, however, was that rather than taking these principles from the classical tradition, they were in most cases reproduced in the distinctive U.S. intellectual climate and reinvented at a more abstract level.

The ambiguous result of this history was that academic sociology gained respectability and efficiency. It took its place in the university curriculum and produced record numbers of publications and practitioners, outstripping its European counterpart, which was many more years gaining general recognition. At the same time, a schism developed with growing tension between the associated polarities of theory and research, science and reform, or expertise and engagement—a tension that provoked healthy debate, but also compromised a clear sense of the sociological purpose. That tension has yet to be resolved.

Illustratively, from about 1930 until 1960, sociology followed two sometimes intersecting paths. Critical research continued. The Swedish economist Gunnar Myrdal was brought to the United States to examine its racial problem; Myrdal's essential qualifications included the fact that he was an objective outsider who explicitly rejected the do-nothing evolutionary theory of Sumner. Yet Myrdal's 1944 classic, *An American Dilemma*, which received public attention, did not jar the prevailing social theories with its claim that racial conflict was built into the social order. On the contrary, social theory became more grandly abstract; especially in the much cited and little used 1951 work, *The Social System*, by Talcott Parsons which maintained vaguely that societies were like all other equilibrium-seeking systems.

This, then, was the setting for the critical and spirited observations of Ralf Dahrendorf (Chapter 1) and C. Wright Mills—the challenge that sociology somehow bring together its general interpretive ideas and its research. Dahrendorf emphasized the replacement of a utopian sociology with another sensitive to social conflict and why questions. Mills thought the grand theory (of Parsons), as well as mindless fact-gathering or abstract empiricism, should be superseded by a publicly relevant sociological imagination. In short, this brings us back to the circumstances of the 1960s that produced a redefinition of the sociological perspective—a new sociology, born of its own social crisis, that began bringing together the classical and modern traditions. That sociology is the subject of this book.

SCIENCE, SOCIOLOGY, AND CIVILITY

The paradoxical reputation of sociology as both threatening and trivial which introduced this chapter now makes sense. To the extent that academic sociology necessarily spelled out the foundations of the discipline, in part by formalizing commonplace observations, it bored the reader looking for new explanations of social problems. Similarly, to the extent that critical sociology at the hands of a Marx or Myrdal explained poverty or racism as a consequence of the normal operating principles of economy and society, it threatened those with particular stakes in the system. What many of sociology's critics and practitioners fail to see is that these features of the discipline are unavoidable. On one hand, it requires its own conceptual language. On the other, if it does the job of analyzing social problems, it is bound to antagonize someone. Sociology, after all, is a social activity.

The inevitable question, then, is how can something be a social activity and an objective science at the same time? The answer is that *all* sciences share this quality and they manage, somehow, by producing humanly fallible results which, nevertheless, can be checked by others. In the 1920s, physicists such as Werner Heisenberg (quoted in Gould, p. 21) had already learned that "Science no longer is in the position of observer of nature, but rather recognizes itself as part of the interplay between man and nature." Later the historian Thomas Kuhn would show how scientific communities behave like other societies, changing their theories (or paradigms) in revolutionary jolts rather than by a steady accumulation of fact. Recently, the paleontologist and writer Stephen J. Gould (1981) has argued that science does not presume to master the enormous variability in nature or to predict in any specific way, as opposed to understanding the general movement of structures. The purported differences between the physical and social sciences, in which the latter are inferior but can emulate the former with more exacting conceptions of causation and powers of prediction, are not such differences after all:

> Science, since people must do it, is a socially embedded activity. It progresses by hunch, vision, and intuition. Much of its change through time does not record a closer approach to absolute truth, but the alteration of cultural contexts that influence it so strongly. Facts are not pure and unsullied bits of information; culture also influences what we see and how we see it. Theories, moreover, are not inexorable inductions from facts. The most creative theories are often imaginative visions imposed upon facts; the source of imagination is also strongly cultural. (Stephen J. Gould, *The Mismeasurement of Man*, pp. 21–22)

The early North American sociologists, as well as those who doubted the possibility of a social science, were therefore misled by an unrealistic model of what science is. Sociology is a science in the unprepossessing sense that it seeks to discover and codify empirical fact, to organize facts in logically coherent structures (theories) that allow interpretations (explanations) to be drawn that may be checked out (verified). Individual sociologists may devote most of their time to one or another of these steps and to the vast technical puzzles each presents. Individuals have their favorite puzzles and regularly plead that either sympathetic discovery or hard-headed verification deserves top priority. But sociology is more than this, and so are all the other sciences in that they involve humanly developed standards of what is true (however well-documented technically) and what is worth study.

Sociology is a distinctive discipline and social activity which, nevertheless, struggles with many of the same problems pervading the rest of society. It asks, for example, how to stem the alienation of an increasingly complex society that infuses even its own ranks. Sociologists understand themselves and others as caught somewhere in the rush of uncomprehended changes similar to those faced by Steinbeck's characters—What is this new situation? Where did it come from? Who or what is responsible? How do we change it? Sociology's promise is a means of transcending those circumstances; of providing, in Mills's words, "lucid summations of what is going on in the world" and how it affects each of us. That is the perspective, the unifying element of the tradition, and the civilizing opportunity.

Sociology's tradition is something to envy—nearly 200 years of investigation, reflection, and action coeval with the great transformation of industrialization, urbanization, bureaucratization, and irrepressible human effort to make modern society livable. The aim of sociology, whatever its divisions, is to foster civility. Civility involves the relations among citizens, one with another and with the body politic, deference or allegiance to the social order befitting a citizen, solidarity of civil rights and obligations. A social order befitting the citizen is our subject. Sociology is thus a moral matter.

SELECTED BIBLIOGRAPHY

BENDIX, RINEHARD (1962). *Max Weber: An Intellectual Portrait*. New York: Anchor Books.

BOOTH, CHARLES (1970). *Life and Labor of the People of London*. New York: AMS Press. (Originally published in 1902–04.)

DIGGINS, JOHN P. (1978). *The Bard of Savagery: Thorstein Veblen and Modern Social Theory*. New York: Seabury Press.

DOS PASSOS, JOHN (1969). *The Big Money*. New York: Signet Classics. (Originally published in 1933.)

DURKHEIM, ÉMILE (1960). *The Division of Labor in Society* (George Simpson, Trans.). New York: Free Press. (Originally published in 1893.)

———(1958). *Professional Ethics and Civic Morals*. Glencoe, IL: The Free Press. (Originally published in 1950.)

FOOTNOTES (1980, March and April). American Sociological Association.

GERTH, HANS, & MILLS, C. WRIGHT (1958). *From Max Weber: Essays in Sociology*. New York: Oxford University Press.

GIDDENS, ANTHONY (1978). Émile Durkheim. New York: Viking Press.

GOULD, STEPHEN J. (1981). *The Mismeasurement of Man*. New York: W.W. Norton.

GOULDNER, ALVIN (1962). Introduction to Émile Durkheim, *Socialism*. New York: Collier Books.

———(1970). *The Coming Crisis of Western Sociology*. New York: Basic Books.

HASKELL, THOMAS L. (1977). *The Emergence of Professional Social Science: The American Social Science Association and the Nineteenth-Century Crisis of Authority.* Champaign: University of Illinois Press.

HINKLE, ROSCOE C. (1980). *Founding Theory of American Sociology: 1881–1915.* Boston: Routledge & Kegan Paul.

KUHN, THOMAS P. (1962). *The Structure of Scientific Revolutions.* Chicago: University of Chicago Press.

MCLELLAN, DAVID (1975). *Karl Marx.* London: Penguin.

MARX, KARL, & ENGELS, FRIEDRICH (1947). *The German Ideology.* New York: International Publishers. (Originally published in 1846.)

———(1959). *Communist Manifesto,* in Lewis S. Feuer, *Marx and Engels: Basic Writings on Politics and Philosophy.* Garden City, N.Y.: Anchor. (Originally published in 1848.)

MILLS, C. WRIGHT (1959). *The Sociological Imagination.* New York: Oxford University Press.

———(1960). *Images of Man: The Classic Tradition in Sociological Thinking.* New York: George Braziller.

NEWMAN, EDWIN (1974). *Strictly Speaking.* New York: Warner Books.

PARK, ROBERT E. (1973, September). "Life History," *American Journal of Sociology, 79,* 251–60.

ROSS, EDWARD A. (1936). *Seventy Years of It: An Autobiography.* New York: Appleton-Century-Crofts.

———(1907). *Sin and Society.* Boston: Houghton, Mifflin.

SCOTT, CLIFFORD H. (1976). *Lester Frank Ward.* Boston: Twayne Publishers.

STEINBECK, JOHN (1939). *The Grapes of Wrath.* New York: Viking Press.

THOMAS, W.I. (1973). Life History. *American Journal of Sociology, 79:* 246–50.

THOMPSON, E.P. (1955). *William Morris: Romantic to Revolutionary.* New York: Pantheon Books.

TOQUEVILLE, ALEXIS D. (1959). *Democracy in America.* New York: Vintage Books. (Originally published in 1835.)

VEBLEN, THORSTEIN (1953). *The Theory of the Leisure Class.* New York: Mentor Books. (Originally published in 1899.)

WARD, LESTER FRANK (1883). *Dynamic Sociology.* New York: Appleton.

Weber, Max (1958). The Protestant Ethic and the Spirit of Capitalism. New York: Charles Scribner's Sons. (First English publication in 1930.)

——(1946). *Politics as Vocation*, pp. 77–128 in Hans Gerth and C. Wright Mills, *From Max Weber: Essays in Sociology*. New York: Oxford University Press.

Weinberg, Julius (1972). *Edward Alsworth Ross and the Sociology of Progressivism*. Madison: The State Historical Society of Wisconsin.

Wiebe, Robert H. (1967). *The Search for Order: 1877–1920*. New York: Hill and Wang.

Wilson, Edmund (1940). *To the Finland Station: A Study in the Writing and Acting of History*. Garden City, NY: Doubleday.

3

Social Class and Inequality

*In the 1930s tenant farmers were a class in decline, displaced
by corporate agriculture, mechanization, and falling commodity prices. Yet they were aware of themselves as a class
and did not go down gently. (Library of Congress)*

PART I
CONCEPTIONS OF CLASS
AND MOBILITY

In the last few years, the news has rekindled a faded awareness of the meaning of class society. A representative headline from the *Los Angeles Times* reads, "Millions Hit Bottom in the Streets."

When darkness falls in downtown Atlanta, they scurry for shelter in the ruins of the "underground Atlanta" night district, lifting themselves into the deserted storefronts that still carry names like Scarlett O'Hara's and the Tutti Frutti Palace.

In New York City, where their ranks are swelling rapidly, they sleep in the steam tunnels under Grand Central Station or in subway cars. One man resides above a heating vent on Park Avenue, sustained by sandwiches and scraps of *haute cuisine* fed him by doormen and high-society cooks.

In Minneapolis-St. Paul, they spend the night on the basement floors of nine churches. In Boston, there is no more room at the Pine Street Inn, the city's oldest and largest shelter. On some nights there, as many as 400 persons are turned away for lack of space on the floor.

These are the homeless Americans: men, women, and children forced onto the streets by physical addictions, the failure of America's mental health programs and, increasingly, by joblessness and economic despair.

A survey at San Francisco's Trinity Episcopal Church, which opened its doors on Dec. 1 to provide shelter for homeless single men, produced a remarkable portrait...40 percent of the men were between 16 and 29 years old. Another 32 percent were between 30 and 39. More startling still, 92 percent were high school graduates, 30 percent were college graduates and 70 percent possessed work skills. The church found that 72 percent had been employed for more than a year before they lost their jobs.

What we are seeing now is a new class of poor.... Our shelters are filled with them—families, good people, productive people from our own communities. These are not the inebriates, not the street people, not the hobos. They're the new homeless, the new poor...the evidence is that a great many of the homeless were just a few months ago stable, responsible people who had homes and jobs but whose world collapsed around them....For the "new poor" of America, those for whom a life of jobless poverty is a completely alien experience, the road to homelessness is long, and losing a place to live is only the last stage.

It is preceded by loss of jobs, foreclosure or eviction from homes, expiration of unemployment benefits, exhaustion of savings, sale of valuables and loss of credit. (*Los Angeles Times*, December 26, 1982)

At about the same time *Architectural Digest: The International Magazine of Fine Interior Design* (December, 1980) reported enviously on the furnishings of a New York City apartment overlooking Central Park. The apartment owner is a Texan and partner in a firm importing porcelain and dinnerware from Japan. His business requires that he spend half the year in the Far East and divide the rest between New York and Dallas. Although he maintains a residence in each place, "he is particularly pleased with the new apartment because the decor represents a distinctive change from his other homes and is, in his words, 'quintessentially New York....I am here mostly in the winter, and naturally wanted something different from what I have in my homes in Texas and in Japan.'"

The living room is appointed in roseate sofas, chairs, and matching walls; the dining room contains oak paneling and a coffered ceiling; a recessed window in the bedroom accommodates two Louis XVI chairs and an English inlaid table. The overall mood is "comfortable, suitable, sophisticated—and not a 'trendy'" aspect.

These portraits contrast an upper and, as the journalists believe, a growing lower class in the United States of the 1980s. The existence of what we unself-consciously call "social classes" is nothing new. The term was in common use well before Marx began writing, although his work and what followed gave it a new importance. Long before Marx's name was known to the public, the gentleman novelist and Conservative prime minister of England, Benjamin Disraeli, wrote in his 1845 novel *Sybil—or the Two Nations*:

> Two nations: between whom there is no intercourse and no sympathy; who are as ignorant of each other's habits, thoughts, and feelings, as if they were dwellers in different zones, or inhabitants of different planets; who are formed by a different breeding, are fed by different food, are ordered by different manners, and are not governed by the same laws.
> You speak of—
> The Rich And The Poor. (Benjamin Disraeli, *Sybil—or the Two Nations*, p. 96)

What may be new these days is a popular style of class analysis convinced that class divisions are widening, rather than narrowing as conventional wisdom has held for perhaps a century in the United States. In the *Atlantic* of July 1983, for example, an article on "The Declining Middle" by Bob Kuttner is introduced by the statement, "With most jobs being created at the top and the bottom of the ladder, America may have difficulty remaining a middle-class society (p. 60). Once denigrated as Marxian mischief, the idea of social class is back in fashion.

The portraits of homeless people who sleep in the subway or laundromats, and the owner of three homes, concerned that his Manhattan apartment appear sophisticated and not trendy are contemporary, even familiar, instances of Disraeli's two nations—between which there is no intercourse, ignorant of each other's feelings, dwellers of different planets. Although it is important to be reminded of these disparities, the key question about class has always been the stability of its structure and the extent of its influence on people's lives: whether distinct classes are converging in a middle mass (a diamond shape as some sociologists of the 1940s envisioned) or polarizing between a pinnacle of privilege and an impoverished mass (in the shape of a pyramid). Disraeli held guarded hope for the former, while contemporary journalists fear that the latter is upon us. The trouble with this question is that it yields to many answers as long as no precise meaning of social class is specified.

WHAT MAKES A SOCIAL CLASS?

This issue was key to the rejuvenation of the classical tradition and challenge of a new sociology in the 1960s (Chapter 2). The new sociology spoke often of conflict, but it usually meant class. The Young Turks claimed that academic analyses dominant for nearly 50 years had emphasized a stable and integrated social system to the point of losing touch with the rapidly changing and conflict-filled post-World War II reality. A revitalized sociology would trace these changes to new arrangements of class and power. Ralf Dahrendorf (1959) explored a new pattern of conflict between labor and management in his book *Class and Class Conflict in Industrial Society*. In *White Collar: The American Middle Classes*, C. Wright Mills (1951) described the historical and political forces that produced a new middle class as well as the mentality of these "rearguarders...a chorus too afraid to grumble, too hysterical in their applause" (p. 353). Slowly, the classical notion of social class developed in U.S. sociology.

The concept social class joins topical issues and modern sociological analysis. The questions that need to be answered have a practical as well as a theoretical aspect. To some, it is obvious that disparities such as those between the homeless and Manhattan apartment owners exist, and the legitimate question that follows is, What does the concept social class add to one's understanding? Is this more common sense or another name for the familiar? Can it tell us where the differences came from and how the homeless and the rich fit into some structure? What is to be said of differences between these conditions that seem to have nothing to do with class, such as differences in individual ability, in lifestyles, race or culture? These are key questions since, at bottom, they ask what the notion of class itself explains. The purpose of this chapter is to answer that question.

Social class is proposed as one of the basic interpretive ideas in sociology, a concept that is also central to the classical legacy. It is a building block, even a cornerstone, in the foundation of sociological interpretation. It should help unravel the bases of social structure, the origins and trends in social inequality. But it does not explain everything, or even a great deal by itself. We do not make our homes on unimproved foundations. To the dynamics of class analysis, it is necessary to add the ideas of status, family, association, state, and other concepts—all the work of subsequent chapters. Here we shall explore the meaning of social class, asking how far it takes us toward a cogent description of social organization and an explanation of social inequality.

Marx on Class

The origins of the term "social class" are inconspicuous. Saint-Simon's mentors and the great English political economist Adam Smith, all writing in the late 18th century, divided society into orders or estates (landowners, commerce and industry, the state). Smith and Saint-Simon subdivided these orders into classes (the various working classes, propertied classes), all rather unsystematically, but also in the first explicit application of the term to economically distinct social groupings. The gradual replacement of orders with classes during the 19th century progressed with the crystallization of industrial society itself and with the declining fortunes of the aristocracy. Adam Smith was a vigorous liberal critic of aristocratic privilege and its economic inefficiencies. He developed the idea that labor was the source of all value which, along with the notion of social class, Marx combined in the most explicit interpretation of classes in capitalist society.

Yet the difficulty with Marx was that he used the term class for many purposes: in an abstract model of the "two great classes directly facing each other: bourgeoisie and proletariat"; in a general historical description of "the owners of mere labour-power [workers], the owners of capital and the landowners [which] form the three great classes of modern society"; in concrete historical studies of the struggles among such multiple classes as rentiers, petty bourgeois shopkeepers, industrialists, workers, financiers, peasants; and in the political sense of consciously organized groups rather than mere individuals living under similar economic conditions. Moreover, when Marx turned to what might have been his definitive statement on the subject in the 52nd chapter of *Capital*, Vol. 3, and posed the question, "What makes a class?" he wrote just five paragraphs and left the manuscript unfinished. Although this opened the way to a continuing debate (Dahrendorf, for example, proposed to rewrite Chapter 52 for him), it is still possible to extract Marx's central point from other works.

Marx's formulation of social class need not be obscure. He began, as we have seen in Chapter 1, with less interest in coining a new term than in deriving the consequences of the competition among capitalists for surplus value. Two important features of competitive capitalism were its tendencies to expand and to rationalize itself (or reduce costs and increase profits through greater efficiency). First, in the interests of expansion, the capitalist mode of production spread by incorporating new activities. It spread, for example, from commercial agriculture and textile manufacture by incorporating small farms, artisan trades and merchant services—by expropriating independent producers along the way. It also spread geographically into backward and colonial areas that were transformed from subsistence and trading economies to suppliers of raw materials to the industry of the advanced areas.

Second, capitalism rationalized itself by creating a division of labor along factory lines. Each component task of production was subdivided, simplified, speeded up, and generally made more automatic, with the result that skilled and craft workers were converted into machine tenders. Mass production was invented for and it worked best on a very large industrial scale in which the worker had an ever smaller part in the total production process. For capitalists, this implied ever keener competition in which the smaller and less efficient were eliminated. For merchants, agricultural smallholders, peasants, and artisans it also meant the progressive elimination of their occupations and ways of life. Many of these people were forced into the ranks of the working class, just as that class was seeing its own jobs degraded by mechanization and other means for exploiting unpaid labor (such as the extended workday discussed in Chapter 1).

In short, old groups were being eliminated and new ones created under exploitive conditions. Marx chose to call these groups social classes, thereby implying several things in answer to his own question, "What makes a social class?" First, social classes are locations in the process of production, similar to but not coincident with the modern notion of occupations. Marx believed that one's location within the social relations of production was the single most important of a variety of influences on one's life. Second, classes are generated in production processes that are themselves changing, old ones waning and new ones forming, which accounts for the fact that descriptions of the classes appropriately change over time. Classes are not static categories whose relative numbers can be compared from one time to another. Third, beyond objective locations, classes under capitalism are experienced social relations; relations that people feel, for example, in alienation or the estrangement from one's labor, other people, and from one's own self. Fourth, the objective condition of "class in itself" may be transformed into an active "class for itself" to the extent that people in similar economic conditions become socially conscious and politically organized.

Classes are potential bases of organization resulting from class struggle. Finally for Marx, class is a value-laden term, a concept that simultaneously analyzes and criticizes society. Just as the term is not static, neither is it purely descriptive.

Weber on Class Situation

Max Weber agreed with Marx about the importance of classes in industrial society, but disputed the idea that they were generated exclusively in the process of production. His differences with Marx on this point stemmed from a more general difference about the underlying forces of historical change. Weber believed that the most important feature of modern society was not the growth and differentiation of classes, which is a continuous process in history, but the expansion of rational bureaucracy— the growth of large-scale, impersonal organizations in all branches of society. As we saw in Chapter 2, Weber understood the expropriation of independent producers as a general process, not limited to the economy, but the essence of the growth of the state and other social institutions (such as business enterprises).

The connection between Weber's general observation and the specific problem of social class lay in the interpretation of expanding capitalism as a process of rationalization throughout society. That is, Weber expected an expansion of bureaucratic organization and in the economy this meant a more complex division of labor. By contrast to Marx, then, he believed that the expansion of capitalism leads to a more diversified class system, including various bureaucratic or white-collar classes, rather than a polarization of two great classes (the owners and workers, or bourgeoisie and proletariat in Marx). Moreover, some of these classes would be better off than before, accounting for the rural to industrial migration patterns he studied.

As a result, Weber introduced a new and more discerning terminology. Class situations (rather than locations in production) are determined with growing rationalization of society and diversification of the division of labor. *Class situation* is defined by the power of groups in the marketplace; the power, for example, of workers and their unions to monopolize a certain skill in the labor market, the power of manufacturers to eliminate competitors in the commodity market, or the power of financiers to dominate the credit market. Weber (1946) claims that class situation is, in this sense, ultimately market situation, thus arriving at an explicit definition of class:

> We may speak of a "class" when (1) a number of people have in common a specific causal component of their life chances, in so far as (2) this component is represented exclusively by economic interests in the possession of goods and opportunities for income, and (3) is represented under the conditions of the commodity or labor markets. (Max Weber, "Class, Status, Party," p. 181)

Weber accomplished a great deal in a few tightly reasoned propositions. He generalized Marx by arguing that classes are formed in entire economy, not just in production. He distinguished sharply between the economically determined classes and status groups (that we shall come to in the next chapter) which also form a hierarchy, but one based on social honor or prestige. And he characterized the way classes arise in markets that are based on economic interests, but comprise all manner of bargaining encounters. Finally, he claimed that the life chances of large aggregates of individuals are determined in these encounters to which each brings different resources—a different amount and kind of power.

People compete, for example, in a market for jobs with different skills and amounts of education, and in a market for commodities with different amounts of capital and credit. In capitalist society, their life chances are determined largely by how well they compete (or use their market power). As social categories, therefore, classes are aggregations of people with similar power in markets. Weber's concept stressed that "always this is the generic connotation of the concept of class: that the kind of chance in the *market* is the decisive moment which presents a common condition for the individual's fate" (p. 182).

In what follows, we shall speak of social classes as large groupings of individuals who share common experiences, life chances, and a culture by virtue of similar situations and power in the marketplace. Crucially, classes are not things, but relationships within and between groups of people. Particular individuals may occupy several market situations at once, but classes are formed by the coincidence of these situations in ways sufficient to produce a common awareness of social position. Classes in this sense are real social and historical groupings, rather than categories for enumerating a population. As the historian E.P. Thompson (1978) says, "We know about class because people have repeatedly acted in class ways" (p. 147).

SOCIAL MOBILITY

In sociology, journalism, and politics, the nature of social class is always a major and hotly debated topic because it reflects judgments about social equality. Class is an academic issue *and* a problem of political ideology. Questions posed in one vocabulary, about social mobility, class structure, and life chances, signify in another the extent to which people enjoy economic freedom and equal opportunity.

The question of social class in the United States has always been surrounded with ambiguity. On one hand, there is a tendency to deny the existence of classes altogether, or to minimize their influence. This comes from the combination of a powerful ideology of social equality and the certain facts that the United States did not begin with the same conditions of privilege and inequality (aristocracy, feudalism) found in Europe where the classical theories of class were formulated. Indeed, major European thinkers confirmed this opinion when they visited or wrote about the United States. Alexis de Tocqueville traveled the country in the 1830s and wrote his famous *Democracy in America* which stressed the openness of U.S. society resulting from an active associational life. Karl Marx wrote for the *New York Herald Tribune* about the undeveloped U.S. class structure. On the other hand, few sensitive observers would deny the existence of social classes in the United States, and many native-born sociologists have spoken harshly of their constricting effects. The Englishman R.H. Tawney (1952) best described the dilemma: "The word 'class' is fraught with unpleasing associations, so that to linger upon it is apt to be interpreted as the symptom of a perverted and jaundiced spirit.... If the word 'class' is one which everyone dislikes, it is also one which no one in practice can escape from using" (p. 53).

The Mobility Controversy

Among the early North American social analysts, Thorstein Veblen was the most forthright class theorist. He viewed history as the long struggle between productive industrial and parasitic leisure classes. In the early 20th century, he believed that the United States had experienced a marked ascension of class exploitation through the force and fraud of vested business interests and absentee ownership (his term for emergent monopoly capitalism). A leisure class had grown to bloated proportions and imposed its own standards of idleness and "conspicuous consumption" on other classes.

Yet Veblen was virtually alone among sociological observers in this uncompromising view. Most sociologists took a more ameliorative position consistent with progressivism. E.A. Ross is revealing in this appraisal, for although he borrowed heavily from Veblen and was one of the more outspoken sociological critics of class privilege, he shared the moderate conclusion of his colleagues that an open class structure was developing with the equalization of opportunity, the redressing pressure of public opinion, and the social reform movement. The dominant interpretation held by Ward, Sumner, Giddings, Cooley, all with a cautionary nod in the direction of the evils of class, was that the United States was moving in the direction of a classless society and had already surmounted the hurdle of a disassociation of economic condition and social class position. The latter, they claimed, now relied more on considerations of status or prestige.

The implicit contrast everyone had in mind was between the United States and the European countries where, they felt, class theories were appropriate. This impression was fostered by an influential article in 1906 by the German economist and historian Werner Sombart. Following the suggestions of Marx and Engels, Sombart explained the absence of a strong socialist workers movement in the United States by the high degree of social mobility between classes. Although there was a socialist movement in the United States, the relative weakness of which resulted partly from state repression, the popularity of Sombart's analysis testified to a strong ideological attachment to principles of egalitarianism. For example, the important book by Reinhard Bendix and Seymour Lipset (1959) on *Social Mobility in*

Industrial Society demonstrated that it is not so much the actual amount of social mobility, which has been significant in all industrializing countries, as "it is the American emphasis on equality as a part of the democratic credo which differentiates American society from the more status-oriented cultures of Europe" (p. 111).

Research on social class in the United States during the 1930s affirmed all these principles. The centerpiece of this work was the "Yankee City Series" by Lloyd Warner (1941) and his associates, an elaborate study of Newburyport, Massachusetts, published in five volumes and summarized in *The Social Life of a Modern Community*. Warner referred to the classes he found in terms of levels (upper-upper, lower-upper, upper-middle, and so forth) emphasizing, in a complete departure from classical definitions, that class position was determined by prestige—the individual's social standing in the eyes of the neighbors. Social mobility was common as individuals tended to move up the prestige ladder by contrast to their parents' standing. With so many moving up, the natural result was a change in the overall structure of social classes; a change in its shape from something resembling a pyramid to something else more like a diamond. The diamond-shaped image was a contribution of Charles Page's (1964) influential book on *Class and American Sociology* which concluded that "'social class' refers to an intracommunal group possessing a distinct status."

Three points are important here. First, the view expressed by most sociologists reflected and contributed to the dominant interpretation of U.S. society. It was not merely an academic opinion, but a widely held evaluation of the open society, in which the experts concurred. Second, it was a conclusion about class that departed from the classical definition of the term. Third, in this work, the very objective of class analysis had shifted from explaining structural change and social action to describing a set of fixed categories or a cross-sectional profile of the classes (indeed, it was at this time that sociologists began speaking metaphorically about social "stratification" rather than about real classes). Apart from these points, the key question is, Is it true? If it is true, the concepts introduced previously are either wrong or inappropriate. If it is not true, the notion of social class drawn from Weber and others may help to explain what is.

Some of the best evidence that U.S. sociologists had mistaken opinions about prestige for real changes in class mobility came from a new breed of social historians who began looking into the actual records on social change. The work of Stephan Thernstrom (1969) is especially important since he restudied, using original census schedules from 1850–80, the same New-buryport (Yankee City) where Warner had conducted his influential research. In *Poverty and Progress: Social Mobility in a Nineteenth Century City*, Thernstrom says, "Warner's inter-pretations rested on assumptions about the past which were demonstrably false" (p. 230); his error lay in the use of ahistorical methods relying on personal notions of prestige ranking, rather than on any solid information about economic condition.

Thernstrom discovered that the working class of 19th-century Newburyport experienced only modest upward mobility, often by the unexpected route of acquiring agricultural property while remaining in unskilled or semiskilled occupations (or by "property mobility" rather than "occupational mobility"), and that this limited upward movement was seldom cumulative in the sense of carrying over from one generation to the next. Indeed, property mobility was usually accomplished at the cost of "sacrificing the children's education for an extra paycheck, and thereby restricting their opportunities for inter-generational occupational mobility" (p. 161). Working-class efforts to achieve a better life produced mixed results, although the central fact was immobility;

these working class families did not remain in a uniformly degraded social position.... On top was a small but significant elite of laboring families who gained a foothold in the lower fringes of the middle class occupational world. Below them was a large body of families who had attained property mobility while remaining in manual occupations, most often of the unskilled or semiskilled variety; these families constituted the stable, respectable, home-owning stratum of the Newburyport working class. At the very bottom of the social ladder was the impoverished, floating lower class, large in number but so transient as to be formless and powerless.... The contrast between the literal claims of the rags-to-riches mythology and the actual social experience of these families thus appears glaring. A few dozen farmers, small shopkeepers, and clerks, a large body of home-owning families unable to escape a grinding regimen of manual labor: this was the sum of the social mobility achieved by

Newburyport's unskilled laborers by 1880. (Stephan Thernstrom, *Poverty and Progress: Social Mobility in a Nineteenth Century City*, pp. 158 and 163)

Newburyport, of course, is just one small town and its working-class experience may be atypical—a consideration that did not prevent the earlier sociologists from generalizing Warner's results. Other community studies were pursued in the 1920s and 1930s, especially the *Middletown* and *Middletown in Transition* series by Robert and Helen Lynd (1937) which shared equal fame with Warner's work. Middletown (Muncie, Indiana) did not demonstrate a great deal of social mobility. On the contrary, the Lynds concluded that mobility opportunities were shrinking noticeably.

Yet a genuine debate persists about the historical experience of social mobility. Results vary depending on the sites and the class origins or destinations chosen for study. The historian Herbert Gutman (1977) studied a rapidly expanding industrial city in the mid-19th century, concluding,

> that the rags-to-riches promise was not a mere myth in Paterson, New Jersey, between 1830 and 1880. So many successful manufacturers who had begun as workers walked the streets of that city then that it is not hard to believe that others less successful or just starting out on the lower rungs of the occupational mobility ladder could be convinced by personal knowledge that "hard work" resulted in spectacular material and social improvement. (Herbert Gutman, *Work, Culture, and Society in Industrializing America*, p. 232)

The differences between Gutman and Thernstrom arise from two sources. One, of course, is that they studied different towns, with different economies, at different periods. The second, however, is more of an artifact. Gutman's method was to examine a select group of successful manufacturers, while Thernstrom's focused on the entire working-class population. To discover that among those who made it, many came from the working class is not the same as saying that many from the working class make it. These kinds of differences have opened a profitable and continuing research debate among social historians and sociologists. In brief, the question that divides both disciplines is whether upward mobility was typical in the U.S. past, contributing to greater class equality, or whether upward mobility was matched by downward and immobility producing more class inequities.

A Critical Assessment

The sociological evidence on this question is rich and controversial, but it also allows some definite conclusions. The first landmark study by Reinhard Bendix and Seymour Martin Lipset in 1959, *Social Mobility in Industrial Society* concluded that occupational mobility was common to all the Western industrial nations; rates in the United States were not markedly different from those in Western Europe, although the belief in mobility was stronger. The qualified interpretation of Bendix and Lipset paled in the epic study of *The American Occupational Structure* by Peter Blau and Otis Duncan in 1967. Recognizing that mobility met with occasional setbacks, Blau and Duncan were forthright about the generality of upward movement.

> The rates of upward mobility in the United States today are still high.... Technological advances have sometimes led to serious economic depressions, which worsened chances of upward mobility and seriously disrupted careers in general, and they have sometimes effected a routinization of formerly skilled tasks, which can only have an adverse effect on mobility. In the long run, however, *technological progress has undoubtedly improved chances of upward mobility and will do so in the future* [italics added]. Technical improvements in production and farming have made possible the tremendous expansion of the labor force in tertiary industries—those other than agriculture and manufacturing—and, particularly, in professional and semiprofessional services since the turn of the century.... This great expansion of the occupational group at the top of the hierarchy, in combination with the simultaneous contraction of the bottom strata, has been a major generator of upward mobility. (Peter M. Blau and Otis Dudley Duncan, *The American Occupational Structure*, pp. 426, 428–29, [italics added])

The conclusion of Blau and Duncan represents the dominant view in U.S. sociology and echoes in a more sophisticated form ideas advanced by earlier generations from Ross to Warner. There are, however, some important qualifications on this conclusion. In the first place, it deals exclusively with occupation, rather than class in a full or proper sense. In the second place, it does not contend with the serious problem of inferring long-term change from cross-sectional data. Particularly troublesome is the assumption that the same occupation means the same thing (for example, about life chances) at two widely separated times.

Social mobility is usually measured by comparing the prestige or standing of the occupations of a contemporary sample with their parents. A white-collar office worker today is assumed to have improved on the condition of his or her employed parent who was a skilled or craft worker, say a cabinetmaker. A manager today is better off than a parent who was a clerk. Generally, white-collar jobs now are better than blue-collar jobs of the past. Much of the research supporting high-mobility rates rests on crude inferences about labor force shifts from manual to non-manual occupations. The problem is that all such inferences are dubious and, in any event, do not look into the actual conditions of the positions compared.

Illustratively, a clerk in 1900 enjoyed a relatively uncommon and rewarding position; far more so than today. In the intervening years the entire occupational structure has shifted upwards. A clerk today, say in a grocery store, does not enjoy the same advantages of 1900; there are more of them now and their incomes relative to other occupations are probably lower. A parent and grown child both holding clerks' positions across time very likely reflect downward mobility rather than immobility. A parent cabinetmaker may have been better off than today's office worker. Similarly, a skilled worker today may enjoy a position far superior to a parent grouped in the same category and even a better position than some of today's managers. The point is that the meanings of these positions change, casting doubt on point-to-point comparisons of presumed mobility and requiring informed evaluations of the actual experience or life chances attached to these positions over time.

Beyond these issues of meaning and measurement, the more serious problem with research, convinced that social mobility is the rule, lies in its focus on occupation rather than class. Classes are social groupings with a common experience, culture, and situation in the marketplace. Occupation is a category that taps group experience only indirectly and constitutes just one, albeit important, dimension of market power. These differences make it easier to study movement between occupations (for example, in the census or sample surveys). But they do not make it impossible to study classes.

Indeed, some of the more lasting studies did just that. Mills's (1951) book *White Collar: The American Middle Classes*, examined the social forces that produced the new middle class of office and corporate workers and described what their lives were like—their work, politics, and styles of life *as a class*. Related popular works by William H. Whyte, *The Organization Man* (1956), and David Riesman, *The Lonely Crowd* (1950), focus on the overconforming world of corporate-employed, suburban-dwelling, "other-directed" people. In all these works, the new middle classes are not markedly better off than the old ones in terms of income or market power; they have not experienced mobility so much as a new kind of middle-level existence entailing restrictions on their freedom. Although their conclusions are debatable, they contribute immeasurably to an interpretation of class and social change.

These studies of social class tell a very different story about mobility from the comparisons of occupational categories. Are the two sets of evidence contradictory? Perhaps not, since the occupational data can be read in very different ways. Harry Braverman's (1974) work on *Labor and Monopoly Capital* interprets the same changes that Blau and Duncan considered upward mobility as a long-run process of labor degradation. Technological change and a once-expanding economy meant that new jobs were created in a middle ground or buffer zone between top management and labor. Initially these jobs granted a privileged market position since specialized and technical labor was "in the earlier phase of its development, at a time when the supply of such labor is only in the process of catching up with the needs of capital accumulation" (p. 407). Later, however, the fundamental condition of wage labor makes itself felt as a mass market of qualified workers is created, driving down relative wages, and as the new jobs themselves become mechanized, all in a cyclical process. Studies that purport to demonstrate upward occupational mobility miss this key development by making cross-sectional comparisons rather than following workers and jobs through time.

Which of the interpretations about mobility (the Bendix and Lipset-Blau and Duncan or the Mills-Braverman) is correct? The answer is enormously complex and still unfolding. It involves many changes that have taken place since these writings. Moreover, labor degradation is far from a uniform process and class determination is increasingly taking place on an international level. There is, however, a clearly emerging answer that supports the second, critical interpretation more than the first about universal mobility.

Much of the argument in support of that conclusion follows in the balance of this chapter. Three factual points about the significance of the new middle class, however, provide some initial closure on the issues presented thus far. First, as Anthony Giddens (1973) has summarized in a lucid book, *The Class Structures of the Advanced Societies*, an important segment of the newly mobile stratum is made up of low-skilled and low-paid clerical jobs, filled increasingly by women who have entered the labor force under discriminatory conditions. The buffer zone at the bottom ranks of clerical and service jobs does not represent mobility so much as a new white-collar proletariat. Second, automation and recession have reduced the ranks of middle-level supervisors and technicians. Third, all of the evidence on job creation in the 1980s indicates that the openings are for a few managers and a great many salesclerks, cashiers, secretaries, stockhandlers, cooks, and so forth—as the journalists have correctly reported, the trend is toward a declining middle class. The class structure is changing to the disadvantage of working people in the middle.

PART II
CLASS EXPERIENCE AND STRUCTURE

The belief that upward social mobility is the destiny of all industrious labor in advanced capitalist society implied another, even more astonishing hypothesis: a new age of the affluent worker. The two interpretations went hand-in-hand. Occupational mobility, it was argued, brought with it a changed consciousness in the working class, a preference and aspiration for middle class (bourgeois) values, or what was called a process of "embourgeoisement." The old working classes allegedly were becoming differentiated, richer, and more like the middle classes. The popularity of this theory was marked, but short-lived. Beyond its ungainly name, embourgeoisement ran into factual trouble. John Goldthorpe (1969) and a research team in England report:

> Our findings show that in the case of the workers we studied there remain important areas of common social experience which are still fairly distinctively working-class; that specifically middle-class social norms are not widely followed nor middle-class life-styles consciously emulated; and that assimilation into middle-class society is neither in process nor, in the main, a desired objective.... Thus, it may be claimed that ongoing trends of change in modern industry are not in fact ones which operate uniformly in the direction of reducing class differences and divisions. (John H. Goldthorpe, 1969, *The Affluent Worker and the Class Structure*, pp. 157–58)

Similar conclusions poured in from other advanced industrial countries where the theory was presumed to apply. Richard Hamilton's (1972) research repudiated the idea of working-class affluence in France and the United States. Working-class families who enjoyed periods of modest prosperity depended on dual incomes that prevailed only during times of full employment, and did not result in any conversion to middle-class values or political preferences. Similar results were found in West Germany and Italy. Nowhere had the miracles of technological advance or the blandishments of middle-class life worked their presumed revolutionary effects on the structures of social class.

THE INJURIES OF CLASS

As evidence refuting the generalized upward mobility and affluent worker hypotheses began to accumulate, a more critical
interpretation gained recognition. Class differences, it appeared,
were large, persistent, and consequential for people's life chances:
their opportunities in education, wealth and income, occupation,
health and longevity, and in moral standing. It is commonplace
to observe that the upper classes enjoy an abundance of wealth,
and worry more about how to shelter it from taxation than
about its sufficiency; while the working classes live precariously
at or below the margin of a decent standard, often depending on
moonlighting or second and third salaries as essential sources of
family income. What is less obvious is that the working classes
living with chronic economic anxiety constitute almost one half
of the U.S. population—not a small minority with only itself to
blame. The truly poor comprise about one quarter of the general
population. Contrary to prevailing myth, the structure of income
inequality that separates the desperate from the comfortable and
affluent has scarcely changed over the past 50 years. The change
that has occurred is mostly cyclical; gains of lower-income
groups secured in periods of national prosperity are purloined
in austerity.

The better one's class situation, the greater the chances of
surviving infant illnesses, living in good health as an adult, and
enjoying an extended life span. The working classes have bad
teeth, poorer health in general, less access to medical services,
and they die five to ten years sooner on average than other
classes. Their work, when they can get it, is more physically
demanding and less respected. Independent of their own conduct,
they are at greater risk of zealous law enforcement, criminal
assault, depredations of the tax collector, and induction into the
military when drafts are in effect. During the Vietnam War, for
example, the working class was greatly overrepresented among
combat troops and, controlling for unequal numbers, suffered
twice the middle-class death rate.

Once again, such vital statistics are generally known. Less
appreciated is that people of the lower classes are taught to bear
a stigma for their station in life, or at least to deal with social
blame as though circumstances quite beyond their control

(birthplace, family background, opportunity, necessity) were matters of their own choice. Their teeth are bad, this attitude of blame supposes, not because they cannot afford the affluent dentist, but because they come from a working class or poverty culture indifferent to personal hygiene. They do manual work, not because they left school to help support a family burdened with illness, but because they have short time-horizons and relish immediate gratification. William Ryan's (1976) marvelous book, *Blaming the Victim*, coined the phrase to designate a middle-class ideology common in schools, welfare programs, and public agencies whereby social problems are interpreted as individual deficits. Neighborhoods are rundown through no fault of the slumlords or developers, but owing to the acculturation of rural migrants in the city. Ryan's phrase can be justifiably extended to the working class who are sometimes blamed for their position and, not least, often blame themselves.

Social classes, in the present usage, do not exist without class consciousness, although the coherence and contents of the latter vary with time and the class involved. *Class consciousness* is a collective awareness of beliefs and attitudes linked to the lifestyle of a class situation and a recognition that these are distinct from other classes. Class consciousness is many-sided, containing elements of pride, rebellion, satisfaction, and humiliation. We shall touch on all of these, but in the case of the U.S. working classes it is important at the start to note the heavy hand of blame that pervades conscious experience.

A sensitive study of *The Hidden Injuries of Class* by Richard Sennett and Jonathan Cobb (1972) discovered the complexity of this experience among Boston workingmen. The workers talked at length about complex and ambivalent feelings regarding their class position. They could take pride in their ability as workers, but regretted their own lack of freedom and of any conferred dignity. They had an innate disrespect for their class situation and they believed that education was the most likely avenue for achieving something better. Yet they also understood the sham of class privilege and the fact that persons with an education were not superior to themselves, least of all as workers. They felt class differences intensely, recognized that those who had gotten ahead through the acquisition of knowledge did so mainly with luck and guile, yet they also blamed themselves for not having been as clever. "If only I had what it takes, things would be different," lamented a shoe salesman. Their lack of success, and self-blame, however, did not mean that they had given up. What is striking is that these working people were determined to recoup a sense of dignity by sacrificing themselves for the betterment of their children.

> The workingmen of Boston almost never voiced resignation in the face of the injuries of class. The people we encountered had a powerful, though complicated, sense of mission in their lives: they were determined that, if circumstances of class had limited their freedom in comparison to that of educated people, they would *create* freedom for themselves. By that we mean that they were resolved to shape the actions open to them so that, in their own minds, they felt as though they acted from choice rather than necessity.... No matter how much the world had enslaved you, in this way you kept alive your dignity. (Richard Sennett and Jonathan Cobb, *The Hidden Injuries of Class*, pp. 120–21)

Much as that self-effacing courage may be admired, it is an unhappy bargain when it carries little real promise for the next generation. In the end, it is a demoralizing dilemma: "Something hidden and perverse is at work in our society so that people lose a conviction of their dignity when they try to take responsibility for either an increase in or a limit on their 'freedom' as society defines that word" (p. 37). As they struggle with this paradox, workers acquire no special esteem for the middle class, nor any expectation of joining it. They covet self-esteem and autonomy on their own cultural terms, but despair of achieving that save through their legacy. From this amalgam of circumstance and feeling, they fashion a consciousness of their class that is debilitating but unresigned.

From Boston to the San Francisco Bay area, the story is similar. Lilian Rubin's (1976) *Worlds of Pain* reports on a California working-class family life pervaded by: the exhaustion of men and women with stultifying jobs, the resentment of economic uncertainty that corrodes personal relations, conflict on the role of the working wife, sexual insecurity, alcohol abuse, and heartbreak over the likelihood that children face more of the same.

> [T]he affluent and happy worker of whom we have heard so much in recent decades seems not to exist....[the realities] call the

lie to the mobility myth we cherish so deeply...one that avoids facing the structured reality that there's no room at the top and little room in the middle...the economic realities of working-class life and the constraints they impose upon living are common ingredients from which a world of shared understandings arises, from which a consciousness and a culture grows that is distinctly working class. Whether in ways of being in the family, in childrearing patterns, in orientations toward work and leisure—common experiences create common adaptations, all responses to a particular set of life circumstances. (Lilian Breslow Rubin, *Worlds of Pain: Life in the Working-Class Family*, pp. 204, 210–11)

Working-Class Life

Yet the hidden injuries and pain of working-class life should not obscure a vital aspect of its consciousness, the wit and spiritual energy that keep people going. Studs Terkel's (1972) book on *Working* allows people to speak for themselves "about what they do all day and how they feel about what they do." Of the result, he says:

> This book, being about work, is, by its very nature, about violence—to the spirit as well as to the body....It is, above all (or beneath all), about daily humiliations. To survive the day is triumph enough for the walking wounded among the great many of us....It is also about a search, too, for daily meaning as well as daily bread, for recognition as well as cash, for astonishment rather than torpor; in short, for a sort of life rather than a Monday through Friday sort of dying. Perhaps immortality, too, is part of the quest. To be remembered was the wish, spoken and unspoken, of the heroes and heroines of this book. (Studs Terkel, *Working*, p. xiii)

Above all, in their work people seek self-esteem. This is the root of varied expressions of class consciousness. What is distinctive about the working classes, however, is that the great majority are forced to accept the trivial and demeaning kinds of work that a rationalized advanced economy is based upon. This is the link between working-class consciousness and social structure, the source of frustration entailed by an all-consuming stress on productivity.

The working classes, like other large groupings of people, are not by nature angry, tormented, and preoccupied by their precarious position in the marketplace. On the contrary, they resemble the middle classes in coming hopefully to their jobs and other encounters in the marketplace. Because of the ways in which production, consumption, and the amenities of life are organized in advanced capitalist societies, however, they experience exploitation, commence to struggle, and discover themselves as classes in the process. Barbara Garson's (1972) book *All the Live Long Day*, describes how this sequence of events takes place. She talked with workers across the country in settings as diverse as a tuna fish cannery and a Ping-Pong factory:

> I have spent the last two years examining the way people cope with routine and monotonous work. I expected to find resentment, and I found it. I expected to find boredom, and I found it. I expected to find sabotage, and I found it in clever forms that I could never have imagined. But the most dramatic thing I found was quite the opposite of noncooperation. *People passionately want to work.*
>
> Whatever creativity goes into sabotage, a more amazing ingenuity goes into manufacturing goals and satisfactions on jobs where measurable achievement has been all but rationalized out.... Almost everyone wants to feel she is getting something accomplished—to see that stack of paddles, the growing pile of dark meat, or to master the job blindfolded since there's not much to master the other way. (Barbara Garson, *All the Live Long Day: The Meaning and Demeaning of Routine Work*, pp. x–xi)

For some, these adaptations to working-class life give way to rebellion in its many forms: sabotage on the job, alcohol and drug abuse on and off the job, truculence in the face of conventional morality, and the defense of workers' rights. Rebellion can be both politically constructive and self-destructive, but it is always a cultural expression. Joseph Howell (1973) spent a year learning about the *Hard Living on Clay Street*, the white families engaged in blue-collar service occupations of Washington, D.C. He noticed that these families were divided into two kinds, the hard living and the settled: "The hard living families on Clay Street did not represent a distinct class or group of people, but rather a variation of life styles within the white working class" (p. 357). Why some families were settled and others bent on hard living was neither predictable nor the focus of Howell's work, although the impression is that the difference was largely circumstantial and reversible (hard living took its toll on the body, a better job came along, or financial burdens eased with children leaving home).

The hard-living families drank heavily, had a history of divorce and presently unstable marriages, evinced violence mainly in tough talk, moved about a lot, valued individualism, and expressed complete alienation from politics. The "sole political comment of the year" coming from one of Howell's Washington neighbors is almost humorous for its belligerence: "President Nixon? Fuck him. That's all I got to say. Course I never thought about it all that much. He's probably doing the best he can with what he's got" (p. 304).

These traits of hard living, however, would be mistakenly understood as personal attributes of the working class. In the first place, they either do not apply or take other forms in the settled families that were usually church-going, teetotaling, and conservative. In the second place, "for some, hard living was rebellion; for others, it was running away from life's problems" (p. 356). Rebellion, then, was just a part of the overall pattern of working-class life, but it was a vigorous part both for the numbers it attracted and for the threat it posed to others.

> Hard living was among other things a way of rebelling against the life circumstances one found himself in. It was as if the individual concluded consciously or unconsciously that there was little to be gained from "fitting in," or from saving for the future. Whatever the future held, it was not worth making sacrifices. Rather, a person should live for the present and get the most out of life now. If something happened to change those circumstances—that is, when the individual felt he did have a stake in society, that the future was promising, that there was a place for him—then there was a tendency to save, to be more cautious, to live a more restrained life. (Joseph T. Howell, *Hard Living on Clay Street: Portraits of Blue Collar Families*, p. 355)

Rebellion is key to understanding one important expression of U.S. working-class culture. In the past that culture has been properly understood as a product of what William Yancey called "emergent ethnicity" or the enactment of an immigrant heritage in the new setting of U.S. urban neighborhoods and industrial workplaces. Today it is changing from an immigrant to a more indigenous working-class culture as younger generations ironically hark back to a supposed tradition of the American West. Its symbols are the pickup truck or four-wheel drive vehicle, the cowboy hat or monogrammed baseball cap, jeans, and fancy belt buckle. This group admires the freedom of the open road and the citizens'-band radio as a collective defense against police, although most of its devotees work in offices and factories. Highways and the ability to outsmart police express independence from oppressive jobs and middle-class standards. In play, tastes run to beer and country music, and in worship to fundamentalism—the interdependent wages and salvation of hard living. Behind the postured urban cowboy or -girl is a cultural statement of a desire for respect and self-determination.

The working class expresses itself in popular culture; in the songs of artists such as Bruce Springsteen whose "Born in the U.S.A." expresses the plight of a Vietnam veteran with no prospects in civilian employment:

> Born down in a dead man's town
> The first kick I took was when I hit the ground
> You end up like a dog that's been beat too much
> Till you spend half your life just covering up
> Born in the U.S.A. (Bruce Springsteen, *Born in the U.S.A.*, Columbia Records)

The Higher Reaches of Class

As class differences assert themselves, their associated cultures diverge. The middle and upper classes have their own cultures and consciousness. These attitudes require less description since they are the familiar, dominant ideas behind much of the interpretation of U.S. society that has been questioned here—the ideas of mobility, the declining significance of class, and the equalization of opportunity. They pervade the mass media, schools, and government, defining appropriate ambitions and blaming other classes for their failure to fulfill those ambitions.

We understand the upper classes mostly as they like to see themselves: competent in matters of finance, generous in charity, public-spirited, rich but not gauche, tasteful (like the Manhattan apartment owner, sophisticated but not trendy), and, with the rare exception of a playboy scion, generally deserving of their exalted position. The upper classes are glamorous; less resented than envied. In business and art, they are indisputably in charge, although it is arguable whether they control politics (an issue reserved for later). There is little doubt that they constitute a self-conscious, socially cohesive group.

In *The Power Elite*, C. Wright Mills (1951) showed that the corporate rich attend the same prep schools as children, go to the same elite universities and law schools, join interconnected firms and social clubs, marry one another, and rotate in the same influential public posts. William Domhoff (1974) has added to this portrait showing, in *The Bohemian Grove and Other Retreats*, how the likes of (former secretary of state) Henry Kissinger and John McCone (former CIA director, head of the commission that investigated the Watts riot, director of Standard Oil of California, and International Telephone and Telegraph) mix socially in the California redwoods with the heads of most major U.S. corporations and government agencies. Since they are enveloped in glamor and envy, the legitimacy of the upper classes is not seriously challenged—or if it is questioned, the blame is laid to mean-spirited socialists.

The upper classes are miniscule in numbers. Their great cultural influence derives from a combination of power and middle-class emulation. In the revealing asymmetry of class relations, emulation seldom works downward, except in affectations of modesty, and works upward mainly for the middle classes. Portraits of middle-class culture in the 1950s showed this most clearly in Whyte's creatures of the organization and suburbia, Riesman's other-directed characters, and the white-collar rearguarders, up for sale in Mills. Middle-class culture has been the bulwark of belief in universal mobility, the fruits of education and hard work, fair play, and the generous distribution of opportunity.

These beliefs were questioned in radical circles during the early part of the 20th century and they faltered for everyone but Little Orphan Annie in the 1930s. In the postwar boom, however, they reasserted themselves forcefully as the sociological observers saw. The cultural pattern, like the bedrock structures of social class, shifts over time. Today it appears that middle-class culture has fallen on hard times, self-doubt, and some social criticism. Education has lost much of its emollient effect on class divisions as the "rewards to education" (characteristically the differential income earned over a lifetime by variously educated categories) have dropped. Inflation and recession have eroded what were thought to be permanent gains in income and career. Home-ownership, the single most important symbol of middle-class position, has grown out of reach for many young couples, even with dual incomes. Others once securely rooted in homes and middle-class lives, as we saw, have been turned out homeless.

Increasing unemployment and job degradation affect both the middle-class material standard and the culture. Confidence in the equity of the system and in one's self are only as stable as their positional underpinnings in the marketplace. Some years ago a revealing study by Douglas Powell and Paul Driscoll (1973) showed the changing mood of unemployed male engineers and scientists. Immediately upon receiving notice that they had been laid off, they were relaxed, even relieved that certain dissatisfactions with their jobs were at least resolved. They were confident of finding another well-paid position soon; enough so that they vacationed a bit while planning the next move. In the second stage, concerted efforts to obtain a job similar to the one they had lost unexpectedly failed for many and, after a few months of this, they were cast into a third stage of vacillation and doubt.

> Doubt begins to undermine the process of decision making. He becomes intensely moody. Relationships with friends deteriorate ...the controlled optimism which produced earlier efforts starts to erode. The unemployed man begins doubting his judgment, second-guessing himself and becoming more self-critical.... Anxiety surrounding these feelings intensifies.... The men have a tendency to lose a sense of who they are vocationally.... They feel a violent rage that sometimes turns back on them in the form of a deep depression. (Douglas H. Powell & Paul F. Driscoll, "Middle-Class Professionals Face Unemployment," pp. 21–22)

In a final stage of malaise and cynicism, they withdraw further from humiliating job interviews and refusals. "I've lost all my drive and don't care.... I'm just staying around the house" (p. 23).

In fact, these unemployed scientists and engineers begin acting very much like working-class people; displaying the resentment and apathy that some social scientists have mistaken for character traits of the less fortunate rather than ego defenses against understandably threatening circumstances. We are reminded of Goffman's description of the "institutional self" (in Chapter 1) with class position, rather than the total institution, providing the supports people use to maintain a particular conception of themselves. These exceptional cases in which institutional props are withdrawn testify to the general importance of class cultures in shaping experience.

In summary, social classes are much more than categories for describing a population. They are socially meaningful groupings that display common lifestyles, a consciousness of kind, and patterned relations with other classes. They figure importantly in the life chances that people enjoy. Taken together they portray much of what we understand as a social structure.

CLASS STRUCTURE AND STRUGGLE

Having described the experience of selected social classes, it is useful to develop a portrait of the overall *class structure*: the set of social groupings defining positions in the marketplace and, most important, the relations between them which reciprocally define the power and circumstances of each.

The U.S. Class Structure

Any portrait of the class structure, as a geometric figure of a set of categories, entails difficulties. On the one hand, classes as acting and self-conscious social groupings vary in cohesiveness and salience. Factory workers and the corporate rich are clear-cut class positions replete with a well-developed consciousness and culture. Middle classes such as the executive-managerial are less internally coherent and more torn by conflicting loyalties to upper-class owners and middle-class colleagues. Combining all these in one structure means slighting to some extent important differences. On the other hand, joining many experiences of market power in one structure requires a common dimension of class comparison, the most convenient being occupational or economic. There is no way to escape these problems if a general portrait of class structure is desired, but it is important to remember that the structure is an approximation in meaning.

The class structure is divided into three levels on the underlying dimension of power in the marketplace, using source of income as a shorthand for designating specific positions. The upper classes include: (1) the propertied rich, often old money; (2) the corporate rich, owners of industry and large corporations; (3) the top financiers and owners of money. The middle classes include: (1) top- and middle-level executives, managers, and technocratic experts of the business and corporate world; (2) owners and proprietors of small businesses that employ small numbers; (3) independent, self-employed business and professional people (lawyers, doctors, accountants, for example); (4) employed professionals and highly skilled workers (teachers, engineers, medical technicians, for example); (5) lower-level supervisors, managers, and foremen. Other groupings, such as farm owners, could be added, although their numbers have declined drastically. The working classes include: (1) industrial and factory workers; (2) trade and construction workers; (3) office workers, attendants and service workers; (4) manual and agricultural labor (of which there are still many now employed by corporate and industrialized agriculture). In addition, perhaps beneath these is a sizable underclass or *lumpen proletariat*, in Marx's words, including the permanently unemployed, migrant, and casual laborers, and some of the career criminals.

The major markets in which these classes compete and develop their varying degrees of cohesiveness are the labor market for

---

TABLE 3–1 Contemporary Class Structure in the United States

A.	*Upper Classes*	2%*
	1. Property owners	
	2. Corporate and business owners, large employers	
	3. Financiers	
B.	*Middle classes*	52%
	1. Executives, managers, technocrats (top and middle levels)	(12%)
	2. Small-business owners and employers	(6%)
	3. Self-employed business and professionals	(7%)
	4. Employed professionals, skilled crafts	(10%)
	5. Supervisors, foremen	(17%)
C.	*Working classes*	46%
	1. Industrial workers	(16%)
	2. Trades and construction	(12%)
	3. Clerks, attendants, office, and service workers	(14%)
	4. Manual and agricultural labor	(4%)

*Estimated percentages
SOURCES: Wright, et al. (1982, December). The American class structure, *American Sociological Review*, 47 709–726; *United States Census of Population*, 1980.

jobs and earned income, the credit market, and the commodity market for goods and services. The most dramatic change in the labor market over the last few generations has been the increase in wage earners by contrast to the declining numbers of independent professionals, tradespeople, farmowners, and small businesspersons. At the same time, however, industrial employment, traditional blue-collar work, has declined with automation and the transfer of production abroad. The industrial working class has been the principal victim, while the technical and skilled middle class and the corporate rich have been the beneficiaries. The market power that industrial workers once had by virtue of their skills and their unions has been severely eroded. The industrial working class of the Midwestern "rust bowl" is losing this struggle, particularly in steel and automobiles, with large reductions in the labor force and in wages and benefits.

Second, in the credit market, the financial upper class recently has enhanced its power with high interest rates, while most of the working and middle classes have either paid that interest or been forced out of the market altogether, as in home buying. Lost power in the credit market has lately been the ruin of many small businesses and of the few remaining farm owners. In the 1980s, the number of bankruptcies, traceable in important part to interest rates, reached its highest level since the 1930s depression. The financiers, however, have also been playing a risky game in high-interest loans, particularly to Third World countries, coming more than once to the brink of international monetary collapse. Domestically, the Federal Deposit Insurance Corporation (FDIC) which insures commercial banks recently reported that the number of banks in serious financial trouble had risen sharply (up from 385 in 1976 to 597 in 1983). Actual bank failures quadrupled in the early 1980s (from 10 in 1981 to 42 the following year).

Third, commodity markets have followed a pattern typified by the growing difficulty in buying a new home. Unemployment, reduced wages, and inflation have cut severely the purchasing power of the middle and working classes. In this sense, such commodities as the education of children are increasingly out of reach, compounding disadvantages in other markets. Meanwhile, with corporate taxes declining as a proportion of national income, middle class taxpayers have been squeezed to the point of tax revolt. The victims of resultant public fiscal crises have been other middle-class civil servants (teachers, for example), working-class service and clerical people, and underclass beneficiaries of public programs for medical care, social security and nutrition, among others.

Class Struggles

These examples show how class situations are determined in markets, and they hint strongly at the forms of exploitation that help to produce open class conflicts. The class situations described illustrate the bases of conflict which, nevertheless, are beneath the surface; the continuing sources of disadvantage and inward struggle that contrast with episodic class fights. The essential point here is that classes take their most decisive form when they come to struggle for changes in these conditions. The historian E.P. Thompson (1978) noted that,

> [C]lasses do not exist as separate entities, look around, find an enemy class, and then start to struggle. On the contrary, people find themselves in a society structured in determined ways (crucially, but not exclusively, in production relations), they experience exploitation (or the need to maintain power over those whom they exploit), they identify points of antagonistic interest, they commence to struggle around these issues and in the process of struggling they discover themselves as classes, they come to know this discovery as class consciousness. Class and class-consciousness are always the last, not the first, stage in the real historical process. (E.P. Thompson, "Eighteenth-Century English Society: Class Struggle Without Classes?" p. 149)

The classical, and once most common, form of open conflict is the struggle between labor and capital; between corporate and industrial owners and the working classes. Other forms are increasingly common today, including struggles between certain upper and middle classes.

A celebrated instance of the first type was the 1972 strike at the General Motors plant in Lordstown, Ohio. The notoriety of Lordstown stemmed from the fact that a new generation of autoworkers confronted the corporate upper class with protests about the quality of their jobs in the face of measures for automating production. The Lordstown factory opened in 1966, billed as a model plant and designed to turn out 60 standard

Chevrolets each hour. The first workers considered themselves privileged to have these jobs and, at an average age of 35, represented the traditional industrial working class. By 1970, General Motors was feeling the competition of foreign imports and converted the Lordstown facility for accelerated production of the Vega economy car. Physically demanding work and high labor turnover by then had altered the workforce to an average age of 25, including many Vietnam veterans, hillbillies, hippies, and minorities—the Woodstock of the working class, some said. With the help of automated welders and paint dipping, the line was now to produce 101 cars per hour. In many instances, this could be accomplished only through more intensive exploitation of labor. Stanley Aronowitz (1973) describes the arduous working conditions:

> For example, within a minute on the line, a worker in the trim department had to walk about 20 feet to a conveyor belt transporting parts to the line, pick up a front seat weighing 30 pounds, carry it back to his work station, place the seat on the chassis, and put in four bolts to fasten it down first by hand-starting the bolts and then using an air gun to tighten them according to standard. It was steady work when the line moved at 60 cars an hour. When it increased to more than 100 cars an hour, the number of operations on this job were not reduced and the pace became almost maddening. In 36 seconds the worker had to perform at least eight different operations including walking, lifting, hauling, lifting the carpet, bending to fasten the bolts by hand, fastening them by air gun, replacing the carpet, and putting a sticker on the hood. Sometimes the bolts fail to fit into the holes; the gun refuses to function at the required torque; the seats are defective or the threads are bare on the bolt. But the line does not stop....."You really have to run like hell to catch up, if you're gonna do the whole job right." (Stanley Aronowitz, *False Promises: The Shaping of American Working Class Consciousness*, pp. 22–23)

The highly publicized technology of the reorganized factory was not per se the source of its productivity. Emma Rothchild (1972) noted, Lordstown technology is based on the speed-up developed by Henry Ford, methods which follow from the earliest techniques of mass production. General Motors tried to gain a competitive edge over Japanese manufacturers by extracting more work from the people on the assembly line, by reducing what was thought to be their idle time. But the new breed of worker rebelled, as one of Studs Terkel's (1972) conversations revealed.

> So what happened? A guy faced up to the facts....If he were young and married, he had to do one thing: protect his pace. He had to have some time. The best way is to slow down the pace. He might want to open up a book, he might want to smoke a cigarette, or he might want to walk two or three steps away to get a drink of water. He might want to talk to the guy next to him. So he started fighting like hell to get the work off him. He thought he wasn't obligated to do more than his normal share. All of a sudden it mattered to him what was fair. (Studs Terkel, *Working*, p. 259)

The result was a bitter strike. The local United Auto Workers union voted 97 percent in favor of a strike and was out for 22 days before reaching an agreement that restored back pay to workers previously disciplined for violating work standards. UAW locals in 10 other GM plants around the country followed suit with strikes related to speed-ups. In the long run, however, little was done to improve working conditions. Grudging concessions were at first made, but as recession and unemployment mounted in the 1970s, the screws of productivity were retightened, accompanied now by actual wage and labor force reductions which the union was forced to accept rather than face plant closings. The long-term result of the Lordstown struggle, and others based on similar issues, was working-class defeat and lost power in the market.

With changes in the economy and increasing production overseas by U.S. multinational corporations, the size of the industrial labor force is declining steadily. The fastest-growing working class is devoted to services and clerical work, much of it in the public sector. Accordingly, since the mid-1960s a common form of class struggle has been the fight for wages and working conditions by public-service unions. James Green (1980) explains that:

> During the fifties, strikes by government employees were rare, but in the following decade 119 walkouts occurred in the public sector, involving 70,000 workers. The strikers ranged from professionals, especially teachers and nurses, to blue-collar workers such as garbage collectors and fire fighters. Violating laws that prohibit public employees from striking, the American Federation of Teachers

adopted militant tactics and gained thousands of new members. The American Federation of State, County, and Municipal Employees (AFSCME) also used the strike effectively, increasing its membership from 182,000 in 1960 to 350,000 in 1967.... City workers faced increasing job pressures during the sixties, whether they were bus drivers wrestling with poor equipment, teachers contending with growing classroom violence, or mental health workers dealing with the large number of people who could not cope with the urban "rat race." While public employees absorbed the human and social effects of urban disintegration, they also faced increasing demands for productivity and efficiency. As public-sector bureaucrats adopted strategies for control used in the private sector, government workers rebelled. Public-school teachers, who had enjoyed a good deal of control on their jobs, fought to remain in charge of their classrooms and to reduce the power of administrators. By the end of the sixties, public employee unions had become powerful.... As a result, demands for productivity in the public sector increased as recession hit during the Nixon Administration in the early 1970s. As wage inflation in the state sector grew, politicians, businessmen, and many taxpayers blamed the public-service unions for the fiscal crisis of the state in the 1970s, even though wage increases for public workers lagged behind those of unionized industrial workers ... government workers were thrown on the defensive. (James R. Green, *The World of the Worker*, pp. 234–235 ff)

The foregoing examples of class struggle touch only the most prominent forms and portray a two-party contest in the labor market. The reality is always more complex. In the first place, the struggles involve additional parties. In the dispute between autoworkers and the corporate owners, the other upper classes side with industrial management. So, too, do many middle-class managers, skilled workers, and technicians—all finding themselves in an ambiguous (in the words of Erik Wright) or conflicting class situation. The struggles of public service workers pit working- and middle-class unionists against other middle-class bureaucrats and taxpayers. The corporate and propertied upper classes have benefited indirectly from middle-class led tax revolts—just as the working and under classes dependent on public services have suffered.

In the second place, class struggles take place in other, interpenetrating markets. In the commodity market, price increases by dominant producers are met with consumer protest or boycott. General Motors met with consumers turning to cheaper imported cars in the commodity market and acted on this problem in the labor market in the specific ways that Lordstown demonstrates.

A topical and instructive example of protest in the commodity market is the utility rate rebellion that spread across the United States in the 1980s. Energy is provided chiefly by publicly regulated monopoly corporations. Nevertheless, these are owned and managed by the corporate rich and financial classes which hold the largest blocks of stock. With rising petroleum prices, inflation, and costly investments in new, often unworkable, nuclear plants, the major utilities began raising their rates, sometimes doubling or tripling the monthly cost to ratepayers. Protests spread and took many forms. Victor Zonana, writing in *The Wall Street Journal*, March 19, 1982, for example, perceived the connection between the struggle and finance capital.

> Rebels are rising in the Pacific Northwest. Sporting nasty buttons, they threaten to undermine banks, to unseat politicians and, for the prime target they call "Whoops," to deal the harshest blow—refusal to pay their bills.
>
> The action is part of the continuing drama centered on the Washington Public Power Supply System. Until now the drama has been set on Wall Street, where investment bankers struggle to patch together financing for the giant public agency, and at two construction sites in Washington state, where mismanagement, snafus and cost overruns killed two of the system's five partially built nuclear power plants.
>
> Now an open rebellion against skyrocketing electric rates is gathering momentum in Washington, Oregon and Idaho communities large and small. Jolted by the doubling and tripling of electric bills and faced with the prospects of similar stiff hikes this year, customers are organizing, marching, packing legislative hearings and withholding payment of rates. (*The Wall Street Journal*, March 19, 1982)

There is little doubt that the poor, elderly, and people on fixed incomes have suffered most from rising utility rates. The *Los Angeles Times* (December 26, 1982) reported "seniors living in bathrooms with kerosene heaters. They don't even turn on their furnace, they don't use lights at night." Nevertheless, the speeches and tactics of the ratepayer revolt suggest that it is largely a middle-class movement. Organized petition drives, bill burnings, sieges on utility commission hearings are the methods of a nonalienated, nonapathetic, politically socialized middle class using the conventional weapons at hand to confront the regulators of monopoly corporations. In many instances, the movement succeeded in winning rate rollbacks or freezes. Although these small victories may not last, they contrast sharply with the recently bleak record of working-class struggles in the labor market.

SUMMARIZING TRENDS

From all these illustrations of class conflict, it appears that both the structure of social classes and the nature of their struggles are changing. In order to conclude this discussion with a sense of what the near future holds, the conception of social class that has served this far need only be applied to current trends. If we can discern the changing shape of markets, and thereby of class relations, we should be able to infer their practical consequences. A good place to begin is in the labor market.

Over the last generation, the labor forces of the advanced industrial countries have changed fundamentally with the rise of a service economy. In the United States, Germany, France, and England, the number of industrial workers has declined. Between 1940 and 1980, the percentage of the U.S. labor force (including middle- and working-class persons) engaged in manufacturing dropped from 34 to 22, while the percentage in services rose from 46 to 68. More revealing is the fact that 90 percent of all the new (public and private sector) jobs created during the 1970s were in services—including in this omnibus category such things as retail trade, banking, government, repair services, and many more.

The economist Emma Rothchild (1981) has captured this change with an impressive contrast. Speaking only of the private economy, from 1973 to 1980, 70 percent of all new jobs were in services and retail trade, and of these 40 percent occurred in just three areas: eating and drinking places, health services, and business services. Considering only the first of these, "the increase in employment in eating and drinking places since 1973 is greater than total employment in the automobile and steel industries combined" (p. 13). By contrast to the old blue-collar jobs, which are unionized and tended to win favorable wages and benefits, the outstanding features of the new jobs include: an overrepresentation of women, low pay, short hours or part-time character, dead-end prospects, and the relative absence of protections and benefits.

> The United States, in sum, is moving toward a structure of employment ever more dominated by jobs that are badly paid, unchanging, and unproductive. (Emma Rothchild, "Reagan and the Real Economy," p. 13)

Two more trends explain and compound the picture. Obviously, the United States continues to be an industrial society and to produce an enormous quantity of manufactured goods. Much of the actual production, however, has moved out of the country in search of cheap labor markets accessible to U.S. multinational corporations. Nearly all of the television sets and radios, increasing proportions of the clothes, shoes, toys, computers, appliances, steel, and even automobiles are all being manufactured in low-wage countries (Taiwan, Mexico, the Philippines, Malaysia, Hong Kong, and so forth) and reimported into the U.S. market under preferential tariff arrangements. Since the 1970s, when this practice became common for the largest U.S. manufacturers, literally millions of domestic jobs have been eliminated and, as the trend continues, the market power and the share of national income going to labor have plummeted. Increasingly, class determination lies in the international division of labor.

Meanwhile, in the altered labor market at home, the second compounding trend is toward further mechanization now in the service economy. Business services are computerized and offices mechanized with word processors and photocopiers. Banks are becoming fully automated. Franchise food operations build standardized outlets (one hesitates to say restaurants) that mechanize assembly-line food. Medical services depend increasingly upon machines for treatment and laboratory analysis. Transportation introduces computerized trains and containerized cargo handling attached to mechanized warehouses. Repair services, notably for automobiles, are dispensed by national chains using factory methods to restore transmissions, tires, brakes, and mufflers. Supermarkets and gas stations are automated to the extent that checkers and attendants can now be replaced by plastic debit cards that effect purchases through electronic communications between banks.

Sociologists such as Daniel Bell have spoken enthusiastically about this process, hailing it as a post-industrial society in which new and exciting jobs will exist in the information industry. If the computer industry is prototypical, however, new jobs are not produced in numbers anywhere equal to those lost. To stay in the competitive race companies go abroad to create their jobs (as in the recent celebrated case of Atari) and their production and programming tasks are further mechanized. Ernest Mandel (1972) has captured better the significance of these changes.

> Far from representing a "post-industrial society," late capitalism thus constitutes *generalized universal industrialization* for the first time in history. (Ernest Mandel, *Late Capitalism*, p. 387)

The broad results of these trends for the structure of classes is now readily observed. As new service jobs replace old industrial ones, work is degraded as a net result. This is not a uniform "de-skilling" process. Some displaced industrial workers and, particularly, new entrants to the labor force get decent jobs in the service or information industry. But the typical transition is from skilled industrial work to attendant or clerk in retail services—illustratively, from steelworker to liquor store clerk. Since fewer of the new jobs are unionized, organized labor as a percentage of the total workforce declines (down from 36 to 19 percent in the last 40 years) and with it the pay and benefit levels of the working class erode. Job security is declining. Real wages in 1978 dropped to levels of the 1960s and the trend has not reversed itself. In summary, for the majority of the population— all of the working classes and middle-class civil servants, small business, and some corporate employees—power in the labor market has declined. With that, of course, their class situations and life chances have worsened.

Class relations have become more polarized, notably during recessionary years. Open class conflict is more likely from now until the end of the century than it was during boom decades after World War II. But the locus of that conflict is also shifting. The struggles of labor and capital in industry are less frequent because the threat of more automation and of offshore production have chastened labor into fighting a rearguard action to protect the remaining jobs even at the cost of wage reductions. Public-service unions are on the defensive as a result of fiscal strains in government. These facts do not mean that conflict has been suppressed, as the utility rate-payers' movement shows. Rather, the conflicts take different forms and are displaced to other market situations.

Recent struggles in the labor market have focused on plant closings: to prevent them, to provide for retraining and community reparations when they occur, or to promote employee buy-outs that would keep firms operating. In the publicized case of the Chicago and Northwestern Railway, venturesome employees successfully bought out and restored the company to prosperity. Few buyouts are as successful, but the idea is attractive to communities threatened by plant closings. All of this suggests that as good jobs become scarce, future class struggles in the labor market will center on the provision and rights of employment. Migrant labor, exported production, plant closings, and automation are specific targets for new organizing strategies.

Finally, class struggle appears in new forms beyond the labor market. It focuses on commodities, broadly understood as housing, education, clear air and water, health care, protection of the poor and elderly. Economic austerity and the suppression of struggles in the labor market have had the ironic effect of spreading the potential for new coalitional struggles. Whole communities suffer from inflation, unemployment, and plant closings. The ratepayers' movement, with its middle-class leadership, is also a civil rebellion aimed at broad local welfare goals. Its largest national confederation, the Citizen-Labor Energy Coalition, includes 200 elderly, community and labor-union organizations. Like the classes themselves, class struggle persists and adapts to the changing structure of the economy.

Social class is a basic interpretive tool in the sociological tradition that provides lucid summations of what is going on in the world. In the process of social mobility, the changing occupational world, and the personal and cultural experience of distinct social groupings, social classes distinguish the foundations of social structure, helping to explain the sources of inequality. An understanding of classes penetrates durable myths about universal mobility and the equalization of opportunity, whether those are presented historically as a steady progression toward an egalitarian society or contemporarily as a placid post-industrial order. The idea of social class uncovers a different and more complex human reality. Classes explain a good deal about why the homeless live alongside the sophisticated. Classes explain power, humiliation, self-satisfaction, hard-won mobility, and the manner in which people struggle for a livelihood with some dignity.

The metaphor of class stratification or census accounts of occupational distribution tell us something about contemporary society, but they also risk obscuring a vivid social life. The world of social class is people making their own culture by acting in class ways. Any metaphor transforms its subject, but we would gain some understanding by replacing class categories or strata with an image of classes as poker players. The players, each with different styles and resources, engage in a high-stakes game governed by rules that favor the house and the highest bidder, but in a game always susceptible to intrepid plays and collective disputations of the rules.

SELECTED BIBLIOGRAPHY

ARONOWITZ, STANLEY (1973). *False Promises: The Shaping of American Working Class Consciousness.* New York: McGraw-Hill.

BELL, DANIEL (1973). *The Coming of Post-Industrial Society: A Venture in Social Forecasting.* New York: Basic Books.

BENDIX, REINHARD, & LIPSET, SEYMOUR MARTIN (1959). *Social Mobility in Industrial Society.* Berkeley: University of California Press.

BLAU, PETER M., & DUNCAN, OTIS DUDLEY (1967). *The American Occupational Structure.* New York: John Wiley & Sons.

BRAVERMAN, HARRY (1974). *Labor and Monopoly Capital: The Degradation of Work in the Twentieth Century.* New York: Monthly Review Press.

DAHRENDORF, RALF (1959). *Class and Class Conflict in Industrial Society.* Stanford: Stanford University Press.

DISRAELI, BENJAMIN (1980). *Sybil—or the Two Nations.* New York: Penguin Books. (Work originally published in 1845.)

DOMHOFF, G. WILLIAM (1974). *The Bohemian Grove and Other Retreats: A Study of Ruling-Class Cohesiveness.* New York: Harper & Row.

GARSON, BARBARA (1972). *All the Live Long Day: The Meaning and Demeaning of Routine Work.* New York: Penguin Books.

GIDDENS, ANTHONY (1973). *The Class Structures of the Advanced Societies*. New York: Barnes & Noble Books.

GOLDTHORPE, JOHN, et al. (1969). *The Affluent Worker and the Class Structure*. New York: Cambridge University Press.

GREEN, JAMES R. (1980). *The World of the Worker: Labor in Twentieth-Century America*. New York: Hill & Wang.

GUTMAN, HERBERT G. (1977). *Work, Culture, and Society in Industrializing America: Essays in American Working-Class and Social History*. New York: Vintage Books.

HAMILTON, RICHARD F. (1972). *Class and Politics in the United States*. New York: John Wiley & Sons.

HOWELL, JOSEPH T. (1973). *Hard Living on Clay Street: Portraits of Blue Collar Families*. Garden City, N.Y.: Anchor Books.

KUTTNER, BOB (1983, July). "The Declining Middle." *The Atlantic, 252* (1), 60–72.

LYND, ROBERT S. & HELEN M. (1937). *Middletown in Transition: A Study in Cultural Conflicts*. New York: Harcourt Brace Jovanovich.

MANDEL, ERNEST (1972). *Late Capitalism*. London: Verso.

MARX, KARL (1963). *The Eighteenth Brumaire of Louis Bonaparte*. New York: International Publishers. (Original work published in 1852.)

———(1981). *Capital*, Vol. 3. New York: Vintage Books. (Original work published in 1894.)

MILLS, C. WRIGHT (1951). *White Collar: The American Middle Classes*. New York: Oxford University Press.

PAGE, CHARLES (1964). *Class and American Sociology: From Ward to Ross*. New York: Octagon House. (Originally published in 1940.)

PORTES, ALEJANDRO, & WALTON, JOHN (1981). *Labor, Class, and the International System*. New York: Academic Press.

POWELL, DOUGLAS H., & DRISCOLL, PAUL F. (1973, January/February). "Middle-Class Professionals Face Unemployment." *Society, 10*(2), 18–26.

RIESMAN, DAVID (1950). *The Lonely Crowd*. New Haven: Yale University Press.

ROTHCHILD, EMMA (1972, March 23). "GM in More Trouble." *New York Review of Books*, pp. 12–18.

———(1981, February 5). "Reagan and the Real Economy." *New York Review of Books*.

RUBIN, LILIAN BRESLOW (1976). *Worlds of Pain: Life in the Working-Class Family*. New York: Basic Books.

RYAN, WILLIAM (1976). *Blaming the Victim*. Rev. ed. New York: Vintage Books.

SENNETT, RICHARD, & COBB, JONATHAN (1972). *The Hidden Injuries of Class*. New York: Random House.

TAWNEY, R.H. (1952). *Equality*. London: George Allen and Unwin. (Originally published in 1931.)

TERKEL, STUDS (1972). *Working*. New York: Avon Books.

THERNSTROM, STEPHAN (1969). *Poverty and Progress: Social Mobility in a Nineteenth Century City*. New York: Cambridge University Press.

THOMPSON, E.P. (1978, May). "Eighteenth-century English Society: Class Struggle without Class?" *Social History*, 3(2), 133–65.

VEBLEN, THORSTEIN (1953). *The Theory of the Leisure Class: An Economic Study of Institutions*. New York: Mentor Books. (Original work published in 1899.)

WARNER, W. LLOYD, & LUNT, PAUL S. (1941). *The Social Life of a Modern Community*. New Haven: Yale University Press.

WEBER, MAX (1946). "Class, Status, Party." In HANS GERTH and C. WRIGHT MILLS (Eds.). *From Max Weber: Essays in Sociology*. New York: Oxford University Press.

WHYTE, WILLIAM H. (1956). *The Organization Man*. New York: Simon and Schuster.

WILEY, NORBERT (1967, August). "America's Unique Class Politics: The Interplay of the Labor, Credit and Commodity Markets." *American Sociological Review*, 32, 529–41.

WRIGHT, ERIK OLIN (1976, July-August). "Class Boundaries in Advanced Capitalist Societies." *New Left Review*, 98, 3–41.

———et al. (1982, December). "The American Class Structure." *American Sociological Review*, 47, 709–726.

4

Social Status and the Struggle for Equality

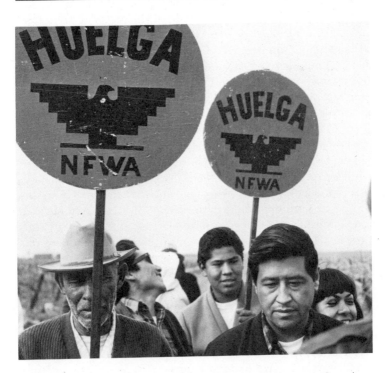

The struggle to unionize Mexican-American farm workers in California brought out their strengths as members of the working class and of a unique status group in America. Caesar Chavez led the struggle, called La Huelga. (© Paul Fusco/ Magnum Photos, Inc.)

PART I
DIMENSIONS OF STATUS

In the fall of 1965, no one in the United States, or in the quietly industrious town of Delano, California, would have hesitated to describe the Mexican-American farmworkers there as working class according to their effort and lower class by their returns. Yet, no one who saw them singularly as workers or expected them to act only as a class would have understood what they were about to do.

During the spring of 1965, Filipino grape pickers in the southernmost parts of the state had walked out of the fields under the leadership of the AFL–CIO Agricultural Workers Organizing Committee (AWOC). Their simple grievance was that as domestic workers they were paid at piece rates, earning an average hourly wage of $1.20, while Mexican guest workers (Braceros) were guaranteed by law $1.40. The AWOC walkout won equal wages, but as farmworkers moved northward to the Great Central Valley with the advancing harvest season, they encountered in Delano the same differential wage scale.

Delano was different in other ways. It was home to a tough-minded community of local growers, many of them second-generation Yugoslavians who had wrested their farms from the semidesert with guts and determination. It was also home to a young Mexican-American community organizer named Cesar Chavez who had come to the central valley on behalf of the Community Services Organization—a populist group animated by the radical methods of Saul Alinsky. The growers were tight-fisted, parochial, and clannish; only two of the 38 commercial farms were absentee-owned by large corporations. The Mexican-American community was bone poor, seasonally employed, and unorganized. Chavez had established the National Farm Worker's Association (NFWA) in Delano which, despite its auspicious name, was a fragile volunteer agency devoted to organizing through provision of essential services such as legal aid, a credit union, and a co-op gas station and garage. In the fall of 1965, Chavez estimated that any militant class action on the part of the NFWA was at least three years away.

The plan Chavez had laid was disrupted when the Filipino-led AWOC struck Delano growers on September 7, 1965 over the differential wage issue. Paternalistic with their workers and contemptuous of labor organization, the growers brought in grape pickers from surrounding towns, many of them also Mexican-Americans. As the chief AWOC organizer explained, "That's when I went to see Cesar and asked him to help me." For Chavez, according to John Gregory Dunne's perceptive book *Delano*, "The strike began three years ahead of schedule."

> Chavez was in a quandary. Relations between AWOC and the NFWA had never been strong. Chavez had twice refused offers to join AWOC, and at the rank-and-file level, there was an undertow of racial antagonism between the predominantly Filipino AWOC and the predominantly Mexican NFWA. More importantly, Chavez was reluctant to incur the risk of failure by committing his ill-prepared forces to a situation he did not control. "That morning of September 8, a strike was the furthest thing from my mind...."
>
> Within the NFWA, however, there was a feeling that if Chavez did not call a strike now, ready or not, he would be forever loath to take the chance. Backed into a corner, his hand forced, Chavez finally decided that it would be far worse to ignore the strike than to join it. On the night of September 16, he called a strike vote. Hundreds of people were packed into the Filipino Hall on the West side of Delano. Chavez stood before the crowd, dressed in work pants and an old sport shirt. "You are here to discuss a matter which is of extreme importance to yourselves, your families, and your community," he said. "So let's get to the subject at hand. A hundred and fifty-five years ago, in the state of Guanajoto [sic] in Mexico, a padre proclaimed the struggle for liberty. He was killed, but ten years later Mexico won its independence. We Mexicans here in the United States, as well as all other farm workers, are engaged in another struggle for freedom and dignity which poverty denies us. But it must not be a violent strike, even if violence is used against us. Violence can only hurt us and our cause. The law is for us as well as the ranchers. The strike was begun by the Filipinos, but it is not exclusively for them. Tonight we must decide if we are to join our fellow workers." (John Gregory Dunne, *Delano: The Story of the California Grape Strike*, pp. 79–80)

So began another chapter in the civil rights struggle and, after a protracted campaign with many reversals, the first successful organization of farm workers in U.S. history. But those enormous achievements are not what makes the story of special interest here. The farmworkers showed the unusual group solidarity and political energy of a movement organized on a common ethnic culture and experience.

The symbols and composition of the Delano strike distinguish it from conventional class struggles. In his successful call for a discussion and strike vote, Chavez, an Arizona-born U.S. citizen, recalled Father Miguel Hidalgo and Mexico's struggle for independence from Spain. As the strike unfolded its participants knew it by the Spanish name—*La Huelga*. Marches and picket lines displayed the flags of Mexico and the United States, but usually as backdrop to the banner of the Virgin of Guadalupe, patron saint of Mexico and symbol of her poor. The Delano strike became a national crusade for the rights of Mexican-Americans and farmworkers, merging at times with the national civil rights movement and drawing support from Gringo liberals. Its profound aspiration was for dignity, the word repeated most often in connection with what the struggle sought.

Once it became clear that the strike would succeed, that farmworkers would at last be organized, the Teamsters Union tried, with some success, to steal the victory by signing agreements with growers. One unwittingly perceptive Teamster official complained of the UFWA, "They're not even a union. They're a civil rights organization." A local grower, more consciously insightful, said of Chavez, "He doesn't want a union, Jack, he wants a social revolution." They were saying, in other words, that Delano was something more than a class conflict.

Reflection on these events from the standpoint of social classes and class struggles produces some analytic discomfort—a suspicion that economic interest and power in the marketplace (the defining features of class in Chapter 3) fail to capture the essence of the farmworkers movement or, for that matter, of the civil rights struggle as a whole. On one hand, although many Mexican-Americans are certainly poor, ill-housed, and underemployed, the inequalities they suffer extend beyond the marketplace. An important part of their plight results precisely from the fact that they are Mexican-Americans; that is, members of a social category whose history of incorporation into the United States and present social status carry disadvantages. Those disadvantages (of prejudice, second-class citizenship, and discrimination) did not originate in the marketplace, although they were later exploited, no doubt amplified, in the labor market. On the other hand, the unifying bases of action by Mexican-Americans are uniquely compounded of a particular history, religion, and ethnic culture that are certainly brought to the marketplace, as in the Delano strike, but not born there. The roots of and responses to social inequality overlap with class issues, but they include much more.

THE MEANING OF STATUS GROUPS

Having devoted the previous chapter to an explanation of inequality based on social class, we now confront a problem. A good deal of the inequality experienced in modern societies stems from sources other than social class. Moreover, when struggles are mounted to eliminate social inequality, they draw their energy and methods as much from the traditions of religion, ethnicity, nationalism, and community, as from the episodic solidarity of social class. We need a broader vocabulary to explain these things.

The classical tradition provides a solution. Karl Marx knew that there were a great many group loyalties that competed with, perhaps obscured, class awareness. Max Weber (1946) went a step further by suggesting that there were other bases of group formation every bit as important as class interest. Weber drew a sharp distinction between *class situation* and *status situation* as conditions that may give rise to organized *social classes* or to *status groups* respectively. Social classes, as we saw in Chapter 3, are based on economic interests and formed by people sharing common life chances in the marketplace. Class is a powerful, but highly specific, basis for group formation. Classes, accordingly, are not communities with diffuse ties of social solidarity for Weber (1946). Status situation and status group are very different; not so much opposed to class as broader unifying conditions resting on more diverse interests. Weber explains the difference:

> In contrast to the purely economically determined "class situa-tion" we wish to designate as "status situation" every typical com-ponent of the life fate of men that is determined by a specific, positive or negative, social estimation of *honor*. This honor may be

connected with any quality shared by a plurality, and, of course, it can be knit to class situation: class distinctions are linked in the most varied ways with status distinctions....In contrast to classes, *status groups* are normally communities. (Max Weber, "Class, Status, Party," pp. 186–187)

The key phrases in this passage are "social honor" and "any quality shared by a plurality." Social honor is roughly equivalent to prestige; colloquially high status or low status. Qualities shared by a plurality are potentially great in number, but those typically singled out for conferral of positive or negative status include race, ethnicity, sex, age, religion, nationality, and the like. Societies differ in the bases upon which they award status. Language, tribe, or regional origin are as important in some as race or sex in others. Among exemplary status groups in history, Weber listed preindustrial aristocracies and craft guilds, slaves, pariah people like Jews, and, in the fullest development, the closed castes of India.

Modern status groups are based on a distinctive set of qualities. Race, ethnicity, and national origin are everywhere important. Religion and language define prominent status groups in some European countries (Belgium, Spain) and Canada. Increasingly sex and age have shifted from potential bases of group formation (status situations) to well-defined status groups. Contemporary pariah peoples in the United States include American Indians, Afro-Americans, Mexican-Americans, and many of the new ethnics (Cubans, Vietnamese). Equally important, of course, are the status groups who enjoy positive estimations of social honor: society people, the jet set, debutantes, the beautiful people chronicled by *People* magazine, or, as C. Wright Mills (1956) called them, "The celebrities....All those who succeed in America—no matter what their circle of origin or sphere of action...[members of] the American forum of public honor" (p. 71).

Status and Class

The defining features of status groups distinguish the concept from class. First, the qualities to which (positive or negative) social honor attaches are diverse—from the seemingly objective signs of race to the subtleties of success. Second, status groups vary in prominence and coherence. Homosexuals, ex-convicts, and priests are bona fide status groups, although they lack the perceived importance of other groups united by ethnicity or gender. Third, as Weber (1946) stressed, "In content, status honor is normally expressed by the fact that above all else a specific *style of life* can be expected from all those who wish to belong to the circle. Linked with this expectation are restrictions on social intercourse" (p. 187). Status groups are identified by the conventions or culture they bear, by distinctive behaviors and customs. In contrast to these status-group characteristics, classes are defined by a more specific quality (power in the marketplace), limited number, and varied lifestyles.

Finally, status groups differ from classes by not obeying the economic logic of the marketplace. Indeed, they may hinder free development of the market. Status represents a monopoly of privilege or disadvantage which is determined by social allocations of prestige rather than profit and loss. For example, low status of blacks and women in the occupational world means that they are not given the opportunity to compete freely with other ethnic groups and males as an unimpaired labor market would dictate. Similarly, celebrities go to the head of the line and command special attention when they sell products or politicians, while ex-convicts form at the rear. People who enjoy high prestige are expected to be above crass material considerations. Weber (1946) captured the point nicely when he said, "The notion of honor peculiar to status absolutely abhors that which is essential to the market: higgling" (p. 193).

In spite of these differences, status groups are less the opposite of classes than they are alternative bases of stratification. Sometimes these contrasting principles of group formation conflict with one another, as in the case of status impeding the free play of the market—hindering, for example, a free labor market in which Mexican-Americans or women have equal access to equal jobs based on their economic value as workers. At other times, the two principles reinforce each other. Status, to some extent, is a commodity that can be bought and sold in the market where it is embodied in automobiles, homes, clothes, baubles, and, generally, a purchasable lifestyle. Nevertheless, disdain for status climbers in some higher circles indicates that honor cannot be bought at will, suggesting again the autonomy of status groups.

Conversely, as Weber noted, "An 'occupational group' is also a status group" (p. 193). Independent professionals (for example, doctors and lawyers) and factory workers are distinct classes in the marketplace who also carry different prestige and constitute, for other purposes, distinct status groups. Within limits, class and status position are complementary. In the case of a successful black businesswoman whose class position engenders some prestige, class and status are noncomplementary. Together they form an incongruity. More tellingly, however, since this woman is apt to enjoy prestige and privilege owing to her success in business, the incongruity is reduced by the greater importance of social class in this instance.

Status groups are arrayed from exalted celebrities to disdained criminals on the unique dimension of social honor. This chapter focuses on the struggle for status and the contribution that status makes to explaining social inequality (that is, what it explains beyond class). For that reason, the focus is also on the large and disadvantaged status groups; on race, gender, and ethnicity. Inferences may be drawn from this material about high-status groups, but their specific situations are treated in later chapters.

Social class and status group, in sum, are distinct, but interactive dimensions of group formation. They combine in different ways depending upon circumstance—the host society, the character of status groups, the fluidity of class structure, and the dynamics of politics. The relative importance of class and status also varies in time and with economic conditions. Weber (1946) hypothesized that "stratification by status" dominates in periods of social and economic stability, while "naked class situation" comes to the fore during "periods of technological and economic transformation" (pp. 193–194). At the end of this chapter, we shall have the opportunity to evaluate this important proposition.

The plain distinction between class and status allows us to supersede barren debates over whether classes exist or class analyses are refuted by the shifting impact of status. Instead, we may assess their relative and shifting importance as joint determinants of social inequality. This avoids the error of confusing prestige with class and mistakenly concluding that stratification by classes is no longer important. If class and status are employed as analytic principles in tandem, it is possible to determine the actual importance of each. Weber's proposition, moreover, provides a foothold on the question of why modern society has witnessed such a dramatic resurgence of status or civil rights' struggles—why the politics of equality dominated the 1960s, yet gave way to the politics of austerity in the 1980s.

STATUS STRATIFICATION IN WORK AND COMMUNITY

Despite the absence of aristocracy and the eventual abolition of slavery, the United States has always had status groups and practiced status stratification. Black Americans have suffered most, but the same process has victimized women, ethnic minorities, the aged, religious and linguistic communities, and a host of others. It is useful to indicate some of the broad outlines of status stratification here, although a more rigorous examination of recent changes and the current situation fits better in a subsequent section.

The Changing Labor Force

Perhaps the boldest statistics in the U.S. recordbooks are those showing that working blacks and women earn less than whites and men—disparities that persist even within the same occupations and educational levels. In 1950, the average black family or individual earned just half the income of whites. Women in general did somewhat better, receiving slightly over 60 percent of the income of men. The postwar years saw a number of important changes, which are demonstrated in a few simple tables. From 1950–80, certain income differences were reduced, while others persisted. As Table 4–1 shows, black-white income differences, especially among women, narrowed. Black family income improved very modestly (from 58 to 63 percent of white families), black men gained (from 55 to 73 percent of white male income), and black women nearly reached income equality with white women (57 to 95 percent). Oddly, within this generally improving picture, women workers as a group lost ground relative to men (down from 64 to 59 percent of male income).

These results involve more than a simple redistribution or convergence of incomes. The class structure and status order

TABLE 4-1 Nonwhite and Female Income for Full-Time Workers as a Percent of White and Male Income, 1955–79

	1955	1959	1969	1979
Black men (percent of white men)	55	54	64	73
Black women (percent of white women)	57	63	82	95
Black families (percent of white families)	58	54	65	63
All women (percent of men)	64	61	61	59*

*Figure for 1978

SOURCES: *Current Population Reports* (1981). U.S. Bureau of the Census, Series P–60, No. 129, Tables 11 & 67; *Perspectives on Working Women: A Databook* (1980, October). Bureau of Labor Statistics, Bulletin 2080, Table 68.

were changing. Table 4–2 shows some of the dramatic changes in the labor force that lie behind the outcroppings of status stratification. As the Total column indicates, more people are full-time workers than ever before. The percentage of the population in the labor force has risen from 59 to 64 percent, representing a much larger increase in absolute numbers given population growth (in the 1980s, there are well over 100 million people in the U.S. labor force, although 7 to 11 percent of those have been unemployed). The modest overall increase, however, is compounded of an actual decrease in the proportion of working men (down from 86 to 77 percent) and, therefore, an enormous compensating increase in the number of working women (up from 33 to 52 percent).

For an understanding of the Women's Movement, it is important to recognize that the greater part of this change took place in the 1970s. In the preceding 20 years, the percentage of working women inched up from 33 to around 40 percent, but in the next decade it moved much faster bringing us to the present circumstance in which over half of all women are employed full-time. From near equality of participation, the reduced number of black working men (down to 71 percent) is greater than that of white men (down to 78 percent). Black women have changed least in this respect; 47 percent were working in 1954 and 53 percent in 1981. The proportion of white women working now is equal to that of black women. In general, the U.S. labor force has become more feminized, closer to parity in sex composition, and more white—owing to big gains among white women and significant losses to black men while their counterparts were changing more slowly.

TABLE 4-2   Civilian Labor Force Participation Rates by Sex and Race
(16 years and over)

January	All men	All women	White men	Black men	White women	Black women	Total
1950	86	33	—	—	—		59
1954	86	34	86	85	33	47	59
1958	84	37	84	83	36	47	59
1960	84	37	83	83	36	47	59
1964	81	38	81	80	37	48	59
1968	80	41	80	77	40	48	59
1970	80	43	80	78	42	50	60
1974	80	45	80	75	45	52	61
1978	78	49	79	72	49	53	63
1981	77	52	78	71	52	53	64

SOURCE: *Labor Force Statistics Derived from the Current Population Survey: A Databook* (vol. II). (1982, September). Bureau of Labor Statistics, Table D-2.

Returning to the question of income differences, the new women entrants to the labor force have been assigned low-paid, low-skilled "women's work" contributing to the erosion of female income as a percentage of male. For example, in the late 1970s, women accounted for 99 percent of all secretaries-typists; 97 percent of all registered nurses; 92 percent of all bank tellers; 87 percent of all cashiers; 71 percent of all elementary and high school teachers; but only 11 percent of all physicians and osteopaths; 9 percent of all lawyers and judges, 3 percent of all engineers. Black women, on average, have longer experience in the job market and have gained access to many of the middle-class female occupations (nursing and teaching, for example). As a result, they have closed the income gap more than black men and certainly more than women in general. But, there is a disturbing irony here. Although black women may have more job experience, they are still paid about the same as white women. Moreover, the gains of black women really mean that they are approaching a women's standard that has been *reduced* slightly as a proportion of men's incomes during the same period. Claims by the Women's Movement about the absence of comparable worth have statistical support.

Table 4-3 completes this picture, indicating the occupational positions of the labor force by sex, race, and Hispanic origin. Although the number of comparisons that can be made within this table is very large, the major ones elaborate the foregoing interpretation of how occupational (and class) stratification interacts with status inequality.

Looking first at the contrasts between white men and women, their proportions are about the same in the professional-technical ranks, but there are more men in managerial and craft occupations, along with many more women in clerical and service jobs—and, of course, the last two are lower paying. These differences are pronounced in more detailed occupational breakdowns, adding force to the claim of discrimination against women in the job market. As suggested previously, the occupational distribution for black women resembles that of white women, although blacks are somewhat less represented in the professional (13 versus 17 percent) and clerical (29 versus 36 percent) categories and more numerous in services (35 versus 18 percent) than white women. Much sharper differences appear between black men and women. Black men are spread mainly and fairly evenly across the categories of craft, operative, labor, and service, categories that are not typical of black women, except for services. Finally, the occupational distribution for Hispanic women is closer to all women and Hispanic men are more like black men (see Table 4–3).

On an impressionistic basis, we may conclude from Table 4–3 what more rigorous statistical analyses discover—namely, that race and sex interact in affecting occupation. That is, there are similarities among the distributions for women irrespective of race and origin, just as there are similarities between blacks and Hispanics by contrast to whites. The patterns are too varied to be captured in any single (or simple) summary precisely because *both* sex and race influence occupation—just as occupations discriminate among workers in varied ways. To illustrate that point with a final irony, all women receive a fraction of male income even within the same occupational category, as shown in the right-hand columns of Table 4–3. White women are slightly better paid than black women (Table 4–1). However, white women receive only about 60 percent of the income of white men, while black women earn 72 percent of the income of black men (as of 1978), with Hispanic women in between at 69 percent—a fact explained by both the lower wages of minority men and the greater similarity of male-female occupational distributions for minorities.

Focusing just on income inequality, status and class (as measured very roughly by occupational category here) have separate *and* combined effects. Moreover, the combined effects vary depending upon the combination. Illustratively, being female is a handicap in the labor market. So is being black or a laborer. But, being a black woman is less of a handicap by contrast to all female workers than being a black man is by contrast to all male workers. At least it is a different kind of handicap, recognizing that black women earn less than black men.

The effects of status stratification are best known through their appearance in the labor market since those inequalities are more tangible, widely felt, readily documented, and open to redress by civil rights' groups and political reformers. Yet social honor affects most aspects of people's lives; often in ways that are more direct because they are unmediated by class and more damaging because they invade personal realms where self-esteem is fashioned. Where and with whom we live, home and community, are as important as the job. Social class has a decisive effect on residential choice, but status groups figure here, too.

Minorities in the Community

In the early 20th century, most U.S. cities embraced a variety of ethnic neighborhoods (shaped by the narrow choices of class and kinship), heterogeneous (though overwhelmingly white) middle-class communities, and the enclaves of luxury that were both white and Christian. Although the privileges of class helped perpetuate this pattern, it was ensured by restrictive covenants—agreements among homeowners that they would not sell to such undesirables as blacks and, particularly, Jews who were the main targets of the covenants since some of them could afford to integrate the neighborhood. Although tightly knit ethnic neighborhoods and restrictive covenants have largely passed from the urban landscape, U.S. cities are more segregated today than ever. Status groups are at the heart of this change.

Residential segregation is a product of two broad trends: the overall urbanization of the United States, made possible by transportation technology and economic centralization, and the migration of southern blacks to northern cities, occasioned by the commercialization of agriculture. In 1900, just 40 percent of

TABLE 4-3   A. Occupational Distribution of Employed White, Black, and Hispanic Workers

	White				Black				Hispanic			
	Men		Women		Men		Women		Men		Women	
	1959	1979	1959	1979	1959	1979	1959	1979	1970*	1979	1970*	1979
Total: Number (in thousands)	39,493	49,674	18,512	35,025	3,972	4,549	2,652	4,321	1,874	2,704	1,019	1,677
Percent	100	100	100	100	100	100	100	100	100	100	100	100
Professional-technical	11	16	13	17	4	9	6	13	8	8	8	8
Managerial-administrative	15	15	6	7	3	6	2	3	5	6	2	4
Sales	6	7	9	7	1	2	1	3	4	3	5	5
Clerical	7	6	33	36	5	7	8	29	8	6	29	32
Craft	20	22	1	2	10	18	1	1	20	21	2	2
Operatives	19	17	16	11	24	26	14	14	27	26	28	25
Nonfarm laborers	6	6	0	1	25	14	1	2	10	12	1	1
Service	5	8	19	18	15	17	59	35	12	14	23	22
Farm	10	4	4	1	15	3	10	1	6	5	2	2

B. Women's, Black, and Hispanic Earnings as a Percent of Other Groups by Occupation, 1979

	Women's earnings as a percent of men's, 1978	Black and Hispanic earnings of men and women as a percent of like-sex whites, 1979			
		Men		Women	
		Black	Hispanic	Black	Hispanic
Total: Number (in thousands)	—	—	—	—	—
Percent	59	65	72	98†	88
Professional-technical	64	75	78	119	77
Managerial-administrative	54	75	75	104	107
Sales	45	57	71	96	107
Clerical	60	78	81	110	95
Craft	61	79	89	—	—
Operatives	59	85	83	104	87
Nonfarm laborers	62	85	97	79	—
Service	62	80	89	113	101
Farm	30	42	74	103	—

*First year available.

†Since these figures are based on mean income, they differ slightly from Table 4–1 based on median income.

SOURCE: *Perspectives on Working Women: A Databook* (1980, October). Bureau of Labor Statistics, Bulletin 2080, Tables 74 and 62; *Handbook of Labor Statistics* (1974). Bureau of Labor Statistics, Bulletin 1825, Table 19; *Current Population Reports* (1981). U.S. Bureau of the Census, Series P–60, No. 129, Table 59.

the U.S. population lived in urban places. Today the figure is 75 percent. In 1910, 80 percent of the black population lived in the South and 70 percent in rural settings. Today 50 percent of U.S. blacks live outside the South and 80 percent live in cities. In short, while the nation became urbanized, the black population became more so, a great part of it moving to northern cities.

In one study of the changing urban population, Reynolds Farley (1970) took the largest U.S. metropolitan areas and compared the relative size of the central city black population in 1950 and 1970. In just 20 years, it doubled from 13 to 26 percent and, updating his figures, was almost 30 percent in 1980. If the Hispanic and black central city populations are combined, they make up 39 percent of the largest U.S. cities. Illustratively, comparing the black in 1950 with the combined black and Hispanic population of 1980, some of the central city changes are: New York, 10 to 45 percent; Chicago, 14 to 54 percent; Detroit, 16 to 66 percent; Washington, 35 to 73 percent; Baltimore, 23 to 56 percent; Miami, 16 to 81 percent. Eight of the top 10 central cities have a combined black and Hispanic population in excess of 40 percent.

The important point in all this is not simply the faster rate of urbanization for minority groups, but their increasing segregation. The Census Bureau measures the urban population in several ways, including the central cities just mentioned and the urbanized area comprising the central city and suburban ring. In a related study, Farley (1977) showed the curious pattern of growth and decline that ends up producing greater segregation. The central cities are losing their white and upper-income groups and gaining blacks, Hispanics, elderly, and people with lower incomes. Some cities have experienced a *net absolute* population loss and, therefore, a very large *percentage* increase in minorities. Meanwhile, the suburbs have grown in *both* black and white populations. But, black suburban population growth has been mainly in either all-black developments or in old suburbs that have shifted to industrial and commercial use leading to white abandonment. Naturally, some middle-income blacks have moved into integrated suburbs, but their numbers are small compared to the all-black new developments and old suburbs. The net result is that the central cities are becoming sharply segregated minority enclaves, while, in Farley's (1977) words, "residential segregation patterns of central cities are reappearing within the suburbs" (p. 527).

The mechanisms through which this pattern of segregation is realized tell us more about status stratification. The sheer cost of housing and availability of jobs account for a good deal strictly on a class basis. Where that does not reach, status discrimination comes into play.

At one time, status discrimination was practiced widely and openly in restrictive covenants and racial cruelty—from refusals to show residential property to minorities in white-only areas to Ku Klux Klan-style cross-burnings in the front yards of blacks who did manage to integrate neighborhoods. With growing legal curbs on such practices, new ones came along in more sophisticated forms of institutional racism—that is, routine practices in law, government, or the private economy which have the effect of racial discrimination, whether or not they are explicitly so intended. Minorities in the housing market found themselves the object of steering; they were shown homes for rent or sale only in segregated neighborhoods or ones in transition due to white flight. The pervasive practice of red-lining got its name from the red lines that lending institutions drew on city maps to indicate areas in which they would make no mortgage loans. Their rationale was that because those areas were in transition, property values were likely to drop once the minorities took over, leaving the lenders with less valuable collateral. The self-fulfilling effect of red-lining was that neither blacks nor whites could purchase homes in central city areas with conventional financing. Once-viable neighborhoods began to deteriorate as older homes were converted to multiple occupancy rental units.

The financial institutions helped create new residential segregation by ignoring the minority home buyer, "disinvesting" in the troubled city, and reinvesting their funds (often generated from inner-city savings and loan companies) in the suburbs where blacks were restricted by costs or steering. As the effects of lending practices took hold, other institutions added their weight, particularly industry and business that began moving to suburban quarters, thereby depriving the cities of jobs. Under the press of black urban migration and institutional neglect, the ghettos enlarged.

The critical point in this example is that class stratification working alone would have produced a different result. Whites and minorities would have been disproportionately mixed in cities and suburbs according to their incomes and market capacities. When status-group considerations compound the process, even high-income blacks have difficulty finding integrated suburban housing. Low-income whites cannot find mortgages or jobs in the cities, even when they want to stay there and maintain their ethnic communities. Status stratification exacerbates and distorts the pattern. It creates anomalies like low-income black suburbs, the exclusion of many middle-income blacks from the average suburb, and once fashionable central cities that have been abandoned by higher-income whites except as daytime (and nocturnally dangerous) centers of commerce and government. This is what Weber had in mind when he said that class and status group sometimes conflict.

We have focused here only on the gross effects of status stratification. Volumes are written on the inequalities suffered by status groups. Jews are still restricted from certain elite clubs. Pacific coast Japanese-Americans were interned and stripped of their land in 1942, not, as we now learn, because they were a wartime security threat, but because they were highly successful agriculturalists. Recently, small fishing towns on the Atlantic and Gulf of Mexico coasts have tried to banish the competition of Vietnamese immigrants. Today, blacks and Hispanics hold less than 2 percent of elective posts, although they account for nearly 20 percent of the population and a majority in many cities and electoral districts. The Equal Rights Amendment failed to win approval of the necessary number of state legislatures. Bills aimed at outlawing employment discrimination against homosexuals have been defeated by conservative groups led by fundamentalist churches. Ex-convicts, handicapped persons, the elderly, and Moslems (especially when they are black) all live with the occupational and civil consequences of disrespect.

The beneficiaries of all this are the dominant status groups: whites, men, Protestants, the middle-aged, and so forth. These are the people who routinely enjoy status honor in the sense of full civil liberties, political representation, job and mobility opportunities. Indeed, one of the peculiarities of U.S. society is that the presumably average American portrayed in the mass media (in the central roles of television shows, for example) is usually a relatively affluent male professional. Several years ago, a popular television show was modeled after the real-life Japanese-American coroner of Los Angeles County. On television, the coroner was a lovable middle-aged white male doctor with a dutiful Japanese assistant. This is the society's model of respect or status honor, although white male Protestant professionals are only about 10 to 15 percent of the population.

The general pattern of individious status distinctions is not new or peculiar to the United States and Western Europe. What is new, and peculiar to the more developed countries, is that discrimination is now recognized as an abridgment of rights. Claims for justice made by status groups have legitimacy in the sense that they can be made, are usually heard, and, if valid, persuade many that they should be redressed. The moral order has changed in the course of this century to the point where equality of status honor is politically a rightful aspiration. Certainly that does not mean that status stratification is being eliminated wherever it is challenged. It does mean that denial of equal rights is no longer taken for granted and readily justified on the basis of some natural law or economic expedient. Opponents are on the defensive.

The rights of minorities and other status groups to equal treatment (and, slowly, to equal outcomes) is no longer debated. The debate has shifted to whether real equality exists. In something of an extreme example of public tolerance, a bill guaranteeing employment rights for homosexuals was recently vetoed by the governor of California after passing both houses of the state legislature. Although this was a defeat of social rights, the veto was defended, not on the basis of principle (that homosexuals should or should not enjoy those rights), but on the allegedly factual claim that sufficient evidence of discrimination did not exist. This change in the cultural understanding of social rights is the result of a political struggle and equality revolution that swept over the United States and Europe in the 1960s.

PART II
THE EQUALITY REVOLUTION

MOVEMENTS FOR EQUALITY

The phrase, "equality revolution," comes from an essay by the sociologist Herbert Gans (1974). Although he was writing in the midst of the controversy, Gans saw a broader meaning.

> Someday, when future historians write the history of the 1960s, they may describe it as the decade when America rediscovered poverty still in its midst and when social protest, ranging from demonstrations to violent uprisings, reappeared on the American scene. But these historians may also note a curious fact, that the social protest had very little to do with poverty.... The social protest that began in the 1960s had to do with *inequality*. So far the demand for greater equality has come largely from the young, from the black, and from women, but other groups have asked for more autonomy or control over their own lives, for more liberty and democracy.... In the years to come, I believe America will face more such demands from many other people, which will be widespread enough that they might be described as an "equality revolution." (Herbert J. Gans, "The Equality Revolution," pp. 7–8)

From a longer historical vantage, in 1950, the British sociologist T.H. Marshall (1964) observed that citizenship has three elements: "the civil, composed of rights necessary for individual freedom, the political right to participate in the exercise of power, and the social element [meaning] the whole range from the right to a modicum of economic welfare and security to the right to share to the full in the social heritage and to live the life of a civilized being according to the standards prevailing in the society" (pp. 71–72). Marshall thought that civil rights were won in the 18th century, political rights in the 19th, and that social rights are the essence of 20th-century movements. Gans and Marshall agree that the struggles over inequality and social rights represent a historical watershed in the philosophical principles of collective action. Although this provides a valuable historical perspective on status struggles, it is also true that the battle for social rights did not begin in the 20th century or in the 1960s. These movements have a long history. What changed in the recent period was that social rights came to be accepted as a legitimate political end.

Civil Rights

The centerpiece of the equality revolution was the civil rights movement. The uniqueness of this period, however, was that other movements grew up to supplement and reinforce one another, notably the Women's and the Peace Movements. Each of these had a long pedigree. Prior to the Civil War, slave rebellions rocked the South (Nat Turner's revolt of 1831, John Brown's Harper's Ferry raid of 1859, and many more), and after Reconstruction civil rights organizations became active in the North (the National Association for the Advancement of Colored People [NAACP] was founded in 1910). Antiwar movements grew from protest of U.S. involvement in the Philippines in 1898 to demonstrations and refusals to serve in the "imperialists'" World War I. The first Woman's Rights Convention was held in 1848 and grew into the women's suffrage movement which reached its zenith in 1920 with the passage of the 19th Amendment and women's right to vote.

In the 1960s these movements reappeared with new vigor and began joining forces to an unprecedented degree. Martin Luther King, Jr., pledged his forces to ending the Vietnam War which was a moral and a black issue. Women formed interracial alliances. People spoke simply of "the movement." The times encouraged other insurgencies: the American Indian Movement, Chicano Power, Gray Panthers, and Gay Liberation. This was the equality revolution.

These years of turmoil changed the face of U.S. society. Yet, if they constituted a revolution of sorts, they did not end in *the* revolution. On the contrary, their peculiar brand of success lay in a new accommodation with conventional society. How is this explained? To be more precise about the question itself, it should be divided into three parts: (1) why did the equality revolution occur in the 1960s? (2) what did it accomplish? and (3) why was it transformed and in some ways reversed in the 1980s? The interaction of class and status contributes much to an explanation.

The immediate background to the civil rights movement included changes, particularly from the 1940s onward, that affected the U.S. population distribution, economy, and a growing moral issue—what Gunnar Myrdal's classic book of 1944 called *An American Dilemma: The Negro Problem and Modern Democracy*. World War II had just been fought to eliminate religious persecution and the doctrine of a superior race, a war in which U.S. blacks played a central role. How could the country continue to deny basic liberties to its minority populations and pretend to call itself the "land of the free"? Myrdal understood this as a corrosive conflict of values; a cultural conflict between manifest racism and the values of social equality. "The American Negro problem is a problem in the heart of the American" (p. xvii).

It was also a dilemma at the heart of the U.S. economy. The modernization of southern agriculture had precipitated much of the black urban and northern migration. Blacks were not only crowding the cities, they were now contributing a large slice of the urban labor force: men as industrial labor and women in services, as the earlier tables show.

The Negro movement had been slowly gaining political strength since before the turn of the century. From the 1890s until 1920, Booker T. Washington urged black education for equal employment opportunities and a National Negro Business League. From 1917, with the formation of the Universal Negro Improvement Association, through the 1920s, Marcus Garvey brought a new militance to the cause by urging "integral nationalism" and a network of self-sufficient black enterprises. The sociologist W.E.B. DuBois left academic life to lead the Niagara Movement and the NAACP, which included white liberals, all working for equal rights. During World War II, a foundation was laid for the modern movement. The Congress of Racial Equality (CORE) was formed in 1942 and joined A. Phillip Randolph's segregated yet powerful Brotherhood of Sleeping Car Porters in demanding employment in wartime industry. Randolph threatened a march on Washington and pressured President Franklin D. Roosevelt to create the first Fair Employment Practices Commission.

Black discontent grew apace of urbanization and wartime industrialization. A rash of race riots in 1919 was repeated in Harlem in 1935 and during the war. Growing black rage in the Northern ghettos was expressed in the sensational novel *Native Son* by Richard Wright (1940) and the urban sociology that

Robert Park inspired. In 1945, St. Clair Drake and Horace Cayton published *Black Metropolis* profiling migration to Chicago and the disenfranchisement of blacks in the northern economy. Indeed, as perhaps the first prominent black novelist, Richard Wright not only shocked white America by portraying the anger of a black youth who killed two whites, but noted that he came to understand the Negro plight by reading the Chicago urban sociologists. In the introduction to *Black Metropolis*, Wright (1945) says that he came to Chicago to tell his story,

> But I did not know what my story was, and it was not until I stumbled upon science that I discovered some of the meanings of the environment that battered and taunted me. I encountered the work of men who were studying the Negro community, amassing facts about urban Negro life, and I found that sincere art and honest science were not far apart, that each could enrich the other. The huge mountains of fact piled up by the Department of Sociology at the University of Chicago gave me my first concrete vision of the forces that molded the Negro's body and soul. (Richard Wright, "Introduction" to St. Clair Drake and Horace Cayton, *Black Metropolis: A Study of Negro Life in a Northern City*, pp. xvii–xviii)

Although it is important to see these links between sociology and the public understanding fostered through art, neither the growing black militance, a moral dilemma, nor the maturing political organization precipitated a civil rights movement at this time. Instead, it was the changing conditions of national politics that lay behind the breakthroughs of the 1950s. The race issue had divided the Democratic party in 1948 when the Southern Dixiecrats split from the party over civil rights issues. As Frances Piven and Richard Cloward (1979) observe in *Poor People's Movements*, "... the Republicans saw opportunities in the difficulties being experienced by the Democratic Party over the race question" (p. 213). Republicans were not sure whether they had more to gain by appealing to dissident southern Democrats or northern blacks. Pushed by President Dwight D. Eisenhower's commitment to civil rights, "... the Republicans finally cast their lot with the potential for gain among northern blacks, for the congressional Republicans were all from northern states where blacks were concentrating" (p. 214). Although the NAACP had promoted legal challenges to discrimination for many years, it was the 1954 Supreme Court decision outlawing school segregation that symbolically began the modern civil rights struggle.

None of this should minimize the prolonged struggle of black people. That history was a precondition of the equality revolution. But as long as the white power structure could ignore the struggle with no risk to its own supports, the revolution could be held off. Economic and demographic shifts culminating in a postwar urban and industrial boom now meant that the race question could no longer be dodged by politicians who hoped to hold their jobs. It was the interplay of the continuing civil rights movement and the changing bases of political power that brought success in the late 1950s and 1960s.

Yet, the changes were far from preordained. The civil rights struggle had to escalate the pressure as it began to do with the Montgomery, Alabama bus boycott in 1955. Suddenly the black struggle was mobilizing thousands of people drawn from its own middle class and Baptist Church leadership, personified in Dr. Martin Luther King, Jr. Montgomery led to the Little Rock, Arkansas, fight for school integration (1957), public accommodation sit-ins (1960), freedom rides including northern and white liberal supporters (1961), and the decisive campaign in Birmingham, Alabama, that brought open clashes between civil rights marchers and southern law enforcement agencies forcing the Kennedy administration in 1963 to act by proposing a comprehensive civil rights bill.

The Civil Rights Act of 1964 did not quell the black uprising. On the contrary, the summers of 1965–68 witnessed the most extensive urban riots in history as the oppression of a century since the abolition of slavery took its violent revenge. The ghetto revolt and President Lyndon B. Johnson's compensatory War on Poverty burned into the political conscience a conviction that blacks and organized minorities had to be accommodated—in part to preserve the social order and its economic base and in part to resolve the moral dilemma. Political and industrial leaders, when challenged and moved to assure their own positions, were among the first to understand this. Blacks won political recognition of their rights.

Mexican-Americans

The struggle of Mexican-Americans bears some similarities to the civil rights movement. One key difference, however, is that instead of arriving in the United States as slaves, Mexicans and their homeland in the Southwest were acquired by conquest in the Mexican-American War of 1848. An enormous territory in then northern Mexico was annexed to the United States (including present-day Texas, New Mexico, Arizona, Utah, Nevada, California, and parts of Colorado and Wyoming—one half of Mexican territory in 1847). Many of its 75,000 residents were more Spanish than Mexican, since by 1848 Mexico had enjoyed only 27 years of independence and the northern settlements dated back to Spanish land grants.

Similarities between the black and Hispanic populations began to appear with the 20th-century trends in migration and urbanization. In 1920, there were about 1 million Mexican-Americans in the United States. By 1960, the number had grown to 4 million, and today it is 12—a figure that includes only citizens and permanent residents. If we add to this other Spanish-speaking people (Cubans, Central and South Americans, Puerto Ricans) and the estimated number of undocumented migrant Mexican workers, the size of the Hispanic population doubles and comes close to the number of blacks. As with blacks, 80 percent of Hispanics in general and of Mexican-Americans now reside in urban areas. As blacks moved from the rural South to urban areas and northern central cities, Mexican-Americans left the rural Southwest for its cities and for the northern climes of Chicago, Denver, and the like. Equally important, rapid urbanization in the Southwest spread to incorporate many of the tattered Mextowns that languished on the outskirts of cities. Table 4–3 shows that employed Hispanics closely resemble blacks in occupations and earnings.

Mexican-Americans pursued uncelebrated struggles for economic and social rights beginning with mutual benefit societies in the 1910s, a League of United Latin-American Citizens (LULAC) in Texas and a militant Confederation of Mexican Workers' Unions in Southern California in the 1920s. World War II provided the same impetus for political organization as it had among blacks. The American GI Forum founded in Texas and the Community Services Organization in California devoted themselves to voter registration, community organization, and discrimination in the late 1940s. The GI Forum was established when a Texas funeral home refused to bury a Mexican-American veteran. Yet it was not until the 1960s that the renamed Chicano movement came to prominence with broad mobilization by the Mexican-American Political Association (MAPA), Viva Kennedy clubs, and the Political Association of Spanish-Speaking Organizations (PASO). Mexican-Americans moved squarely into the civil rights movement with the stimulus of black pride and strong affinities for the youthful and Catholic symbols of the Kennedy administration.

Mexican-Americans differed from blacks in the scope and divisions within their movement. An established middle class pushed successfully for electoral representation through the older groups. Chavez and the farmworkers focused their efforts on unionization, allying more with church, labor, and Anglo liberal groups than with Chicanos. In New Mexico, the intrepid *Alianza Federal de Mercedes* led by Reies Lopez Tijerina captured a county courthouse to protest the expropriation of Mexican lands and grazing rights. The Raza Unida Party organized in South Texas, taking control of Crystal City through local elections and aiming for repeat performances elsewhere. A youth movement spawned Brown Berets in the urban barrios and the student-based MECHA (*Movimiento Éstudiantil Chicano de Aztlan*).

Despite their differences, the gains by Chicanos matched those of blacks because, in each case, they accrued as much from the changing political environment as from the strategies of the movements themselves. As the Democratic administrations of the 1960s sought new urban constituencies and loyalists for their War on Poverty, Mexican-Americans became valuable allies—particularly as swing voters in large states like Texas and California. In a revealing analysis, Craig Jenkins and Charles Perrow (1977) conclude about the farmworkers something that was true for Chicanos as a whole. The 1960s did not differ greatly from earlier periods in the level of minority protest, "What had changed was the political environment—the liberal community was now willing to provide sustained, massive support for insurgency.... The dramatic turnabout in the political environment originated in economic trends and political realignments that took place quite independent of any 'push' from insurgents" (pp. 263, 266). Once more, this should not detract from the courageous stand of Mexican-Americans, but emphasize the necessary interplay of movement demands and divisions in the political elite that require reformed coalitions.

The Feminists

The Women's Movement, as we have seen, began in the 1830s and continued to the present with periods of quiescence during the abolitionist struggle of the 1850s and after suffrage in 1920. The modern movement coincided with the equality revolution and is conveniently dated by the much-heralded book of Betty Friedan, *The Feminine Mystique*, in 1963. Friedan argued that women, credited with some general competence and independence through the 1940s when they played key roles in wartime and defense industries, were denigrated in the next 15 years. The feminine mystique comprised a set of ideas that added up to a patronizing celebration of femininity in the exclusive role of housewife and mother. Much of the responsibility for this change in women's roles Friedan (1963) assigned to the mass media and,

> Experts [who] told them how to catch a man and keep him, how to breastfeed children and handle their toilet training, how to cope with sibling rivalry and adolescent rebellion; how to buy a dishwasher, bake bread, cook gourmet snails, and build a swimming pool with their own hands; how to dress, look, and act more feminine and make marriage more exciting; how to keep their husbands from dying young and their sons from growing into delinquents. They were taught to pity the neurotic, unfeminine women who wanted to be poets or physicists or presidents. They learned that truly feminine women do not want careers, higher education, political rights—the independence and opportunities that the old-fashioned feminists fought for....All they had to do was devote their lives from earliest girlhood to finding a husband and bearing children. (Betty Friedan, *The Feminine Mystique*, pp. 15–16)

Beyond capturing the mood of a generation—the "problem with no name" that haunted and rang true for many women and some men—Friedan locates the problem in time and hints at its causes. A change had occurred around 1945 and another one was in the offing. *"In the fifteen years after World War II*, this mystique of feminine fulfillment became the cherished and self-perpetuating core of contemporary American culture" (italics added, p. 18). Yet by placing so much emphasis on experts and media stereotypes, Friedan does not satisfactorily explain the timing of the changes. Why did the experts and media begin promoting the feminine mystique after World War II?

Without pretending to have a complete answer to the question of why the feminine mystique flourished after 1945, it seems plausible that the changing economy and social structure explains a good deal. Large numbers of servicemen returned looking for jobs, some of which women had been holding or might compete for. Women were not needed in the labor force, at least not in their wartime numbers. Consequently, many women were removed or demoted from these good-paying jobs and occupational sex-typing was restored to some extent.

At the same time, U.S. industry had to convert from a wartime economy to peacetime production. This required creation of a massive new domestic market in products for the home and family (automobiles, appliances, television sets, and so forth). An emphasis on domestic production for home and family consumption suggested the importance of homemakers to whom the media could appeal with its products and stereotypes. A key segment of the postwar economy was precisely the construction of suburban housing, assisted by government financing. Women were now needed in a social role that provided the demand and symbol of the suburban consumer family. Moreover, a baby boom followed World War II, providing a good many more young mothers with larger families to whom the media and manufacturers could appeal with the suggestion that they should consume. The economy required, or at least benefited hand-somely from, the newly conceived feminine role.

The rebirth of the feminist movement in the 1960s was also assisted by the equality revolution. A conventional explanation is the presumed explosion of women in the labor force. This, no doubt, is part of the picture and one reason that the feminine mystique was irritating to so many women. But, as the previous tables show (especially Table 4–2 under the "White women" column), women in the labor force during the years prior to the new movement edged up only gradually and did not take off until the 1970s. Changes in the number of working women alone do not explain the resurgent feminist movement.

What caused *The Rebirth of Feminism*, as Judith Hole and Ellen Levine (1971) entitled their informative book? Consistent with the previous observations about social movements in the 1960s, the new feminism was occasioned by the interplay of women's advocacy and political groups that moved, however reluctantly, to incorporate new constituents. The advocacy drew upon the facts that the new feminists were mainly educated, white, middle-class, typically employed women. To the extent that these women did participate in the labor force, they experienced inequality more acutely than working-class women. As may be inferred from Table 4–3, most employed women were assigned to the lower rungs of the occupational ladder or generally to working-class positions. Working-class, black, and Hispanic women may have accepted that as normal, while the typical recruit for the new feminism understandably perceived it an injustice given their reference group of middle-class working men. Consequently, it was not so much the numbers of women who were now working, but, as Gans (1968) says, the experienced inequalities of their circumstance. In *Woman's Estate*, Juliet Mitchell (1971) develops this interpretation by adding that the inequality went further to include a contradiction between the idealized femininity and the productive role women were expected to fulfill in the workplace and the home. Even homemakers would find it difficult to look feminine and build a swimming pool with their own hands.

In the changing political environment, many women had been active in the civil rights movement (and encountered discrimination even there), acquiring organizational skills and a clear sense that the rights of women were an integral, if neglected, part of that movement. Just as Democratic administrations had sought the support of blacks and Hispanics in a new coalition, women were courted, particularly in 1961 when John F. Kennedy created a President's Commission on the Status of Women. As Judith Hole and Ellen Levine (1971) point out,

> Kennedy had appointed Esther Peterson, a member of his campaign staff, and a long-time labor lobbyist, to head the Women's Bureau. It was she who originated the idea of a President's Commission, and it was she who convinced Kennedy to set it up. Some of the suggested "political" reasons for establishing such a Commission are: it would allow Kennedy to discharge political obligations to women who had worked hard for his election in 1960 (none of whom, with the exception of Peterson, had been appointed to policymaking positions in his administration); it would result in the creation of a strong political block (women) to campaign for Kennedy in 1964; it could be used to get his administration "off the hook" on the Equal Rights Amendment which, as in the past, had been included in the Democratic Party platform...since Kennedy

was beholden to labor for electoral support and labor was dead set against the Amendment. (Judith Hole and Ellen Levine, *The Rebirth of Feminism*, pp. 19–20)

This commission, of course, did not initiate or fully represent the new feminist movement. But it did signal encouragement for women to join the growing liberal coalition and it advanced measures (such as the Equal Pay Act of 1963 and Title VII of the 1964 Civil Rights Act that prohibited race and sex discrimination in employment) which came to define many aims of the movement. The National Organization for Women (NOW), founded in 1966 with Betty Friedan as its first president, drew many of its initial supporters from the commission and developed a bill of rights focused largely on employment issues, along with advocacy of the Equal Rights Amendment and women's control of their reproductive lives. The new liberal political coalition did not dictate the aims of the feminist movement, but it had a great deal to do with explaining when and why that movement was reborn.

Explaining the Revolution

We may now return to the first of three questions posed earlier, namely, why did the equality revolution occur in the 1960s? Obviously, there is no simple explanation for so complex an event. Several sets of causes operated at once and converged. First, changes in population and social structure formed a backdrop to the decade. The most dramatic of these was migration and rapid urbanization; prompted on one hand by the commercialization of agriculture, and reflected on the other by growing differentiation between central cities and suburbs. After World War II, educational levels advanced rapidly as returning veterans with the GI Bill and others began attending college in record numbers. The birth rate and family size increased for a time. The ratio of men to women in the labor force changed slowly, until the 1970s, when the shift toward parity became dramatic. And the economy boomed, despite cyclical recessions, on the basis of postwar consumer demands and international trade. It was, in economist John Kenneth Galbraith's phrase, an "affluent society." But prosperity was unequally distributed along class lines as long as the major status groups continued to suffer economic discrimination.

A second set of forces was political in nature. The social structural changes disrupted the traditional and New Deal bases of political power. Rural and Southern political districts lost population and, with reapportionment, their political leverage. Voter registration drives enfranchised minorities, many for the first time. All of the disadvantaged status groups saw their opportunity to organize from below in this fluid situation. The Democratic party, given its reliance on the South and working-class districts in the cities, was most shaken by these changes and moved more decisively than the Republicans to reorganize from above. But Republicans saw the opportunity to profit from Democratic losses and began promoting civil rights. In a relatively short time, the political scene became a competitive struggle among divided elites for the allegiance of the newly emboldened status groups. There was a democratic opening— short-lived, perhaps, and not an opening at the top, but a huge change in the numbers of people who were allowed into the mainstream and whose right to be there was established.

The last set of forces behind the equality revolution was sociological. It involved changing ways in which people experienced their circumstances and defined their rights. As Gans (1968) said, the social protest of the 1960s had to do with inequality. Status groups perceived their lack of equality in relation to others—whites, Anglos, men. And they argued that such inequalities should not exist on the basis of cultural values including justice, freedom, dignity, liberation. When Gunnar Myrdal (1944) characterized the American dilemma as a conflict of cultural values, he saw ahead two decades to the wellsprings of the equality revolution. Blacks and Mexican-Americans served in the war to end the moral blight of racism. The Supreme Court of the United States said that these people should receive equal treatment. Women, too, served in that war and in industrial jobs on the homefront. Several presidents (Eisenhower, Kennedy, Johnson) seemed to say that they deserved equal employment opportunities. As these status groups were activated by cultural values, each could draw on a rich subcultural history of political organization and struggles for justice. And, paradoxically, as the political system continued to maintain many barriers to equality, its own opportunism also encouraged in other ways the minority insurgency.

LEGACY OF THE EQUALITY REVOLUTION

Returning to the second of three questions posed earlier, what did the equality revolution accomplish? In one sense, I have answered this in the claim that a democratic opening occurred and a new conception of social rights was established. What about the more concrete effects in the areas of income, education, and employment, which were the specific targets of so much movement activity?

Contrary to some critics, minorities, and particularly blacks, made important material gains in the 1960s that were not reversed in the recessionary 1970s and early 1980s. That statement is controversial and viewed in some quarters as an apology for the racism and sexism that undeniably persist. Consequently, much care is required in assessing the changing pattern of inequality. In fact, the picture is complex. Gains in some areas have been offset by losses in others. Some clear gains have not reached parity, and improvement often means slightly less inequality. At bottom, large inequalities among status groups still exist— racism and sexism (and ageism) are still routine practices and lively moral issues, but the pattern has changed. Unless we examine carefully the pattern, which includes important improvements, we shall fail to understand the contemporary nature of inequality.

As Table 4–1 showed, and evidence from the early 1980s confirms, black individuals, particularly women, have made substantial gains in income, although they have not reached equality. Table 4–3 showed near parity of black and white women, with Hispanic women behind blacks, at the same time that women in general lost ground slightly to men. That last trend is caused by women entering the labor force more rapidly and occupying lower rungs of the occupational ladder. Black men closed ground on whites more slowly, but there are differences here by education. Young black, male high school graduates earned 74 percent of their white counterparts in 1979, while college graduates were at 84 percent. Among blacks the most disturbing statistic is a decline in median family income from 60 percent to 56 percent of white median family income between 1971 and 1981. This seemingly inconsistent fact is a result of the higher rate of single-parent families among blacks and, therefore, fewer two-income families.

Against these mixed accomplishments in income, a pattern of unalloyed gains appears in other important areas. In education from 1970–82, the proportion of black high school graduates increased faster than for whites; blacks went from 53 to 79 percent and whites from 76 to 87 percent. The number of blacks completing college rose from 6 to 13 percent between 1970 and 1982. Whites increased from 17 to 25 percent in the same period. This is typical of what gains mean in this context. By 1982, the percentage of black college graduates was only about half of the white figure, *but* it had increased from one third of that figure in 1970. Similarly, in 1979, the average black family had financial assets (home and savings) amounting to just one third of white families, *but* the proportion had doubled from one sixth in 1967. The black-white gap in occupational prestige has narrowed, especially for women. Black registered voters have increased over the past decade and nearly equaled white proportions in 1982 (73 and 76 percent respectively).

In a valuable article by the same Reynolds Farley mentioned previously, the question is posed, "Have the gains of the 1960s disappeared in the 1970s?" The significance of the question lies in the fact that the 1960s witnessed an economic boom when minorities would be expected to gain, if only by trickle-down, while the 1970s saw a recession in which some sociologists claim minorities were bound to lose (on the principle of last-hired, first-fired). Farley's challenging conclusion is that this did not happen. His book, called *Catching Up* (1983), shows that gains continued through 1980, along with some losses, particularly in black male employment.

Finally, some status inequalities either did not improve with the equality revolution or they got worse. Gaps in the income and occupational levels of women and men have not narrowed significantly. Black males in the labor force have declined, and this is due in large part to the increasing rate of unemployment among black youth. In 1954, the unemployment figures for black and white youth (16–24 years) were 15.8 percent and 9.9

percent respectively—a difference of 5.9 percentage points. In 1980, the comparable figures were 26.4 percent and 12.0 percent or a much larger difference of 14.4 points. In the area of residential segregation, John Logan and Mark Schneider (1984) reanalyzed for 1970–80 the previously mentioned absence of black gains with suburbanization. Once again, suburban blacks were found mainly in older and declining communities, while white suburbs had gained few black residents: "The typical pattern appears to have been consolidation of black population in segregated communities" (p. 875).

From this mixed bag of results, can we arrive at any unambiguous conclusions about the accomplishments of the equality revolution? The answer is yes, and it comes in three parts. First, on a number of measures, the circumstances of disadvantaged status groups improved (e.g., women's participation in the labor force, black income and education). Second, on other measures, the situation remained the same (e.g., residential segregation, women's occupational levels) or got worse (e.g., women's income differential and black youth unemployment). Third, the overall change defies simple additive description because the core explanation for the shifts is the changing interaction of status group characteristics, class, and the measures of inequality. We encountered this circumstance previously in the description of status stratification, and it applies as much to how the pattern changes.

The dominant pattern can be illustrated rather simply with some of the discoveries by Erik Olin Wright and Luca Perrone (1977), who have compared the effects of class and status stratification. The familiar facts are that race (black), sex (female), and low education all mean low income. There are relatively few blacks and women in such higher-class positions as management (managers and executives are considered a distinct grouping within the middle class in Chapter 3). However, comparing just those people who have become managers, black and white males have similar incomes, which are significantly greater than the incomes of female managers. Sex differences among managers are considerably greater than the race differences. The fact that this may not be true for a different (nonmanagerial) occupation constitutes another kind of interaction. More generally, Wright and Perrone conclude,

The *class differences* between workers and employers are *considerably greater* [italics added] than the differences between men and women or between blacks and whites within the working class...racial discrimination operates more in sorting people into class positions in the first place than in giving them lower incomes for lower levels of education and skills once they are in a class position. (Erik Olin Wright and Luca Perrone, "Marxist Class Categories of Income Inequality," pp. 53–54 ff)

William Julius Wilson (1978) has made the same point in a book whose controversial title, *The Declining Significance of Race*, has misled some critics. Although Wilson has been charged with minimizing the pernicious effects of race, which he does not do, his central point is the new interactive pattern. The changing significance of race for Wilson means that by contrast to 1940 when race was close to the sole determinant of black life chances, today class influences combine with race and, in some circumstances, override them.

The key point in my argument, based upon the ensemble of evidence, is that *status and class operate jointly* on the outward consequences of inequality (income, wealth, residence). The effect of the equality revolution has been *to reduce certain status-group disadvantages* which, nevertheless, have been *replaced* in many instances by *class inequalities*. Status-group inequality has lessened in some respects, but class inequality has reasserted itself, sometimes canceling the categorical gains of working-class minorities.

CONTEMPORARY STATUS GROUPS

The last of our three questions about the equality revolution asks, Why was it transformed and in some ways reversed in the 1980s? The answer should begin with a qualification. The movements discussed here were never united with one another or even within their own ranks. As early as 1869, the Women's Movement divided into two camps: an assertive wing headed by Susan B. Anthony and Elizabeth Cady Stanton who founded the National Woman Suffrage Association, and the more respectable branch gathered around Lucy Stone and the American Woman Suffrage Association. In 1920, blacks were split between the Booker T. Washington moderates emphasizing education for integration and Marcus Garvey's black nationalism. The same tendencies characterized Mexican-American civic associations such as LULAC by contrast to the labor movement activism of the Confederation of Mexican Workers.

The divergence appears again in the 1960s. Civil rights groups agreeably divided in tone and strategy between the mainline NAACP-Urban League-Southern Christian Leadership Conference (SCLC) and the militant Student Nonviolent Coordinating Committee (SNCC)-Black Panthers. Similarly, the Mexican-American Political Association (MAPA) and the Political Association of Spanish-Speaking Organizations (PASO) took the moderate side by contrast to the Brown Berets. The Women's Movement was different, less publicly divided than organizationally segregated with mainliners in the National Organization for Women (NOW) and radical feminists gathered in a variety of decentralized support groups.

The equality revolution was special because of the relative unanimity within and between status groups. For a decade or so, the movements were in step. There were overarching interests, notably the peace movement that unified liberal and civil rights groups. Black and white women joined hands. Differences within groups were set aside as the NAACP and SNCC participated in the same freedom marches. But the unity was short-lived. Nascent splits that appeared in the late 1960s began to separate groups in the next decade. Actually, two things began to happen in the mid-1970s—a general demobilization of the movement and a fragmentation of surviving loyalists.

The Costs of Progress

The most important division across status groups was between those who responded to concessions, deciding to work within or for the system, and those who endeavored to push the movements beyond a victory of political compromises. I want to avoid any implication that the partisans of these divergent movement strategies can be understood as compromisers, sell-outs, or true believers. As the gains of the equality revolution were registered and the movements looked toward an agenda for the 1970s, good arguments were made for each divergent strategy. Movement participants had no way of knowing that reversals were in store and, had they seen this coming, it is not at all clear that one or another strategy could have avoided that fate. If hindsight tells us anything, it is that the revised course of the 1970s and 1980s was set by conditions in the broader society rather than by the movements themselves.

The civil rights movement reached a turning point precisely because it succeeded in its legislative and legal aims. The 1964 Civil Rights Act was an enormous achievement, not least because it came through a recognition by the political parties that their own futures depended upon a new guarantee of social rights. Blacks followed the victory with massive voter registration drives and political pressure for inclusion in President Lyndon B. Johnson's Great Society programs. As Frances Piven and Richard Cloward (1979) perceptively remark, "The disintegration of the movement was inevitable given the integrative impact of the very concessions won" (p. 253).

Ironically, demands for Black Power were mounted after this stage of the struggle for civil rights. Stokeley Carmichael and Charles Hamilton (1967) explained, "The concept of Black Power rests on a fundamental premise: Before a group can enter the open society, it must first close ranks... solidarity is necessary before a group can operate effectively from a bargaining position of strength in a pluralistic society" (p. 44). Piven and Cloward (1979) conclude that black power actually contributed to the integrative thrust of the movement. "Defined in this way the concept was especially suited to the ideological needs of a black leadership stratum seeking to exploit the new possibilities for electoral and bureaucratic influence" (p. 253). One study of the demise of the Congress on Racial Equality (CORE) by August Meier and Elliott Rudwick (1975), for example, indicates that the new antipoverty programs of the Johnson administration began hiring civil rights activists and leaders who felt that their positions ruled out continued participation in protest organizations.

The incorporation of many blacks into ameliorative programs, in combination with the documented gains, understandably led to a conservative appraisal of the changes by some middle-class blacks. Thomas Sowell's (1983) widely heralded book *Ethnic America* argues that black gains were actually generated by the operation of a competitive economy in which discrimination had proved inefficient and government programs beneficial to only a few. Christopher Jencks (1983), among others, has demonstrated the many fallacies in this argument. What is significant about it for present purposes is that during the 1970s the U.S. economy and social structure changed in ways that created an audience receptive to Sowell's viewpoint—a socially mobile black middle-class which had, indeed, worked hard for its gains and a group of conservative politicians who wanted to give credit for that achievement to the free enterprise system.

Mexican-Americans made gains in the 1960s and found themselves, like blacks, incorporated into reform programs. Indeed, when the militant spark went out in the civil rights movement, all status groups faced a new political prospect. Just as the change was setting in John Womack (1972) noted,

> Chicanismo has left many in the movement cold, like those... who gladly call themselves Chicanos but reckon that a new alienation would ruin la raza. And it has scandalized the LULACs, GI Forumites, MAPAs, and PASOs, who now have their investments in "Mexican Americanism." Since their first encounter with him the nationalists have repelled Chavez, who is committed far beyond Atzlan to building solidarity among farmworkers of every complexion. (John Womack, Jr., "The Chicanos," p. 15)

In some respects, the problems of Mexican-Americans were different from those of blacks. They had not suffered slavery or constitutional disenfranchisement. They enjoyed a strong cultural heritage in their southwestern communities, the base upon which their movement was founded—albeit one that was lost for some through migration and urbanization in what Octavio Paz (1961) called a *Labyrinth of Solitude*. By the 1970s, Mexican-Americans had their own U.S. senators and representatives. This is not to say that they suffered less from discrimination; only that they responded to it in ways that necessarily differed from blacks. Beyond electoral gains, many Mexican-Americans found positions in education, particularly in programs for bilingual education mandated by the federal government. By the mid-1970s, Chavez and the United Farmworkers had won their struggle for legally recognized unions in California. In Texas, the Farah Slacks workers gained national recognition and a boycott-supported victory for their union—with the support of the Catholic church and Amalgamated Clothing Workers. While programs devoted to Chicano studies wrestled with undeniably vexing questions of cultural identity, these working-class movements were helping to create a new one.

In the 1980s, fragmentation in the Chicano movement is less a product of the conservative reaction of a Thomas Sowell than it is a statement about the effects of integration. The artful autobiography of Richard Rodriguez (1983), *Hunger of Memory*, is the story of a boy raised in Sacramento, California in the 1950s by hard-working middle-class parents and parochial school teachers. The confusion Rodriguez faced stemmed from the fact that the private Spanish language of his home was discouraged in the public setting of his education. He was torn several ways. As a scholarship boy, he enjoyed the benefits of concessions to disadvantaged minorities, although he had gained an excellent parochial education.

Rodriguez represents a minority within the Mexican-American minority. The barrios of Sacramento include many truly disadvantaged youths and, coincidentally, 50 years earlier had produced Ernesto Galarza, who earned a Ph.D. at Columbia University in the 1930s, directed a branch of the Pan American Union, returned to his native state in 1946 to work for the unionization of farmworkers, and wrote the autobiography of a *Barrio Boy* (1971). The differences between Galarza and Rodriguez show the changing conditions of Mexican-American generations and something of the present divisions within their communities. Galarza chides the shrinks who have spread the rumor that Mexican-Americans have lost their self-image. "I, for one Mexican, never had any doubts on this score. I can't remember a time when I didn't know who I was" (p. 2). Rodriguez complained of an experience that came much later when he was treated as something he was not, simply because he had a Spanish surname. His identity problem stemmed from well-meaning, compensatory affirmative action programs aimed at the inequalities of poverty and social class, but awarded on the basis of ethnicity, thereby including studious middle-class Chicanos. His experience is not typical, but it does help to explain the source of contemporary divisions among Mexican-Americans.

Finally, the most publicized fragmentation has been within the Women's Movement—a split between radical feminists and the career and political women who continue to support NOW.

Ironically, although it was Betty Friedan's (1963) book on *The Feminine Mystique* that did so much to advertise and articulate the aims of the women's movement in 1963, her 1981 sequel, *The Second Stage*, attacks the *feminist* mystique as the new barrier to liberation. The radical feminists, according to Friedan, go too far with their sexual politics and repudiation of male and female needs for intimacy in the family. Feminists answer that their aim is real equality for women and an egalitarian family. The difference is that Friedan and her colleagues argue for the dual-career family in which men and women play mutually supportive roles. Men and women should take advantage of flexible economic arrangements to meet their mutual career needs and rely more on self-help than on government programs. Unreconstructed feminists argue that this plan retreats from the original and unmet aims of women's equality in the face of political unpopularity and would reinforce gender as a social tracking system.

If these brief descriptions serve to persuade that the current thrust of status-group politics is a reversal, from an equality revolution in the 1960s to fragmentation and compromise in the 1980s, the question returns, Why? The foregoing explanation for the rise of the equality revolution relied heavily on political changes in the broader society. The same applies here. The fragmentation of status-group politics resulted precisely from the gains it won—new employment opportunities, broader political representation, marginal to significant improvements in economic circumstance, a piece of the action. Recall, once more, Gans's (1974) observation that the equality revolution "had very little to do with poverty" as opposed to the inequality experienced by status groups that enjoyed fewer advantages than their reference groups. Once the political system, for its own reasons, began responding to these claims in ways that made a difference for some, it won converts. Blacks who saw their income increase, women who began getting jobs, Mexican-Americans who unionized or entered the educational establishment—many of these the leaders of the equality revolution—knew that they had gained something worth preserving.

It is also true that the benefits of these status-based movements are not broadly distributed. Particularly, they touch only indirectly the bases of *class privilege*. Richard Rodriguez (1983) is correct when he notes that,

Remarkably, affirmative action passed as a program of the Left. In fact, its supporters ignored the most fundamental assumptions of the classical left by disregarding the importance of class and by assuming that the disadvantages of the lower class would necessarily be ameliorated by the creation of an elite society. The movement that began so nobly in the South and the North came to parody social reform. Those least disadvantaged were helped first, advanced because many others of their race were more disadvantaged. (Richard Rodriguez, *Hunger of Memory: The Education of Richard Rodriguez*, p. 151)

But, it is equally true that this was not the fault of the status groups who fought the equality revolution with the weapons they had at hand—namely the ethnic, gender, and cultural resources that enabled them to unite and act against great odds. We have to bear in mind two conclusions despite the moral tension between them: the equality revolution made a difference, winning converts to the system that embraced it and splitting its original foundations. But it did not begin to wash away the footings of class inequality.

This lesson was made acute by a worldwide recession in the mid-1970s that reaffirmed class divisions and further divided status groups as those who had made their own gains fought to hold on to them. Unemployment climbed to 11 percent in 1982 and real income dropped with inflation. Those who had advanced during the previous decade came to realize that they now occupied a new class position with its attendant interests. Status groups made the equality revolution and social classes captured it.

The 1980s, accordingly, witnessed another experience. Class inequalities returned with a vengeance, but status anxieties did not disappear. On the contrary, a far-flung backlash to the equality revolution appeared. In defense of a status hierarchy that had been under siege, traditional values were reasserted: religious fundamentalism, patriotism, family, sexual probity (with anti-abortion linked to several of these), free enterprise, an ethical defense of capitalism. All of these resurgent values bloomed in the political process to the advantage of conservative Republicans. The shift was facilitated by more than an imprecise backlash. On one hand, dominant status groups reorganized themselves: men's rights, reverse discrimination, racial quotas, abortion, busing versus neighborhood schools, all became passionate concerns. On the other hand, many of the very beneficiaries of the equality revolution joined the establishment in position and in principle. Many Hispanics became Republicans; some blacks and women who attained better positions took on the values attached to the new status rather than to the movement that had made it all possible. The balance of political power shifted.

CLASS AND STATUS

The preceding chapter argued that a resurgent pattern of class stratification characterizes the United States in the 1980s. More evidence of the sort reviewed in this chapter supports the same conclusion. Writing in the *New York Times* for March 14, 1984, the economist Lester Thurow indicates that if the U.S. middle class is defined by households with an income of $15 to $25,000 (a very rough definition for sociological purposes, but an indicator), then the size of that stratum has shrunk. Between 1967 and 1982, it was reduced from 28.2 to 23.7 percent of the population. During the same period, households with incomes in *both* the lower and the upper income ranges increased. That is, household income tended to become more polarized between rich and poor. The same conclusion was reached in a later study by the Urban Institute in Washington, D.C. From 1980 to 1984, average real income rose 3.5 percent, which was still lower than previous four-year periods in the last few decades. Nevertheless, within this average, the bottom 20 percent of the wage earners saw their incomes drop by 8 percent, while the top fifth gained 9 percent. In short, the income gap widened appreciably. A Census Bureau report, "Money Income and Poverty Status of Families and Persons in the United States: 1983," came to essentially the same conclusions, emphasizing recent modest increases in both median family income and the percentage of families living in poverty.

Now, if we add to these indirect measures of class the facts reviewed here about status-group gains that have not been reversed during the same period, the resultant picture is one of a reorganized class and status structure. The current hierarchy is more balanced by race and sex *and more rigidly stratified* by material rewards and life chances. Class differences are more often the bases of sharp inequalities than are status differences.

The new and large question we are left with after this analysis is why these shifts occur in the relative importance of class and status determinants of inequality. Max Weber hypothesized that they are produced by changes from economic stability (and stratification by status) to "technological and economic transformations" (and class stratification). Weber qualified this by admitting that "only very little can be said" from our present knowledge about why such changes occur. Weber's proposition is generally supported in the postwar United States—the economic boom and technological advance that prevailed in this period did help to break down a pattern of status stratification and push the class situation into the foreground. But Marx's expectation that classes would become more polarized with advancing capitalist development is equally plausible on the evidence.

The problem with both of these grand generalizations is that they miss the key discovery in this material, namely, the *constant interaction of class and status* in a pattern of reciprocal influence. The economic and technological transformations that Weber stressed have recently brought *class* back to the forefront of stratification. Yet a similar transformation in the early part of this century that modernized Southern agriculture had the effect of reinforcing race *status* as a feature of the urban and industrial economy. Moreover, at any given time, it is the combination of class and status characteristics that explains the life chances of particular groups—explains, for example, why black women made more progress than black men or women in general during the equality revolution.

Stated more simply, it is the interaction of class and status that reveals the *nature* of any system of social stratification; that tells us how racist, sexist, or class-based that system is.

When we ask, then, what determines the blend of class and status, the clear answer from this material is politics—the political struggles of groups who find it necessary or effective in a given situation to organize themselves on the basis of class or status themes. Political struggles based on class or status take different forms, drawing on economic groups or on religious and cultural influences. And they seek different ends, material benefit or social rights. These differences, indeed, the ultimate success of the struggles, depend on the structure of political power in society including what appears in this analysis as the moral dilemmas and political strategies of ruling groups.

In summary, the status group is an essential parallel to social class in any sociological analysis of group formation, political action, and social inequality. The relative importance of class versus status changes over time, requiring an explanation of its own and reminding us of the maxim that adequate sociological explanations must also be historical. The main result of this analysis, however, is that class and status cannot be disaggregated and each weighed for its individual importance. This is because the most discerning explanations of social action or inequality derive from the interaction of class and status, an interaction that is causally specific to certain situations and changing in ways that mark off distinctive eras. Failure to understand this principle has led to many unnecessary controversies between social reformers (militants for working class solidarity versus pragmatists for ethnic-religion coalitions) and social analysts (Marxists versus culturalists). Once the interaction principle is understood, however, better explanations are generated and new questions come forward.

As the studies in this chapter show, during the last 20 years an equality revolution was fought, and in some senses won, for the twin reasons that the status groups fighting it had the cultural energy of justice on their side and the elites who accommodated it discovered their own interests in a new class order. The state was changing and with it the social structure.

SELECTED BIBLIOGRAPHY

BANKS, OLIVE (1981). *Faces of Feminism: A Study of Feminism as a Social Movement*. Oxford: Martin Robertson.

CARMICHAEL, STOKELEY & HAMILTON, CHARLES (1967). *Black Power: The Politics of Liberation in America*. New York: Random House.

DRAKE, ST. CLAIR & CAYTON, HORACE R. (1945). *Black Metropolis: A Study of Negro Life in a Northern City*. New York: Harcourt Brace Jovanovich.

DUNNE, JOHN GREGORY (1967). *Delano: The Story of the California Grape Strike*. New York: Farrar, Straus & Giroux.

FARLEY, REYNOLDS (1970, January). "The Changing Distribution of Negroes within Metropolitan Areas: The Emergence of Black Suburbs." *American Journal of Sociology*, 75(4), 512–29.

———(1977, April). "Trends in Racial Inequalities: Have the Gains of the 1960s Disappeared in the 1970s?" *American Sociological Review*, *42*(2), 189–208.

———(1983). *Catching Up: Recent Changes in the Social and Economic Status of Blacks*. Cambridge, MA: Harvard Univ. Press.

FRIEDAN, BETTY (1963). *The Feminine Mystique*. New York: W.W. Norton.

———(1981). *The Second Stage*. New York: Summit Books.

GALARZA, ERNESTO (1971). *Barrio Boy*. Notre Dame, IN: University of Notre Dame Press.

GANS, HERBERT J. (1974). "The Equality Revolution." In Herbert J. Gans, *More Equality* (pp. 7–35). New York: Vintage Books. (Work originally published in 1968)

GREBLER, LEO, MOORE, JOAN W., & GUZMAN, RALPH C. (1970). *The Mexican-American People: The Nation's Second Largest Minority*. New York: Free Press.

HERMALIN, ALBERT I., & FARLEY, REYNOLDS (1973, October). "The Potential for Residential Integration in the Cities and Suburbs: Implications for the Busing Controversy." *American Sociological Review*, *38*(5), 595–610.

HOLE, JUDITH, & LEVINE, ELLEN (1971). *The Rebirth of Feminism*. New York: Quadrangle Books.

JENCKS, CHRISTOPHER (1983, March 3). "Discrimination and Thomas Sowell." *The New York Review of Books*, *30*(3), 33–38.

JENKINS, J. CRAIG, & PERROW, CHARLES (1977, April). "Insurgency of the Powerless: Farm Worker Movements (1946–1972)." *American Sociological Review*, *42*(2), 249–268.

LOGAN, JOHN R., & SCHNEIDER, MARK (1984, January). "Racial Segregation and Racial Change in American Suburbs, 1970–1980." *American Journal of Sociology*, *89*(4), 874–888.

MARE, ROBERT D., & WINSHIP, CHRISTOPHER (1984, February). "The Paradox of Lessening Racial Inequality and Joblessness Among Black Youth: Enrollment, Enlistment, and Employment, 1964–1981." *American Sociological Review*, *49*(1), 39–55.

MARSHALL, T.H. (1964). *Class, Citizenship, and Social Development*. Garden City, NY: Doubleday Publishing. (Originally published in 1950)

MEIER, AUGUST, & RUDWICK, ELLIOTT (1975). *CORE: A Study in the Civil Rights Movement, 1942–1968*. Champaign: University of Illinois Press.

MILLS, C. WRIGHT (1956). *The Power Elite*. New York: Oxford University Press.

MITCHELL, JULIET (1971). *Woman's Estate*. London: Harmondsworth.

MYRDAL, GUNNAR (1944). *An American Dilemma: The Negro Problem and Modern Democracy*. New York: Harper & Row.

PAZ, OCTAVIO (1961). *Labyrinth of Solitude*. New York: Grove Press.

PIVEN, FRANCES FOX, & CLOWARD, RICHARD A. (1979). *Poor People's Movements: Why They Succeed, How They Fail*. New York: Vintage Books.

RODRIGUEZ, RICHARD (1983). *Hunger of Memory: The Education of Richard Rodriguez*. New York: Bantam Books.

SOWELL, THOMAS (1983). *Ethnic America: A History*. New York: Basic Books.

STACEY, JUDITH (1983, Fall). "The New Conservative Feminism." *Feminist Studies 9*(3), 559–83.

WEBER, MAX (1946). "Class, Status, Party." In Hans Gerth and C. Wright Mills (Eds.). *From Max Weber: Essays in Sociology* (pp. 180–95). New York: Oxford University Press.

WILSON, WILLIAM JULIUS (1978). *The Declining Significance of Race: Blacks and Changing American Institutions*. Chicago: University of Chicago Press.

WOMACK, JOHN, JR. (1972, August 31). "The Chicanos." *The New York Review of Books, 19*(3), 12–18.

WRIGHT, ERIK OLIN, & PERRONE, LUCA (1977, February). "Marxist Class Categories and Income Inequality." *American Sociological Review, 42*(1), 32–55.

WRIGHT, RICHARD (1945). Introduction. In St. Clair Drake & Horace B. Cayton, *Black Metropolis: A Study of Negro Life in a Northern City* (pp. xvii–xviii). New York: Harcourt Brace Jovanovich.

U.S. BUREAU OF THE CENSUS (1983, July). *America's Black Population: 1970–1982*. Washington, DC: U.S. Government Printing Office.

U.S. BUREAU OF LABOR STATISTICS (1980, October). *Perspectives on Women: A Databook*. Washington, DC: U.S. Government Printing Office.

Social Organization and the State

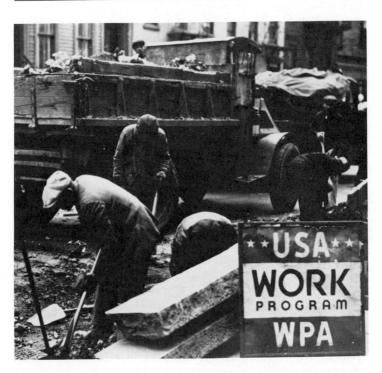

The public works programs sponsored by the Work Progress Administration produced the nation's highway system and urban renovation on a scale unmatched since the Depression. (The Bettmann Archive)

PART I
PURVIEW OF THE STATE

On Long Island, New York, in the fall of 1983, an infant was born severely handicapped, yet destined for notoriety. Baby Jane Doe, as she became known to the world, was delivered with an open spinal cord, fluid on the brain, an abnormally small head, and an underdeveloped brain. With routine care, she would live perhaps two years. Surgical intervention to close the hole in her back and drain the excess brain fluid might extend her lifetime. She would never be "human." Her parents anguished over what to do; discussed it with their doctors, friends, and clergy. In the end, they decided against surgery.

Baby Jane Doe's condition was told to a lawyer and anti-abortion activist by an anonymous informant. The lawyer, a specialist in litigation on behalf of newborns, filed suit in the New York State Supreme Court claiming that the infant's right to life was being violated, that the court had a responsibility to take the decision out of the hands of the parents and to require the doctors to perform surgery. The state court rejected this argument, noting that the lawyer was an outsider with no standing in the case or right to sue. That did not end the public drama. The lawyer went to federal court demanding an injunction that would force the hospital to fight any parent's choice to reject life-prolonging surgery.

More important than the lawyer's tenacity, however, was a decision by the federal government to enter the now publicized case on behalf of the people of the United States. The government brought suit against the hospital, where Baby Jane Doe lay quietly through all this, seeking access to her medical records. The government's case was based on the Rehabilitation Act of 1973 which includes a provision (and here an unanticipated consequence of the equality revolution) stating that it is illegal for any institution receiving federal aid to discriminate on the basis of race, creed, color, religion, ethnic origin, or *handicap*. The government requested access to medical records in order to determine whether the infant was a victim of discrimination by virtue of being denied medical treatment solely because of her handicap. Baby Jane Doe's mute life became a civil rights issue because the administration decided to contest the judgment of attending physicians and the family at the behest of politically organized prolife groups. The family found itself face-to-face with the state in a tormented contest over who bore ultimate responsibility for the unfortunate baby's life.

Cases like Baby Jane Doe's are commonplace with large hospitals and obstetricians. Traditionally, they have been handled in a manner determined by the doctors and family. There is no question that grotesquely malformed and hopelessly retarded infants are allowed to die, just as it is true that modern medicine and extraordinary efforts are now devoted to abnormal newborns who were once written off. Down's syndrome or mongoloid babies once discounted at birth or permanently institutionalized are now raised in families. Although prolife groups claim that there are 300 victims of infanticide each year, no consensus exists on what to do with babies like Jane Doe—who decides and who bears the costs for the prolongation of life?

The federal government has no position on what should become of the life prolonged by nondiscrimination. Indeed, it is still a mystery how discrimination could be established. Since the treatment involved would never be administered to an infant without the handicap, it is difficult to say that it is denied solely because of the handicap. Without answers to such thorny issues, and with the officials steadfastly pursuing public jurisdiction over these decisions, the only suggestion agreeable to physicians and government is the establishment of quasi-official bio-ethical committees composed of clergy and medical, legal, and ethical experts to judge individual cases. However the issue is resolved, it represents a significant extension of state authority into the realm of personal choice.

This illustration refers knowingly to "the state" despite the elusiveness of the term. In ordinary usage, it ranges from a vague synonym for government, to a critical composite such as the welfare state or capitalist state, and, in the extreme, a futuristic nightmare like the vision of George Orwell's novel *1984*—an oppressive, big-brother state based on the complete usurpation of individual will. Orwell's allegory, written in 1948, transposed two digits and projected a trend toward enforced conformity into an imaginary totalitarian state that made decisions for individuals, provided them diversion, and brooked no independent thinking or unofficial recollection of history. Orwell provided a warning rather than a prediction. When 1984 came, his warning was as important as ever, although events appeared differently. The purview of the state, as Orwell saw, had expanded enormously—it had even marched into family and medical choices—and so, as Orwell hoped, had the conflict over what the state should and should not do.

THE STATE

The state is both a set of *organizations* possessing *legitimate authority* and an *institution*. Organizations, public bureaucracies, and agencies possess legitimate authority when, in the eyes of the citizens, they have the right to command (as do the police or Internal Revenue Service). Institutions exist at a higher level as established ways of doing things. Representative government, for example, is a way of exercising public authority, and marriage a way of organizing companionship and reproduction. Organizations are concrete representations of institutions, but institutions are foremost ideas about how society should be organized. This standard sociological usage differs from such vernacular phrases as mental institution, which confuses an important distinction. By distinguishing between concrete organizations and institutional ideas, it is possible to investigate how one influences the other and how both change under a variety of influences.

Organizationally, the state includes government in all its branches and levels. It is the Congress and the executive departments, as well as state, county, and municipal governments. But the state is more than representative governing institutions. It is also the military, police, public financial institutions (the Treasury and Federal Reserve Board), the courts and officers of the court (lawyers), prisons and welfare agencies, regulatory commissions, public utilities, and a variety of independent agencies whose authority stems from government (the Federal Deposit Insurance Corporation, Environmental Protection Agency, National Science Foundation, Federal Election Commission, Commission on Fine Arts). When nongovernmental bodies act to ensure that public mandates are carried out, as bio-ethical committees might do, they act for the state.

As an *institution* linking these diverse organizations and agencies, the state is the expression of an established and legitimate way of conducting the public's business. As Alan Wolfe (1974) puts it in a valuable article on the theory of the state, the state is embodied in public bureaucracies, "yet that thing called government can only do what it is supposed if behind it is an apparatus responsible for the reproduction of the social system within which the government operates. That other thing, which cannot in fact be directly touched or seen, is the state" (p. 149). More simply, the state is civic authority, law and administration, as it is practiced by a great variety of organizations.

This chapter develops three general themes about the state and society: (1) that the state is a crucial determinant of social organization, particularly in modern societies—although conventional sociology has neglected this fact, leaving an important part of its own responsibility to disciplines such as political science; (2) that the state has vastly expanded, particularly in the 20th century, in tandem with the maturation of industrial capitalism; and (3) that the state is presently changing in fundamental ways owing to a crisis of the welfare state as an institution.

Social organization, defined in the standard text by Leonard Broom and Phillip Selznick (1968), "is the pattern of individual and group relations" in a society; relations that ensure cooperation as well as those that "isolate people and groups and that foster disharmony" (p. 14). These relations exist in interpersonal behavior (in social roles), groups (families, peer and work groups), and in broader settings (communities, organizations, bureaucracies). Social organization is a pattern of relationships with many loci, a pattern that is constrained by basic human needs (nourishment, reproduction, and so forth) and the requisites of social order (production, law, and so forth). Accordingly, it is a pattern negotiated from the bottom up and the top down. Social organization includes those patterned relationships we learn in families, schools, churches, communities, careers, and political life.

The connection we want to pursue is that between the state and social organization. Social life is led mostly in organized settings; in work, for example, to which we bring social relationships developed in family, school, and community. Historically, family and community were interwoven and, together, pretty much exhausted social organization of the preindustrial "world we have lost" (to borrow a phrase from the English historian Peter Laslett). In modern society, by contrast, we are less engaged by family and community, more so by school, work, career, and organizational life. The state, in turn, has steadily taken responsibility for regulating all of these institutions. Stated differently, contemporary society presents us with a world that is organized differently owing to the intrusion of the state into so many other institutional spheres. Social organization is changing in consequential ways that we can only get at by reconceiving the institutional order; seeing it as a new set of relationships in which the state is critical in its own right and a potent influence on the character of other institutions.

Social thinkers have struggled with this issue, usually by posing grand typologies. Émile Durkheim, as we saw (Chapters 1 and 2), viewed industrial society as moving toward state centralism by eliminating the "intermediate powers" that promoted group cohesion and associational life (and also curbed anomie). His contemporary, Ferdinand Tonnies, noted the same shift from personal bonds and community life to a more formal and distant society—or, in his own German terms, from *gemeinschaft* to *gesellschaft*. Max Weber spoke of the transition from traditional to rational-legal authority. More recently, North American sociologists, including C. Wright Mills, suggested a shift from local to mass society. With certain variations, all these polar types claim that the old order is disappearing mainly as a result of the decline of the institutions of community and association or the buffers between family and state.

These formulations have the virtue of capturing the general sense that something important is afoot, that the world is changing rapidly around us in ways that we do not fully understand. They also have a few drawbacks. They tend to ignore the pole that Durkheim identified as the state, concentrating on what is supposedly disintegrating below. They disagree on the implications of the change, some anticipating more, involuntary (Orwellian) integration and others less. And, according to a good deal of research, they are factually in error. All those intermediate groups are not disappearing so much as changing in function. The expected mass society did not develop, although the society organized around class and state that did come seems no more agreeable.

THE STATE IN SOCIAL LIFE

If the foregoing terms are necessarily abstract, it will be useful to indicate some of the countless and often unacknowledged ways in which the state affects our daily lives. In U.S. society, there is a peculiar ambivalence about the state. On one hand, we may think about it very little or think it a nuisance, a source of bureaucratic meddling in private affairs if not an Orwellian beast. On the other hand, we want a strong state to protect us from foreign and domestic enemies and to guarantee a far-flung collection of rights. We are ambivalent about many things that the state does, except when it ensures our own interest. The sociological implication of that somewhat obvious statement is that from an individualistic standpoint, we tend not to understand the causes of state expansion since our interests appear limited and stable. Ralph Miliband's (1969) important book, *The State in Capitalist Society*, opens with the observation,

> More than ever before men now live in the shadow of the state. What they want to achieve, individually or in groups, now mainly depends on the state's sanction and support. But since that sanction and support are not bestowed indiscriminately, they must, ever more directly, seek to influence and shape the state's power and purpose, or try to appropriate it altogether. It is for the state's attention, or for its control, that men compete; and it is against the state that beat the waves of social conflict. This is why, as social beings, they are also political beings, whether they know it or not. It is possible not to be interested in what the state does; but it is not possible to be unaffected by it. (Ralph Miliband, *The State in Capitalist Society*, p. 1)

Consider some of the ways in which the state routinely affects our lives.

Life. As the Baby Jane Doe case indicates, the state has recently entered the field of supervising the care of newborns to ensure the prolongation of any life, or at least of those lives that an arm of the state (such as a bio-ethical committee) may decide have a right to prolongation. This initiative furthers standards that the state has already set limiting legal abortions by barring their performance under federal medical assistance programs. In some instances, therefore, the state has assumed the responsibility for deciding who lives.

Death. As the Baby Jane Doe case was argued in the New York courts, a young woman in California was legally restrained from allowing her own life to expire. Elizabeth Bouvia, a cerebral palsy victim and quadriplegic from birth, who had nevertheless completed college and married, decided that she no longer wished to live totally dependent on others. She entered a hospital asking to be kept comfortable while she starved herself to death. Having already admitted her, but refusing this request, the hospital was in the uncomfortable position of being able neither to put her out on the street nor to force feed her without legal authority. In a ruling sought from the California Superior Court, the judge said that Ms. Bouvia "does have a right to terminate her existence, but not... with the assistance of society." The hospital won state support to force feed her as long as she remained (later she left the hospital, but changed her mind about wanting to die). This is not a unique case. Contrary to popular belief, neither the suffering individual nor the family can choose to terminate an unconscious or painful life without medical sanction. We cannot simply pull the plug where doctors and hospitals are concerned. They must make or approve that choice and their approval is constrained by state and court-established precedents on medical malpractice. In the end, the state still watches over us, regulating where burials are permitted or ashes spread.

Marriage and divorce. The state, of course, grants licenses for marriage and officially confers divorce, in both instances under terms that bind the partners to legal responsibilities (monogamy in marriage or child support in divorce). People may enter into marriages without the consent of the state, as common-law and homosexual marriages demonstrate, yet those unconventional unions are not free of state influence. In the eyes of the state, a common-law marriage becomes legal after seven years, meaning that spouses may call on the state to intervene in the relationship, say to require alimony after separation or legal inheritance with the death of one partner. Conversely, since the state does not recognize homosexual marriage, those couples are not entitled to the forms of intervention just mentioned or to certain marital privileges such as joint ownership of property. People can marry with or without the state, but the state's attitude toward the union has personal consequences in both cases.

Child rearing. The state cannot dictate how families must raise their children, but under a variety of circumstances it may usurp parental responsibility (in cases of family destitution, unfit parents, child abuse). Conversely, parents may relinquish the duties of child care to the state by convincing the appropriate authorities that a son or daughter is incorrigible. Beyond the extremes of family disruption, parents cannot keep minor children out of school or put them to work without the risk of state intervention. The government tries to require conventional forms of medical care for children. In one case of a Seventh Day Adventist family that chose prayer over chemotherapy for a child with cancer, the government lost a court contest to overrule the family since that was held a violation of religious freedom. Presumably, a family choice based on another standard with fewer constitutional safeguards could be reversed.

Sex. Studies of sexual behavior dating from the Kinsey reports in the 1950s show that people routinely engage in practices that are illegal in certain jurisdictions (e.g., oral copulation, homosexuality). In general the state, particularly the police, confines its attention to prostitution when it regulates sexual conduct. Yet the state may call upon authority to intervene under other circumstances, such as questions of public health. Concern about the transmission of AIDS (acquired-immune-deficiency syndrome that impairs the body's capacity to resist infection), which is statistically more common among homosexual and bisexual males, led San Francisco officials to close gay bathhouses. AIDS occurs in other populations, for example, drug addicts, and it is transmitted in heterosexual contact, yet the sexual behavior of such other affected populations has not been regulated; indicating both a selective application of health measures and a potential for broader state intervention.

Schooling. The state is now responsible for most primary and secondary schools as well as much of the advanced education in colleges, universities, graduate, and professional schools. People are trained for specific jobs in the military, in special manpower programs such as the recently terminated CETA (the Comprehensive Employment and Training Act), and with the help of government loans (once titled and justified as national defense loans). Governments at various levels are also involved in "credentialing" schools or determining that they meet certain standards of content, coverage, and competence in their programs. Among other things, this involves assuring that schools are offering courses of instruction mandated by the state. Even private schools and universities are critically dependent upon the federal government for financial support (through program and research grants).

Occupational life. By itself and in collaboration with professional associations, the state sets standards for a variety of occupations and participates in the process through which people are permitted to practice. Medical doctors, real estate agents, accountants, attorneys, building contractors, civil servants, and many more are required to pass state-supervised examinations before legally pursuing their occupations. Public school teachers and counselors must obtain a state credential based on specific training. Psychologists and beauticians are licensed by the state. State supervision affects not only who may enter a vast number of occupations, but also their conduct and the circumstances under which the right to practice a profession may be withdrawn.

Leisure life. Even our recreation is shaped by state control. Camping permits, wilderness passes, hunting and fishing licenses all precede certain uses of the outdoors. Some hobbies such as operating a ham radio require licenses. The state regulates when and where people can drink and dance.

Travel. Where leisure life may include travel to foreign countries, the state issues passports and keeps tabs on exit and re-entry, including the personal property one may travel with. Until recently, U.S. citizens were barred from legal travel to certain countries (Cuba, Algeria, Albania, North Korea, North Vietnam). Even today, there are restrictions on who can travel to Cuba (researchers and relatives of Cuban nationals) and at least one New York travel agency is under investigation for sending tourists. Yet, there are more mundane ways in which the state regulates travel, notably by requiring licenses to operate automobiles and airplanes, licenses that depend upon state examination and are subject to revocation for misconduct or physical limitation.

Income and wealth. For most people who enjoy an income or net worth above a certain minimum, taxes are the most forceful reminder of state authority. We are taxed not only by the many levels of government and charged for all those licenses, we are also taxed in ways that vary with our lifestyles. All wage-earners are taxed according to a theoretically progressive schedule: the greater the income, the greater the tax bite. That principle, however, is compromised by another; the greater the income, the more available are opportunities for tax exemption and shelters. Low-income people who cannot afford to buy a home must rent, with no tax advantage. Higher income people can purchase homes and deduct mortgage interest payments from their income taxes. Tax laws have discriminated against people according to marital status. Credit buying in general, business-related expenses and travel, educational costs, all carry class-biased tax benefits and begin to suggest the incentives for a consumer lifestyle.

Retirement.   As in work, the state influences how people spend their retirement. All those who pay into the Social Security fund are eligible for retirement income. The state determines the level of that income as well as the addition (and, more recently, the subtraction) of associated benefits such as medical care. Social Security sets limits on any additional earned income. Retired people who have difficulty living on their pensions and want to supplement that income must forgo part of their retirement pay or break the law by not reporting extra earnings, even when those just meet essential living expenses (property taxes or food and medical bills that have risen faster than retirement incomes). The state's generosity determines how well or poorly 36 million Social Security recipients live.

Times of need.   In 1983, the Census Bureau published a report centered on the impressive datum that 30 percent of the U.S. population currently receive direct benefits from the federal government. Social Security and Medicare top the list of these benefits, but they are followed closely by (means-tested) programs for the needy such as Food Stamps and Medicaid. Studies of cyclical poverty, such as those carried out at the University of Michigan, show that in the United States, during any given eight-year span, one family in 10 is poor over *all of those years,* but more than one third of all families are poor *for at least one* of the eight years. Accordingly, a substantial number of people at one time or another depend upon state benefits for unemployment, disability, aid to dependent children, or food stamps.

Once receiving those payments, the individual's life is subject to close official scrutiny and stigma. Welfare recipients are required to follow budgets drawn up by social workers, and mothers of children receiving aid cannot live with whom they please.

Military service. Many countries require some form of national service. The United States has enforced a military draft or some alternative service in recent years of war and peace. Universal draft registration now in effect represents the potential for broad service demands which, if the equality revolution continues, could include women. Drafted military service has previously fallen disproportionately on the less privileged classes, although that began to change with the Selective Service lottery system. At present, about 30 million people (13 percent of the population) are active members or veterans of the military services.

Property. The state regulates how we use our property, not to mention how it is acquired, taxed, and disposed of. One's home may be a castle, but that does not mean that a moat with crocodiles can be built around it. Zoning laws and use permits define what can be done with real property; a suburban lot cannot be turned into a farm or business, at least not if the neighbors object.

Consumption. State agencies provide consumer protection against unsafe products and fraud. Presumably, products sold to the public must meet standards set by the government, such as those for automobile safety. We are taxed differentially on consumer goods, including a judgmental luxury tax, while the state subsidizes certain (for example, agricultural) producers to control prices. Various rates and fees, such as for shipping or utilities, are set by the state.

Information. Modern societies are increasingly dependent upon the electronic media for information. The airwaves, in turn, are considered public domain under state supervision. Broadcasting requires a license and adherence to a state-enforced code. In the United States, three large corporations dominate radio and television broadcasting, and a fourth public system is the only general source of variation in coverage or editorial slant. New networks require large amounts of capital and state certification, neither of which is easy to get, as the battle over cable television franchises shows. The state does not control the news in any Orwellian sense, but it has a great influence over how that news reaches the public.

Religion. The First Amendment of the U.S. Constitution begins, "Congress shall make no law respecting an establishment of religion, or prohibiting the free exercise thereof." What constitutes a religion or its free exercise, however, is sometimes a matter of dispute. Recently, the state has denied the normal tax-exempt status of churches to new and prosperous fundamentalist groups who use their facilities for profit-making activities. The Heavyweight Champion of the World was once stripped of his title (the state regulates sports, too) for claiming military draft exemption as a conscientious objector. Many COs have served jail terms for failing to persuade the state of their religious convictions. Conversely, courts have set aside convictions of immigrant Jamaicans who use drugs in their religious-cult ceremonies.

Politics. In the past, the state has proscribed political freedom by legal harassment of radical parties. Recent legislation to reform political campaign practices and reduce the candidates' dependence on wealthy contributors has done little to stem those contributions, but it has made the amount of public funding available to a party or candidate a function of performance in past elections. Public financing for political campaigns, much of it for television advertising, is pegged to popularity, meaning that new and less appealing ideas are at a disadvantage in the state-regulated marketplace.

Environment. State responsibility has extended to the air we breathe. Health hazards of pollution and the depletion of natural resources have brought the state into the business of regulating use of the natural environment. Since the potential sources of environmental damage are vast, the state must create special agencies to deal with air pollution, toxic and nuclear waste, contamination of waterways and aquifers, use of chemicals in industry and agriculture, depletion of the ionosphere, and an orbiting junkyard of spent space equipment. The manner in which the state deals with environmental abuse affects the individual's health, enjoyment, and pocketbook.

Conduct. A final and somewhat open-ended category of expanded state influence has to do with the ways we conduct ourselves. Although it would appear that state authority ends with the rights of individuals to live the way they please within the law, reality belies appearance. People can be committed to state mental hospitals less because their behavior is exceptional by normal standards than because it offends family or associates from whom the state entertains commitment petitions. Through its agencies and oversight, the state confers the status of ex-mental patient, ex-convict, or ex-GI; statuses that affect the individual and the treatment he or she is accorded by others. As in all of the previous examples, the consequences of extended state influence may be good or bad from the standpoint of the individual or particular social groups. Typically, that evaluation differs among people and over time. The point here is that, for good or ill, the role of the state in modern society has grown to such an extent that any appreciation of social organization must begin with this fact.

The foregoing list is weighty, apropos of a burdensome subject. It names 20 different ways in which the average person is affected by the state, intimating both the pervasiveness of, and the mixed feelings we have about, state regulation. The list could be expanded or recombined—a profitable exercise for anyone who questions the state's influence on our daily lives. Once that fact is established, it will also be clear that the world was not always organized in this fashion; that the vast expansion of the state is recent historically, explaining, perhaps, why social science has yet to absorb the changes into its analytic schemes.

There was a time when the functions of the state were minimal by today's standards. In the United States, there were no public schools until the 1820s, when they were started in New York exclusively for children of the indigent classes. The first operating state university began in 1795 with the University of North Carolina, but it was not until the 1860s and the public land-grant college (Morrill) act that the major state systems of higher education took shape. The first state mental hospital opened (or closed) its doors in 1835 in Worcester, Massachusetts. Social welfare was a function of families, churches, and mutual societies until the late 19th century. Roads, steam and electrical power, worker housing, and, generally, all of the industrial infrastructure considered today as essential public services were once provided by factory owners themselves.

Personal income tax, the source of almost half of U.S. government revenues, did not exist until 1913 and another 30 years passed before it was withheld from wages. What is called in some quarters the welfare state did not take its definitive form until the unemployment crisis and economic depression of the 1930s. During previous periods of recession and high unemployment in 1893, 1914, and 1921, Congress failed to approve bills providing federal aid to the unemployed. In *Regulating the Poor,* Piven and Cloward (1971) note, "During the severe depression of 1914–15, for example, it was left to the New York Association for Improving the Condition of the Poor to initiate work projects for the unemployed in New York City" (p. 48).

All this changed with the New Deal policies of Franklin D. Roosevelt, beginning in 1932. Particularly, it changed with the Social Security Act of 1935 that created federal responsibility for unemployment insurance, old-age pensions, and aid to the unemployable (the blind, orphaned, and aged not eligible for pensions). The New Deal had precedents from the period of Reconstruction after the Civil War and from the Progressive Era, but it was a qualitative break with the past in its redefinition of state responsibility. Once the state accepted the principle that it was responsible (at least as a regulator) for the public's economic and social welfare, its exponential growth and its entry into issues as far-flung as consumer and environmental protection were ordained.

Two summary points can be drawn from all this: first, that the state influences individual and group life ubiquitously and, second, that this is new in the sense of being a rapid expansion of its scope in the 20th century. The latter implies that the new role of the state had identifiable causes, some of which are hinted at with the observation that state expansion followed economic crisis. If this much is granted, the three themes that introduced this chapter now appear as three questions that must be answered: (1) what explains the growth of the state? (2) what are the implications of that growth for social organization? and (3) how are state-society relations changing—where are we headed? These questions are treated in the next three sections.

Answers to the first question are easier once the ideological underbrush is cleared away. An intuitive sense of its importance has led conservative, liberal, and radical social critics to cast the state in the image of their respective demons. Although its origins are kinder, the term "welfare state" typically occurs in conservative criticism of big government, misguided initiatives that undermine free enterprise, and costly expenditures that should be replaced by workfare. A new variation on this theme is Christopher Lasch's (1977) pejorative "therapeutic state," the extensive social service agencies staffed by liberal professionals who are allegedly destroying the family. Liberals like John Kenneth Galbraith and Gunnar Myrdal point even-temperedly to the "new industrial state" or the "postwelfare state" as the unavoidable creature of advanced capitalism that requires a broadly planned economy. Ralph Miliband, Gabriel Kolko, and other radicals understand the "capitalist state" as a marriage of big business and government, a means of rationalizing the economy and stabilizing politics in a manner that safeguards the elite interests of both in a new "political capitalism."

There is truth in each of these views, rather more in the last, I believe. But there is also much simplification. Group perceptions can be mistaken, but it is instructive to find that sharply opposed political camps separately view the state as a tool of their antagonists. The problem is partly perceptual and partly a result of complexity. The state serves many contradictory interests and sometimes contradicts itself. Moreover, caricatured liberal and conservative positions contain their own contradictions.

This is apparent if we return for a moment to the case of Baby Jane Doe. Conservatives generally stand for less government intervention and more free choice; liberals favor state responsibility for the general welfare. Yet the conservative pro-life groups that took up the baby's case want the state to ensure the rights of infants and to outlaw abortion. The liberals who stood up for the Doe parents insist on individual choice free of state coercion. The pro-life debate is not unique in this respect. Conservatives and liberals differ uncharacteristically on questions like farm subsidies, defense spending, loans to large corporations, and so forth.

The lesson to be drawn from these examples is that the state cannot be properly understood as merely the instrument of particular, and sometimes contradictory, interests. Marx was certainly wrong in his polemical writings when he said, "[T]he executive of the modern state is but a committee for managing the common affairs of the whole bourgeoisie." The state is more than that for several reasons. First, its own legitimacy depends upon the fact or appearance of serving the people. Second, concrete actions that appeal to one constituency, such as the pro-life conservatives, are bound to antagonize liberals and other conservatives (for example, some doctors, hospital and health-insurance managers). By attempting to find the least hazardous path through this thicket, the state is bound to act in ways that do not represent anyone. For example, in the Doe case the government did not intervene to save the baby, but to establish its own right to review medical records. Third, in the near impossible task of trying, or claiming, to represent all groups, the state develops its own distinct interests in legitimacy and political support.

PART II
STATE ACTION

During the first year of its operation in 1789, the U.S. government collected $5.72 million in revenues and spent $5.78 million. By 1982, the budget was $728 billion, which exceeded federal income by over $100 billion. Times had changed with 200 years of inflation and the expansion of the union from 13 to 50 states, but neither of those changes matches the budget, which increased 146,000 times over. What changed was the number of obligations the state had assumed. Moreover, much of the expansion occurred in recent years. Leaving aside periods of civil and world war when expenditures skyrocket, the greatest increases came in the 1930s and 1960s. Federal expenditures increased 1,000 percent between 1955 ($64 billion) and 1981 ($660 billion)—when inflation rose about 300 percent—and it doubled between 1976 and 1982.

A simple picture of federal finances is provided in Table 5–1. Of the $617 billion in 1982 revenues, most came from the combined sources of individual income and social security (insurance) taxes (almost $500 billion). Corporation income taxes amounted to 16 percent of what individuals paid and 8 percent of total revenues—figures down from the 30 percent and 14 percent respectively in 1979. By far the largest federal expenses are social (income) security ($248 billion); defense spending ($187 billion); and interest on the national debt ($100 billion).

In 1981, government at all levels employed 16 million people. A useful indicator of state expansion over time is the proportion of the total labor force employed by government. Table 5–2 shows how this has climbed steadily from 7 percent in 1900 to a high of 19 percent in 1975. That is, in 1975, nearly one employed person in every five worked for government, most of them at the state and local levels. Between 1975 and 1981, a time of recession and government fiscal strain, the percent of the labor force in government (though not the absolute number) dropped slightly from the 1975 high. The far right-hand column shows that the overall steady growth is punctuated by periods of rapid expansion: notably between 1930–40 (2.3 percent); 1950–60 (2.1 percent); 1960–70 (2.3 percent). From 1960 to the onset of decline in 1975, the increase was 3.7 percent.

TABLE 5-1 Summary of U.S. Government Receipts by Source and
Outlays by Function, Fiscal Years 1979 and 1982
(millions of dollars)

	1979	Percent	1982	Percent	Percent Difference
Net receipts					
Individual income taxes	$217,800	46.7	$298,111	48.3	+ 1.6
Corporation income taxes	65,700	14.1	49,207	8.0	– 6.1
Social insurance taxes and contributions	141,600	30.4	201,132	32.6	+ 2.2
Excise taxes	18,700	4.0	36,311	5.9	+ 1.9
Estate and gift taxes	5,400	1.2	7,991	1.3	+ .1
Customs duties	7,400	1.6	8,854	1.4	+ .2
Miscellaneous receipts	9,200	2.0	16,161	2.6	+ .6
Total	$465,900	100*	$617,766	100	
Net outlays					
National defense	117,700	23.8	187,397	25.7	+ 1.9
International affairs	6,100	1.2	9,983	1.4	+ .2
General science, space and technology	5,000	1.0	7,096	1.0	0
Energy	6,900	1.4	4,844	.7	– .7
Natural resources and environment	12,100	2.5	13,086	1.8	– .7
Agriculture	6,200	1.3	14,808	2.0	+ .7
Commerce and housing credit	2,600	.5	3,843	.5	0
Transportation	17,500	3.5	20,589	2.8	– .7
Community and regional development	9,500	1.9	7,410	1.0	– .9
Education, training, employment, and social services	29,700	6.0	25,411	3.5	– 2.5
Health	49,600	10.0	74,018	10.2	+ .2
Income security	160,200	32.4	248,807	34.2	+ 1.8
Veterans' benefits and services	19,900	4.0	23,973	3.3	– .7
Administration of justice	4,200	.9	4,648	.6	+ .3
General government	4,200	.9	4,833	.7	– .2
General purpose assistance	8,400	1.7	6,161	.9	– .8
Interest	52,600	10.7	100,777	13.8	+ 3.1
Undistributed offsetting receipts	– 18,500	—	– 29,261	—	
Total	$493,700	100	$728,424	100	

*Some columns total slightly more or less than 100 due to rounding error.
SOURCE: U.S. Treasury Department, Bureau of Government Financial Operations, 1980, 1983.

191

TABLE 5-2 Total Nonagricultural Labor Force and the Number (in thousands) and Percent Employed by Government

Year	Total	Federal government	State and local government	Total in government	% in government
1900	15,178	—	—	1,094	7.2
1910	21,697	—	—	1,636	7.5
1920	27,434	—	—	2,371	8.6
1930	29,434	—	—	3,148	10.7
1940	32,376	—	—	4,202	13.0
1950	45,197	1,928	4,098	6,026	13.3
1960	54,189	2,270	6,083	8,353	15.4
1970	70,880	2,731	9,823	12,554	17.7
1975	76,945	2,748	11,937	14,686	19.1
1981	91,543	2,772	13,282	16,054	17.5

SOURCE: *Handbook of Labor Statistics* (1983). (Table C–1); and *Historical Statistics of the United States.* U.S. Bureau of the Census.

From the combined tables, two conclusions are suggested. In the mid-20th century, state expansion proceeded at an unprecedented peacetime rate. Second, the times of greatest expansion coincided with social and economic unrest and its aftermath. Simplifying a bit, these were the times of depression and the equality revolution—periods followed by vast new state responsibilities that are reflected in the costs and personnel of government.

STATE AND ECONOMY

Yet the state did not grow in isolation. The same years witnessed an enormous expansion and concentration of the economy. The two went together. A pivotal book on the U.S. economy, by Paul Baran and Paul Sweezey (1966), describes it as *Monopoly Capitalism.* Those who object to the phrase recognize, nevertheless, that if many branches of industry and commerce are not strictly monopolized by single firms, there has been an inexorable trend toward *oligopoly* during the 20th century. This trend, like the growth of the state, has been steady, but also punctuated by periods of accelerated concentration. One of these occurred in the 1890s, another in the 1920s. The most dramatic shift toward oligopoly came in the post-World War II boom, roughly from the mid-1950s to 1970.

Taking a midpoint of these changes, in 1962 there were about 180,000 manufacturing corporations in the United States. Yet, of that very large number, just the 20 biggest firms owned 25 percent of *all* manufacturing assets; the largest 200 corporations (about one tenth of 1 percent of the total number) owned 56 percent of all the assets. Using a slightly different measure, in 1925 the 100 largest manufacturing firms held about one third of all manufacturing assets. That figure rose to 42 percent in the early 1930s when the trend slowed and was even reversed slightly. In the mid-1950s, it began moving upwards again such that by 1970 the 100 top corporations held one-half of all manufacturing assets. The same result is obtained by taking the top 500 firms or, say, all those with assets over $10 million. At present, more than 80 percent of all corporate wealth is held by about 1 percent of all firms (including banks and large retail firms along with manufacturers). Concentration has grown markedly during the 20th century, notably in periods of great prosperity.

The figures on growth and concentration indicate something quite opposite conventional wisdom or the myth of free enterprise. Two facts are especially striking. First, periods of prosperity (the 1920s and the postwar boom from the late 1940s to the early 1970s) do not lead to greater competition or to enhanced opportunities for small businesses but to greater concentration by the corporate giants—their invasion of new realms of the economy once reserved for local and family firms. During cycles of depression (the 1930s and late 1970s to early 1980s), the largest firms have trouble and competition is restored slightly. Second, the expansions of state and economy are not opposed to each other, big government does not hamper business expansion. On the contrary, big business and big government foster each other. This is suggested by their coincident historical timing in which state expansion follows closely on periods of economic concentration.

The principal reason for state expansion has been its widening role in the economy. State intervention in the economy is aimed at promoting the conditions of general prosperity, meaning, specifically, the conditions of stability and continuing economic growth. Doubtless, the state does many things that widen its role in society, such as supporting the arts, leisure, or basic research, but its efforts to regulate the economy account for most of the expansion. In the United States and Western European countries the economy, of course, means an advanced capitalist economy. As Ralph Miliband's (1969) book *The State in Capitalist Society* argues, state intervention in these countries has a very specific purpose:

> State intervention in economic life in fact largely *means* intervention for the purpose of helping capitalist enterprise. In no field has the notion of the "welfare state" had a more precise and apposite meaning than here: there are no more persistent and successful applicants for public assistance than the proud giants of the private enterprise system. (Ralph Miliband, *The State in Capitalist Society,* p. 78)

Yet the tasks of helping capitalist enterprise or ensuring the conditions of prosperity are much more involved than simply providing tax breaks to big business or lavishing a huge chunk of the federal budget on defense industries. The key to understanding the state's expanding role in the economy is in providing the *conditions of stability and continuing growth.* As we have seen, these conditions include: the provision of mass education and a skilled work force, the physical infrastructure of transportation and energy, a population sufficiently prosperous to provide a home market of consumer demand, a global presence that ensures foreign markets and raw material supplies, support for scientific and technical innovation, labor peace, and mechanisms for dealing with the unfit or the casualties of economic competition (the disabled, unemployed).

The defining feature of advanced capitalist society is that these responsibilities, once shouldered by individual firms and local philanthropies, are now awesomely beyond the capacity of private initiative. The state is the only body big enough and generally accepted for this role. This proposition, which is plausible at face value, is made even more obvious by the history of those periods of accelerated state expansion.

One of the few laws of history is the cyclical pattern of capitalist development—the long waves of prosperity and recession that the Russian economist N.D. Kondratieff discovered dating back to the late 18th century. Although economists and historians (including Kondratieff) cannot explain it, this 50-year cycle has been recurring on a worldwide scale from the 1780s down to the recession and crisis of the 1980s. Among other things, the cycles seem to occur with major wars at their peaks followed by a primary recession, a short recovery blip, and a long secondary depression. For present purposes, state expansion accelerates during these troughs devoted to re-creating the conditions for prosperity.

In recent U.S. history, the great eras of protest and reform corresponded to the cycle; Populism and the Progressive Movement belonged to a crisis around the turn of the century, the New Deal and equality revolution coincided with the Great Depression of the 1930s and its subsequent post-World War II recovery boom. By this I do not mean that protest and reform are caused by economic crises in any simple way, or that they are caused by what the state does to solve economic crises (a somewhat more plausible alternative if singular explanations were sought). Rather, I mean that the occasions for a new role of the state begin with the general problem of how to restore social stability and economic growth in a new set of circumstances.

The historical argument cannot be provided in detail here and, indeed, has been the subject of many excellent books. Concerning the progressive era, Gabriel Kolko's (1963) *The Triumph of Conservatism* and James Weinstein's (1968) *The Corporate Ideal in the Liberal State, 1900–1918* show that the foundations of the modern U.S. state were laid in the first two decades of this century with measures to regulate business enterprise. Particularly, the Federal Trade Commission and antitrust legislation were designed to restrain ruinous competition, the near monopolies of Standard Oil and a few railroads, but not to hamstring big business as a whole. On the contrary, the Progressive Era, including the urban reform movement aimed at big-city machine politics, fashioned a new form of political capitalism in which the general interests of business prevailed. Indeed, the major business associations were the architects of the new regulations designed to bring stable growth and social peace. The state regulated those interests (through interstate commerce rates and franchises) in an undertaking that also significantly expanded its own size and function.

More important from the standpoint of the sheer volume of state activity, if not for the precedent of intervention, was the response to the depression crisis of the 1930s. The New Deal

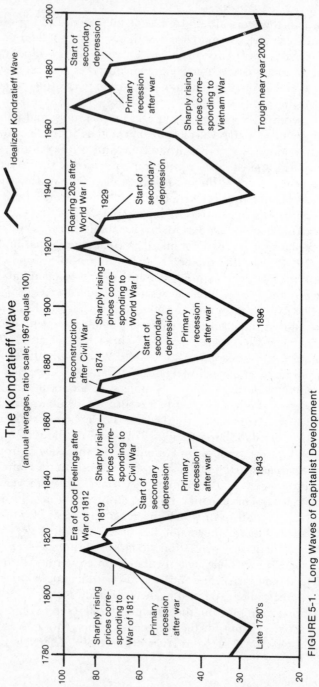

FIGURE 5-1. Long Waves of Capitalist Development

SOURCE: Media General Financial Weekly (1974)

created an important part of contemporary federal and state bureaucracy through the Social Security Act of 1935. The key feature of this legislation was its recognition that private charity could not handle the massive unemployment crisis of the 1930s (12–15 million people out of work representing well over one third of the labor force); that the federal government had to take responsibility for relief and for restoring confidence to business and agriculture. The social insurance programs that constitute the largest category of current federal expenditures (and the second largest category of taxes) began in 1935 and were expanded, for example, with medicare in the 1960s. The purpose of the New Deal, however, was less to create a "welfare state" than to restart the economy by providing relief, jobs, and consumer demand along with concessions to industry and labor. Once signs of recovery began to appear in the late 1930s, direct relief for the unemployed was converted to work relief, the wages for work relief were reduced so as not to appear more inviting than private employment where it existed, and relief or welfare was steadily redefined as shameful for all but the disabled, and poor mothers—and in practice it was even made shameful for them.

The central question in this discussion has been: What explains the growth of the state? One blunt answer is that the state expands in response to the demands of the economy, including both popular protest and financial crises. This is not the only answer, as we shall see below, and the relationship between state and economy is not one-directional. The state is both a source of private economic growth and a problem-solving response to conflicts generated in that growth. The state and economy thus merge in a way that makes it impossible to speak of one thing causing another. As Gabriel Kolko (1963) concludes his study:

> The crucial factor in the American experience was the nature of economic power which required political tools to rationalize the economic process, and that resulted in a synthesis of politics and economics. This integration is the dominant fact of American society in the twentieth century, although once political capitalism is created a dissection of causes and effects becomes extraordinarily difficult. (Kolko, *The Triumph of Conservatism: A Reinterpretation of American History, 1900–1916*, p. 301)

If that much of the argument has been demonst ated, the next question is, what are the implications of state expansion for social organization?

STATE AND SOCIETY

State influence is scarcely confined to the economy as the previous illustrations show. The state invades, or at least guards, the frontiers of social life. The question is less whether the state affects everyone's daily affairs than how and to what extent it transforms social organization. This could be answered in countless ways. I shall focus on two representative topics that bring the question close to home: family and school.

Invasion of the Family

Family sociology, once a rather dull backwater of the discipline, has lately become a lively and quarrelsome arena precisely because of competing claims about how the state has altered this venerable institution. The debate joins feminists, conservatives, and conventional family specialists. Many issues are captured in the compound question: Where is the family headed, toward dissolution or adaptation? Conservatives argue that it is in danger of losing its traditional role owing to permissive child rearing, two-career parents, or because of meddling in its province by social service agencies of the state. The last point is the theme of Christopher Lasch's (1977) popular book *Haven in a Heartless World: The Family Besieged,* a book that argues that "the family has been slowly coming apart for more than a hundred years" owing largely to a "tradition of sociological study" that reflects and shapes "the shattering impact of policy—the impact of the so-called helping professions—on the family" (p. xiv).

Feminists are split on the significance of recent changes, some of which are attributed to their own movement. The new conservative feminists (as Judith Stacey [1983] refers to the latest position of Betty Friedan and others) also believe that the family is threatened, perhaps by too much equality—that its nurturing and emotional support activities are disappearing as family structure is made a public issue by radical feminists. The latter argue that the family should and probably will survive, but in a new form, free of patriarchy and based upon real equality of the sexes.

Conventional family specialists often remain aloof to these quarrels. They claim that the basic nuclear family of husband, wife, and children has succeeded the extended family with many relatives living together. But the nuclear family itself has shown remarkable durability, persisting despite divorce, the generation gap, the sexual revolution, and the feminist movement. The family adapts to a changing environment, to the economy in particular, but does not change in the dramatic ways that conservatives bemoan or feminists desire.

As the debate goes on, family structure is changing. The typical family—composed of a married couple, minor children in the home, and one working spouse—in fact, is now a rarity. Only about 17 percent of all U.S. families fit this description. By the early 1980s, for example, 62 percent of all married couples had both husband and wife employed, up from 50 percent in 1970 and 40 percent in 1960. Most of the change is due to wives joining the labor force for the first time (Chapter 4) or returning to work after child-bearing, rather than any appreciable increase in the number of married couples. Between 1975 and 1979, the number of married couples increased by 2 percent, while the number of families with employed wives jumped 14 percent. Among married couples, 95 percent of the husbands work, as do 67 percent of the wives. Birth rates edged up in the early 1980s after a low ebb in the mid-1970s, but at least for the near future they will remain low by the standards of the immediate postwar decades. Similarly, marriage rates rose in the 1970s and early 1980s after unusual lows during 1955–65. Divorce rates have risen steadily throughout this century. The pattern, in sum, indicates that contemporary families are marrying, divorcing, remarrying, and working more so than in the past.

The nuclear family clearly persists, as family sociologists claim, but closer inspection reveals that it persists in a form rather different from what was once typical.

The special nature of today's nuclear family stands out when compared to earlier forms. If the two-career family is new in the annals of the nuclear family, the nuclear family itself is a product of recent history. In preindustrial societies, the family embraced a wide circle of relatives and household workers. Indeed, the household was the unit of economic activity, the site of the job, combining productive and reproductive functions. Peter Laslett's (1965) *The World We Have Lost* describes the preindustrial English household using as a prototype a London bakery where 14 people (including the baker, his wife, children, servants, journeymen, and apprentices) all lived and worked together.

> The only word used at that time to describe such a group of people was "family." The man at the head of the group, the entrepreneur, the employer, or the manager, was then known as the master or the head of the family. He was father to some of its members and in the place of father to the rest. There was no sharp distinction between his domestic and his economic function. His wife was both his partner and his subordinate, a partner because she ran the family, took charge of the food and managed the women servants, a subordinate because she was woman and wife, mother and in place of mother to the rest.
>
> The paid servants of both sexes had their specified and familiar position in the family, as much part of it as the children but not quite in the same position.... [T]he division of dwelling place and working place was no recognized feature of the social structure of the towns which our ancestors inhabited. The journey to work, the lonely lodger paying his rent out of a factory wages or office salary, are the distinguishing marks of our society, not theirs. (Peter Laslett, *The World We Have Lost*, pp. 2 and 14)

The English preindustrial family closely resembled patterns found throughout the Western world and especially in the colonial United States. In 1790 the average U.S. household contained 5.8 persons, by 1980 the figure had dropped to 2.8. The historical forces that altered that pattern to the nuclear and two-career family residing in a home distinct from the workplace are manifold and conveniently summarized in the master themes of industrialization and modernization. For present purposes, however, the state played an essential role in the transformation, perhaps a leading role.

The transformation involved a shift from large, multipurpose, and interdependent family units to small, single-purpose, self-supporting, and private ones. In effect, this meant that certain (but by no means all) family responsibilities were lost (or located elsewhere) as the new family responded to incentives to streamline itself. The state facilitated this transformation by creating institutional alternatives to family functions: public schools for the education of children, social insurance for support in old age or unemployment, relief and welfare for needy women and children, asylums for the ill, social workers and probation officers for the errant, public training and employment for the corrigible and able-bodied men.

The state had no conspiratorial aim in fostering policies that had the effect of transforming the more communal, extended family to the nuclear family—no conscious purpose to reduce and "privatize" the family as an end in itself. Rather, the modern state intended to reform social life in a manner consistent with economic growth and prosperity. The growing demands of the economy—such as mass education and a consumer society—as well as the perils of economic competition—such as recession and unemployment—overwhelmed the capacities of the traditional family. Specialized public institutions were best suited for these new tasks. Conversely, the nuclear family was a more efficient unit for producing and socializing children to assume their place in the social order.

As industry was rationalized for the production of mass consumption goods, the "privatized" household became the logical market for a standard set of necessary possessions—a set that was duplicated, expanded, and frequently replaced in each home. That fact is commonplace to any observer of family consumption patterns. What may be less obvious is that the state pioneered this materialistic frontier with policies that reshaped the family. The best example in contemporary U.S. history is housing. Through the Federal Housing Authority (FHA), GI loans, and their successors, the state subsidized with mortgage loans the massive suburbanization that made the single-family home a statistical and normative standard. In a typical year, the federal government spends on public housing a small fraction of the billions it allows in tax deductions for mortgage interest payments. The nuclear family has become a normative criterion underpinning social policy. As Eli Zaretsky (1982) concludes his analysis of this change, "'the family,' in the conventional sense of a private, self-supporting nuclear unit, was to a large extent created, or at least reconstituted, by the modern state" (p. 192).

Controversy over the nature and plight of the black family provides ironic support for this interpretation. In the fall of

1965, the federal government released a soon-to-become-famous study written by Daniel Patrick Moynihan (1965) entitled, *The Negro Family: The Case for National Action.* The Moynihan Report urged, on one hand, true equality for blacks, and reasoned, on the other, that the roots of inequality lay in the black family. Beginning with the depradations of slavery, the report argued, the black family has been abused in ways that produced a record and a culture of family failure. The record is found in high rates of divorce, desertion, illegitimacy, female-headed households, and welfare dependency. The culture of a mother-centered or matrifocal family purportedly causes high rates of delinquency, school dropout, drug use, unemployment, and so forth.

The record cited in the report is accurate and continues in the 1980s. The analysis, however, was sharply disputed, particularly the interpretation that a family culture somehow produced all that pathology. William Ryan, in his memorable phrase, called it "blaming the victim" and critical sociologists showed that there was really no direct connection between having been raised in a matrifocal family and individual delinquency or the rest. Delinquents (et cetera), including white youths, come from all sorts of families, but mainly from the poor and unemployed. Moreover, many poor families that have not experienced slavery (white and Hispanic) also show the statistical face of a matrifocal family. That is, the matrifocal family appears a pattern and plight of lower classes rather than particular status groups. Many believed that the analysis was wrong.

The lower-class black family has a distinctive profile that is more likely a result of poverty and inequality. It takes the form of high male unemployment, low-level occupations, and welfare codes that disqualify families with an able-bodied male in the household. In short, because of discrimination, black families do not enjoy equal access to consumer society or the protections and subsidies of the state. Important from an interpretive standpoint, middle-class black families that have gained such access conform to the nuclear family pattern.

Once again, that is not news. What is revealing, however, is the fact that blacks have developed their own community institutions and culture for coping defensively with a hostile state and environment, *including the extended family.* We have learned, from 1939 onward with the publication of E. Franklin Frazier's (1939) *The Negro Family in the United States*, that black families include centrally located grandparents, uncles and (especially) aunts, cousins, and friends that have "fictive kin" status—all knitted together in mutual support. Apropos of pathology, blacks have a lower suicide rate than whites because, if Durkheim's theory is right, they have a higher degree of group cohesion. As Frank Riessman (1966) says in his criticism of the Moynihan Report, "the Negro has responded to his oppressive conditions by many powerful coping endeavors. He has developed many ways of fighting the system, protecting himself, providing self-help and even joy. One of the most significant forms of his adaptation has been the extended, female-based family" (p. 475). The lower-class black family is the exception proving the rule of state influence on the nuclear family pattern.

Forming and Reforming the Schools

The social organization of schooling parallels in many ways the economy and family. Beyond intervention, since the late 19th century the state has taken major responsibility for the once private and family chores of education. Beyond responsibility, beginning with the Progressive Era at the turn of the century, the state has reorganized the nature of schooling in ways consistent with its general program of social reform. In *Education and the Cult of Efficiency*, Raymond Callahan (1962) shows that the key to school reform was in the pressure put on administrators to reorganize educational institutions in the likeness of business corporations—to make them run like factories and produce graduates fitted for their place in corporate and state bureaucracies.

Although school administrators had little sense of how factories operated, they obligingly adopted the familiar organization that seemed to suit the dictates of scientific management: compulsory schooling, regular long hours, required attendance, penalties for absenteeism and tardiness, standardized work (curriculum), time-budgeted instruction, performance ratings (grades), skills analysis (testing), an academic and vocational division of labor (tracking), earned promotion, a chain of command from classroom teacher to principal, dismissal for noncompliance with authority, and the broad ideological defense of these methods founded on the dogma of "achievement"—the certainty that educational performance determined occupational success and future earnings.

Higher education has not escaped these reforms. The state has influenced the character of education in colleges and universities beginning with the creation of the land grant college system, the GI bill that sent a new kind of student to college in the veterans of World War II, and the vital research and program funds that universities continue to receive from government. Among the consequences of this support, colleges and universities were encouraged, first, to maintain a program of research that served state-suggested public needs. Since the state reflects political pressures, this often meant the needs of private enterprise, such as the agribusiness agenda for land-grant colleges and their research, documented in Jim Hightower's (1972) book *Hard Times, Hard Tomatoes*. Second, it meant that a curriculum was designed to serve the occupational demands of the corporate and state economy—business and public administration, social work, engineering, education itself. The liberal arts took a backseat to the marketable areas of specialization. Today, something called general education (humanities, arts) fights a rear-guard action against such curiosities as a newly discovered computer science for a place in the curriculum.

Around 1970, a new plateau was reached in higher education as slightly over 50 percent of all high school graduates went on to college. Although an active military draft at the time encouraged the high figure, and the percentage slipped back a few points in subsequent years, the coming-of-age of the postwar baby boom marked a permanent change to mass higher education. For 20 years, from the mid-1950s to mid-1970s, community colleges, private and state colleges, and universities expanded (and overexpanded) to meet the new demand. With the laudable achievement of mass higher education, however, a crisis set in. The students were unhappy, even rebellious.

Although much of the rebellion was aimed at the Vietnam war and only happened to be staged on the campuses, educators correctly read a lesser theme of educational criticism in the student movement—including university war-related research. Tellingly, students described the university as an "education factory" and, in (former University of California President)

Clark Kerr's approving phrase, the "multiversity" became an epithet in dissident mouths. But the students were not the only ones unhappy. Some educators saw the mass invasion of the university as a threat to its standards, perhaps to its status, and often as the very cause of the unrest (beleaguered administrators tended to take all this personally and failed to see what a threat Vietnam was to participants in the student movement).

As is usually the case in higher education, the crisis called for a study. From 1967 to 1973, the Carnegie Commission on Higher Education labored over a multivolume answer to university ills. It made many recommendations, but their central thrust was to limit the numbers coming into the universities and to encourage a new division of labor in higher education by segregating ordinary training for the masses from research and advanced instruction for the privileged. In the commission's words:

> "Elite" institutions of all types—colleges and universities—should be protected and encouraged as a source of scholarship and leadership training at the highest levels. They should not be homogenized in the name of egalitarianism. Such institutions, whether public or private, should be given special support for instruction and research, and for the ablest graduate students; they should be protected by policies on differentiation of functions. (*Priorities for Action: Carnegie Commission on Higher Education, Final Report,* 1973, p. 30)

Samuel Bowles and Herbert Gintis (1976), after reviewing the commission's conclusion in *Schooling in Capitalist America,* ask, "Whatever became of equality of educational opportunity?" Obviously it did not fit with the new demands that the state and economy were placing on the elite universities—demands for new research, marketable technology, and advanced scientific training—least of all when the universities that should be doing this work were in the throes of political dissent. Better to shunt the average student (who the educational planners may have pictured, mistakenly, as more prone to political action) to the community college or the state college system. Indeed, the major state systems began implementing this recommendation. Students judged less promising were diverted to the community colleges or, as some called them, "the high schools with ashtrays." Whatever else it meant, in this case the less promising clearly included the less affluent and minorities, creating a new problem for universities trying to meet their affirmative action goals.

The justification for all this, Bowles and Gintis (1976) observe, was "starkly reminiscent of the arguments made for high-school stratification [i.e., vocational schools] during the progressive era" (p. 209).

Reforming the schools seems an insatiable urge. No sooner had higher education gotten used to the fallout of the Carnegie Commission bomb than a spate of warnings appeared about the deterioration of primary and secondary schools in the early 1980s. Best known, perhaps for its alarming title, is *A Nation at Risk: The Imperative for Educational Reform* prepared by a National Commission on Excellence in Education (three others produced by various task forces at about the same time were *Action for Excellence, Making the Grade,* and *Educating Americans for the 21st Century*). In each case, the condition of public education was described in ominous tones: "the educational foundations of our society are being eroded by a rising tide of mediocrity," "a real emergency is upon us," a "disaster." The language suggests that something catastrophic had occurred, a setback on the order of a Russian sputnik that prompted similar excitement in 1957.

The reports vary on precisely what had happened. Descriptions of the emergency ranged from falling test scores to apathetic or undisciplined kids. The crux of worry, however, jumps out of *A Nation at Risk* in the observation that education must stress excellence if we hope to "keep and improve the slim competitive edge we still retain in *world markets*" (italics added). In short, the looming disaster is economic and the sobering evidence of a narrowing competitive edge is not a Russian satellite but a galaxy of Japanese consumer goods. The connection is made clear in a set of comparisons showing how Japanese kids got smarter: they attend school 220 days a year against our 180; they spend three times as many hours studying science in high school; 95 percent of their high school students graduate versus 73 percent of ours. Accordingly, the recommendations that follow focus on a more demanding regimen of school routines and, particularly, a larger dose of scientific, technical, and computer training.

The critics, mostly public officials, business executives, school administrators, and professors, see another difficulty at the root of the disaster and any practical solution—namely, incompetent teachers. Allegedly, school teachers are recruited from the lower levels of college graduates and lack preparation for math and science teaching. A solution to that problem is envisioned in a master teacher program that rewards good teaching with pay differentials, although there is no clue as to how that teaching would be evaluated. Teachers become convenient scapegoats. No attention is given to class size, declining salaries, growing workloads, or what actually goes on in the classroom. The responsibilities of parents, school officials, and taxpayers play no part in the problem or its solution. Indeed, there is a striking similarity between the problem conceived materialistically as a disappearing competitive edge in world markets and the solution as monetary incentives for more spirited teaching performance.

In the end, it is the reports themselves that perform badly. Between the hyperbole and scapegoating, the basic analytic questions are not posed. Should a competitive edge in world markets be the aim of education? Are the Japanese doing well because of their schools (or because they make cars that don't fall apart)? If the United States has lost its competitive edge in world markets, how is that the fault of school kids and poorly paid teachers, rather than the business people who were in charge when it happened? If the schools are doing poorly, why not pay teachers more, give them paid leaves to learn new subjects, reduce class sizes and workloads, rather than giving incentive pay to a few who would introduce cutthroat competition into the schools?

Obviously, the answer to these questions is that the alternatives are costly. In the absence of any probing analysis or unflinching commitment of thought and money to education, the reports provide crass business sense. The recommended dominance of technical subjects in a new curriculum is a modern re-creation of the parody Charles Dickens gave us with Mr. Gradgrind's school of "the facts" in *Hard Times*. At bottom it is not only an exercise in blaming the schools for circumstances far beyond their control, it is one more illustration of how schooling is construed as a servant of the state and the economy.

For good or ill, the state's role in shaping the social organization of the family, school, and other institutional foci of our lives is decisive, if sometimes indirect. Social organization is changing in ways that affect and sometimes make uncomfortable individual lives—families become more isolated and less convivial, schools more bureaucratically regimented in competitive pursuit of material ends. Through these intermediaries, the state weighs on the individual. The root influence is a complex union of state and economy.

These developments summarize in a focused context what grand theories describe as the parallel evolution of bureaucracy and oligopolistic capitalism. This material portrays a pattern of reciprocal causation in which the economy generates crises due to its own competitive drive, the state responds to those crises with more adaptive policies that influence social organization (families and schools, for example). But the state also takes the lead by refashioning the institutional rules governing the economy, social life, and the state itself. The direction of these changes is not determined by the requirements of any one institution; not by economic conditions alone, for example. Rather, change is a result of interacting causes: institutional demands and social group conflicts. These principles are demonstrated in our final theme, the direction of change.

THE CRISIS OF THE STATE

Sociological theories have talked about the great transformation from community to society beginning with Durkheim and Tonnies, continuing through the once-fashionable notion of mass society, and resting today with the theory of the state. In that enterprise, the theories have lucidly portrayed the historical experience and a few have explained pieces of it. Marx was certainly right, and ahead of his time, when he analyzed the trend toward a concentration of capital. Weber added a key element left undeveloped by Marx when he argued that the state expanded "in a complete parallel to the development of capitalist enterprise through gradual expropriation of independent producers. In the end the modern state controls the total means of political organization."

In one essential respect, however, these grand theories mislead by failing to dwell on the conflicts that attend the process of centralization—conflicts that are important not simply because they may slow the pace of the process, but because they define the nature of its outcome. Concretely, this means that the family has not been eliminated by the state (or by the helping professions as Lasch (1977) maintains) or the schools made willing lackeys of the corporation (as Bowles and Gintis (1976) sometimes imply). Instead, families, schools, and many other institutional loci of human endeavor have felt the conflicts and resisted, struggled, acquiesced without enthusiasm, lost grudgingly, or generally responded in ways that also determine the emergent nature of social organization. All of these intermediate powers are altered, but not eliminated, and their alteration involves a struggle.

This generality takes substance in social organizational forms such as the lower class and black matrifocal family which illustrates how family and community steel themselves for self-defense, and even flourish, in a hostile setting. Frank Riessman's (1966) essay "In Defense of the Negro Family" observes that,

> In response to the deficiencies of the system the Negro has developed his own informal system and traditions in order to cope and survive. Storefront churches, the extended family, the use of the street as a playground, the block party, the mutual help of siblings, the informal know-how and self-help of the neighborhood, the use of peer learning, hip language, the rent strike and other forms of direct social action are just a few illustrations. (Frank Riessman, "In Defense of the Negro Family," pp. 477–78)

White families cope in other ways, such as cooperative schools and day care for two-career couples, new kinds of paid work within the home (the underground economy), house husbands, and experiments in communal living. The two-career family has not been eliminated and may even be facilitated by the maligned helping professions in matters of child care and extended-day schools, making it durable but different from the traditional nuclear family. Schools resist and adapt with new programs (many teachers have taken their own scarce time to learn the mysteries of computers), alternative schools, and perseverance in teaching old skills like writing, all despite corporate pressures. When the yoke of the state gets heavy, taxpayers revolt. Students revolt, demanding something different from what government and schools have offered and, in the cases of Vietnam and the "multiversity," they sometimes succeed. None of these responses can reverse the concentration of the state and economy, but together they mediate the impact of those forces on daily life.

Financial Crisis

The final irony in this long story of state power is that just as we have come to understand how the state has penetrated our institutions and communities, the state itself has fallen into a crisis of financing and of legitimacy. Its material capacity for intervention is drying up as fast as its conferred right. The fiscal crisis of the state is elegantly outlined in James O'Connor's (1973) book of the same title. Put simply, the expanded operation of the state, much of it in support of private enterprise, becomes too costly, particularly when profits from government assisted activities are privately appropriated. The growing costs of big government, new agencies to protect the environment, renew the cities, or finance private health care, are socialized in the sense of being created at taxpayer expense. Meanwhile, the private beneficiaries of these services profit, such as the doctors and hospitals whose social, insurance-supported costs have sky-rocketed. But there are limits, a political limit set by rebellious taxpayers and a structural limit posed by recession, such as the one that began in 1974 and precipitated the fiscal crisis.

From the mid-1970s onward, the state found itself faced with the need to cut back on services and personnel, beginning with services to the poor (social security payments, school lunches, eligibility under medicare). Much more than a temporary strain, the state began reversing the historical drift of expansion, began to shed some of its responsibilities by reprivatizing services. While that might have pleased many interests, the familiar problem was that the reorganization followed lines of class and status privilege.

Leafing back to Table 5–1, the effect of the fiscal crisis is evident in federal budget changes from 1979 to 1982. In just three years, the costs of government increased by one third (inflation was a large part of the increase, but O'Connor (1973) argues convincingly that inflation is also caused by the forces behind the fiscal crisis). The growing tax burden was shifted from corporations to individuals, and therefore to middle-income individuals who pay a disproportionate share. As a percent of total revenue, individual income taxes increased 1.6 percent, social insurance by 2.2 percent, and corporate taxes dropped 6.1 percent. Expenditures on corporate defense contracting increased (1.9 percent), along with the costs of income security, elevated by unemployment and recession. The biggest increase, however, was in interest on the national debt (3.1 percent) since the fiscal crisis was dealt with partly by new deficit spending. The other alternative, cutting state services to poor and middle-income groups, was pursued with greater force. Spending on education, training, employment, and social services was cut most (−2.5 percent), followed by lesser but cumulatively substantial reductions in programs for the environment, energy, transportation, community and regional development, veterans' benefits, and general purpose assistance (−4.5 percent in total).

A fair summary of the change is that lower-income people paid a greater share of state expenditures—which went disproportionately to the wealthy—and bore the brunt of reduced services. In part, this change reflects the contrasting values of the Carter and Reagan administrations. But the fiscal crisis is a deeper structural problem. It began five years before the Reagan administration (although several years elapsed before it was reflected in the budget) and similar social consequences appeared at the state and local levels. As the Kondratieff long waves suggest (Figure 5–1), particular administrations do not control these economic cycles as much as respond to them with a limited range of stylized policies.

Changes in state financing reflect the circumstance of crisis, rather than determine its direction. The more important qualitative shift of the 1980s is summarized in the awkward phrase "reprivatization." That is, a reversal of expanding state responsibility is taking place through actions that return certain functions to the private economy on a profit-making basis. Medical care has been provided mainly through private insurance plans, but recent efforts are aimed at reducing the coverage of medicare and hospital support in preference to profitable operations. Hospital ownership is rapidly turning into an oligopolistic industry controlled by three or four major health-care provider corporations. Corporate giants like Xerox, American Telephone and Telegraph, and General Electric are awarded government contracts to discover more efficient ways to operate school systems. The problems of the cities are turned over to urban-development corporations. The military is hiring private companies to do its maintenance work. These arrangements may, indeed, prove more efficient. The issue they raise, however, is whether the individual taxpayer should have to support them and what the equitable responsibility of the state is to its citizens.

Legitimacy Crisis

This raises the other side of the crisis of the state: its declining legitimacy in the eyes of the citizenry. Opinion polls over two decades show an eroding trust in government and in public officials—a trend going far beyond one fading Watergate. A fiscal crisis is not produced by disembodied structural forces, but by social unrest as evidenced in taxpayer revolts and ebbing consumer confidence. In growing unison, conservatives question the propriety of the welfare state and liberals doubt its equity. Nobody really knows where it is going.

Social scientists do know some important things. The state and economy, with all their effects upon social organization, must inevitably restructure themselves in the 1980s and 1990s. Some of the implications of this fact are discernible.

In the not-distant past, agriculture employed nearly half the population of the developed societies. Today the United States can feed itself and a good many others through the efforts of 3 percent of the population. More important, where industry once grew in a process that steadily incorporated a larger labor force, it now advances with labor-saving technology. The new computer technology requires less labor for its production. The central importance of these facts is that previously the distributional mechanisms of the state and economy were connected directly to the job. That is, the mechanisms that raised money for social programs such as Social Security and Unemployment Insurance and distributed those benefits according to eligibility criteria were based on the condition of long-term, steady, well-paid jobs throughout the economy.

As industry and profits expanded and concentrated, an improved standard of living *did* trickle down to the general population in the developed countries. State guarantees of social welfare were linked directly to employment or indirectly to the programs maintained by working people and by employers on a per capita worker basis. Now, however, with a precipitous decline in the number of jobs that are needed in the productive segments of the economy, the linchpin of the distributional mechanism falls out. In its absence, the only way to provide for the well-being of increasing numbers of people is through direct-transfer payments or what has been called welfare—a system that was never designed for large numbers and, indeed, was to be supported by a fully employed work force.

The final and noteworthy conclusion is that the welfare state, as it has been conceived, will not work in our technological future. The methods that solved social crises in the recent past are now impractical. This assessment implies several things about the immediate future: (1) state fiscal problems will continue beyond what some saw as only a temporary recession—government faces a longer term revenue squeeze; (2) this means continuing reductions in the services and programs the state has supported— reductions that will spread from the working classes and cost the middle classes in such fields as medical care; (3) together, the foregoing imply pitched political struggles over budgetary levels and what the state will support; (4) somewhere down the line a new mechanism for supporting the state will be developed in the political struggle and, although we cannot envision what that will be, it is safe to say that its terms will command the energies of policymakers in the coming decades.

In the short run, this means that we can anticipate growing inequalities that affect middle-income groups as well as the poor and minorities. The system will not reorganize itself simply through a demonstration of its contradictions. The meaning and occasion of structural crisis is found in the social crisis. The late 20th century is going to be a period marked by the same kind of social unrest and wholesale state reorganization that attended the Great Depression and New Deal crisis. When a solution is found, it will involve the state as a more intimate part of social organization.

SELECTED BIBLIOGRAPHY

BARAN, PAUL A. & SWEEZEY, PAUL M. (1966). *Monopoly Capital: An Essay on the American Economic and Social Order.* New York: Monthly Review Press.

BOWLES, SAMUEL & GINTIS, HERBERT (1976). *Schooling in Capitalist America: Educational Reform and Contradictions of Economic Life.* New York: Basic Books.

BROOM, LEONARD & SELZNICK, PHILLIP (1968). *Sociology.* (4th ed.). New York: Harper & Row.

CALLAHAN, RAYMOND E. (1962). *Education and the Cult of Efficiency: A Study of the Social Forces That Have Shaped the Administration of the Public Schools.* Chicago: The University of Chicago Press.

FRAZIER, E. FRANKLIN (1939). *The Negro Family in the United States.* Chicago: University of Chicago Press.

GALBRAITH, JOHN KENNETH (1967). *The New Industrial State.* New York: Signet Books.

KOLKO, GABRIEL (1963). *The Triumph of Conservatism: A Reinterpretation of American History, 1900–1916.* New York: Free Press.

LASCH, CHRISTOPHER (1977). *Haven in a Heartless World: The Family Besieged.* New York: Basic Books.

LASLETT, PETER (1965). *The World We Have Lost.* London: Methuen.

MILIBAND, RALPH (1969). *The State in Capitalist Society.* New York: Basic Books.

MOYNIHAN, DANIEL PATRICK (1965, March). *The Negro Family: The Case for National Action.* Office of Policy Planning and Research, U.S. Department of Labor. Washington, DC: U.S. Government Printing Office.

O'CONNOR, JAMES (1973). *The Fiscal Crisis of the State.* New York: St. Martin's Press.

PIVEN, FRANCES FOX & CLOWARD, RICHARD A. (1971). *Regulating the Poor: The Functions of Public Welfare.* New York: Vintage Books.

Priorities for Action: Carnegie Commission on Higher Education, Final Report (1973). New York: McGraw-Hill.

RIESSMAN, FRANK (1966, March–April). "In Defense of the Negro Family." *Dissent,* 266–267. In LEE RAINWATER & WILLIAM L. YANCEY (Eds), *The Moynihan Report and the Politics of Controversy* (pp. 474–478). Cambridge, Mass.: MIT Press.

RYAN WILLIAM (1976). *Blaming the Victim.* New York: Random House.

STACEY, JUDITH (1983, Fall). "The New Conservative Feminism." *Feminist Studies, 9,* 559–583.

WEINSTEIN, JAMES (1968). *The Corporate Ideal in the Liberal State, 1900–1918.* Boston: Beacon Press.

WOLFE, ALAN (1974, Winter). "New Directions in the Marxist Theory of Politics." *Politics and Society, 4,* 131–159.

ZARETSKY, ELI (1982). "The Place of the Family in the Origins of the Welfare State." In BARRIE THORNE & MARLYN YALOM (Eds.), *Rethinking the Family: Some Feminist Questions* (pp. 188–224). London: Longman.

6

Country and City

Strip mining brought jobs and a temporary boom to Appalachia, but destroyed farms and pushed once independent mountain people off the land and into the "little Kentucky" slums of Cincinnati, Baltimore, Chicago, and Detroit. (© Arthur Tress)

PART I

THE NATURE OF URBANIZATION

Hillbillies tell one of the diagnostic stories of urbanization. They tell it literally in oral histories of their experience and figuratively in what they represent as a social category. If we hope to understand the process that transforms rural societies into urban-industrial worlds, we must be able to explain the fate of hillbillies and similar people.

Urbanization, the growing concentration of a population in cities, is a story of the displacement and social reorganization of people: farmers, immigrants, small-town folk, and the colorful but disappearing breeds of lumberjacks, miners, and cowboys. The story of hillbillies is a revealing cross section of this process; an experience of traditional rural independence, regional despoliation, struggle for a self-sufficient way of life, and defeat at the hands of a centralizing corporate society. In many ways, the history of hillbillies parallels the transformation of North America summarized in the master process of urbanization. An imaginary line connecting the first British explorations of the Carolina coast in the 1580s and urban life in the 1980s would run straight through the society of southern Appalachia.

A sociological understanding of this experience begins by reflecting on the term "hillbilly." In its present general usage, the term refers derisively to people of the Southern mountain regions; their alleged rascality, lack of culture and education, loose morals, fondness for alcohol, clanishness, and penchant for living in the trash-infested "little Kentuckys" of Northern cities. With the exception of a slumming indulgence of hillbilly music, the popular image is pejorative. That stereotype, however, is recent and at odds with the regional origins of the term.

As late as 1900, the *New York Journal* felt obliged, with some indifference to geography, to inform its readers that "a Hill-Billie is a free and untrammelled white citizen of Alabama, who lives in the hills, has no means to speak of, dresses as he can, talks as he pleases, drinks whiskey when he gets it, and fires off his revolver as the fancy takes him." Yet the term has a longer and more complimentary provenance. Southern Appalachia (the Virginias and Carolinas, Eastern Kentucky and Tennessee, and

Northern Georgia) was populated beginning in the late 17th century by British escapees and freed bondsmen from the Eastern seaboard plantations. The hardy survived in this wilderness by adopting the ways of their Choctaw and Shawnee Indian neighbors—clothes made from the skins of game they hunted, the tomahawk, and Indian corn which they grew and distilled with the Scottish whiskey brewer's skill. Like Daniel Boone, they lived in family clans no closer than sighting distance of their neighbors' chimney smoke. British fondness for the name William, Bill, and the diminutive Billy provided the eponym for the society of hill people—"hillbillies" in local parlance was the affectionate counterpart of the "mountainmen" and women who earned the nation's esteem in the Revolutionary War.

As the rustic and insular society prospered, the more successful river-bottom agriculturalists acquired a few slaves and became merchants. Incipient classes and neighbors were divided by the Civil War: yeomen farmers and frontiersmen siding with the Union and prosperous farmer-merchants with the Confederacy. Legendary feuds began with the depredations and vendettas of the war, imposed as they were on an austere and clan-centered society. Whiskey production was the only source of cash income and commerce with the external world. Indeed, the isolation and feuding of kinship clans led to inbreeding and a small factual basis for the image of mental retardation. As the *New York Journal* piece suggests, however, the ridiculing hillbilly stereotype was still ill-formed in 1900.

Apparently the shift in the nation's esteem from mountainman to hillbilly occurred with the growing commercial contact between Appalachian society and the industrializing Midwestern and Northern cities. In the 1870s, national demand for hardwoods brought timber buyers into the mountains who dealt the guileless frontier people out of their forests. Later, particularly from 1912–27, rapacious coal companies bought mineral rights for trifling sums and converted hillbillies into rent-paying, commissary-indebted miners living in company towns. No wonder that mountain people, lured by the opportunity for a regular cash income exceeding anything they had known, came to be called dumb hillbillies by the industrial North. Now the stereotype flourished with the lovable morons of the Lil' Abner comic strip, the querulous Hatfields and McCoys, the fatuously clever

"Beverly Hillbillies" of television, and the barbarians in James Dickey's novel and film, *Deliverance.*

The Southern Appalachian coal boom was stilled by the Great Depression, but out-migration was small simply because there was no place to go for a job. Instead, the relief came to the mountains and stayed, converting the once independent frontier into an enclave of welfare dependency. The mines revived during World War II, but afterwards they were increasingly mechanized. Successful struggles by the United Mine Workers from the 1930s onward encouraged the now-conglomerate coal companies to eliminate as many miners and company towns as possible. So began the mass exodus to the "little Kentuckys" in Baltimore, Cincinnati, Chicago, Detroit, and points beyond. Harry Caudill's (1962) masterful *Night Comes to the Cumberlands* observes, "The same industry which required seven hundred thousand men to provide the nation's coal in 1910 was able to provide all of the same fuel required by a vastly larger nation in 1958 with fewer than two hundred thousand men" (p. 263). With the introduction of strip mining in the 1950s, most of the remains of a culture were bulldozed away with the coal, soil, towns and people.

Southern Appalachian migrants found jobs in the cities to the north, but not better lives. Families and women were strained by the confinement of working-class neighborhoods, as Harriet Arnow's (1954) novel *The Dollmaker,* about a Kentucky family in Detroit, showed. Jobs were often scarce, temporary, and poorly paying for those equipped, if at all, with a miner's skills. In a collection of interviews by Todd Gitlin and Nanci Hollander (1970), *Uptown: Poor Whites in Chicago,* hillbillies tell their own stories. John Dawson, who found work through "labor [contracting] companies" describes employment conditions:

> They's a poor class of people that come to Chicago and come to different cities like Detroit, Chicago, New York, Los Angeles, and places like this that they thought that when they got there that they could just walk in and get a job of work that would pay 'em big money, but places like these slave-labor markets hurt a lot of those people trying to make a decent living for their families. There's a lot of people that comes here with a family and they find out they can't get a job where they can make a living and don't have enough money to pay for theirselves. All right, they hop over here and they think, "Well, I can make a living in this place here," and they don't

know that the place is only paying one-twenty-five, one-thirty an hour till they get out there. Well, in fact they wind up with about a dollar an hour when they get off the job. They cain't feed their family. Well, they get the attitude, the hell with it, and that's the cause of a lot of people from the South that just don't give a damn....

It wasn't like it is back home. Most of the class back home, you walk in a plant whether they know you or not and if they give you a job you can explain to the personnel manager that you had to have some money at the end of the week or had to have some money the next day after you work. Well, he would make arrangements for you to get money to live on till you drawed a payday. Well, these plants here won't do that, for they've got this cutthroat with these slave-labor markets here, they get their labor to them much cheaper. (Todd Gitlin and Nanci Hollander, *Uptown: Poor Whites in Chicago*, pp. 90–91)

Dawson lived in an Uptown apartment where the landlord failed to provide heat and where Dawson's child contracted lead poisoning from paint peelings. After a fight with the landlord, he moved to another apartment.

At that time we had a nice manager there, when we moved in. We stayed there about four months, very nice manager. This woman she was from Kentucky, had some kind of sickness and the doctors advised her to go back to a different climate, you know. And she left and went to a different climate. So they got one of these damn smart-asses in to manage the buildin'. And she had the attitude that Southern people were all dogs. So I had the attitude that she was just a sonofabitch. And I just told her there in the hall one afternoon, she was runnin her damn mouth, and I just told her in the hall, I said, "Well, what in hell you think you're talking to?" I said, "I ain't no dog." I said, "I'm makin more money right now than you make." I said, "I ain't askin for a damn thing." I said, "I ain't got to rent in this buildin." (Todd Gitlin and Nanci Hollander, *Uptown: Poor Whites in Chicago*, p. 84)

Hillbilly migration was just one stream that joined a current of blacks, Hispanics, motley immigrants, and other poor whites. The United States became a rapidly urbanizing society during the decades around the turn of the century. In the *Grapes of Wrath*, John Steinbeck (1939) described the migratory flight of people from Oklahoma's Dust Bowl in the depression years. Okie tenant farmers, evicted "under the tractor's blade," took to the highways. "Highway 66 is the main migrant road...the path of a people in flight, refugees from dust and shrinking land, from the thunder of tractors and shrinking ownership" (pp. 127–28).

Hillbillies and Okies describe one important side of the urbanization story, but certainly not the only side. Other people from comfortable circumstances were drawn to the cities by hopes of social mobility. Flights from oppression by Russian Jews, or from famine by Irish peasants, combined with the English weavers' pursuit of opportunities to ply their acquired industrial skills or, in the phrase of U.S. sojourners from small towns, to "get into something."

Whatever the group motives for migration, urbanization fundamentally reorganizes individual and social life. The seemingly neutral urbanization process generalizes a great many forces that break up rural societies and shape the emerging cities in decisive ways. Understanding that process requires a close examination of the conditions that produce urbanization, rather than exclusive attention to what happens to people once they reach the city. City and countryside help explain one another— there is no adequate urban sociology apart from a rural sociology. The hillbilly experience, for example, encapsulates an important part of the meaning of urbanization and urban life. Urbanization is a process, a global process and the hallmark in many ways of the modern world. But it is also an abstraction built from the uprooting experience of hillbillies, Okies, peasants, workers, and sojourners around the world.

URBANIZATION

Urbanization refers to the *redistribution* of a population, a shift in the proportion living in cities rather than in villages and rural areas. Urbanization, therefore, involves a distributional change in the population of some geopolitical unit—whether that unit is a country, a state, or the world as a whole. Since urbanization is defined by the shifting percentage of a population residing in cities versus rural areas, its measurement requires specification of what constitutes a city. This is no simple matter since the notion of a city conveys something physical (the size and density of a population) and something social (an urban culture or way of life). The issue needs treatment in two parts, beginning here with a description of urbanization as a worldwide population phenomenon. The next section focuses on how sociology conceives of urbanism as a social form.

Two facts about the modern world, and particularly the 20th century, distinguish it from much of recorded history: It is predominantly an urban world and it got that way rapidly. Demographers, who study populations and their changes, have used two standards for measuring world urbanization. The first is a fixed standard applied to all countries. Defining urban places as settlements with 20,000 or more inhabitants, in the year 1800 just 3 percent of the world's population was urbanized. During the 19th century, largely as a result of industrialization, this began to change, affecting first the more developed parts of the globe in Europe and North America. In the 20th century this change accelerated. The demographer Kingsley Davis (1955) puts it pointedly:

> Compared to most other aspects of society—e.g., language, religion, stratification, or the family—cities appeared only yesterday, and urbanization, meaning that a sizable proportion of the population lives in cities, has developed only in the last few moments of man's existence. (Kingsley Davis, "The Origin and Growth of Urbanization in the World," p. 429)

Table 6–1 shows that in 1920 there were 266 million people (of the then-total world population of 1.84 billion) living in cities of 20,000 or more. Most of these were in the more developed or industrialized regions. This absolute number represented 14.3 percent of the world's population. The more developed regions had 29.4 percent of the populations in cities and the less developed regions 5.8 percent.

From 1920 to 1975 enormous changes took place. In just 55 years the total world urban population doubled (from 1.86 to 3.94 billion) while the urban population increased well over four times (from 266 to 1,169 million). This combination meant that in percentage terms the world's urban population increased from 14.3 to 29.7 percent. The more developed areas, led by North America, passed the 50 percent mark in urbanization while the less developed areas, led by Latin America, urbanized even faster—although they started from and reached lower overall levels (from 5.8 to 20.3 percent). From 1800 to 1970, world population increased four times, but the number living in cities increased 50 times over. As a result, the urban population of

TABLE 6-1 World Urban Population and Population Growth Based on the Fixed Standard of Urban Places Comprising 20,000 or More Inhabitants, by Region: 1920-75.

	1920	1930	1940	1950	1960	1970	1975
World population total (absolute numbers				(Percentages)			
in billions)	(1.86)	(2.07)	(2.30)	(2.52)	(2.99)	(3.58)	(3.94)
World urban total (absolute numbers							
in millions)	(266)	(338)	(432)	(533)	(760)	(1,010)	(1,169)
World total	14.3	16.3	18.8	21.2	25.4	28.2	29.7
More developed major areas	29.8	32.8	36.7	39.9	45.6	49.9	52.1
Europe	34.7	37.2	39.5	40.7	44.2	47.1	48.2
Northern America	41.4	46.5	46.2	50.8	58.0	62.6	65.4
Soviet Union	10.3	13.4	24.1	27.8	36.4	42.7	46.4
Oceania	36.5	38.0	40.9	45.7	52.9	57.9	57.1
Less developed major areas	6.9	8.4	10.4	13.2	17.3	20.4	22.2
East Asia	7.2	9.1	11.6	13.8	18.5	21.7	23.7
South Asia	5.7	6.5	8.3	11.1	13.7	16.0	17.4
Latin America	14.4	16.8	19.6	25.1	32.8	37.8	40.5
Africa	4.8	5.9	7.2	9.7	13.4	16.5	18.1
More developed regions	29.4	32.6	37.0	40.0	46.0	50.5	52.8
Less developed regions	5.8	7.0	8.6	11.4	15.4	18.5	20.3

SOURCE: W. Parker Frisbie (1977), The scale and growth of world urbanization. In John Walton and Donald E. Carns (Eds.), *Cities in change* (2d ed.). Boston: Allyn & Bacon.

1970 was larger than the entire world population of the early 19th century. Moreover, the world's urban population doubled between 1920 and 1950; and it doubled again in the shorter span from 1950 to 1975.

Table 6–2 introduces the second, variable standard that demographers use to measure world urban population. Here "urban" means those places that nations themselves consider cities. The evident result of this self-defined standard is to raise the percentages (for example from 14.3 to 19 percent urban in 1920). Another difference in Table 6–2 is that past trends are used to estimate urban population growth through the year 2000. The results are bracing, but not incredible. Although the percentages are higher than those in Table 6–1, the trend is much the same: a steady increase in worldwide urbanization, led

TABLE 6-2   Estimated Percentages of Urban Population as Nationally Defined, in the Total Population of the World and Major Areas, 1920, 1940, 1960, 1980, and 2000

Major Area	1920	1940	1960	1980	2000
World total	19	25	33	46	51
More developed areas	40	48	59	70	80
Europe	46	53	58	65	71
Northern America	52	59	70	81	87
Soviet Union	15	32	49	68	85
Oceania	47	53	64	75	80
Less developed major areas	10	14	23	32	43
East Asia	9	13	23	31	40
South Asia	9	12	18	25	35
Latin America	22	31	49	60	80
Africa	7	11	18	28	39
More developed regions	39	47	60	71	81
Less developed regions	8	12	20	30	41

SOURCE: *Growth of the World's Urban and Rural Population, 1920-2000.* United Nations, Department of Economic and Social Affairs, Population Studies, No. 44.

by the developed areas, and a narrowing gap between the more and less developed. In both tables, the 1920 figures show the developed regions roughly five times more urbanized. By 2000, the difference will be just double. If the estimate is right, by the year 2000 the less developed areas will be as urbanized as the industrialized world was in the 1950s.

Urbanization, therefore, is a massive, world process that uproots people and reorganizes societies. It suggests that an ensemble of new and adaptive experiences, including the hillbilly's, characterizes millions of people in recent history and at present. Urbanization also refers broadly to the advent of a new kind of society, economy, and culture. But what kind?

THE CITY

The nature of the city and the social meaning of urbanism have always engaged sociologists. Lively debates focus on whether urbanism represents a society coercively organized according to the needs of capitalist economic development and, therefore, an experience of personal alienation from traditional bonds; or a new culture of liberation from rural and small-town parochialism—the touchstone of modernity. For some, urbanism is a segmented and impersonal way of life, for others, a blessed toleration of diversity. From debates and research prompted by such questions, a coherent urban sociology has emerged, based on the classical tradition and recent accomplishments in urban political economy.

Defining Features

What is a city? The meaning of that term is far from obvious. Cities have existed for perhaps 5,000 years, or so the legends and archeological remains of the Middle East suggest. Cities were the centers of great civilizations in Egypt, Mesopotamia, India, and Mayan Central America before the rise of Athens, Rome, and the other European latecomers to the urban world. Is there a conception of the city that embraces these historical forms and the modern metropolis?

Max Weber (1969) posed this question in an essay on the nature of the city. He noted the existence of many definitions that "have only one element in common: namely that the city consists simply of a collection of one or more separate dwellings but is a relatively closed settlement" (p. 23). Most definitions center on the size and density of a settlement, but Weber rightly observed that "in terms of what it would include and what it would exclude size alone can hardly be sufficient to define the city" (p. 23). For example, small but densely settled commercial centers could be excluded and large sprawling settlements included by this standard. Instead, Weber looked to the *activities* of cities as the hallmark of their distinctive characteristics. Of these he discovered three.

First, cities are settlements where there is a regular exchange of goods. "The market becomes an essential component in the livelihood of the settlers" (p. 24). No settlement could be called a city unless its inhabitants possessed a local market which met their daily needs with locally produced or acquired goods. "In the meaning employed here, *the 'city' is a market place*" (italics added, p. 24).

Although economic activity is a necessary component of the definition, alone it is incomplete. "The mere fact that merchants and tradesmen live crowded together carrying on a regular satisfaction of daily needs in the market does not exhaust the concept of the city." Second, and historically, cities have also been the locus of *political and administrative authority* over the urban hinterland, and that authority is used in ways that ensure the prosperity of the local market. In Weber's words, the "politico-administrative aspects are conceptually fused with pure economic aspects and conceived as forming one whole" (p. 30). Indeed, the fusion of market and political authority is essential for the city's survival, growth, and prosperity. Cities characteristically develop practices for dealing with the countryside that include "regulations in the interests of permanently and cheaply feeding the masses and standardizing the economic opportunities of tradesmen and merchants" (p. 31).

With reference to the first two activities, Weber spoke of "the city as the fusion of fortress and market...the politically oriented castle and economically oriented market" (pp. 35–36). The third element is a population of citizens who enjoy rights and status of their association, what Weber called the "urban community." The urban citizenry are united in a corporate unit administered by authorities whom they elect.

In sum, a city has three defining features: market, administrative center, and community. The virtue of Weber's definition is the fusion of demographic (population) and economic conditions with a special form of association, or community, and the recognition that these become fused in political activity. Cities do not simply well up on the land. They are created by groups of people with political and economic goals. This should be the central proposition of any urban sociology and the fact that it has sometimes been forgotten has only meant that it is periodically rediscovered, most recently in a renewed emphasis on urban political economy.

If Weber was right, the rapid, even revolutionary, changes in world urbanization must have produced far-reaching changes in economy, politics, and social organization. Specifically, political and administrative practices must have been devised to regulate the urban marketplace and to organize the urban community. Urban social research in the early 20th century, however, understood this only vaguely. The sociological study of cities did not begin with any clear or singular conception of its subject. Much of that research was produced in the United States where Weber's ideas were slow in gaining recognition.

Urban Ecology

More important, the pragmatic North Americans focused on urban social problems which had a special urgency about them in the political and intellectual climate of Progressivism (Chapter 2). A rich and energetic urban sociology developed in this setting; particularly, in Chicago where reform-minded researchers gathered at Hull House, the University of Chicago, and in the city's motley ethnic neighborhoods. The Chicago sociologists had a natural laboratory and a purpose. Some of their work was scientifically pretentious or conceptually misplaced, but it began to provide the raw material from which our current understanding is fashioned.

One wing of the Chicago school pursued a scientific description of basic urban forms and processes. In search of a proper metaphor from the physical sciences, Robert Park and Ernest Burgess (1925) hit on the notion of ecology—which means the science of relationships between organisms and their environment. They proposed an urban ecology in which the city landscape, perhaps even its institutions and ways of life, could be understood as adaptations to the environment. In this naturalistic metaphor, the city is an agglomeration of people in space governed by ecological processes. Human communities perform in a spatial setting the essential functions for survival such as production, distribution, and consumption. The form and life of the city arise from processes of dominance and competition that govern the functions.

Illustratively, Park and Burgess depicted the city as a set of concentric circles and zones: the innermost devoted to business and commerce, industry and worker housing in the next zones of transition, followed by a ring of middle-class neighborhoods, and upper-class residences at the periphery. Whether or not the picture fitted precisely every city, the point was that urban life could be explained by ecological competition over land use and function.

After unsuccessful efforts to find a similar land-use pattern in cities other than Chicago, new models were proposed. A sector theory said that the concentric rings were sometimes cut by wedges that form as cities grow and, particularly, as the lower class moves into areas abandoned by the upper class fleeing the city's bustle to the outer rings or suburbs. A "multiple nuclei"

FIGURE 6-1. Three Models of City Growth

SOURCE: C.D. Harris, & Edward L. Ullman (1945, November). The nature of cities. *The Annals, 242*, 7–17.

theory countered that urban growth leads to a patchwork of specialized zones rather than a geometric design; some activities benefit from contiguity and others want insularity. Different models seemed to fit different cities and histories of urban growth, casting doubt on the explanations given for the generality of each. Underneath all these portraits, however, was the basic (some even said the subsocial) idea that urban form obeyed certain physical or economic *forces*—that it followed a general process governed by dominance and competition.

With its appearance of rigor and tangible results, urban ecology continued to have a strong impact until research began attacking its conceptual foundations. While some research offered more refined land-use models, other work claimed to uncover specific causes for variety in the urban landscape. For example, an important study by Everett C. Hughes (1928), a Burgess student, observed that Chicago did, indeed, have a clear-cut land-use pattern, but one did not have to resort to mysterious, subsocial forces to explain it. The pattern reflected instead the interests and political muscle of the Chicago Real Estate Board. Business influence and realtor practices determined which zones were set aside and promoted for specific uses—including where the lower classes and minorities should live and where they were prevented from living. To the surprise of no informed citizen, city politics had more to do with urban structure than ecological competition. Another study of Boston noted that "sentiment and symbolism" were the reasons for maintaining the Boston Commons park in the middle of prime urban real estate and an exclusive residential area in the heart of the city. The urban form is determined in a market of property values, but that market is decisively affected by politics, civic values, and, no doubt, by conflicts between those two.

In short, research along the lines of Weber's ideas about the marketplace, political control, and the urban community appears more discerning than other accounts based on population growth and naturalistic metaphors. The notion of an urban ecology was appealingly simple and stimulated a great deal of informative descriptive work. Its drawback was a failure to *explain* anything, and that stemmed from its retreat into the vagaries of some supposed "master process" (here, dominance and competition). This is not to say that the research of the early, ecologically minded urban sociologists was wrong. Only that it needed to be fitted to a different explanatory model, one that was only beginning to emerge at the time.

Urbanism

Another related wing of the Chicago school of urban studies was advanced by W.I. Thomas, Park himself, and, preeminently, by Louis Wirth (1938). Wirth was part of the generation of progressive reformers in Chicago during the early 20th century and his special interest was in the social psychology of city life—"urbanism as a way of life," in his words. Wirth took one leaf from Weber's book by defining "the city as a particular form of human association." His influential view of what human association involved in the urban setting was that,

Characteristically, urbanites meet one another in highly segmented roles. They are, to be sure, dependent upon more people for the satisfaction of their life-needs than are rural people and thus are associated with a greater number of organized groups, but they are less dependent upon particular persons, and their dependence upon others is confined to a highly fractionalized aspect of the other's round of activity. This is essentially what is meant by saying that the city is characterized by secondary rather than primary contacts. The contacts of the city may indeed be face to face, but they are nevertheless impersonal, superficial, transitory, and segmental. The reserve, the indifference, the blasé outlook which urbanites manifest in their relationships may thus be regarded as devices for immunizing themselves against the personal claims of others. (Louis Wirth, "Urbanism as a Way of Life," pp. 152–53)

Wirth equated this condition with Durkheim's description of anomie. Yet, as he went on to describe the effects of urban density and heterogeneity, he noted that "different parts of the city acquire specialized functions, and the city consequently comes to resemble a mosaic of social worlds in which the transition from one to the other is abrupt. The juxtaposition of divergent personalities and modes of life tends to produce a relativistic perspective and a sense of toleration..." (p. 155). There is a deliberate irony in Wirth's description of urban life. Urbanites are involved with more people and groups than rural folk, although that involvement is divided into many specialized relationships, none especially deep. Such, however, is the cost of toleration, or freedom from the oppressive parochialism of rural life.

When Wirth generalized his social psychology to the urban landscape, the result was a similar variety of segmented communities. The many segmented roles of the individual urbanite had a direct parallel in the specialized communities that comprised the city And the parallel extended further with the inference that segmentation produced ill effects. Specialized, but fragile, institutions took over industrial, educational, and recreational activities causing "the weakening of bonds of kinship, the disappearance of the neighborhood, and the undermining of the traditional basis of social solidarity" (p. 160). Wirth envisioned what later writers would call a mass society, including a strong connection between "virtual impotence as an individual" and the appeal of mass movements.

Wirth stimulated a great deal of research with his provocative ideas and confident assertion that "all these phenomena can be substantially verified through objective indices" (p. 160). The overwhelming result of that research, however, is that urbanites are not the segmented, anomic beings he described. On the contrary, they have ties to local community institutions, a neighborhood life mirrored by the community press, and geographically extended networks of "primary contacts." Urbanism, in short, is a much more engaging and social way of life than the pessimistic theory suggested. Yet, if Wirth was refuted on that score, his more lasting influence was to encourage countless chronicles of the "mosaic of social worlds." Many of the classics in urban sociology were produced in this milieu; studies of the texture of city life as it appeared in the social world of hobos, the organization of street-corner gangs, or the recreation afforded by taxi-dance halls.

Wirth's contribution is not tainted by his pessimism or anti-urban views. Ironically, he characterized the city as anomic for generations of followers who dug up vivid evidence of community bonds. It is also true that urban life is harshly impersonal for the poor or black who are not welcome in the mainstream of occupational and civic life. But that is not what Wirth and other students of urbanism intended to explain. The problem with urban social psychology is not that it fails to observe the social disorganization of communities or the pains of underprivileged life, but that it falls back on oddly mechanical explanations for those facts, such as the purported effects of population density, size, and heterogeneity. Political and economic exploitation, for example, play no part in individual or community troubles.

The two wings of the Chicago school, with all their valuable research contributions, came to grief in the 1960s. An urban crisis suddenly appeared which the earlier theories did not expect and could not explain. Urban riots spread from Watts to Washington because of anger rather than anomie. Central cities were deteriorating into sprawling ghettos rather than zones of transition. Social problems had less to do with population heterogeneity than with race and class inequality. A new framework for explaining urban society was needed and, fortunately, was close at hand.

Urban Political Economy

A new urban social science emerged from the crisis, one less concerned with repudiating earlier traditions than with subsuming them under a holistic *political economy* that Weber would have recognized. The new approach builds on the classical tradition and the Chicago school, applying the wisdom of both to a condition of worldwide urbanization, itself new and uncharted. As a framework, urban political economy involves five tenets:

1. Urbanization and urbanism must be explained, rather than taken for granted or glossed over vaguely as results of industrialization, population growth, or heterogeneity.

2. Since, by definition, urbanization is a process of change, its analysis must include historical development and the shifting relationship between urban and rural society.

3. The economy, changing practices of production and market exchange, is an essential determinant of urban life.

4. The contending broad forces of population and economy intersect in politics—political action resolves conflicts and assumes an independent determining role, particularly in the state.

5. The experience of urban life arises in group responses to these forces, responses that may alter the urban condition through politic struggle and cultural invention.

Illustratively, such specific urban processes as residential segregation, community organization, or class and ethnic politics are understood in connection with the economy and patterns of political control. The new urban social science deals with change, particularly as it grows out of conflicts between and among classes and status groups. These conflicts are the basis of the political process and increasingly the business of the state. Changes in the economy are politically generated and mediated. Political and social changes are in no sense independent of the economy.

Concretely, studies of land use and the spatial distribution of productive or residential areas are of value, provided they are understood as the result of historically changing economic strategy and political influence—rather than dubious ecological processes. There is an urban way of life, one situated in group action and urban social structure—rather than flowing from population size, density, or heterogeneity. Community studies of the slum or suburb are the blood of urban structure, but they make something more than anecdotal sense only when we can explain why such divergent neighborhoods existed in the first place and how they became segregated.

The first chapter of this book suggested that the sociological method has less to do with discovering previously unknown facts than with developing the implications of facts from an interpretive standpoint. Accordingly, the definition and framework proposed for analyzing cities suggest that the process of urbanization will work itself out differently under historically different political and economic conditions. In a particular country such as the United States, the pattern of urbanization and the experience of urban life should change over time. Similarly, in broad comparisons of the developed and underdeveloped countries which live under wholly different economic and political circumstances, cities should reflect a different structure. If the proposed framework does its job, we should be able to identify and explain these differences. The next two sections explore that proposition.

PART II
COMPARATIVE PATHS

A. URBANIZATION IN THE DEVELOPED COUNTRIES: THE U.S. CASE

By world standards, urbanization in the United States is unique. In the historically brief span of 200 years since the first population census, the number of people living in cities has risen from virtually none to almost all—from 5 to nearly 75 percent urban. These figures vary with the particular definition of urban, and the U.S. Census offers several.

Dating from an earlier era, the census defines the "urban population [as] all persons living in urbanized areas and in places of 2,500 or more inhabitants outside urbanized areas." Although this is a minimal definition more appropriate for the early 19th century, the census retains the category for purposes of comparison. Closer to present standards, an urbanized area is defined as a central city with a population of 50,000 or more and its surrounding closely settled territory or urban fringe. Yet even this is outmoded with the modern megalopolis that includes millions spread over areas that sometimes cross state lines. As a result, the U.S. Bureau of the Census developed the category, "standard metropolitan statistical area" or SMSA, corresponding to "a metropolitan area [having] a large population nucleus [the urbanized area], together with adjacent communities which have a high degree of economic and social integration with that nucleus." Tables 6–3 and 6–4 describe U.S. urbanization with these categories.

Table 6–3 traces urban growth from 1790 when the nation included just under 4 million people, of whom only 5 percent lived in towns or cities larger than 2,500. The figures show the rate of urban growth and distinct periods of accelerated increase. Two cautions are necessary for reading the table. The precise definition of "urban" shifted with each census and the total land area of the country kept expanding with annexation of frontier territories. The latter had the effect of reducing the urban average since it added new people to the U.S. population total, but seldom any towns of important size. With that in

TABLE 6–3   Urban Population of the United States: 1790–1980

Current Urban Definition	Total U.S. Population	Percent Urban
1980	226,545,805	73.7
1970	203,211,926	73.5
1960	179,323,175	69.9
1950	151,325,798	64.0
Previous urban definitions		
1960	179,323,175	63.0
1950	151,325,798	59.6
1940	132,164,569	56.5
1930	123,202,624	56.1
1920	106,021,537	51.2
1910	92,228,496	45.6
1900	76,212,168	39.6
1890	62,979,766	35.1
1880	50,189,209	28.2
1870	38,558,371	25.7
1860	31,443,321	19.8
1850	23,191,876	15.3
1840	17,069,453	10.8
1830	12,866,020	8.8
1820	9,638,453	7.2
1810	7,239,881	7.3
1800	5,308,483	6.1
1790	3,929,214	5.1

SOURCE: *Census of Population,* Vol. 1 (1980). *Characteristics of the General Population.* U.S. Department of Commerce, Bureau of the Census.

mind, the increasing urban population is all the more impressive, particularly in the period from 1840 onward. Generally, there are two major periods of urbanization: the first from 1850–1930 (especially the middle years of 1880–1910) and the second from 1950–70. In the last decade or two, urbanization has slowed perceptibly, perhaps as a "ceiling effect" is reached.

Table 6–4 provides another angle using the SMSA standard. The interesting sidelight here is that the urban population (2,500+) and SMSA figures are very similar (73.7 percent and 74.8 percent), indicating that the vast majority of urbanites live in the very large cities. This is also apparent from the near doubling in the absolute number of SMSAs in the last 40 years (from 168 to 318). The pattern requires historical explanation.

TABLE 6-4   U.S. Population in Standard Metropolitan Statistical Areas (SMSAs): 1940–80

	Number of SMSAs	Total Population in SMSAs (in thousands)	SMSA Population as a Percent of Total United States
1940	168	69,535	52.8
1950	168	84,854	56.1
1960	212	112,885	63.0
1970	243	139,419	68.6
1980	318	169,431	74.8

SOURCE: *Statistical Abstract of the United States (1982–83)*, 103d ed. U.S. Department of Commerce, Bureau of the Census.

The Historical Development of U.S. Cities

The historical and contemporary experience of urbanization in the United States is usefully divided into four periods, each with its distinctive urban form, function, and conflicts: (1) the *commercial city* (colonial times to 1850); (2) the *industrial city* (1850–1930); (3) the *corporate city* (1930–60); and (4) the *world city* (1960 to the present). Each period and urban form is described as it appears chronologically in a current of historically changing influences on the city. Distinct conflicts mark each period and its evolution to the next. The first three periods are adapted from a lucid article by David Gordon (1978) and used to summarize a rich history. The fourth period is contemporary, even futuristic, and is reserved for discussion in a final section.

In keeping with the framework, the U.S. city in each period is a result of the interacting forces of the economy, polity, and community. Changes in the economy in some ways demand reorganization of the urban system, but alone they do not determine it. Change is implemented by the political process that responds to economic demands and community conflicts. It is the resolution of these forces in distinct social and spatial forms that defines each period. Moreover, the transition from one period to another is marked by conflict among these spheres. The changing character of urban life as well as the nature of the evolved present require treatment from the standpoint of historical sociology.

During the first 200 years of U.S. history, four commercial cities dominated: New York, Philadelphia, Boston and Baltimore. In 1790, these four port cities included 67 percent of the country's urban population. The early cities were devoted principally to foreign trade and the commercial marketplace. Artisan crafts existed, but no significant industry. Later, when the textile industry began to grow in the 1820s, it located in New England towns with available water power—in Lowell, Lynn, Waltham, and Lawrence, Massachusetts, and around Philadelphia.

The Commercial City

The commercial city centered around the port itself, the business of the docks and shipping. The occupational structure included merchants and their retainers, artisans, and laborers in transportation work (seamen, dockworkers). Most business establishments were small and, much like the bakery in Laslett's *The World We Have Lost* (1965), combined work and the extended family in one place. Social classes and economic activities were closely integrated in a maze of narrow streets that crossed at irregular angles. Street life flourished and the city gave, in the words of historian Sam Bass Warner (1972), a feeling of the unity of everyday life. The only obvious segregation placed the itinerant poor in shanties and rooming houses on the outskirts.

Under these conditions, the urban population grew slowly. Indeed, from 1690 to 1790 it actually dropped (from 9 to 5 percent) as a result of westward movement and new agricultural settlement. Until independence, the number of cities held fairly constant, since England granted charters for the legal establishment of towns and followed a policy of minimizing the number of commercial centers that might compete in trade.

Social conflict in commercial cities focused on customs, trade restrictions, and the impressment of seamen into British maritime service. Pauline Maier's (1970) description of popular uprisings in the 18th century indicates that "[W]hen the press was of long duration, moreover, or when it took place during a normally busy season, it could mean serious shortages of food or firewood for winter, and a general attrition of the commercial life that sustained all strata of society in trading towns" (p. 12). In cities such as Boston, the urban mob frequently served as an extralegal arm of the community preventing grain exports that might result in food shortages. An accumulation of such conflicts led to the American Revolution in which the commercial cities played a leading role.

After independence, the cities expanded rapidly without any fundamental change in economic activity. Among the important commercial cities, only Philadelphia converted to a center of industry. In the absence of English control, the big cities competed for trade dominance with one another and with newer commercial towns that began to flourish. The result was a growing prominence of New York which enjoyed the special advantage of connections to inland markets through the Erie Canal. By 1860, New York controlled most foreign trade and took its present place as the country's financial capital.

The transition from commercial to industrial city in the mid-19th century was produced by a number of intersecting forces. Until about 1830, U.S. industry was concentrated in the smaller New England towns and devoted mainly to textiles. As the country grew, industry diversified under tariff protections from European imports. A key problem for industrial development was the shortage of a skilled and disciplined labor force. The United States had not yet produced its own industrial working class. New England textile mills relied on British immigrants and, later, young women from rural areas who lived in company dormitories and operated spinning machines (the Lowell Girls, for example). The labor shortage was exacerbated by free land in the West and attractive alternatives to tedious factory work.

Yet the methods of industrial production and the demands of the internal market were also developing. Steam-powered machines made the urban factory possible and a protected, expanding home market promised successful diversification of manufacturing. Equally important, the state began building an urban infrastructure of roads, canals, and the all-important railway for the profit of private firms. Governments at all levels intervened in the economy with enormous subsidies to the railroads. Historian Carl Degler (1959) estimates that between 1850 and 1870 the state made cash loans to the railroads totaling $150 million and awarded them more than 180 million acres of public land as rights-of-way.

At the same time, the first massive wave of immigrants was arriving. From 1820 to 1880, roughly 15 million people came to the United States, mainly from the British Isles and Northwestern Europe. As Table 6–1 reflects, this period witnessed a sharp increase in the populations of the older commercial cities as well as the rapid development of new industrial-market hub cities such as Chicago, Detroit, Minneapolis, Kansas City, St. Louis, and Omaha. Immigrants and railroads were essential ingredients of the industrial city, but the encouragement of both was a political policy choice.

Vast as these changes were, they neglect the most traumatic social and political reorganization that laid the basis for urban-industrial society, namely, the Civil War. The Civil War was fought over slavery, but slavery was only one manifestation of the conflicting economies of North and South. Northern industrial development by 1860 had reduced its dependence on textiles and, consequently, on Southern cotton. As it diversified and moved toward the Midwest, industry looked for new markets and a political alliance with Western agriculturalists, themselves fearful of competition from slave-based plantation agriculture. North and West struck a bargain predicated on mutual support for free land and the tariff—an agreement that joined the prime interests, respectively, of the West and the North in opposition to the South. Assessing the causes of the Civil War, Barrington Moore concludes that "[T]he focal point of the difference was slavery.... [but] The more fundamental issue became more and more whether the machinery of the federal government should be used to support one society or the other... the American Civil War was the last revolutionary offensive on the part of what one may legitimately call urban or bourgeois capitalist democracy" (pp. 136, 112).

The Industrial City

With the end of the Civil War, the industrial city began to boom—and to suffer periodic recessions. From 1870 to 1930, the U.S. population tripled while the number of workers in manufacturing increased five times. The urban population increased from 20 to 56 percent. A major determinant of population and urban growth was the new or second wave of immigration drawn mainly from eastern and southern Europe (Italians, Greeks, Poles, Russians, Slavs in general and many Jews). In just 14 years, from 1902 to 1916, the number of new immigrants exceeded all that had arrived in the 60 years from 1820–80.

The new industrial city relied on the controllable immigrant labor force. Industries preferred the big cities where labor was abundant, cheap, and easily disciplined. The U.S. working class was formed in the cities largely from immigrant stock. It was at this stage that the urban ecology described by the Chicago sociologists developed, through no accident, since Chicago was the prototypical industrial city. Factories were centrally located along railroad lines and shipping channels. A business and shopping district formed the city center. Wedged among these two were the working-class neighborhoods as close as possible to the factory gate or trolley line. The middle and upper classes now preferred living at a peaceful distance from the noise, stench, and crowds in the center. Unlike the commercial city, the industrial city was segregated by social class and economic activity.

In *The Jungle* (1906), Upton Sinclair provided a memorable portrait of urban life in the industrial city and, specifically, of Chicago at the turn of the century. An extended family of Lithuanian immigrants settles in an ethnic community near the stockyards, buys (and later loses) an overpriced house on contract. Then, a son drowns in a pothole in the street, the family finds and loses jobs until its few survivors learn the corrupt ways of union and machine politics. The validity of Sinclair's grim picture is supported by the writings of Jane Addams who created the first settlement house in the same neighborhood to deal with urban social problems. The work of Hull House, in turn, figured prominently in the first volume of the *American Journal of Sociology* published in Chicago in 1895. As the work of Thomas, Park, Wirth, and others filled in the factual foundations for novelists and reformers, a general and critical understanding of the industrial city grew out of the Chicago experience.

Each period had both a characteristic urban form and pattern of conflict. The important conflicts occurred in the cities and in rural areas, the fortunes of which were severely affected by urbanization. The reorganization brought on by urban industrial society produced a generation of social conflict unprecedented before or since. From the late 1870s until World War I a mortal struggle was fought in the countryside and the cities, the stakes of which were nothing less than the kind of society the United States was going to be.

In the Old South, Texas, and the Great Plains, an agrarian revolt rose against concentrated capital. Following the debt-financed Civil War, the federal government adopted a harsh deflationary monetary policy the results of which benefited bankers and finance capital, but severely contracted farm prices, credit, and income. Farmers were forced into a crop lien system, pledging anything from 20 to 50 percent of their next crop in exchange for seed, fertilizer, and provisions from the "furnishing man" (or, to black farmers, simply "the man"). When the crop came in, many farmers were scarcely able to settle accounts and others went further behind as farm prices continued falling. Large numbers lost their farms and were forced to migrate to the cities or to remain as tenant farmers in the service of local lenders who consolidated land ownership. Farm tenantry and sharecropping, which had been infrequent and largely the fate of black farmers prior to 1870, rose to 25 percent of all farmers in 1880 and 38 percent by 1910. In selected regions like the Old South, Iowa, and Kansas, half the farmers were reduced to being tenants by the depression years.

In the late 1870s, rural society responded with The Farmer's Alliance, a cooperative mass movement opposed to the railroads, credit merchants, and the money trust. Alliance men and women set up cooperative stores, warehouses, credit bureaus, and procurement and marketing arrangements. A series of Alliance newspapers like the *Rural Citizen, American Nonconformist,* and *Progressive Farmer* argued their case to the general public while hundreds of traveling lecturers carried to the small towns and farms the details of an Alliance plan to reform the U.S. Treasury and save the family farm. In their political demands, the Alliance sought "such legislation as shall secure to our people freedom from the onerous and shameful abuses that the industrial classes are now suffering at the hands of arrogant capitalists and powerful corporations" (quoted in Goodwyn, p. 53). They endeavored to unite with the Knights of Labor and the fledgling union movement in a general strike against the railroad. With their own cooperatives, they boycotted local merchants and lenders. At its peak in 1890, the Alliance included 400,000 members in thousands of chapters from Georgia to the Dakotas.

In the end, The Farmer's Alliance was defeated by government indifference, the opposition of finance capital, and the movement's own recourse to a People's party that was absorbed into the Democratic party. Far from assisting the innovative cooperatives or ameliorating the plight of the family farmer, government programs favored the more prosperous commercial farms and, later, the emergence of agribusiness. As Lawrence Goodwyn's (1978) study of *The Populist Moment* concludes,

> The collective effort of twentieth-century agricultural legislation ...was to assist in the centralization of American agriculture at the expense of the great mass of the nation's farmers. The process of extending credit, first to the nation's most affluent large-scale farming interests, and then in the 1920s to sectors of the agricultural middle class—while at the same time denying it to the "whole class" of Americans who worked the land—had the effect of assisting large-unit farming interests to acquire title to still more land at the expense of smallholders. Purely in terms of land-ownership patterns, "agri-business" began to emerge in rural America as early as the 1920s, not, as some have suggested, because large-scale corporate farming proved its "efficiency" in the period 1940 to 1970. In essence, "agri-business" came into existence before it even had the opportunity to prove or disprove its "efficiency." In many ways, land centralization in American agriculture was a decades-long product of farm credit policies acceptable to the American banking community. (Lawrence Goodwyn, *The Populist Moment: A Short History of the Agrarian Revolt in America*, pp. 268–69)

Small towns suffered with the decline of the family farm and the rise of mechanized corporate agriculture linked more directly to national and urban markets. Many of the towns simply disappeared as younger generations out of necessity migrated to urban educational and career opportunities. Others persisted, but without a viable economic function that could maintain local investment and the amenities of small-town life. A little-known study by C. Wright Mills and Melville Ulmer, "Small Business and Civic Welfare" (completed in 1946 for the U.S. Senate Special Committee to Study Problems of American Small

Business), concluded that "in small-business cities the environment was favorable to the development and growth of civic spirit" (p. 126) and to local welfare as measured by health, housing, church membership, and public expenditures on cultural facilities. For the same committee in 1946, the anthropologist Walter Goldschmidt (1978) compared two agricultural towns in California's Central Valley. One based on large-scale farming had a more unequal structure of income and social class, and it performed poorly on measures of civic welfare.

The consistent conclusion of such research is that, whatever amenities the cities themselves generated, agribusiness and urbanization marked the eclipse of a small-town way of life conducive to the public good. Many people in addition to the radical populists of the 1880s realized this. In *The Resisted Revolution,* David Danbom (1979) describes how the Country Life Movement fought to preserve the farm towns, but lost to federal policies that promoted industrialized agriculture.

No better example is found in U.S. history of how a changing industrial economy, with zealous political support, produced a sharp increase in urbanization and a new kind of city. Many of the costs of this accomplishment were visited on rural society, farms, and small towns, indicating once more that the urban and rural change in relation to one another. The costs of urbanization are poorly understood because the city is mistakenly studied as independent from rural society.

The political defeat of the agrarian revolt, in tandem with agricultural mechanization and commercialization, contributed to a huge internal migration. The labor force engaged in agriculture fell from 60 percent at the outset of the industrial city to just under 40 percent at the turn of the century, continuing steadily downward to the present level of 3 percent. Farmers joined hillbillies and immigrants in the explosive urban growth of 1890 to 1920. In the cities, however, the new industrial society generated a related set of conflicts centered on the labor question.

Until the mid-1880s, labor unrest was confined mainly to the mines and railroads. In 1886, something new happened. The Farmer's Alliance joined the Knights of Labor in the Great Southwestern Strike against the Missouri-Pacific Railroad. Indeed, 1886 became known as "the year of the great labor uprising."

Previous years had averaged 500 strikes involving 150,000 workers nationwide. In 1886, the figures climbed to 1,400 strikes joined by 500,000 people. The labor economist John Rogers Commons called it "a great movement by the class of the unskilled which had finally risen in rebellion.... The movement bore in every way the aspect of a social war" (quoted in Zinn, p. 267). On May Day, the recently formed American Federation of Labor called a general strike in support of the eight-hour day that attracted 350,000 sympathizers nationwide.

During a large demonstration two days later at the McCormick Harvester Works outside Chicago, police fired into the crowd of strikers and killed four. A protest rally was called for the following evening of May 4 in downtown Chicago's Haymarket Square. When 180 police began to move on the crowd, a bomb exploded killing seven officers and several bystanders. The Haymarket Massacre is legendary for what it told about the forces of reaction to labor unrest. At the urging of a Citizen's Committee, eight anarchists, seven of whom had not even attended the rally, were arrested as instigators of the bombing. Although no evidence was produced at their trial as to who threw the bomb, four of the anarchist leaders of the Working People's Association were hung for the deed. The labor wars continued with such celebrated instances as the Homestead, Pennsylvania, strike at the Carnegie Steel Plant in 1892 and the Pullman strike near Chicago in 1894, where Pinkerton detectives and the Illinois National Guard attacked and killed strikers. The Haymarket, Homestead, and Pullman cases only highlight a 30-year labor struggle that lasted until World War I with no resolution.

Although organized workers eventually won their demands for the eight-hour day, an adequate wage, and social security, most of those gains came in the 1930s as a consequence of government action following the depression. The principal result of the great labor uprising at the turn of the century was a new stage of social reorganization—the transition from industrial to corporate city. With the first major corporate mergers of the late 1890s, new conglomerate firms began to decentralize industrial production. Although suburbs had formed in the late 19th century as middle- and upper-class residential areas, it was the movement of industry escaping labor unrest that gave the greatest impetus to suburban growth. David M. Gordon (1978) quotes a revealing illustration from Graham Taylor's 1915 book on *Satellite Cities: A Study of Industrial Suburbs:*

> In an Eastern city which recently experienced the throes of a turbulent street-car strike, the superintendent of a large industrial establishment frankly said that every time the strikers paraded past his plant a veritable fever seemed to spread among the employees in all the work rooms. He thought that if the plants were moved out to the suburbs, the workingmen would not be so frequently inoculated with infection. (Quoted in David M. Gordon, "Capitalist Development and the History of American Cities, pp. 49–50)

The Corporate City

The corporate city gained its characteristic features as a result of industrial decentralization. As large corporations diversified their production and came to dominate larger shares of the market, they were able to integrate specialized activities on a nationwide basis. Management, production, and marketing could take place in different locations with some efficiency. Corporate headquarters might remain in the central city, but new plants in outlying areas could be linked into national transport networks. Decentralization was all the more convenient when suburban governments cooperated with low taxes, land acquisition, noninterference in labor politics, and when skilled workers followed to the new industrializing suburbs. No doubt, the workers who could live and be employed in the suburbs found the move a pleasant change and a valued symbol of their own social mobility. But it was not their preferences or the appeal of green grass that created the suburbs. The corporate city assumed its decisive and familiar shape as a result of depression era and postwar state policies. Confronted with the depression crisis and supported by unprecedented congressional majorities, the New Deal administration began to rebuild the economy in a manner that also built the corporate city.

The Democratic party was rebuilt in the same process, particularly as it appealed for political support from the urban working classes and status groups: second-generation immigrants, blacks, Catholics, union members. But Roosevelt's New Deal programs successfully reached out for a broader coalition that included business and suburban interests as well as farmers and the Old South. New Deal (and Truman's subsequent Fair Deal) policies for rebuilding the cities included: federal mortgage insurance that stimulated single-family home construction; urban renewal that eliminated blighted inner city areas of working-class housing to make room for downtown commercial development; public works such as roads, bridges, waterfront projects, libraries, and municipal buildings that employed many of the depression's jobless; and limited amounts of public housing. Democratic administrations were never hostile to the corporate interests that continued to make their headquarters in the cities. Although public housing was promoted for the urban poor, it was made palatable in exchange for programs that channeled far more costly government subsidies to single-family housing through the private mortgage market and construction industry.

Despite the inclusiveness of this progrowth coalition, political interests were acquiring new and higher stakes in what John Mollenkopf (1983) calls *The Contested City*. Republican administrations returning in 1952 had their own metropolitan constituents: suburbanites, real estate developers, corporations. Ironically, many of these were precisely the beneficiaries of depression era policies and their contribution to economic recovery. Typical among those beneficiaries were second- and third-generation ethnic families who had moved to the suburbs and enjoyed some social mobility. In the process, however, their political allegiance changed. Splits developed in the old Democratic progrowth coalition. The Republican policy alternatives emphasized urban renewal with little compensatory low-cost housing, freeways and the interstate highway system, and unalloyed suburban development.

At bottom, the urban policies that created the corporate city were manifestations of political party struggles as each party addressed social and economic problems in different ways. The New Deal worked through reform-minded local officials, bypassing wherever possible the old machine politicians. Eisenhower Republicans built their base in the suburbs and in the newer Western cities. Kennedy's New Frontier and Johnson's Great Society appealed once more to old and big cities, now dominated by less mobile working-class ethnics, blacks, the new

Hispanic immigrants, the elderly—minorities in general who were willing to join as citizen participants in inviting Community Action Programs. Nixon's New Federalism was a characteristic switch back to "impartial" support of the cities in the sense of abandoning support for the inner city and the urban crisis in favor of formula funding to state and local governments for projects of their own choosing (revenue sharing rather than antipoverty programs). And so, the pendulum swung in narrowing arcs during the Carter and Reagan administrations as urban policy receded in the face of recession. In a capsule summary of the progrowth coalitions that built the corporate city, Mollenkopf (1983) concludes,

> Over the five decades since the New Deal, the web of federal urban development programs and the intricate national-local political coalitions woven largely by Democratic political entrepreneurs succeeded in reshaping American cities and establishing the Democrats as the nominal majority party. With federal program tools, local progrowth political coalitions...transformed old industrial cities into modern administrative centers populated by corporate headquarters, advanced corporate service firms, hospitals, universities, and other service institutions. The same programs hastened the displacement of industrial investment to the suburbs and the newly developing regions of the country. These successes dissolved the urban conflicts of the industrial city and helped build the modern Democratic party, much as Franklin Roosevelt and his New Deal entrepreneurs had hoped.
>
> It is hardly surprising that changes of this magnitude also generated new kinds of urban conflict which the founders of the New Deal could not anticipate. Seeing Democratic successes, Republican national political entrepreneurs and the conservative coalition in Congress sought to blunt the political efficacy of Democratic programs while substituting alternatives designed to reinforce their own constituencies. Suspended between this conservative opposition and the divisions of interest among their own urban supporters and within their party, Democrats could preserve only programs which reinforced market trends. (John H. Mollenkopf, *The Contested City*, p. 254)

The contemporary urban landscape is dominated by the mature corporate city. It appears as an aging and generally neglected core, save for the commercial central-business district. The outer city and expanding suburbs flourish with new housing, sources of employment, and the characteristic shopping centers linked by freeways. Paradoxically, city savings-and-loan associations have red-lined local neighborhoods and reinvested (or "disinvested") the money of their urban depositors in suburban development projects, while city taxpayers pay for the urban services that support downtown business establishments and commuters' jobs. Metropolitan regions are now segregated by class, ethnicity, age, and economic function.

Yet the social life of this segregated metropolis seldom conforms to popular images of a pathologically disorganized inner city slum and a blandly homogeneous suburb. Beginning in the 1950s, a new folklore grew up in the mass media about the pleasures and restrictions of suburban life. In a favorable light, they were pictured as conducive to a family-centered lifestyle, church-going, neighborliness, and leisure—the American Dream for a deserving postdepression and postwar generation. But critics, such as William H. Whyte, Jr. (1956) in *The Organization Man,* argued that suburbs encouraged standardization, status anxiety, conformity, and cultural degradation—the "split-level trap" of commuters and unliberated women who pilot station wagons between schools, shopping centers, and the veterinarian.

A series of sociological monographs challenged both kinds of description, albeit with little effect on popular stereotypes. In *The Levittowners,* Herbert Gans (1967) reported on the ways of life and politics in a new suburban community in New Jersey. The residents and their styles of life were no more homogeneous than their urban counterparts. In fact, most of the new suburbanites came from city neighborhoods and did not significantly alter their lives in the move. As suburbanites they maintained quasi-primary relations with their neighbors, generally enjoyed their new homes, and conformed mainly to standards, such as keeping a well-groomed lawn and exterior, because they agreed with them. People who reported important changes in their lives, such as more involvement in child rearing, also said that the changes were intended and among their reasons for moving to the suburbs. Bennett Berger's (1960) study, *Working Class Suburb,* in California reached similar conclusions. New suburbanites maintained their (mostly Democratic) political preferences, went to church as seldom as ever, socialized mainly with kin, saw their future as pretty much like their past, and their homes as the fulfillment of a dream. The evidence from Gans, Berger, and others showed that the lifestyles of the suburbs were more a consequence of social-class position and age than of any attributes of the suburbs themselves.

Stereotypes of urban social disorganization have proven equally distorted. In Chapter 1, Gerald Suttles's work on *The Social Order of the Slum* was discussed with reference to method. That exposition made clear, nevertheless, that Chicago's West Side community was consciously organized around principles of a provincial morality, personal safety, self-respect, and group membership, the sum of which produced a pattern of ordered segmentation.

Another study and modern classic by Herbert Gans (1962), suggestively entitled *The Urban Villagers,* found similar patterns in Boston's West End. The neighborhood included a plurality of first- and second-generation Italians along with a mixture of other ethnic groups, employees of a major hospital, and sundry artists and bohemians: "various ethnic groups, the bohemians, transients, and others could live together side by side without much difficulty, since each was responsive to totally different reference groups... life in the area resembled that found in the village or small town, and even in the suburb" (p. 15). Italians lived in fairly close-knit kin and friendship groups and valued their community, not least for the quality of housing it provided at reasonable rents. Gans described the West End as a "peer group society" because most relationships were with people of the same sex, age, and life-cycle status. As in the case of his Levittowners, the distinctive features of the urban village derived from these social class and life-cycle considerations, rather than any purported influence of ethnicity or the urban neighborhood per se.

The social conflicts generated by the corporate city and signaling the start of its present transformation began in the 1960s. Essentially, they revolved around the consequences of metropolitan segregation and urban decline. The main similarity they bore to their predecessors of agrarian revolt and labor struggle was that change penalized some while rewarding others. The first victims were the inner-city poor and minorities who saw their neighborhoods cannibalized by urban renewal and abandoned by public and private investment. Urban riots, as we saw in Chapter 1, were protests against unemployment, exploitative merchants, police, and the lack of public services such as transportation, affordable housing, and hospitals.

But the conflict went far beyond destructive rage. Neighborhoods also organized using the Great Society's palliative Community Action Programs as vehicles for what Daniel Bell and Virginia Held (1969) called a community revolution. The community revolution was precisely an effort by blacks and the urban poor to wrest power from the political system, although it was articulated in the more acceptable language of "participation" in a crazy quilt of organizations: local planning boards, committees for local control of schools and police, community development corporations, employment task forces, youth service agencies, welfare rights groups, and many more.

Emboldened by the participatory blandishments of the Great Society and by contemporaneous Vietnam protests, the community revolution expressed itself in direct action. Marches for jobs and housing took place. Neighborhood defenders camped on proposed urban renewal sites to prevent housing destruction or unwanted new uses. Welfare and renewal agencies were occupied, even trashed. And small victories were won because liberal Democrats in Washington and in city hall seeking new bases of urban political support were also part of the revolution. Bell and Held (1969) capture the complexities of this process in a passage about the contestants and their varied strategies.

> What some of the social scientists only dimly sensed quickly became a reality: that for the indigenous leaders of the poor, particularly the militant blacks, the movement for "participation" became a drive for "power." This challenge was aimed at the local political machines, and was correctly understood as such by the local politicos. In San Francisco, black leaders succeeded early in 1965 in taking over control of the poverty program, and they sought to use the program to build a political base for black control. Plans were laid to have a part-time community organizer for almost every block and a full-time organizer for every eight blocks. Little of the monies went into services for the residents. In the political struggle within the black community, and between it and city hall, the original black leaders lost out. In Philadelphia, a program dominated by independent blacks was pulled back to city hall influence, though not with total city hall control. In New York City, the situation was reversed. The Poverty Program was used by the Lindsay administration to build a new political base by putting the black militants on the community action payrolls, tying them in with the Urban

Action Task Forces, and using them as a battering ram against the older political machines. (Daniel Bell and Virginia Held, "The Community Revolution," pp. 152–53)

The community revolution died a slow death after 1968 as the Nixon administration withdrew political support from the inner cities in favor of another coalition with the suburbs, states, and Western Sunbelt cities. Added to the recession of the 1970s, this change marked not only the defeat of the inner cities, but also of entire cities in the Northeast and Midwest whose economies were based on heavy industry. Detroit, Cleveland, Pittsburgh, Akron, Gary, Buffalo, and many more became known as the rustbowl in a fitting analogy to the Oklahoma dustbowl and the 1930s depression.

The recessionary damper on industrial production and growing imports of foreign steel and automobiles combined in the stagnation for the older cities. The changing economy encouraged new growth in the Sunbelt that benefited from petroleum and high-technology industries. Local officials in the declining cities joined auto and steel workers in protest of plant closings. Without national political support for protections against the closings, however, they had little chance of saving their communities—except in rare instances where employee buyouts of industry could be financed and made profitable. Youngstown, Ohio is typical of these dying towns.

A sense of gloom pervades this city. Youths moping on street corners call it a ghost town. One of every eight people in surrounding Mahoning County is on welfare, and, government officials add, almost 60,000 people are unemployed in the metropolitan area of 500,000.

It wasn't always this way. Mahoning Valley steel mills around this eastern Ohio town helped build America and win two world wars. At one time, more steel was made in Youngstown than in any other city in the United States.

The plants are dead or ill for a number of reasons. Workers blame industrialists for not investing money in archaic plants. Steel executives concede they made mistakes but also point to salary demands, foreign imports brought here at below cost and environmental regulations.

[an ex-union leader observes], These are people who did everything right.... They went to college. They went to church. They bought into the system. Now what? We're wasting people....[And an unemployed steelworker], They say high tech will come here. What do I know about computers? How are they going to teach someone like me something like that. A 20-pound sledgehammer is what I know. I know gears. I don't even know how to play Atari. And maybe 30 percent of the people I worked with in the mill couldn't read or write. I guess we're down. ("Portrait of a Dying Steel Town," *Sacramento Bee*, September 11, 1983)

What one observer called the "manufacturing Appalachia of the Midwest" is part of a broader national phenomenon—the latest transition from the corporate to the world city.

The World City

The world city is presently in the making and something to be observed less as a mature physical form than in its emerging apex. The term comes from John Friedmann and Goetz Wolff (1982) who provide a description and some examples.

As cities go, they are large in size, typically ranging from 5 to 15 million, and they are expanding rapidly. In space, they may extend outward by as much as 60 miles from an original centre. These vast, highly urbanized—and urbanizing—regions play a vital part in the great capitalist undertaking to organize the world for the efficient extraction of surplus...[they reflect] the mode of their integration into the world economy...[and] include such metropolises as Tokyo, Los Angeles, San Francisco, Miami, New York, London, Paris, Randstadt, Frankfurt, Zurich, Cairo, Bangkok, Singapore, Hong Kong, Mexico City, and Sao Paulo. (John Friedmann and Goetz Wolff, "World City Formation: An Agenda for Research and Action," pp. 309 and 310)

Just as the industrial and corporate cities came to constitute a new apex at the top of an urban hierarchy that retained smaller towns with specialized, realigned, or residual functions, so the world city overarches and reorganizes persistent national cities. The effects of world city formation can be seen locally in economic shifts that move production to the Sunbelt or abroad at the convenience of multinational corporations. The deindustrializing of North America expresses in a critical way the rise of a new urban system. Older cities like Youngstown may wither or, like Boston, attract a piece of worldwide production and marketing for high technology. World cities such as Los Angeles become a magnet for domestic migrants, multinational corporate headquarters, and the new ethnics: Asians, Middle Easterners, Hispanics. Armenians and Salvadorans, for example, have their own communities in Los Angeles. There are some parallels between the formation of industrial cities in the early and world cities in the late 1900s. The key difference, however, is that today's world city follows the dictates of a global political economy and grows at the expense of the older industrial and corporate cities.

The process of urbanization, as we have followed it through U.S. history, conveys a clear lesson: Cities are not ecological things that obey natural laws or subsocial processes. Neither are they expressions of any unique cultural urbanism independent of social classes and political struggles. Rather, as Weber saw, they are the fusion of markets, political authority, and community. They assume distinctive shapes and styles in pursuit of economic and social aims defined by the polity and community. Cities and their carrying urban systems change in the interplay of these influences. As the urbanization process moves forward, it destroys much that is in its path, including rural societies and urban forms that it previously built. Urbanization does not systematically degrade society, but successively reorganizes it by realigning social classes, status groups, and ways of life in response to the political economy of each stage.

There are winners and losers in the process. The industrial city supplanted the dominant merchants of the commercial city, destroyed Southern agrarian society, and displaced the family farmer. Industrialists, financiers, and a largely immigrant working class initially benefitted. The corporate city abandoned the working class and ethnic minorities of central cities in favor of downtown commerce and the suburban complex of new industries and homeowners. With the emergence of the world city, entire metropolitan areas in the Northeast and Midwest, including their largely industrial labor forces, are being left behind in a movement of multinational corporations and jobs to the Sunbelt and abroad. Urbanization makes plain to the eye how societies change and what the consequences of those changes are in a calculus of social wellbeing.

B. URBANIZATION IN THE THIRD WORLD

The world city includes as a hinterland and economic extension parts of the developing world in Africa, Asia, and Latin America. This was true of previous city forms, but today's links are more direct and essential. If the pessimistic Youngstown steelworker actually looked for a job with the Atari Company, he would find that it had moved. The company recently shifted its production to Taiwan and Hong Kong at the expense of 1,700 jobs in Santa Clara, California, which retains, nevertheless, the corporate headquarters. This contemporary example continues a long record of foreign participation in the economies and urban development of Third World cities.

Tables 6–1 and 6–2 show that urbanization in the developing areas, particularly Latin America, has increased in the last 60 years at a rate exceeding that of the more developed regions. A larger proportion of the world's total urban population now lives in the less developed countries. The great world cities of New York, Moscow, London, and Tokyo are all smaller than Shanghai, Calcutta, Mexico City, and Seoul. Among those likely contenders, the world's largest city may soon be Sao Paulo, Brazil.

A Different Path

Yet the appearance of cities in the Third World is unprepossessing at best. At worst it is one of seldom-relieved poverty, makeshift shacks, open sewers, bleeding sores, and idle humanity. If we look beneath that appearance, as Gans and Suttles did in the United States, a more livable, if still poverty-stricken, picture emerges. In broad terms, however, cities of the Third World have not developed along a trajectory established in Europe and North America. In a sociological sense, there is no universal rural-urban continuum or generally applicable Western model of urbanization. Specifically, Third World cities have not passed from a commercial to industrial stage and beyond. Their development has followed a very different path—one that needs to be described and explained.

Table 6–5 contrasts the labor-force distribution in the United States and major Latin American countries in various years that

TABLE 6-5   Labor-Force distribution in Selected Countries (in percent)

		Primary: Agriculture, Fishing, Forestry	Secondary: Industry, Construction, Mining	Tertiary: Services, Commerce, Administration, Transport
United States	1860	59	20	21
	1900	38	30	32
	1950	12	33	55
	1980	3	30	67
Argentina	1925	32	20	48
	1960	22	21	57
Brazil	1925	68	12	20
	1960	52	13	35
Chile	1925	37	21	42
	1960	25	17	58
Colombia	1925	65	17	18
	1960	49	15	36
Mexico	1925	70	11	19
	1960	53	17	30
Peru	1925	61	18	21
	1960	54	15	31
Venezuela	1925	63	10	27
	1960	32	12	56

SOURCES: *Statistical Abstract of the United States* (1980). U.S. Census Bureau, 1982. Cardoso, Fernando H. & Reyna, Jose Luis (1968). Industrialization, occupational structure and social stratification in Latin America. In Cole Blasier (Ed.), *Constructive change in Latin America*. Pittsburgh: University of Pittsburgh Press.

represent early and, by national standards, mature industrialization. This comparison reflects dramatically a pattern of difference between the advanced industrial countries and the developing world in general. The pattern is this: In the United States, the industrial era beginning around 1860 leads to a steady decline in the (primary) agricultural labor force with a concomitant rise in the (secondary) industrial *and* the (tertiary) commercial-services sector. In the mid-period of industrial maturation (say around 1900) employment across the three sectors is relatively even, although by 1950 the industrial labor force stops growing and services grow alone.

In the developing countries of Latin America, which raised their industrial production significantly from 1925 to 1960, industrial employment scarcely grows at all. Reductions in agricultural employment owing to mechanization and commercialization are taken up almost exclusively by the burgeoning service sector (and by unemployment). Put simply, the developing countries do not experience a three-stage process of modernization, from agrarian to industrial to services, in employment terms. Instead, their labor forces shift from mainly agricultural to mainly commercial and service-based. Combining this pattern with the contemporaneous fact of rapid urbanization, the result is that Third World cities are dominated by a bloated or overcrowded service sector and its twin, high rates of underemployment.

A Different Experience

The tables portray in structural terms what observers see in the streets of Third World cities—a great many seemingly idle people, a profusion of petty traders (lottery ticket sellers, shoeshine boys, fruit sellers, vendors of clothing and toys), people with only their bodies to sell, and others up to no good. The question, then, becomes where do these urban masses come from or, more precisely, why did the industrial sector fail to grow as it did in the more advanced countries?

The answer is the subject of many volumes devoted to development economics and the sociology of underdevelopment. It is summarized briefly in the notion of Third World dependency in the global political economy. The first fact of the somewhat euphemistically named Third World is that it was incorporated into the world economy by imperialism. The Spaniards in Latin America; the French, Belgians, Germans, Portuguese, and English in Africa; the English and French in Asia; the North Americans in the Philippines, Caribbean, and Central America—all went to those societies in search of plunder, raw materials, captive markets, and client states. They did not go to promote local resources or industry for the purposes of internal development. On the contrary, their intervention typically destroyed local artisan industry where it existed and substituted, through coercive colonial policies, local consumption of European and North American manufactured goods in exchange for exported primary products from the mines and fields. Third World countries "developed" as appendages or enclaves of the core nations of the world economy, and in that sense they were typically misdeveloped from the standpoint of a healthy or balanced local economy.

The pattern of dependent urbanization continued after the formal end of colonialism. Industries were created in the developing countries, but often under the ownership or control of foreign interests, seeking now to dominate world markets without the costly political apparatus of colonialism. Naturally, the methods by which this ambition was pursued varied greatly around the world. Some developing countries succeeded in avoiding its worst effects and even in gaining limited autonomy. The dominant pattern, however, was market control by the advanced nations through exportation of their own industrial goods or through offshore plants that manufactured products for local consumption in the Third World.

Foreign-controlled industry did three things to misdevelop Third World economies: (1) it used advanced industrial production methods, capital-intensive or inappropriate technologies that employed very few people; (2) it concentrated on high profit and luxury markets, failing to industrialize mass consumption goods; and (3) it competed with potential national industrialists, discouraging local investment while taking its own profit out of the countries. A national industrial class did emerge in many countries, often in joint ventures with foreign firms. But that class was generally subservient to the wishes of foreign capital, forced to adopt the same, capital-intensive methods. This prevented the developing countries from generating industrial employment as a source of national development, which is reflected in the table.

The supposed overurbanization of Third World cities now makes sense. It involved, on one hand, too many people forced off the land by commercially mechanized agriculture and flooding into the urban economy and, on the other hand, too many people for the dependent city to productively employ.

The physical results of this process are the extensive slums and squatter settlements observed from Lagos to Lima. Unlike U.S. cities, where poverty and unemployment are concentrated in the decaying inner cities, urban areas in the Third World display vast "peripheral" belts of unserviced, self-constructed housing. Worldwide patterns vary, but in the more urbanized

Third World, such as Latin America, central cities have been maintained as the locus of government, business, and elite residence. With overcrowding, suburbs have also grown for the rich and poor. In such major metropolitan areas as Mexico City, however, the downtown core has been renovated and poor neighborhoods bulldozed to make room for high-rise apartments and offices. Central plazas built in the 1530s are still administratively and commercially central places in most Latin American cities, despite the growth of suburbs and even shopping centers. The city has not been abandoned and the old charm endures alongside the plaintive poverty.

The ecology of Third World cities arises from a social process of rural-to-urban and intraurban migration. Migrants from smaller towns and the countryside come to the city with some prior knowledge of their opportunities, even with a job, acquired from kin networks that have preceded them. Among rural migrants who have lost land or employment, it is typically the more qualified who head for the city. Initially they live with kin or in centrally located boardinghouses. In Latin America, particularly, recent urban migrants have organized themselves for land invasions, setting up literally overnight new squatter settlements on public or private vacant land. Over time, available sites are found farther from the central city. With initiative unexpected by governments or planners, the squatters design their own neighborhoods, appoint committees for sanitation and local control, collectively build their own homes, and begin negotiations with local authorities for the provision of basic services: water, sewage, streets, lighting, transportation, and even legal title to the land. Like a tree trunk with successively newer rings, Latin American cities present a cross section of one-time land invasions, the oldest of which have become well ordered middle-class communities.

The late anthropologist Oscar Lewis is still the best English language source on the urban life of the migrant poor. Published in 1959, his account of *Five Families* in Mexico City is studded with representative descriptions of how people cope with uncertainty and scarcity. In the enterprising Gutierrez family, for example, everyone including the children worked in some way to support their one-room *vecinidad* apartment. Among the extended family living together, the mother did laundry at a communal wash basin and sold towels to laborers around the city, two of her children assisted or sold newspapers, an older son drove a city bus, another was a mechanic's helper, and the father sold toy water bottles of his own invention, candy from his apartment doorstep, and invested in a television set which he charged neighborhood children to watch. With the proceeds of all these endeavors the family got by, saved a few pesos, and hoped one day to purchase a lot. Lewis's ethnography tells of other more affluent families in the restaurant and construction businesses, but they all have in common a close family life and an existence devoted mainly to meeting the material necessities of urban life.

Indeed, one is struck by certain similarities between Lewis's *vecinidad* in Mexico City and Herbert Gans's (1962) urban village in Boston. Although the content and precariousness of urban life are different in the two cases, the "villagers" are similar in their cohesive ties to family and neighborhood, a tolerable existence within the limits of their social class position, a culture associated with humble circumstances, and their dreams of social mobility. The main differences in urban lifestyles and communities are explained by the social and economic structure in which the city itself develops. Discussing the differences between urban and suburban lifestyles in the United States, Gans (1962) makes an observation that is equally true for cross-national comparisons.

Characteristics [such as family, peer, or neighborhood ties] do not explain the causes of behavior; rather, they are clues to socially created and culturally defined roles, choices, and demands. A causal analysis must trace them back to the larger social, economic, and political systems which determine the situations in which roles are played and the cultural content of choices and demands, as well as the opportunities for achievement. These systems determine income distributions, educational and occupational opportunities, and, in turn, fertility patterns, child-rearing methods, as well as the entire range of consumer behavior. Thus, a complete analysis of the way of life of deprived residents of the inner city cannot stop by indicating the influence of low income, lack of education, or family instability. These must be related to such conditions as the urban economy's "need" for low wage workers, and the housing market practices which restrict residential choice. The urban economy is in turn shaped by national economic and social systems.... (Herbert J. Gans, "Urbanism and Suburbanism as Ways of Life: A Re-evaluation of Definitions," pp. 641–42)

When we trace back the characteristics of urban life in Third World cities to the economic and political roots, their causes are found in a distinctive pattern of development within an inter-dependent world system—specifically in the historical development of dominant and dependent countries (as we shall see in more detail in the next chapter).

Illustratively, Lewis's families live the way they do and make do with the limited choices they have because rural living provides few opportunities for economic survival and the cities present few industrial or solid working-class jobs. Instead, the cities offer many small niches for enterprising souls in the overcrowded economy of commerce and services. The common plight of underemployment will allow very few to purchase the suburban lot of their dreams, but it has inspired many to organize themselves to acquire by invasion and by negotiation the rudimentary amenities of urban life.

CONCLUSION

The advantages of the framework I have called the urban political economy are that it supersedes useful approaches of the past and explains both historical and comparative differences in the experience of urbanization.

The urban structure of a given country such as the United States is revealed as a product of shifting economic and political forces. Urban communities take shape under these influences and create different worlds of experience for the slum dweller and suburbanite. Political choices figure as prominently as economic dictates in shaping these worlds. People struggle with their condition in ways that make culture and spark social conflict. Those responses change urban and rural life, even in failure.

Comparison of U.S.–Third World urbanization suggests that Max Weber (1958) was right when he defined the city as a special kind of economy fused with political power and community. The physical form and social experience of urbanism vary with the concatenation of these forces, starting with the fundamental conditions of economic production and political control that so clearly distinguish the North American and Third World cities. The hillbilly and the landless peasant come to their respective cities for similar reasons: to find work denied them at home. Initially at a great disadvantage in the city, many of them survive, building new lives and distinctive communities. But the opportunities presented to those lives and communities are determined politically and by the fortunes of societies within a global political economy.

SELECTED BIBLIOGRAPHY

BELL, DANIEL, & HELD, VIRGINIA (1969, Summer). "The Community Revolution." *The Public Interest, 16,* 142–77.

BERGER, BENNET (1960). *Working Class Suburb: A Study of Auto Workers in Suburbia.* Berkeley: University of California Press.

CAUDILL, HARRY M. (1962). *Night Comes to the Cumberlands: A Biography of a Depressed Area.* Boston: Atlantic Monthly Press.

CHANDLER, ALFRED D., JR. (1977). *The Visible Hand: The Managerial Revolution in American Business.* Cambridge: Harvard University Press.

DANBOM, DAVID (1979). *The Resisted Revolution: Urban America and the Industrialization of Agriculture, 1900–1930.* Ames: Iowa State University Press.

DAVIS, KINGSLEY (1955, March). "The Origin and Growth of Urbanization in the World." *American Journal of Sociology, 60,* 429–37.

DEGLER, CARL N. (1959). *Out of Our Past: The Forces that Shaped Modern America.* New York: Harper & Row.

FIREY, WALTER (1947). *Land Use in Central Boston.* Cambridge: Harvard Univ. Press.

FRIEDMANN, JOHN & WOLFF, GOETZ (1982, September). "World City Formation: An Agenda for Research and Action." *International Journal of Urban and Regional Research, 6* (3), 309–43.

GANS, HERBERT J. (1962). *The Urban Villagers: Group and Class in the Life of Italian-Americans.* New York: Free Press.

——— (1962). "Urbanism and Suburbanism as Ways of Life: A Reevaluation of Definitions." In ARNOLD M. ROSE (Ed.), *Human Behavior and Social Processes: An Interactionist Approach* (pp. 625–648). Boston: Houghton Mifflin.

—— (1967). *The Levittowners: Ways of Life and Politics in a New Suburban Community.* New York: Vintage Books.

GITLIN, TODD & HOLLANDER, NANCI (1970). *Uptown: Poor Whites in Chicago.* New York: Harper & Row.

GOLDSCHMIDT, WALTER (1978). *As You Sow: Three Studies in the Social Consequences of Agribusiness.* Montclair, NJ: Allenheld, Osom. (Originally published in 1947.)

GOODWYN, LAWRENCE (1978). *The Populist Moment: A Short History of the Agrarian Revolt in America.* New York: Oxford University Press.

GORDON, DAVID M. (1978). "Capitalist Development and the History of American Cities." In WILLIAM K. TABB & LARRY SAWERS (Eds.), *Marxism and the Metropolis: New Perspectives in Urban Political Economy* (pp. 25–63). New York: Oxford University Press.

HUGHES, EVERETT C. (1928). *A Study of a Secular Institution: The Chicago Real Estate Board.* Unpublished doctoral dissertation, University of Chicago.

LEWIS, OSCAR (1959). *Five Families: Mexican Case Studies in the Culture of Poverty.* New York: Basic Books.

MAIER, PAULINE (1970, January). "Popular Uprisings and Civil Authority in Eighteenth-Century America." *The William and Mary Quarterly* (3d series), *27*, 3–35.

MILLS, C. WRIGHT & ULMER, MELVILLE (1946). *Small Business and Civic Welfare,* in Michael Aiken and Paul E. Mott (1970). *The Structure of Community Power.* New York: Random House.

MOLLENKOPF, JOHN H. (1983). *The Contested City.* Princeton, NJ: Princeton University Press.

MOORE, BARRINGTON (1966). *Social Origins of Dictatorship and Democracy: Lord and Peasant in the Making of the Modern World.* Boston: Beacon Press.

NASH, GARY B. (1979). *The Urban Crucible: Social Change, Political Consciousness, and the Origins of the American Revolution.* Cambridge: Harvard University Press.

PARK, EZRA E., BURGESS, ERNEST W., & McKENZIE, RODERICK D. (1925). *The City.* Chicago: University of Chicago Press.

WARNER, SAM BASS, JR. (1972). *The Urban Wilderness: A History of the American City.* New York: Harper & Row.

WEBER, MAX (1969). "The Nature of the City," in Richard Sennett, *Classic Essays on the Culture of Cities.* New York: Appleton-Century-Crofts.

Wirth, Louis (1938). "Urbanism as a Way of Life." In Richard Sennett (Ed.), *Classic Essays on the Culture of Cities* (pp. 143–64). New York: Appleton-Century-Crofts, 1969.

Zinn, Howard (1980). *A People's History of the United States.* New York: Harper & Row.

7

The World System

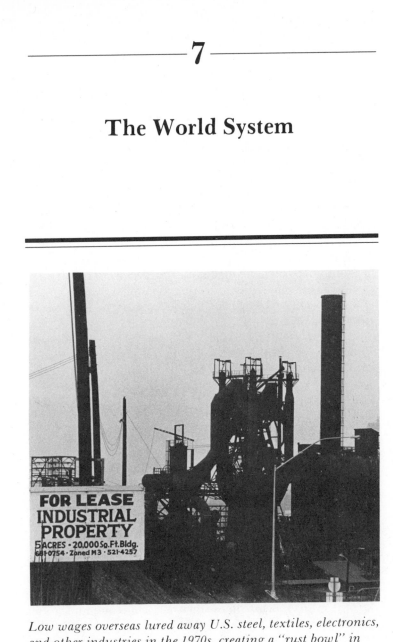

Low wages overseas lured away U.S. steel, textiles, electronics, and other industries in the 1970s, creating a "rust bowl" in America that is still plagued with unemployment and uncertainty. (© Bob Adelman 1983)

PART I
SCOPE

The International Telephone and Telegraph Company (ITT) epitomizes the transnational corporation, that distinctively 20th-century organization that moves money, goods, and information across national boundaries with the impunity of a shark in territorial waters. ITT is a modern empire unto itself; an ensemble of more than 300 companies employing 400,000 people and operating in 70 countries. Yet, unlike IBM and some transnational giants identified with a principal product, ITT is elusive, appearing at some times as a voracious conglomerate and at other times as a disjointed set of firms held together only in a computer's memory. ITT is massive yet formless. It typifies a new way of organizing the world economic system on an axis that cuts across national boundaries, political communities, and corporate identities.

At this writing ITT is the 16th largest U.S. company with annual sales of $16 billion: smaller than General Motors, Exxon, and IBM, but larger than Western Electric and United Technologies. On a world scale of economic entities constructed in the 1970s, ITT was the 42d largest economic entity with annual earnings that exceed the gross national product of countries like Thailand, New Zealand, Israel, Chile, or Ireland, and the income of international companies like British Petroleum, Volkswagen of Germany, and Toyota.

ITT was not always such a formidable player in international business. The company was founded by Sosthenes Behn, a resident of the Virgin Islands when the United States bought them from Denmark in 1917. Behn was a sugar broker who acquired a small Puerto Rican telephone company for a bad debt. Quick to see its potential, he expanded the operation by gaining a national telephone and telegraph franchise in Cuba and, soon after, in Spain. Through expansion and acquisition of other companies during the 1930s, Behn came to own major telecommunications systems in other Latin American countries, England, France, Sweden, Belgium, Switzerland, and, in collaboration with the Nazi government, in Germany. The company's shadowy reputation began with the discovery by U.S. intelligence agencies that even after Pearl Harbor, ITT stayed in close touch with Germany through its subsidiaries in Spain and Argentina and actually manufactured communications equipment for the German army. In fairness, ITT made money by helping both sides during World War II—enjoying all the while the protections of a U.S. company and corporate citizen.

Despite Behn's intrepid diplomatic style and freebooting business methods, in the 1950s ITT was still principally a telecommunications company ranking just 52d among U.S. corporations. From 1959–77, however, the company made radical changes under the leadership of Harold Sidney Geneen, rising to ninth place among U.S. corporations at the height of its expansion and becoming a special kind of transnational. Anthony Sampson's (1980) book describes a meeting with Geneen and the vision behind *The Sovereign State of ITT*.

> He had admired the British Empire and was sorry it had been given up so hastily. Why didn't the British government support the White Rhodesians?... He went on to talk about America's difficulties with the rest of the world—how her oil supplies were in danger and how eventually she might need to move into the Arab countries to protect them. As he warmed to his tirade, his whole frame came to life; he began gesturing, pointing, and laughing, his fingers darting around, touching his nose, his ear, his chin, as if weaving some private spell; his greeny-brown eyes twinkled, and he grinned and laughed like a gargoyle. He seemed no longer a dark-suited, owlish accountant, but more like an imp or a genie. I noticed that a clutch of vice presidents were standing around listening, watching him carefully: they laughed when he laughed and nodded when he nodded.
>
> Businessmen, he explained, are the only people who know how to create jobs and make work for people; he was responsible for 400,000 employees, all over the world, and it was his duty to lobby governments on their behalf as effectively as he could. What do governments know about providing jobs? Why does the American government waste time with antitrust questions when it should be supporting the big corporations that are battling with the Japanese and contributing to the balance of payments?...I had begun for a moment to get the feel of being inside this amazing corporation, to glimpse it through the eyes of the master and followers. From their camp they looked out on a world benighted with prejudice and unreason; where governments were merely obstructing the long march of production and profit; where nations were like backward native tribes, to be placated, converted, and overcome.

Yet on the other side...I had the powerful impression that this company was accountable to no nation, anywhere, and held together and inspired by one man, against whom no one cared to argue. A man, moreover, who in spite of his famous accounting skills and discipline yet had the unmistakable style of a buccaneer. (Anthony Sampson, *The Sovereign State of ITT*, pp. 16–18)

The transnational empire that Geneen created retained at its core the telecommunications of a score of European and Latin American countries. But Geneen's strategy for acquiring subsidiaries was designed to simultaneously strengthen ITT's holdings in the United States and to interweave those with a variety of complementary global businesses. Ideally, ITT should be self-sufficient in natural resources, finance, and marketing, and invulnerable to the uncertainties of national politics. The takeovers came in rapid succession including many household words in U.S. business: Avis Rent-a-Car, Sheraton Hotels, Continental Baking (makers of Wonder Bread and Hostess Twinkies), Apcoa (parking lots), Howard Sams (owners of the Bobbs-Merrill Publishing Company), Levitt (developers who built Levittown, the New Jersey suburban community that Herbert Gans studied), The Hartford Insurance Group, Aetna Finance, Canteen Corporation of America (a major operator of vending machines), Scott's Lawn Products, Pennsylvania Glass Sand (a manufacturer of ceramics and silicon products), Rayonier (a firm producing rayon, wood cellulose, and paper from its own million-acre timber properties in the United States and Canada), and several hundred more firms devoted to everything from dog food to secretarial schools.

Size, diversity, and geographical spread are vital, but alone are not what make the transnational firm distinctive as an actor in the global political economy. Rather, those features allow firms like ITT to operate relatively independent of national regulation and to outcompete purely domestic firms. The global conglomerate can buy and sell from itself, or simply pretend to do so, thereby affecting the import-export balances of independent countries through computerized intercompany transfers. The same mechanism allows transnationals to conceal the true value of financial transactions (and taxes owed in one country or another) through advantageous misstatements of the value of goods moving from one country-firm to another (transfer pricing). Moreover, a transnational like ITT can supply its Levitt housing project in Paris with lumber from its Rayonier timberlands in Canada. It can (and does) leverage its sales of Rayonier paper pulp to Argentina by indicating that the amount of Argentine beef purchased by Continental Baking depends upon reciprocal arrangements. Naturally, wherever ITT executives travel in the empire, they stay at Sheraton hotels, rent Avis cars, and communicate over their own telephone lines.

FIVE STORIES

On the last Monday of every month, a Boeing 707 takes off from New York to Brussels, with sixty ITT executives aboard, including Geneen or one of his deputies, with a special office rigged up for him to work in. They stay in Brussels for four days, enveloped in their own company capsule, spending most of their time in one of the marathon ITT meetings.

A meeting is a weird spectacle, with more than a hint of Dr. Strangelove. One hundred and twenty people are assembled in the big fourth-floor room, equipped with air-conditioning, soft lighting, and discreet microphones. The curtains are drawn against the daylight, and a big screen displays table after table of statistics. Most of the room is taken up with a horseshoe table, covered in green baize, with blue swivel armchairs and a name in front of each chair, with a bottle of mineral water and a volume of statistics. In the chairs sit the top men of ITT from all over Europe, like diplomats at a conference: in the middle are the senior vice presidents. Among them, swiveling and rocking to and fro in his armchair, surveying faces and gazing at the statistics, is an owlish figure behind a label saying Harold S. Geneen.

The tension of the meetings is not simply the tension of its members as they face the cross-questioning. It is also the inevitable tension of a group of directors from four thousand miles away trying to run an empire.... It is in Brussels that the observer can best watch the behavior, coloring and nesting habits of the curious new species, multinational man.... Defying geography is an essential condition, and an executive may even find himself ordered from Europe to New York just for lunch.... In this nomadic existence, telephones become an obsession, not only because ITT makes them but because they abolish distance and provide a reassuring link with home base. The more uprooted the way of life, the more dependent

> the multinational managers become on their company, which forms
> the carapace within which they travel.... It is a self-contained world.
> ...Inside these giant organisms the differences of nationality seem
> often less important than differences of company. (Anthony Samp-
> son, *The Sovereign State of ITT*, pp. 95–99ff.)

Socially and geographically, it is a very long way from the
horseshoe table in Brussels to the garbage dump in Cali, Colombia.
Yet Harold Geneen and a Colombian scavenger named Oscar
work two sides of the same transnational street. Oscar is in the
recycling business. He works the municipal dump in Cali along
with 400 others who search incoming loads of trash for rags,
bones, glass jars and bottles, sundry reusable household items or
industrial scraps, and waste paper. The paper is sold to a buyer
at the site who, in turn, sells it in bulk for recycling to local
industries, including two large firms that do an international
business in cartons, packaging, paper products, and publishing.
As Chris Birkbeck (1978) describes:

> Oscar is 29 years old and came to Cali 5 years ago with his mother,
> sister, and nephews. Having worked in a variety of jobs in the city,
> in early 1975 he decided to try his luck as a garbage picker on the
> dump....Oscar struck up a relationship with Orlando, a fairly
> enterprising dealer who did not buy at the dump but had a waste
> paper business very close to it. Orlando gave Oscar the money
> necessary to buy waste paper on the dump each day, and in addition
> fixed a price at which he himself would buy the material from
> Oscar. In many ways Oscar was little more than an employee of
> Orlando, being paid on a piece work basis but having some room to
> maneuvre. However, after five months Orlando ran into problems
> owing to a temporary downturn in demand for waste paper in the
> city. (Chris Birkbeck, "Self-employed Proletarians in an Informal
> Factory: The Case of Cali's Garbage Dump," pp. 1180–81)

Later, the wastepaper market revived and Oscar managed to
become a buyer himself, although his economic fate was uncertain when Chris Birkbeck wrote this account in 1978. Oscar and
Orlando are in one sense petty entrepreneurs, buying and selling
recyclable material at a small profit. Since the only market for
their main product is the local paper industry, in another sense,
they are disguised wage-workers; but workers who lack any
employee benefits or protections against risks such as unemployment, and who are thrown on their own resources when the

demand for paper falls. The flexibility to use or dispense with these informal workers is a great convenience to local firms, insulating them from the costs of maintaining a regular work force in slack times and thereby producing a cost saving that enables local firms to remain competitive with the transnationals.

In Cali, Colombia, local industries that purchase recyclable paper are even more directly connected to transnational corporations including ITT. The ITT subsidiary, Rayonier, sells pulp paper and, depending upon its price, demand for wastepaper in Cali will fluctuate. Moreover, one of Cali's most prominent firms, Caravajal, in addition to manufacturing paper products, also publishes children's books for companies based in the United States. Hallmark and Price/Stern/Sloan Publishers both commission Caravajal to print their pop-up book versions of *Snow White, The Night Before Christmas*, and other classics (capitalizing on the lower costs of publishing these intricately designed works abroad). The Bobbs Merrill subsidiary of ITT is also a major producer of children's books for the U.S. market. Presumably, the success of Bobbs Merrill in domestic competition with firms like Hallmark would adversely affect the publishing business in Cali and, accordingly, the demand for recyclable paper from the dump. Such are the intricacies of the global economy.

Following the web of international business to another example, on the opposite side of the continent, Brazil is an industrial power in the region and major coffee exporter, competing with Colombia in the world commodity market. In recent years, however, the Brazilian economy has gone from a self-proclaimed miracle to the world's most aggravated case of debt crisis. Brazil presently owes $100 billion to international banks. Interest on the debt alone, if it could be paid, would cost Brazil one half the annual value of all its exports or 40 percent of its gross national product—sources of income that are vitally needed in programs for the nation's poor majority.

In part, Brazil's debt crisis resulted from costly imports including petroleum, basic parts for automobile assembly (by Volkswagen, Ford, General Motors, Fiat, and Chrysler), high technology, and luxuries. Key exports from Brazilian industry such as steel and shoes did not balance this trade deficit. As the crisis developed, government spending increased in an effort to stimulate the economy in the long run, although its short-run effect only aggravated matters by reducing state revenues that might be applied to the debt. International lenders, including many U.S. banks, imagined Brazil a good risk and were happy to fill the gap, until the possibility began to loom that the country would default on its loans. At that point, the U.S. and Brazilian governments, on the advice of the International Monetary Fund (IMF), began to consider the gloomy and unpromising solutions.

In broad outline, the recommended austerity program contained two provisions. While the debt crisis was eased with a renegotiated payment schedule, the Brazilian government would have to reduce substantially its domestic spending and the trade balance would have to be shifted. The latter condition, of course, meant that Brazil would have to sell more than it bought from countries such as the United States. This involves many social repercussions on both sides of the equator. To the south, "the poor are still suffering, but new tax rises, designed to reduce Brazil's budget deficit, have hit middle-income taxpayers hardest. Cutbacks in cost-of-living increases have squeezed white-collar salaries."

> Wiza Leitao, a 38-year-old schoolteacher, is typical of white-collar workers here. A year ago Mrs. Leitao was struggling but was able to continue her middle-class ways. In recent months she has had to give up some of these trappings. First went language classes, swimming lessons and therapy sessions for her children. She had to sell her car to pay the rent. More recently, she pawned her jewelry and silverware and moved into a less-expensive apartment. Her weekly menu has far less variety than it used to. And she has taken out a loan.... [Ms Leitao sees her plight in political terms] "To change the economic situation in our country, you have to change the president, change the ministries and change the system. They've made a disaster out of the economy." (*The Wall Street Journal*, June 22, 1984)

But, for the moment, the bankers are breathing a bit easier as austerity measures have taken hold and Brazilian exports have closed the trade deficit. The crisis has been forestalled, however, at the expense of the real income of the Brazilian lower and middle classes and to the detriment of certain U.S. manufacturers.

Welpro Inc. of Seabrook, N.H., a 50-year-old maker of women's dress shoes, will cease operating July 1, Stanley Barr, president and son of the company's founder, told the 250 employees at noon today.

Mr. Barr said the decision was made in response to Wednesday's decision by the United States International Trade Commission not to give tariff protection to American shoe manufacturers. He said he and his brother were going out of business "before we run out of cash" to meet the payroll.

[Another shoe manufacturer] complained that while imports were flooding the United States, American producers were rebuffed abroad by embargoes and duties foreign countries placed on American-made footwear. Brazil, the biggest supplier of the American market, will not allow American shoes to be imported, while Taiwan and South Korea, the second- and third-largest suppliers to the United States, levy duties of more than 50 percent on American-made shoes. (*New York Times,* June 8, 1984)

Steelworkers in Youngstown, Ohio echo the same complaint, pointing to rising steel imports from Japan and Brazil as a major cause of their town's demise (Chapter 6). Meanwhile, transnational companies like ITT exacerbate the problem from the standpoint of domestic manufacturers and unions by going abroad with new production facilities in order to take advantage of lower labor costs.

Coming full circle, actions taken to protect U.S. jobs against undermining by cheap imports have feedback effects on people and jobs in the Third World. Recent restrictions on imported textiles, for example, would bar apparel assembled by stages in two countries. Millions of sweaters sold in the United States are affected since they are first knitted into panels in China and later finished in Hong Kong.

Chen Choi Ling runs a knitting machine. She works six days a week, earns pretty good money and hopes to visit Hong Kong one day. Miss Chen never heard of protectionism or import regulations, and she does not see how she could figure in any trade dispute.... She lives with her parents and two sisters on a small farm, and earns enough—about $60 a month—to support them all.

But Miss Chen and 500 other women at the Shenzhen [China] knitting factory here just across the border with Hong Kong stand to lose their jobs when the United States imposes new textile import restrictions. (*New York Times,* September 3, 1984)

Harold Geneen, Oscar the scavenger, Wiza Leitao, Stanley Barr, and Chen Choi Ling begin to personify the interrelated constituents of the modern world system. The ambitious concept "world system" correctly assumes that the global economy is increasingly interdependent—a system in which the political and economic interests of nations, citizens, and transnational corporations intertwine like snakes in a sack.

A system means an ensemble of parts whose action can be explained only in their relation to other parts and a whole governed by specifiable interrelationships. The physical environment, for example, is an ecological system. The modern world system suggests, and the illustrations demonstrate, that the advanced and developing nations are palpably interdependent; that old-fashioned rivalries between relatively independent nations or empires are now replaced by crossnational class conflicts (international bankers versus schoolteachers in Brazil and steelworkers in Ohio) or contests between transnational corporations and national states. The modern world system demonstrates, moreover, that there can no longer be a national, or otherwise parochial, sociology. Classes, status groups, the state, all of the fundamental social categories take on a distinctive aspect by virtue of their inclusion in a changing world system. Modern sociology is necessarily international sociology.

DEVELOPMENT IN THE WORLD SYSTEM

In the last 10 or 15 years, sociology has rediscovered the global conditions that determine national prosperity or poverty. Although this revival has greatly enhanced our ability to explain differences in national development, it should not obscure the centrality of such insights in the classical tradition. In 1776 Adam Smith explained *The Wealth of Nations* by their comparative advantage in international trade. In the first volume of *Capital*, Karl Marx disputed Smith and the idea that nations trade freely on the basis of their natural advantages. Instead, he argued, capitalism reorganizes the economic activities of nations to suit its own demands for an international market.

> To understand the course taken by this change, we do not need to go back very far at all. Although we come across the first sporadic traces of capitalist production as early as the fourteenth or fifteenth centuries

in certain towns of the Mediterranean, the capitalist era dates from the sixteenth century. (Karl Marx, *Capital*, V. 1, pp. 875–76)

The development of capitalism depended upon many vital conditions such as the creation of wage labor, but in its fully developed industrial form, it was fundamentally an international system. Marx describes how handicraft production in India was destroyed by British colonial policy in order to create a market for English textile factories. In the new system, India was assigned the role of producing cotton "just as Australia, for example, was converted into a colony for growing wool."

> A new and international division of labour springs up, one suited to the requirements of the main industrial countries, and it converts one part of the globe into a chiefly agricultural field of production for supplying the other part, which remains a pre-eminently industrial field. (Karl Marx, *Capital*, V. 1, pp. 579–580)

In the early years of North American sociology, with neglect of the classical tradition (Chapter 2), the study of development waned. The result, as Anthony Giddens (1973) notes, "essentially severed social theory from the concerns which originally inspired all of the most prominent social thinkers—the nature of the transformation which destroyed 'traditional' society and created a new 'modern' order" (p. 17). After World War II, and with the emergence of new nations in Asia and Africa, sociologists returned to the study of development. At first, however, the developing nations were cast in the interpretive terms of modernization theory—itself largely a product of social evolutionary theories.

Modernization and Underdevelopment

Modernization was ahistorical, taking for granted the idea of a nation, rather than understanding it as a historically created form of society—in the manner, for example, that the new nations were created out of former European colonies. Modernization theory held that nations develop according to a single model defined by such (Western) experiences as capital formation and investment, innovation, entrepreneurship, and, eventually, industrialization. In the metaphors of the time, nations take off at a point when those conditions are secured and then move along a Western developmental continuum—the stages of which are established by the history of the now-industrialized countries. New nations can imitate that success if only they get themselves together: abandon their traditional ways, acquire a dose of the achievement motivation that supposedly did so much for U.S. growth, educate themselves, have fewer children, and take on the mental outlook of modern people.

Most of these modernization formulas were nonsense. If traditionalism sometimes deterred economic development, in many cases, such as family-based saving and enterprise, it promoted it. Moreover, the theory never explained how once prosperous societies became *underdeveloped* and how others were prevented from developing by the imperial designs of the advanced societies. In that sense, the social science of the more developed countries itself tended to be imperialistic, blaming the poor nations for their own plight. In other parts of the world, however, more discriminating explanations of underdevelopment were being fashioned.

In Brazil, Florestan Fernandes suggested that the principal obstacle facing the poor nations was their dependency upon the political and economic conditions set by the advanced countries. In Argentina, Raul Prebish and the ECLA (the UN Economic Commission on Latin America) school pointed more concretely to the deteriorating terms of trade that the poor countries exporting raw materials were forced to accept from the rich industrial nations that controlled demand. In Sweden, the same Gunnar Myrdal (1957) who had studied racism in the United States, explained the existence of *Rich Lands and Poor* through the "principle of circular and cumulative causation." In the world system, nations that are poor or dependent upon the rich are also the least able to break out of the poverty cycle; "the play of the forces in the market normally tends to increase, rather than to decrease, the inequalities between regions" (p. 26). In the sharpest statement of this general idea, Andre Gunder Frank (1969) declared,

> that in contrast to the development of the world metropolis which is no one's satellite, the development of the national and other subordinate metropolises is limited by their satellite status... the regions which are the most underdeveloped and feudal-seeming today are the ones which had the closest ties to the metropolis in the past.

(Andre Gunder Frank, "The Development of Underdevelopment," pp. 9 and 13)

With the growing worldwide influence of these ideas stressing Third World dependency, North American sociology began to question the modernization theory, particularly after the publication of Immanuel Wallerstein's (1974) *The Modern World System*. Wallerstein's volume, the first in a projected series of four, captured much of the momentum of dependency theory in a treatment of development based on detailed historical scholarship. Wallerstein avoids the jargon and polemics of dependency theory, presenting at the same time a model that is holistic and intuitively appealing.

> A world system is a social system, one that has boundaries, structures, member groups, rules of legitimation, and coherence. Its life is made up of the conflicting forces which hold it together by tension, and tear it apart as each group seeks eternally to remold it to its advantage.... It is the peculiarity of the modern world-system that a world-economy has survived for 500 years and yet has not come to be transformed into a world-empire—a peculiarity that is the secret of its strength...capitalism as an economic mode is based on the fact that the economic factors operate within an arena larger than that which any political entity can totally control. This gives capitalists a freedom of maneuver that is structurally based. It has made possible the constant economic expansion of the world-system, albeit a very skewed distribution of its rewards. (Immanuel Wallerstein, *The Modern World System*, V. 1, pp. 347 and 348)

The world system is composed of a core of advanced and dominant states, a periphery of dependent and mainly exploited states, and a semi-periphery of buffer states that deflect the political pressures which would otherwise be directed at the core. Since the rise of the modern world system in the 16th century, the nations occupying these positions have shifted, but the system has persisted. Today's core includes the United States, Western Europe, Japan, and other advanced countries. The periphery, of course, is composed of the poor nations of Africa, Asia, and Latin America. Semiperipheral or buffer states include industrialized countries in the developing world such as Brazil and Israel, as well as poor countries within the developed regions such as Ireland and Spain. Although these states are closely interconnected as an economic system, they are not politically integrated; no central authority governs their competition and conflict. Far from a defect, however, the absence of political integration is a necessary condition of its economic expansion.

Commercialism

Historically, the world system took shape as the dominant European states acquired the transportation technology and the political machinery necessary to sustain colonialism. With navigation skills taken over from the Portuguese, Spain became the first core power of the world system in the early 1500s. Spain colonized South America and portions of North America, the Caribbean, and the Philippines, all in the interests of its empire. Spanish conquistadors and friars took their Christian civilization around the world less for the salvation of heathens than for the commercial enhancement of the Crown. The greatest prize of the early expeditions was the gold and silver bullion taken from mines or from Indian shrines, in Mexico, Peru, and Colombia. In Latin America and the Caribbean, where precious metals were not found, the Spaniards took up production of sugar, indigo, cacao, beef, and sundry products that were in demand in Europe. Typically, production depended upon enslaving Indian labor and the indigenous populations died off at alarming rates from overwork or European diseases. The slave trade conducted by various European countries was designed to provide or replenish the labor supply in the colonies. In other places, such as the Philippines, Spanish colonialism was devoted chiefly to the transshipment of goods (spices and Chinese porcelain) from the East via the *Manila Galleon* which docked in Acapulco.

In this initial stage, little thought was given to any authentic or self-sufficient development of the colonies themselves. Their function was to supply the empire with what it could not get as cheaply elsewhere, rather than to produce what would meet local needs. Cities were located in places of strategic control over the extractive economy and were discouraged from trading with one another in preference to funneling their surplus to the center. In these ways, the colonies were misdeveloped from the start.

Ironically, Spain did not develop either, in the sense of profiting from the empire or reinvesting in the economy at home. As a result, the Spanish Empire began to collapse in competition with the Dutch and English, and with the eventual independence movement in Latin America. Although her commercial power waned, and Spain later lost her place in the core, the nature of the world system remained the same under the trade policies of England, Holland, and other European states. Just as in Spanish-America, the colonies of these new core powers (India, Egypt, Macao, Curacao, and so forth) did not develop in any autonomous fashion.

Imperialism

The first real transformation of the world system came 300 years after its creation with the development of industrial production in the 19th century. Led by England, industrializing nations such as France, Germany, and the United States began looking to actual and potential colonies for raw materials and for markets. What was new and critical at this stage was that the core powers needed a dependable supply of certain raw materials (cotton, minerals, timber, and so forth) and foreign markets for *industrialized*, capital goods. The colonies had to be developed now as something more than passive suppliers or commercial enclaves. They had to supply raw materials needed by industry in the core, and to do so in ways that generated a sufficiently strong market in the periphery for the purchase of manufactured (consumer and, especially, capital) goods. The historian E.A. Brett (1973), discussing British-East Africa trade, put the problem succinctly.

> At the colonial end this system required that each territory find one or more primary products in demand on world markets....At the British end it required export-oriented industry capable of taking advantage of the opportunities created by new colonial markets....The problem was one of creating demand by expanding colonial primary production. (E.A. Brett, *Colonialism and Underdevelopment in East Africa: The Politics of Economic Change, 1919–1939*, pp. 73–74)

The industrializing core powers acquired a new and more aggressive interest in both the size of their colonial possessions and in the development of each in the very restricted sense of a lively market for the manufactured exports of the core. This meant, first, a new rush to acquire colonies: the "scramble for Africa" among England, France, Germany, Belgium, Holland, Spain, and Portugal, as well as the U.S. military campaign to replace Spain in the Philippines and Caribbean. Second, it meant a more active involvement of core states in the domestic economies of the colonies; a colonial service to oversee local political affairs and production policies, managed investments such as in railroads that would consume core capital goods and market local products more efficiently. Above all, it meant a growing and critical *inter*dependence, core rivalries with a potential for global conflict (as World War I is sometimes interpreted), and a more tightly integrated world system. All of these features defined a second stage, after the long era of trade and commerce, in the development of the world system—a stage based on industry and empire.

Multinationalism

Since the mid-20th century, the world system has been undergoing another major transformation. Outwardly the change is represented by the end of formal colonialism and the emergence of the new nations in Africa and Asia, the world dominance of the United States from 1945 to 1975, and the appearance of the transnational corporation. Beneath these appearances, however, is the more fundamental fact of a *global reorganization of production*—the shift of economic power away from nations and national capital, and toward vertically integrated transnational firms whose operations and choices about production and marketing are based on a global financial strategy. It is the world of international companies such as ITT, but also a world in which U.S. firms export their production facilities to manufacture goods abroad in cheap labor markets for reimportation and sale in U.S. markets. Capital is internationally mobile, and so is the labor that migrates from the Third World to the corporate farms and factories of the advanced countries. This is the era of multinationalism.

The new stage is no more favorable to the underdeveloped nations of the periphery than the last two. On the contrary, to the extent that transnational firms operate in a large number of countries, they may be less obliging in particular ones. Where

England, for example, once had a heavy stake in Kenya's domestic prosperity as a supplier and market, the transnational firm manufacturing color television sets in Taiwan for export to the United States and Europe may find that labor is now cheaper in Malaysia or Ireland is offering a tax haven from which shipping costs are lower. Taiwan, which faithfully provided a stable political environment and enthusiastic workers, is dispensable when those exist elsewhere at cost savings. Taiwan supplies nothing unique and its internal market is inconsequential from the transnational standpoint.

With the exception of politically important semiperipheral states such as Brazil and the petroleum exporters, the underdeveloped countries face enormous competition and protected markets in the advanced states when they endeavor to develop their own export industries. Typically, industrialization in the underdeveloped countries is limited, dependent on costly imported components (machinery or parts), and competitive neither in home markets nor as exports. Peripheral states are usually stuck with just their primary products for export (food or minerals). Faced with no other alternative, the poor countries try to produce as much of their one or two export crops as possible, meaning that domestic food production drops and starvation increases. Moreover, as the ECLA school showed, even the demand for these primary products tend to deteriorate as the cost of manufactured goods increases. The problem is summarized, using hypothetical figures, with the situation in which a tractor that could be acquired in 1960 for 50 bags of coffee now requires 1,000.

Naturally, the world cannot be neatly divided into categories like core, semiperiphery, or periphery with distinctive functions assigned to participants. Rather, those categories highlight processes that govern the relations among states. In the concrete world system there are countries, including China and the Soviet Union, that deliberately keep their distance from international capitalism. Their socialist economies based on state ownership of production and central planning, nevertheless, make cooperating with the world capitalist system convenient on many occasions—for example, when China wants to acquire Western technology or the Soviet Union needs grain. Many states practice nonalignment and espouse economic nationalism, but their leverage varies from the independent stance of oil exporters to the diplomatic suasion of important, yet dependent hemispheric powers such as India or Mexico. And there are pure client states which depend for their political stability and economic survival on major powers such as the USSR or the United States—from the Eastern bloc to Taiwan and South Korea.

In summary, since its inception in the 16th century, the world system has evolved from trade and *commercialism* based on state and merchant capital to *imperialism* resting on national industrial capital, and, presently, to *multinationalism* centered on international production and finance capital. The world system of the late 20th century is characterized by: concentration of capital in the giant transnational corporations, the majority of which are U.S.-based, although others are European, Japanese, and merged hybrids; growing monopolies and government supervision of trade; a more active role of the state in international investment; greater tension with the socialist states, despite occasional trade agreements; and the steady development of an internationally determined class structure.

PART II
INTERDEPENDENCE

When the modern world system enters into social and economic analyses, it is usually for the purpose of explaining why the Third World remains poor and exploited at the hands of imperialism and dependency. This line of argument is useful and has explained a good deal that modernization left obscure. Yet, oddly, the same worldly analyses are seldom applied to the advanced nations. In the United States, for example, recessionary cycles, inflation, and unemployment are more often understood as the growing pains of a postindustrial society than as the fruits of a world system changing at its core.

If the essential premise of a world system analysis is that development is a global process, and if this requires, in part, a closer examination of how the practices of the advanced countries have contributed to the underdevelopment of the periphery, it also requires that equal attention be given the structural transformations of the advanced societies that stem from their participation in an interdependent world economy.

THE SCALE OF MULTINATIONALISM

Since participation in the global economy could mean a great many things, let us focus the question and introduce some evidence about the magnitude of foreign investment, using the United States as the leading example among the advanced countries. Table 7–1 shows the growth in U.S. foreign investment since 1950 by world regions. The most impressive feature of these data is the enormous increase shown across the top line. The value of U.S. corporate investment more than doubled with each decade and, by 1982, increased 20-fold since the end of World War II. Second, and contrary to some popular notions, the great bulk of this investment is in the other advanced nations (especially Canada and Western Europe), rather than the less developed regions of Africa, Asia, and Latin America. In fact, the proportion of total direct investment in the developing (poor) nations has been declining from about one half of the total in 1950 to one quarter in 1982.

TABLE 7–1   U.S. Direct Investment Position Abroad at Year-End
(millions of dollars)

Country	1950	1960	1970	1976	1982
All countries	11,788	32,788	78,178	137,244	221,343
Developed countries	5,697	19,328	53,145	101,150	163,076
Canada	3,579	11,198	22,790	33,927	44,509
Europe	1,733	6,681	24,516	55,906	99,877
Japan	19	254	1,483	3,787	6,872
Australia, New Zealand, and South Africa	366	1,195	4,356	7,529	11,818
Developing countries	5,735	12,032	21,448	29,050	53,157
Latin America and other Western Hemisphere	4,576	9,271	14,760	23,536	33,039
Africa (excluding South Africa)	147	639	2,614	2,802	5,069
Middle East	692	1,139	1,617	-3,210	2,703
Asia and Pacific (excluding Japan, Australia, and New Zealand)	320	983	2,457	5,922	12,347
International and unallocated	356	1,418	3,586	7,044	12,660

SOURCE: *Survey of Current Business* (1983, August; 1977, August; 1962, August).
U.S. Department of Commerce.

A full appreciation of the changing character of the modern world system requires that we look behind these figures. Specifically, three major interpretive points help explain what is going on here.

1. The particular U.S. firms that are overwhelmingly responsible for increases in foreign investment are the corporate giants, rather than any cross section of domestic business. Fewer than one tenth of 1 percent of all U.S. corporations receive one half of all business profits earned abroad. The same tiny fraction (1/1000) claims 90 percent of all foreign tax credits provided by the U.S. government. When these facts are combined with the trend toward a growing concentration of corporate ownership within the United States (Chapter 5), where most of the world's largest firms are based, the obvious result is a growing *international capitalist oligopoly*.

2. In the 1950–82 period covered by Table 7–1, the composition of U.S. foreign investment has changed. In the earlier years, the investment was diversified in the sense of a balance among portfolio investments (stocks, shares in foreign enterprises, public

bonds, and so forth) and the direct ownership or control of firms. By the mid-1970s, nearly 80 percent of all investment was direct, that is, made up of companies that operated in other countries but were totally owned or effectively controlled by U.S. parent firms. The significance of this is that U.S. investment has expanded rapidly by buying out firms that were operating successfully under national ownership in their own countries. This means that U.S. investment abroad has *not* gone into new or complementary ventures requiring large capital or techno-logical expertise. On the contrary, it has invaded branches of national economies which domestic capital had already success-fully developed—facts that contradict the conventional justifi-cations of U.S. foreign investment: for example that it transfers technology, complements local efforts, or lends economies of scale.

3. The data in Table 7–1 underestimate both the amount and the impact of foreign investment in the developing countries. On one hand, for tax purposes U.S. firms understate the value of their holdings and conceal them through intracorporate transfers. On the other, U.S. companies operating abroad often raise much of their capital from local sources, meaning that the amount of money which the firm itself has invested is far less than the value of the enterprise controlled. From the standpoint of Third World (public or private) corporations *and states*, the U.S.-based transnationals present an imposing presence. As we have seen, an ITT or General Motors may be richer and more powerful politically than the host nation, circumstances that severely compromise national sovereignty and the capacity of developing countries to regulate the transnationals in their midsts. With their ability to shift production and capital from one country to another, or seek protection from U.S. laws as a last resort, international corporations elude host-country authority over their operations.

From the standpoint of the U.S. economy, international bus-iness for many years proved highly advantageous. There is no doubt that much domestic prosperity, though unequally shared by the corporate rich and the middle and working classes, derived from business abroad. For many years automobiles, steel, a host of consumer goods, and, preeminently, agricultural commodi-ties, produced in the United States or in U.S. subsidiaries abroad, provided through foreign sales a great deal of employment and income at home. Harry Magdoff's (1966) revealing book *The Age of Imperialism* argues that upwards of 20 percent of corporate income derives from foreign sales, and the figure rises to 50 percent with the addition of military purchases by the U.S. and foreign governments.

The reported earnings on foreign investment by U.S. firms have climbed from about 10 percent of the total after-tax profits of all domestic nonfinancial corporations in 1950 to 20 percent, a figure that has remained steady from the mid-1960s until the present. Reported figures, however, again understate true earnings abroad, because they include only income that is sent home (or repatriated), not profits that are reinvested abroad, moved to other-country subsidiaries, or concealed. How much national income really originates abroad is, therefore, guesswork, but it is probably 25 percent of what U.S. citizens and corporations earn from all sources.

THE CONSEQUENCS

International capital has been lucrative for all classes until recently. Since the 1970s, a steady *reversal* of the advantages that accrue to the advanced countries from the global economy has set in. The new winners in this game are not the developing countries, but the transnationals themselves or what some observers call an international capitalist class. Barry Bluestone and Bennett Harrison (1982) describe the change as *The Deindustrialization of America*—the export of U.S. industrial production to offshore plants or runaway shops located in enclave economies of the semiperiphery or in cheap labor markets of the Third World.

The observant U.S. consumer knows that there are no radios or black-and-white television sets "made in America" anymore—although large numbers are sold there. Similarly, color television sets, shoes, shirts, jeans, sweaters, toys, glassware, cassettes, calculators, all manner of electronic products, increasing numbers of automobiles, steel, and countless other items sold domestically are manufactured abroad by U.S. transnational corporations. These firms go abroad with production plants, in the first instance, to reduce their wage bills from, say, the $25–40 per day plus employee benefits paid in the United States to the $3–5 daily wage without benefits paid to foreign workers. Second, host countries are happy to attract these sources of employment and typically offer tax breaks to the transnational firms. Common offshore production sites are in Latin America (Mexico, Puerto Rico, Jamaica), the European semiperiphery (Spain, Ireland, Scotland, Portugal), and, especially, Asia (Hong Kong, Taiwan, India, Singapore, Malaysia, South Korea, Philippines, Thailand). As if these benefits were not enough, the U.S. government waives most of the duties on the products reimported for sale and even insures nominally U.S. businesses operating abroad against loss of property.

As the list of reimported products suggests, it is not just any industry or subdivision of a larger industrial firm that will profit from moving abroad. First, the more easily and cheaply the product can be transported, the more likely that its production will be exported (clothing, footwear, electronic components). Bulky products, like the Ford Motor Company's Escort "world car" made in Spain, may be manufactured abroad when the intended market includes a variety of equidistant, third-country sites. Generally, industries producing for the mass consumption market typify the runaways. Second, it is the actual production activities (fabrication, assembly, testing) that are more apt to be exported, rather than management, clerical and financial activities, or research and development.

Now the significance of these two points for the domestic labor force is that most of the jobs being exported are ones that traditionally defined the U.S. working class—the factory jobs of blue-collar, ethnic, and minority workers. In the last decade, reports of a growing number of plant closings, runaway shops, and abandoned towns have been chronicled in the news media. The devastating effects of multinational production on the U.S. domestic economy are not confined to outmoded industry or even to the rustbowl.

> Sioux City Still Suffers After Its Top Employer Moves Business Abroad.
>
> Ever since the Zenith Radio Corp. pulled out of here, the local economic picture has been dark.

The unemployment rate has soared to the highest level in Iowa. The city's biggest auto dealer says repossessions are up sharply. Home building has come to a halt. "I've shut down and laid everybody off," says Jon Winkel, a local builder. "Everybody I know is in the same situation."

Zenith was the biggest employer in this manufacturing and meatpacking town of 80,000 population. When business was going strong, nearly 2,000 workers made parts for stereo and television sets in a huge plant on the edge of town. But Zenith closed the plant a year ago. It moved its business to Mexico and Taiwan to compete better with Japanese and other imports to the U.S., and the 1,400 remaining workers were out on the street.

"I think it could have been avoided," complains Frances Sorensen, who worked at Zenith for 22 years. "I have no ill feeling toward Zenith. It's the federal government's fault. They aren't putting high enough duties on imports."

Zenith and Sioux City aren't unique in having problems with import competition. In industries as diverse as steel, shoes, textiles and electronics, the same competition is taking place, and communities across the U.S. are losing jobs. Television makers alone say import competition has claimed 60,000 jobs in more than a dozen cities over the past few years. During the past 18 months, Zenith has cut back operations in Glenview and Paris, Ill., Springfield, Mo., and Watsontown, Pa., in addition to closing the Sioux City plant.

Besides affecting the laid-off workers, the closing dealt a blow to small-business men who supplied the plant with parts. "It really hurt me," says Harry Sachau, whose storefront company in South Sioux, Neb., makes antennas. "Zenith was two-thirds of my sales," he says. "I ran about $250,000 of business with them a year. When the plant closed," he adds, "I went from 32 employees to eight...." Some prominent people have been caught in the rubble. Three of the biggest home builders in town have gone out of business. Longstanding real-estate firms have been financially shaken, too. (*The Wall Street Journal*, April 5, 1979)

Warner Communications, Inc. is a transnational firm that grew from the Warner Brothers movie company to a conglomerate with publishing, home video, and a computer branch that included Atari—the once profitable creator of Pac-Man. Although Warner eventually sold Atari, in early 1983 it was attempting to revive the ailing firm by moving abroad.

Atari to Idle 1,700 At California Site, Move Jobs to Asia.

Atari, Inc. said it is permanently eliminating 1,700 of its 7,000 jobs in Santa Clara, Calif., so it can move manufacturing plants to Hong Kong and Taiwan, where it already has facilities.

The employees are nonunion workers involved in making home computers and video games. Production of essentially all of Atari's home-computer products and home video games will be moved.

"This will enable us to keep prices at attractive levels."... While declining to compare specifically costs in the Far East with those in Santa Clara, the spokesman said costs in Asia will be "substantially less. Wages are an important factor in the equation, and so are taxes, real estate and other costs." (*The Wall Street Journal*, February 23, 1983)

The stunned reaction to Atari's announcement arose from the belief that computers and California's Silicon Valley together symbolized the wave of future employment, the place where outmoded blue-collar workers would be absorbed.

Politically, Atari symbolized the notion that high-technology employment could replace jobs lost in U.S. basic industries—that gleaming factories in the Silicon Valley of California could absorb workers from the devastated industrial "rust bowl."...(F)iring a quarter of its U.S. workforce and shifting production overseas seemed an ironic blow to the notion that high-tech jobs might be waiting for laid-off auto and steel workers. (*The Sacramento Bee*, March 7, 1983)

As these illustrations show, there are at least two sides to the problem of exported jobs. Organized labor argues that profit-hungry transnationals have unpatriotically abandoned U.S. workers for Asian sweatshops, although they still want privileged access to the home market. The federal government, it is charged, shows its probusiness colors by enabling the runaway shop with special provisions in the tariff laws. The result is growing unemployment and degradation of the labor force, while transnational profits continue to mount.

International firms, on the other hand, argue that global competition forces these moves; that without access to cheap labor offshore, Japanese imports into the United States and other third-country sites would undersell the U.S. transnationals, damaging the entire domestic economy in the long run. Moreover, they allege, business abroad actually creates new jobs at home in the areas of management and sales that counterbalance losses in production. In many senses both sides are right because they speak from different positions in what is ultimately a contradictory global political economy; contradictory in that the aims of one group can be attained only at the expense of the other.

This is not to say that every claim of the protagonists is correct. On several key issues, it is possible to evaluate competing claims drawing on available research. A central question is the matter of job loss. Does exported production produce a *net* loss of employment in the United States or do new headquarters activities of the transnationals generate an equal or greater number of compensatory jobs?

The initial studies of this question using data from the 1960s were crude in methods and preconceived about conclusions. One conducted under AFL–CIO auspices found that about 500,000 jobs were lost to the domestic economy from 1966–69, based on what *would have been* had U.S. firms produced at home what they reimported from their offshore plants. Conversely, a group from the Harvard Business School polled firms about their operations at home and abroad, reporting that 600,000 new domestic jobs were created in connection with improved export business. These studies talked past one another by posing hypothetical conditions that ignored the question of net gains or losses. The U.S. Senate Finance Committee ordered a more rigorous analysis by Robert Frank and Richard Freeman (1978) which concluded that "the net impact of foreign investment by U.S. multinationals is a substantial domestic employment demand reduction" (p. 156). Whatever compensating trends exist (and they are real), the net loss has accelerated in the late 1970s and 1980s due to the global recession. Bluestone and Harrison (1982) estimate the net loss at 2.5 million jobs per year.

Given the controversy between researchers in sympathy with business or labor over whether there was really any *net* job loss, it is significant that no one argues the substantial *displacement* effect on the labor force due to exported production. That is, everyone is agreed that the jobs that are lost come from the categories of the skilled blue-collar trades and semiskilled factory work. Exported jobs tend to be in the more labor-intensive, traditional manufacturing fields that formerly absorbed the labor of less affluent workers and ethnic minorities. Although some new clerical and managerial positions replace these losses, it is doubtful on an individual basis that redundant workers can be retrained to qualify for those jobs involving completely different skills. Recall the unemployed Youngstown steelworker who lamented being unable to "play Atari." To the extent that the displaced blue-collar industrial workers are reabsorbed at all, it appears to be in low-paying and nonunion jobs in the service economy—in fast-food chains and the like.

This massive shift in the workforce implies that the share of national income going to labor declines as the share going to capital increases; and a study for the U.S. Senate by Peggy Musgrave (1975) confirms that reasoning. This shift toward greater inequality is a fairly straightforward result of there being fewer well-paid, unionized industrial workers and thus a downward movement in average wages, yet no long-term slackening of corporate profits—particularly for the transnational firms.

To summarize these specific developments in broader sociological terms, the internationalization of capital has transformed the class structure of the United States and other advanced countries; just as it has long been a determinant of the class structures of the developing countries. The evidence shows how corporate oligopoly is strengthened while organized labor is penalized by the overseas flight of production. On one hand, the domestic labor force is *professionalized* with the creation of a few new positions in the clerical, sales, management, and engineering fields. On the other hand, it is *degraded* with a great deal of job loss and displacement to low-paying service sector positions. The overall result is a growing polarization of the class structure in advanced societies.

Finally, and key to the interpretation of these changes, class determination operates increasingly on an international scale. These changes demonstrate convincingly that we do not live in a postindustrial society so much as in a *global political economy* with a new and changing international division of labor. If industrial production is increasingly assigned to certain peripheral zones of the world system while the core is reserved for professional and managerial work, that does not mean our lives are any less affected by social classes that are now international— quite the contrary.

TABLE 7-2   Foreign Direct Investment Position in the United States at Year-End (millions of dollars)

Country	1962	1970	1973	1976	1982
All countries	7,612	13,270	30,556	30,182	101,844
Canada	2,064	3,117	4,203	5,859	9,823
Europe	5,247	9,554	13,937	19,916	
United Kingdom	2,474	4,127	5,403	5,699	68,514
Europe excluding United Kingdom	2,773	5,427	8,535	14,217	
Japan	112	229	152	890	8,742
Other	189	369	2,264	3,518	14,765

SOURCE: *Survey of Current Business* (1983, August; 1977, October; 1973, February). U.S. Department of Commerce.

The world system is a matter of daily experience for citizens of the advanced and developing countries alike. When the U.S. dollar is strong, for example, prices are cheaper if we travel abroad, but U.S. exports, including the leading category of agricultural products, are more expensive in world markets, thus reducing demand, profits, and jobs. A weak dollar makes exports more competitive abroad, but it raises the price of gasoline, coffee, and other imports. The strong dollar and high interest rates in recent years have attracted a great deal of foreign investment to the United States. Table 7–2 shows the trend in this *cross-penetration* of international capital over 20 years.

Behind the facades of Main Street America, foreign investors have taken over a variety of domestic firms. The Korvette retail chain was purchased by a French group of investors, while Canadians were trying to buy Woolworth's. U.S. banks have been a favorite acquisition for European, Japanese, and Middle Eastern capital needing a base of operations. Office buildings and urban real estate are common speculative ventures for foreign investors, but their entry into farming and agricultural property has caused the greatest concern.

> Such household staples as Alka-Seltzer, Baskin-Robbins ice cream and Libby's canned food are produced by foreign-owned companies in the United States. In recent years foreign conglomerates have bought such American institutions as Saks Fifth Avenue, A & P grocery stores and Howard Johnson's restaurants and hotels.

Farmers have complained that well-heeled foreigners have bid up the price of agricultural land to the point where it becomes too expensive for Americans.

And even as foreign-held deposits in U.S. banks have grown, foreigners have also turned to buying the banks themselves. State [of California] Banking Department officials estimate that when Midland Bank Ltd. of London completes its takeover of Crocker National Corp., parent of Crocker National Bank, almost one quarter of California banking assets will be under foreign ownership. (*The Sacramento Bee,* December 7, 1981)

This cross-penetration of international capital has increased rapidly in recent years. Comparing Tables 7–1 and 7–2, as late as 1960 foreign investment in the United States was less than 20 percent of U.S. investment abroad; by 1982 it was 46 percent. The trends reflected in Tables 7–1 and 7–2 combine, also, in a growing number of joint ventures by the leading transnational firms based in the United States, Japan, and Europe. Toyota-General Motors and Fiat-American Motors are manufacturing automobiles for the North American market, while U.S. and Japanese high-technology firms are cooperating in some areas as they compete fiercely in others.

In summary, the decisive forces shaping the structure and inequality of social classes are international. Their present effects include the elimination of industrial jobs and polarization of classes. Capital and corporate ownership move in a direction of concentration and interpenetration. The global economy is becoming less a series of national economies than a joint venture dominated by the richest nations and the largest transnational corporations, themselves increasingly independent of nations.

The modern world system is predicated on a basic contradiction between national and transnational interests. If offshore production benefits the U.S. consumer, foreign worker, and transnational firm, it penalizes the domestic manufacturer, U.S. worker, and local community. If U.S. and Japanese firms cooperate to produce for home markets with domestic labor, then French and German manufacturers suffer. At bottom, there is no roundly beneficial solution to these contradictions, short, perhaps, of a global political authority that might regulate conflicts in the best possible compromise. But, it is precisely with this dilemma that modern states struggle—protecting home markets (which Japan does extensively) or enforcing international agreements that benefit the advanced countries (as the United States does through the IMF). Just as international capital reshapes social classes, it changes the nature of the state.

THE STATE AND THE WORLD SYSTEM

On September 4, 1970, Salvador Allende Gossens won a plurality of the popular vote (36.6 percent) in a three-way election for the Chilean presidency. Under the Chilean constitution, the failure of any candidate to receive a majority vote required a runoff election in the national congress. Nevertheless, there was every reason to expect that congress would follow the people's choice when it met seven weeks later. Allende's narrow popular victory delighted supporters in his own Socialist party, in the Popular Unity coalition that backed him (including the small Communist Party, liberal Social and Christian Democrats), and leftists from other Latin American and European countries. At the highest levels of the U.S. government, however, the election produced panic over the prospect of a democratically elected socialist government in a closely allied Latin American country. Henry Kissinger, who was national security advisor at the time, wrote in his memoirs that "Nixon was beside himself," and of Kissinger an associate said, "Chile scared him" (quoted in Hersh, p. 39).

Concern was not limited to White House inner circles. At ITT, Harold Geneen was also worried, and for good reason. Since Geneen took charge of the corporation in 1959 it had suffered reversals in Latin America—indeed, these were partly responsible for Geneen's strategy of expanding through the acquisition of U.S. domestic firms. In Cuba, Fidel Castro expropriated one of ITT's oldest telephone subsidiaries without compensation and others were taken over by public corporations in Brazil and Peru. In Chile, however, ITT profitably operated the Chiltelco national telephone and telegraph system, employing 6,000 workers in an enterprise which the parent company valued at $150 million, as well as two Sheraton hotels, a publishing house, and an international telegraph company.

Business and International Politics

The involvement of ITT and the U.S. government in a campaign to destabilize Chilean politics is one of the more unsavory chapters in foreign affairs. Shortly after the September election, Geneen decided that ITT was prepared to spend an amount of money "up to seven figures" on cultivating opposition to Allende's election by the Chilean Congress. John McCone, the former head of the Central Intelligence Agency, was now employed as a member of the ITT board of directors. Geneen asked McCone to pass the suggestion of destabilization along to Kissinger, to the new CIA director Richard Helms, and, one would surmise, to Nixon. ITT's plan was vague, but it included creating economic chaos in Chile through a boycott of loans and investment from abroad, accompanied by support for the opposition press and dissident groups. Presumably the instability would show that Allende could not govern the country and persuade the national congress to elect the more acceptable runner-up.

It was clear, too, that ITT would have welcomed a military coup. All of this became public knowledge when confidential company memos were leaked to the syndicated columnist Jack Anderson and subsequently published in newspapers all over the world. Anderson's revelations led the U.S. Senate to establish a subcommittee on multinational corporations that held hearings and unearthed these and similarly damning details. It became clear, for example, that just as ITT later pressed for covert destabilization of the Chilean government, it also conducted negotiations with Allende's administration for joint-ownership of the telephone company. When ITT's secret memos were published in Chile, national reaction was so bitter that Allende promptly expropriated the firm. At that point, ITT went to the U.S. government agency that insures business abroad, the Overseas Private Investment Corporation (OPIC), asking compensation under the law for the "unprovoked" seizure of its property.

The bungling of ITT affected very little beyond fouling the corporation's own nest and reputation. Unknown to ITT, the U.S. public, or the State Department, the White House was pursuing its own desperate effort to stop Allende. In *The Price of Power* (1982), Seymour M. Hersh, an investigative reporter for the *New York Times*, provides detailed evidence that Nixon and Kissinger directed a CIA plot to block Allende's election and, later, to overthrow his government. Helms told the Senate Intelligence Committee that Nixon proposed a CIA operation in Chile that, in the president's language, would "make the economy scream." If it should prove costly, Nixon assured Helms that he could make "$10,000,000 available, more if necessary" (quoted in Hersh, p. 41). Hersh writes, "Nixon had specifically ordered the CIA to get rid of Allende. Helms told [an] associate that there was no doubt in his mind at the time what Nixon meant" (p. 43).

Overtly, the administration sponsored an economic boycott of Chile that included the cutoff of U.S. aid, an end to World Bank loans, blocked shipments of the Chilean copper mined by U.S. firms (Kennecott and Anaconda) and curtailment of other Chilean sales abroad. Covertly, money and personnel were dispatched to Chile for the purpose of encouraging domestic strikes (by truckdrivers and housewives), an anti-Allende press campaign, and support for a military takeover. Three years after assuming office, Allende was killed in a military coup. No investigator has yet shown a direct link to the United States, although it is a plausible inference that known destabilization efforts could have gone that far. It is undeniable that the Nixon administration, as in the Watergate affair, took illegal measures to destroy Chile's constitutional government between 1970 and 1973. The Senate Intelligence Committee reported that the administration spent $8 million on its campaign against Allende. Concerning the motive behind these actions, Hersh concludes, "Richard Nixon was primarily protecting the interests of his corporate benefactors, Jay Parkinson [of Anaconda Copper], Donald Kendall [of PepsiCo], and Harold Geneen" (quoted in Hersh, p. 58).

The case of Allende's Chile is dramatic, but far from unprecedented. Since the turn of the century and the neocolonial acquisition of Panama, Puerto Rico, and the Philippines, the United States has used military and economic power abroad to foster international business. What was done in Chile was more than an aberration of the administration responsible for Watergate. Similar tactics were used previously in Guatemala and

Iran to depose liberal regimes in the 1950s. In the 1980s, U.S. attention shifted to Central America with efforts to destabilize the leftist government of Nicaragua and undermine a regional peace treaty that granted legitimacy to Nicaraguan and Salvadoran rebel demands for nonintervention. Nevertheless, political intrigue tells a limited portion of the story of power in the global political economy. The standard activities of U.S. government and international agencies are equally instructive since they show how domination is accomplished in a routine manner.

Political Management of International Conflict

Until recently, the U.S. Congress approved a yearly foreign-aid bill after much conservative hand-wringing and liberal self-congratulation. Conventional wisdom supposes that foreign aid is a gift from the taxpayers to the less fortunate people of the world. The first part is right—but the gift, or about 90 percent of it, as congressional studies show, is aid for the purchase of U.S. products by foreign countries. In the vernacular, it is "tied aid"; funds (including loans) that recipient countries are required to spend on such developmental needs as can be met with U.S. goods and services. Foreign aid is provided to developing countries to build dams with U.S. construction equipment and engineering firms, to start factories with U.S. machinery, and to feed the hungry with U.S. grain. Some of these projects may have constructive effects. Many do not since they preempt local production or make the countries dependent on imports. The point here is that the projects also provide a captive market and indirect subsidy for U.S. business.

A number of public programs complement the subsidies based on foreign aid. Under provisions of the Tariff Schedules of the United States, commodities manufactured in offshore plants and reimported for sale in this country have all tariffs waived and duties are paid only on the "value added" in foreign assembly. The transnationals are awarded a decided edge over domestic or foreign firms that produce for the U.S. market. Moreover, the federal government insures U.S. firms operating abroad against loss through unprovoked nationalization by foreign governments—and even against provoked ones, judging from the ITT experience. The federal government supports a

Border Industrialization program with Mexico that encourages offshore production contiguous to national territory. Free Trade Zones are supported in friendly countries and within U.S. borders. In short, public programs for assisting international capital are abundant.

A program of Worker Adjustment Assistance extends the benefits of government protection to people who lose their jobs as a direct result of foreign competition. Workers who qualify receive extended unemployment benefits and opportunities for job retraining. This assistance, however, is palliative, short term, difficult to qualify for, and funded at a small fraction of the costs of subsidies to capital. In a related vein, organized labor has pressed for more protection of jobs, but favorable action in selected areas seems to come only when the forces of business and political circumstance combine with labor. For example, in mid-1984 the shoe and steel industries both applied to the government's International Trade Commission (ITC) for import curbs on their foreign competitors. The shoemakers' request was rejected, while the jointly submitted petition of the United Steelworkers of America and Bethlehem Steel Corporation resulted in a favorable recommendation to the president and a strongly worded suggestion that foreign steel producers "voluntarily restrain" imports into the United States.

The global economy has become so closely integrated that national states frequently find themselves caught between the conflicting interests of transnational corporations and those of domestic capital and labor. As the preceding examples suggest, the state frequently sides with international capital—but not always. At times the political costs of unemployment and plant closings are too high. In addition to a strong bias in favor of international business, state policy on a given issue depends on the specifics of time and circumstance.

Illustratively, for many years the U.S. government has turned a blind eye on the problem of illegal immigration. The availability of relatively low-paid labor, particularly on a seasonal basis, was highly beneficial to U.S. agriculture and, lately, to the service economy and small-scale manufacturing. Workers at home who suffered through the loss of jobs or from a general downward pressure on wages tended to be the least organized politically. Moreover, the internationalization of labor suited the transnational interests of such allied nations as Mexico that export workers. A ready supply of undocumented workers suited all the dominant interests and the state, accordingly, took a passive regulatory stance.

Recently, however, circumstances have changed. Agricultural labor requirements in the United States have dropped while unemployment has risen. Undocumented workers who decided to stay in the country (often poor Mexicans, other Latins, Haitians, and Asians) grew in number and began to make demands on urban communities and public services. A new set of interests joined organized labor in support of stronger measures to control migrant labor. Proposed legislation included unprecedented penalties for the employers of undocumented workers. For the first time, the state was willing to buck the interests of agribusiness, service-sector employers, the labor-supplying countries, and Hispanic political groups because a vocal coalition of labor, local government, and middle-class public opinion now favored a change. Although the legislation has so far been snagged on congressional division over employer sanctions, the terms of the debate have shifted markedly.

State influence spreads far beyond domestic issues. A number of nominally international agencies set policies for the global economy which serve the special interests of the advanced countries. One of the most important of these is the International Monetary Fund (IMF), created in 1944 to foster economic exchange and stability among the North Atlantic member nations. The organization which began as a source of technical advice and "drawing rights" to meet balance-of-payment deficits was soon converted into an arbitrator of domestic policies in the Third World. The transformation was accomplished by the IMF assuming a greater role in evaluating the credit-worthiness of countries applying for loans to its sister institution, the World Bank. During its first 30 years, the IMF fostered policies for the developing nations that stressed economic (and political) stability and the consumption of exports from the advanced countries. IMF ideology suggested that "free trade" was the answer to underdevelopment, even when that trade was coerced by discretionary World Bank loans and even when it stifled autonomous development.

Beginning in the early 1970s, the IMF was forced to alter these policies in the face of a mounting Third World debt crisis. Worldwide recession and substantial petroleum price increases forced the developing countries to borrow heavily from the World Bank and from international private banks. As the debt and interest rates rose, it became clear that the banks had a crisis on their hands. The developing countries could not borrow fast enough to pay just the debt service on past loans. The danger in this situation was that defaults or long-delayed interest payments on the loans threatened the stability of the world financial system and the prosperity of many of the largest U.S. banks.

The IMF swung into action with a series of renegotiated debt-payment plans and new short-term loans. More important, it instituted austerity programs for the debtor countries intended as long-term solutions. Governments were advised to reduce expensive imports and domestic spending, and to apply their cash savings to debt payments. Hardships were imposed on the poor and middle-income as Third World governments were obliged to cut food and petroleum subsidies to consumers, reduce wages, and eliminate public projects that provided employment. But the amount that could be generated from those savings alone would not significantly reduce debts running to 50 (Argentina) or 100 (Brazil) *billion* dollars. The IMF answer was that Third World countries had to expand their exports.

As sound economic advice, the IMF prescription had only one flaw. More than 40 developing countries were on the IMF's critical list. At the same time, Third World exports were being urged as a practical solution, the advanced countries were suffering recessions and protecting home markets from cheap imports or expanding their own exports. The contradictions loom once more. The IMF and U.S. banks want Third World countries to export so they can pay their debts, but that means countries such as the United States will have to import goods that compete with domestic manufacturers and jobs. In effect, the IMF recommends that everyone sell more to everyone else. Obviously, it is not sound economic advice that is being offered, but a political response to the contradiction that the IMF has not been able to conceal—the fact that prosperity for some in the capitalist world economy comes at the expense of others. The structure of the world system is revealed in such economic policies and state actions.

An appropriately complicated example illustrates the contradictions of global economic politics. Brazil is the world's leading debtor country and a producer of high-grade steel, but no oil. The United States has been importing some Brazilian steel to the disadvantage of its domestic industry. In the summer of 1984, the Reagan administration was looking for needed support in traditional labor strongholds. A solution of sorts appeared in the Middle East.

> The United States government guaranteed $425 million of loans to help Iraq build an oil pipeline through Jordan only after Iraq revised the proposal to include large quantities of American steel pipe....
>
> The Export-Import bank (which provides direct credits and credit guaranttes for overseas purchasers of American products) was initially opposed to giving financial guarantees for the pipeline because it believed that the Iran-Iraq war posed excessive financial risks.... Those reservations were overcome when Iraq agreed to order about $100 million worth of American steel pipe....
>
> The episode shows the role that steel politics is playing this election year. "You can bet this order is going to be played hard up and down the steel country.... That's a very substantial piece of business. It represents about 10 percent of last year's total steel exports."
>
> Iraq's willingness to buy American steel rather than cheaper steel from West Germany, Japan, or third world exporters was taken as an indication of its desire for a stronger American participation in the project.
>
> Iraq had approached the London subsidiary of Bechtel Group, Inc. last spring. The San Francisco-based engineering and consulting concern, which has strong links with the Reagan administration, is the prime contractor in the $1 billion pipeline project.
>
> Bechtel had been headed by Secretary of State George P. Schultz before he came to Washington. Defense Secretary Caspar W. Weinberger was vice president and general counsel for Bechtel before coming to the Pentagon.... (T)he Iraqis wanted a substantial American participation in the pipeline principally as an "insurance policy" against any future action by Israel against the pipeline. In 1981, Israel bombed an Iraqi nuclear reactor. (*The New York Times*, July 16, 1984)

Several conclusions about the politics of multinationalism and the changing state may be drawn from these examples. The domestic policy of states is increasingly affected by the global economy. The state in developing countries is forced to compromise the interests of its own working classes and national manufacturers in policies that benefit transnational firms, international agencies, and banks. In concrete instances, the state in advanced countries must take sides over the conflicting interests of transnational capital and domestic capital and labor. In the Iraq deal where these seem to coincide, U.S. banks with outstanding loans to Brazil would suffer. A parallel contradiction prevails internationally where advanced countries want to revitalize debt-ridden economies and to expand their own markets at the same time. An arrangement in which Brazil swapped steel pipe for Iraqi oil would have helped the debt crisis, but not the U.S. administration's political problems. There are no ready solutions to such dilemmas short of an effective world political authority. Yet the privileged nations resist that alternative with grudging support for the United Nations and self-interested insistence on the IMF's short-term crisis management. Meanwhile, the world system drifts toward deeper crises.

THE NORTH-SOUTH FUTURE

The conceptual framework based on a world system has several distinct advantages over conventional theories of development and modernization. Two such advantages have already been elaborated. First, the world system provides a rich and holistic scheme for describing the modern world; a framework that is capable of incorporating and connecting the economic circumstances of people, firms, and countries around the world. Second, it explains the origins of unequally distributed prosperity and poverty worldwide; explains those through the workings of global capitalism as a historically evolved system. A third advantage is that the framework provides concrete solutions for an equitable form of international development. The gap between rich and poor nations widens with time as an economic and political consequence of the present structure of the world system. That trend, however, is not inevitable. Practical proposals exist that would change matters.

In 1980, a prestigious Independent Commission on International Development, headed by former West German Chancellor Willy Brandt, issued a report entitled, *North-South: A Program for Survival.* The report's key premise was that world peace and survival in the face of ecological and nuclear threats depended on a new pattern of international cooperation. The report addresses the "North-South divide as broadly synonymous with 'rich' and 'poor,' 'developed' and 'developing'" (p. 31)—after some arbitrary rearranging that puts China with the South and Australia with the North. The North-South language is intentionally designed to supersede presumably outmoded notions of East-West conflict and stress that the socialist countries must be a part of any new world order:

> The crisis through which international relations and the world economy are now passing presents great dangers, and they appear to be growing more serious. We believe that the gap which separates rich and poor countries—a gap so wide that at the extremes people seem to live in different worlds—has not been sufficiently recognized as a major factor in this crisis. It is a great contradiction of our age that these disparities exist—and are in some respects widening—just when human society is beginning to have a clearer perception of how it is interrelated and of how North and South depend on each other in a single world economy. Yet all the efforts of international organizations and meetings of the major powers have not been able to give hope to developing countries of escaping from poverty, or to reshape and revive the international economy to make it more responsive to the needs of both developing and industrialized countries.
>
> The nations of the South see themselves as sharing a common predicament. Their solidarity in global negotiations stems from the awareness of being dependent on the North, and unequal with it; and a great many of them are bound together by their colonial experience. The North including Eastern Europe has a quarter of the world's population and four-fifths of its income; the South including China has three billion people—three quarters of the world's population but living on one-fifth of the world's income. In the North, the average person can expect to live for more than seventy years; he or she will rarely be hungry, and will be educated at least up to secondary level. In countries of the South the great majority of people have a life expectancy of closer to fifty years; in the poorest countries one out of every four children dies before the age of five; one fifth or more of all the people in the South suffer from hunger and malnutrition; fifty percent have no chance to become literate.
>
> Behind these differences lies the fundamental inequality of economic strength. It is not just that the North is so much richer than the South. Over 90 percent of the world's manufacturing industry is in the North. Most patents and new technology are the property of

multinational corporations of the North, which conduct a large share of world investment and world trade in raw materials and manufactures. Because of this economic power northern countries dominate the international economic system—its rules and regulations, and its institutions of trade, money and finance.

The South has called for a new regime to protect the commodities which they export against price-falls and fluctuations. The North has only slowly moved towards this.... Exports of manufactures are important for developing countries' industrialization, but the North is raising obstacles against these too.... Current trends point to a somber future for the world economy and international relations ...poverty and hunger... mounting debts and deficits... major tensions between countries competing for energy, food and raw materials.... And overshadowing everything the menacing arms race. (*North-South: A Program for Survival*, pp. 30–47ff.)

The balance of the 300-page report is devoted to solutions. Although the distinguished authors are far from naive, many of their recommendations contrast sharply with current practice. They suggest, for example, a large-scale transfer of resources to developing countries, elimination of tied aid, IMF reforms that respect the domestic social and political objectives of developing countries, greater access to markets in the industrialized countries for exports from the South, priority for the needs of the poorest countries, and better prices for raw materials—in short, a New International Economic Order.

In many senses, a new order is emerging, although so far it does not resemble the hopes of the Brandt Commission. The unrivaled power of the United States in world affairs from 1945–75 is certainly diminishing in the face of industrial competition from Japan and Western Europe. Producer associations such as the Organization of Petroleum Exporting Countries (OPEC) gained influence in world affairs, although that has not been used in the interest of other developing nations. The "high technology future" is an arena of intense competition as France, England, and Germany attempt to make inroads on Japan and the United States.

The old mechanisms of domination are faltering. Third World debt has become so enormous, and implicated so many financial institutions in the advanced countries, that the threat of default forces compromise. Argentina, for example, has refused to accept IMF terms that threaten its own fledgling democracy. A new sense of autonomy and needed reform exists in the developing countries and parts of Europe. While the United States waged war with a social revolution in El Salvador and a postrevolutionary mixed economy in Nicaragua, socialist governments have come to power in five countries of Southern Europe: France, Spain, Portugal, Italy, and Greece. The world system is undergoing fundamental realignment. If a New International Economic Order does not promise rapid equalization of world prosperity, it suggests an unprecedented challenge.

CONCLUSION

Meanwhile, the core responds in its own ways. Increasingly, the placeless transnational corporation is the seat of global economic power rather than the nation state. Transnational corporations like ITT and Atari take full advantage of the protections offered by their nominal citizenship, but show little allegiance when it comes to moving their capital or production around the world.

The class structure that emerges with multinationalism includes menial workers in the Third World enclave economies, displaced workers in the core, and a new class of international capitalists. Yet as the fortunes of the transnationals flourish, the *relative* prosperity of the advanced nations declines. The late 20th century presents a global society with a global class structure and globally patterned inequalities of wealth and poverty. Alone that might suggest equalization and cause for some optimism. But the new inequalities are also more intense, dividing the developing countries into a smaller privileged elite and a larger impoverished citizenry, just as they invade the developed nations.

The commendable Brandt Commission report has yet to redirect international development policy. Indeed, the drift is in another direction. Contemporary policies on international development, encouraged by powerful agencies such as the IMF, stress government frugality with little mention of its human consequences. Meanwhile people persevere living in the conditions that result.

> The government economic policies that have drawn such praise from Mexico's international creditors were not on Jésus Sanchez's mind today as he sifted through the municipal garbage dump here, scavengering scrap to sell to feed his family.

Mr. Sanchez says that on an average day he can gather enough old bottles, cardboard and newspapers in his scuffed canvas sack to earn about 400 pesos, the equivalent of $2.16. It is enough to feed his family of eight with tortillas and chili, he said, but not much more. Last year there was milk nearly every week for the children; this year, with the price nearly two-thirds higher, it is a luxury.

Reduced government spending on items such as salaries, subsidies and public works translate into immediate hardship here.

Mr. Sanchez, who is 60 years old, said he once worked in construction and other odd jobs, and his deeply lined face has a leathery look. With construction in the city at a virtual standstill and other jobs scarce, the dump here is now his only source of income. (*The New York Times*, July 7, 1984)

The world system is a grand abstraction, yet one that vividly connects Mr. Sanchez, Mexico, and the poor countries with international banks and corporations. When these connections are laid bare, solutions for world development readily appear to participants in the North-South struggle. And with those solutions, the bedrock obstacles also appear in an international politics of inequality. This, at least, focuses the conflict and the agenda for a New International Economic Order, although it cannot forecast the outcome of the struggle.

SELECTED BIBLIOGRAPHY

BIRKBECK, CHRIS (1978). "Self-Employed Proletarians in an Informal Factory: The Case of Cali's Garbage Dump." *World Development, 6* (9–10), 1173–1185.

BLUESTONE, BARRY & HARRISON, BENNETT (1982). *The Deindustrialization of America.* New York: Basic Books.

BRETT, E.A. (1973). *Colonialism and Underdevelopment in East Africa: The Politics of Economic Change, 1919–1939.* London: Heinemann.

FRANK, ANDRE GUNDER (1969). "The Development of Underdevelopment." In *Latin America: Underdevelopment or Revolution* (pp. 3–17). New York: Monthly Review.

FRANK, ROBERT H. & FREEMAN, RICHARD T. (1978). "The Distributional Consequences of Direct Foreign Investment" in *The Impact of International Trade and Investment on Employment,* William G. Dewald, ed. Washington, DC: U.S. Government Printing Office.

GIDDENS, ANTHONY (1973). *The Class Structure of the Advanced Societies.* New York: Barnes and Noble.

HERSH, SEYMOUR M. (1982, December). *The Price of Power: Kissinger in Nixon's White House*. Excerpts published in *The Atlantic*, pp. 31–66.

MAGDOFF, HARRY (1966). *The Age of Imperialism*. New York: Monthly Review.

MARX, KARL (1977). *Capital* (Vol. 1). New York: Vintage Books. (Originally published in 1867.)

MUSGRAVE, PEGGY B. (1975). *Direct Investment Abroad and the Multinational: Effects on the United States Economy*. U.S. Senate Committee on Foreign Relations, Subcommittee on Multinationals. Washington, DC: U.S. Government Printing Office.

MYRDAL, GUNNAR (1957). *Rich Lands and Poor: The Road to World Prosperity*. New York: Harper & Row.

North-South: A Program for Survival (1980). Cambridge, MA: MIT Press.

PORTES, ALEJANDRO & WALTON, JOHN (1981). *Labor, Class, and the International System*. New York: Academic Press.

SAMPSON, ANTHONY (1980). *The Sovereign State of ITT*. New York: Stein & Day.

WALLERSTEIN, IMMANUEL (1974). *The Modern World System: Capitalist Agriculture and the Origins of the European World-Economy in the Sixteenth Century*. New York: Academic Press.

8

Social Control, Deviance, and Rebellion

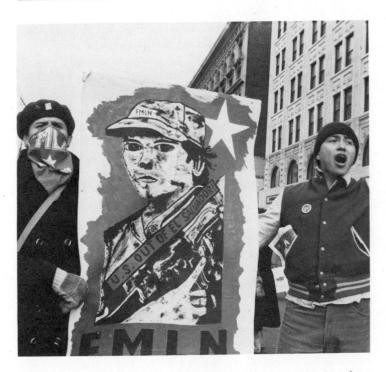

From the Spanish-American War to the current U.S. involvement in Central America, protest has altered domestic politics and international relations. At their most dramatic, protest movements can transform society, as occurred during the Vietnam War. (© Susan Melselas/Magnum Photos, Inc.)

PART I

THE NATURE OF CONTROL

Social control is a fitting subject for this final chapter since it operates through and summarizes many processes discussed previously. In a general sense, social control refers to the means by which groups influence or direct individual members. In context, therefore, social control deals with the means by which class privilege, status-group honor, and the authority of the state, family, church, or association are maintained and sometimes altered. Social control focuses on the circumstances under which people conform to group expectations, the bases of that consensus, and how it is enforced—resulting in conduct judged as deviant in the individual and rebellious in the group. This takes in a lot of territory.

Concretely, every group, association, and institution in society exercises social control or tries to influence its members to some degree: families teach and sanction moral standards, schools do the same while encouraging achievement, churches preach, jobs prescribe and reward particular types of behavior, professional groups define their own ethics and expel rule-breakers, political groups rally their followers around causes, the law and its enforcing agencies define the ultimate boundaries of acceptable conduct. Individuals, in turn, gear their action to all sorts of influences that groups control—rewards, values, customs, esteem, punishment, obligations, recognition, and fear. Although each of these poles of the social control relationship seems so diverse as to defy any organized analysis, this chapter proposes to illuminate the nature of social control by linking it to the structures of class, status, and the state.

A fruitful starting point is the way we think about social control or, more precisely, what people believe society has a right to demand of individuals. Most people agree that a certain amount of social control is essential for the efficient and harmonious operation of social life. We need laws that protect us from scoundrels, agreed upon rules for operating an automobile or a government, and shared goals that orchestrate business or education. We agree, in short, to a social contract that guarantees individuals certain satisfactions provided they play by the rules.

Yet we are ambivalent about the appropriate subjects and limits of social control. There ought to be more law and order, we say, but less restraint on individual liberty; more vigilance of the public interest, but less bureaucracy; civilization without regimentation. Among social critics worried about the proper balance, modern society is alternately portrayed as verging on the barbarous struggle of children that William Golding described in *The Lord of the Flies* or George Orwell's oppressive *1984*.

Ironically, these opposing views err in the same fashion by posing the problem as one of more or less social control, with dangers at each hypothetical extreme. That is, they mistakenly assume that society possesses a coherent set of master values or compatible interests that are implemented to a greater (regimented) or lesser (anarchic) extent. This misconception is promoted by certain social theories that overstress the potent effects of an integrated value system or a unified power elite to the neglect of conflict and competition. Although folklore, fiction, and theory all illuminate different surfaces of social control, none highlights the whole crystal. Social control involves more than a presumably unified set of expectations dictated from the top down.

A topical example demonstrates the point developed fully in this chapter. Today, abortion is a major issue; a conflict over social control in the most intimate way and a battleground on which political fortunes are being decided. Twenty or 30 years ago, abortion, though practiced with some regularity, was morally taboo—a deviant act. With the development of the Women's Movement and pressures for population control, however, values began to change in some quarters. A new women's right to control over their own bodies was asserted by some and disputed by others. Doubtless those favoring abortion were affected by changes in the economy, increased levels of female employment, the trend toward smaller families, and liberalizing sexual mores. Those opposing abortion were equally affected by status threats to the traditional family and homemaker role and by a resurgence of religious commitment which followed on rapid social change.

In 1973, the U.S. Supreme Court ruled that states could legalize abortions on demand. Pro-life and pro-choice forces entered into a conflict that involves churches, feminists, men, state agencies, medical and insurance businesses, and, not least, rival political factions. More than a decade later, the conflict has intensified. Massive pro and con political rallies mark the anniversary of the court's decision. Candidates for the highest offices make direct appeals to abortion opponents or women's political groups. Anti-abortion vigilantes have bombed and burned 30 clinics in defiance of the Supreme Court and its secular law. Women and men anguish over what to do about an unwanted pregnancy, finding little comfort in the crossfire of irreconcilable values and injunctions of social control. Common values may exist in more sublime choices, but real values often conflict with one another. Political and business elites and the general public are divided within their own ranks. Neither our theories nor our popular images of social control shed much light.

The abortion controversy is not unique. Major social issues such as civil rights, war, and social welfare exhibit the same profile. None of this denies the importance of social control, but urges that it be understood as a contentious, problematical, and, in the end, a political process. All sorts of groups in society attempt to influence or control people in ways that proceed from organized interests. Typically, they encounter opposition for a variety of reasons. Social control emanates from group interests at the top, bottom, and around all sides of society. Coming from powerful groups, social control has a better chance of success, but that does not avoid stalemates, as in the case of abortion, or fragile agreements. The value of this conception of social control is that it avoids deterministic interpretations of social life, appreciates the diversity of social motivation, and reckons with the struggles people endure as they labor to define and act upon moral grounds. Social control is no more nor less than the public expression or politics of morality. Values and power affect social control, but in ways that are worked out in contingent situations (rape, gross fetal defects, or pregnancy-related threats to the mother's life, for example, are contingencies that change the meaning of abortion).

The argument that follows specifies the outlines of social control situations (the constraints of class, status, and the state) as well as the main kinds of contingencies that govern those situations. In place of the conventional views shared in theory and fiction, *social control* is defined here as the negotiated and reciprocal obligations among participants in collective actions that derive from group support and influence conduct broadly construed as moral. It is a social contract which, depending upon shifting circumstances, may vary from quite oppressive conditions to liberal compromises and even stalemate. The kind of theory that applies here is one that accepts the role of values and power, but emphasizes, with the sociologist Herbert Blumer (1962), that collective action arises from the "fitting together of individual lines of action" (p. 184). The appropriate imagery is neither a war of all against all nor the big brother state, but Leo Tolstoy's vision in *War and Peace* that history unfolds "in accord with the will of the hundreds of thousands of individuals who [take] part in the common action."

This chapter develops the argument and its implications through four straightforward propositions: (1) social groups attempt to set standards for acceptable and deviant conduct, although these efforts vary widely in the sense of successful control; (2) the state is the fundamental, but not exclusive, agent of social control; (3) social control exercised mainly by the state follows lines of class and status group privilege; (4) attempts at control commonly meet with noncompliance, resistance, or outright rebellion.

INDIVIDUAL DEVIANCE AND THE POLITICS OF SOCIAL CONTROL

Deviant behavior, at first blush, is characterized by violations of the demands of social control. Deviants include criminals who break the law, homosexuals or eccentrics who flout convention, the mentally ill evidently incapable of understanding or acting rationally, people who abuse drugs or children, even ideologues who preach Nazism or communism. In each instance, there are *social control agencies,* from police to the mental health center, especially commissioned to identify, admonish, treat or punish.

The question of what constitutes deviant behavior, however, is quickly complicated by the unsystematic application of social control. Eccentrics and, increasingly, homosexuals enjoy some tolerance, particularly if they occupy positions of social honor—celebrities or artists, for example. Vigilantes in the abortion clinic or New York subway are not always considered criminals by sympathizers and courts. Drunkenness is acceptable in an entertainer whose act features it as humor, but not in the family doctor or accountant. Oddballs who have money or caretakers are just odd; those who are unprotected or on the streets are mentally ill persons requiring confinement when that is available. Moreover, some people who act deviantly escape notice and are not treated as deviants, while others who do not engage in those acts but are suspected of them are treated as deviants.

Two critical implications follow from these observations. First, social control is a group or public response to behavior, or anticipated behavior, that varies widely in its severity or the sanctions it carries. Second, deviance is a socially conferred label applied only to some of those who engage in deviant acts and to others who do not engage in those acts. Deviance is defined by the social reaction to conduct, rather than conduct per se. The implications require elaboration.

Social control may be passive in the manner of settled standards that prescribe appropriate and deviant conduct, or active in the sense of consciously applied rules. The first form belongs to culture as represented in social groups. The second lies in the domain of social control agencies such as police, courts, legislatures, and a variety of nongovernmental bodies—churches, reform groups, guardians of public morals, advocates of legalizing this or banning that.

Deviance

Social control, conceived in this way, is characteristically an interactive and contingent process. Certain social groups and institutions, for many reasons, endeavor to set standards for the rest of society—to play the role of "moral entrepreneurs." To the extent that they are legitimate rule-makers (legislatures, for example) or rule-enforcers (courts), or to the extent that they enjoy status and power (ministers, psychiatrists, bosses), they are more likely to successfully define and sanction deviant conduct. In this process, groups articulate norms or group-defined expectations of individual behavior. The limits of acceptable conduct are suggested and, thereby, the boundaries of the moral order are sketched. But the actual effect of prescribed rules, the real moral universe, depends on how seriously the rules are taken by people, what power backs them, what other rights temporize them, how systematically they are enforced, and the manifold contingencies of particular situations. *Deviance,* according to Howard S. Becker (1975), is defined in the following terms:

> Social groups create deviance by making rules whose infraction constitutes deviance, and by applying those rules to particular people and labeling them as outsiders...deviance is not a quality of the act the person commits, but rather a consequence of the application by others of rules and sanctions to an "offender." The deviant is one to whom that label has successfully been applied; deviant behavior is behavior that people so label. (Howard S. Becker, *Outsiders: Studies in the Sociology of Deviance,* p. 9)

This fertile statement gives a new meaning to concrete events that would otherwise appear as morally inconsistent. Homicide, for example, is often considered a moral absolute—universally recognized as the ultimate crime and severely sanctioned in all cases. Yet mercy killings are sometimes considered justified. And the rules change. Recently several battered wives have been exonerated in the killing of their husbands. Tax evasion, drunk driving, and dope peddling are formally serious crimes. Yet how serious they are in practice, as measured by the actual punishment they draw, depends on: whether the tax evader is a big corporation, the husband of a vice presidential candidate, or a religious nut such as the jailed Reverend Moon; whether the alleged drunk driver is a laborer, the county sheriff, or a famous lawyer such as F. Lee Bailey; whether the dope peddler is a black slum youth, a white suburban Dr. Feelgood, or a colorful industrialist such as John DeLorean—who was indicted for cocaine trafficking in a well-publicized FBI campaign against celebrity dopers and found innocent by a jury persuaded that FBI entrapment was the more grievous deviant act. These examples only begin to suggest the kinds of contingencies that determine whether the deviant label is successfully applied.

Now, if the study of individual deviance concludes that society's reaction determines what is deviant behavior, then the important questions become: how does certain conduct come to be regarded deviant, when do courts and control agencies punish, why don't those things happen on other occasions that involve similar individual acts? If deviance no longer appears as a quality of conduct per se, but as a social reaction to certain conduct under certain circumstances, then the social process of rule-making and rule-enforcement becomes key. That is a big step and a far-reaching implication. John Kitsuse (1962) provides the most cogent summary of how sociologists understand deviance.

> In modern society it is difficult or impossible to derive theoretically a set of specific behavioral presuppositions which will in fact be normatively supported, universally practiced, and socially enforced by more than a segment of the total population. Under such conditions it is not the fact that individuals engage in behaviors which diverge from some theoretically posited "institutional expectations," or even that such behaviors are defined as deviant by the conventional and conforming members of society. A sociological theory of deviance must focus specifically on the interactions which not only define the behavior as deviant but also organize and activate the applications of sanctions by individuals, groups and agencies. For in modern society the socially significant differentiation of deviants from non-deviants is increasingly contingent upon circumstances of situation, place, social and personal biography and bureaucratically organized agencies of social control. (John I. Kitsuse, "Societal Reaction to Deviant Behavior: Problems of Theory and Method," p. 256)

This insight is enormously helpful in sorting out seeming inconsistencies in who is and who is not considered a social deviant. Its implications, however, are much broader. The idea can be extended beyond the usual confines of social control agencies and individual deviance to the general relations of *state and society* by recasting the relations between social control agencies and individuals in terms of the state and such major social groupings as classes and status groups. The state is the chief arbiter of social control, maintaining social order through manifold agencies, both public and private (Chapter 5). Yet the state does not monopolize social control or successfully contain dissent and rebellion. It is, however, in the interplay of state power and dissent that the most general features of social control are found. Some examples of the parallels between individual and political deviance will clarify this avenue of generalization.

Deviance and Politics

The societal reaction view of social control suggests that political deviance, like its "pathological" cousins (crime, mental illness, and so forth), arises in a process that defines certain behaviors as a threat to established order. Reaction to the threat takes different forms such as identifying and prosecuting political deviants (traitors, bribe-takers, pacifists), suppressing dissent, or reorganizing state power depending, once again, on situational contingencies. Illustratively, high officials involved in the Watergate scandal, for a number of reasons including their ambitious rivals and a growing distrust of President Richard M. Nixon, came to be defined as criminals rather than overzealous campaign aides. Watergate justice never held Nixon publicly accountable, and a minor figure, the intrepidly defiant ex-spy Gordon Liddy, drew the longest prison sentence. But, once President Nixon had felt obliged to say, "I am not a crook," it was clear that the social reaction had turned against the highest officials of the state and many would pay with the sufferance of a deviant label. Contingencies such as status and contrition mediated the link between apparently culpable action and sanctioned deviance. In most respects, the discretionary process of judging wrongdoing, disparagingly called "politics," was the same as that accorded so-called behavioral disorders. This suggests, again, that deviance and social control suffuse all of social life, rather than operating only at the bizarre fringes.

In an earlier epoch, partly through the energies of onetime Congressman Nixon, screenwriters, professors, and state department officials were black-listed for alleged (and unproven) loyalties to the Communist party. In both of these cases, what explained the official proceedings was less the gravity of political corruption (the Teapot Dome scandal saw more of that) or of dissent (as when real communists were politically active in the 1930s) than national crises which demanded the reform of state power. In the Watergate case, for example, the crises included an unwinnable war in Vietnam, landslide Democratic party defeats, and the first of the 1970s recessions.

Yet states are not always so successful in prosecuting a new class of deviants and thereby reaffirming organizational principles. Under other circumstances, alleged culprits successfully redefine charges of wrongdoing. They revolt and the state teeters on the edge of suppressing rebellion, negotiating peace, or suffering revolutionary transformation. The American revolutionaries of 1776 said they were not treasonous subjects of George

III or delinquent taxpayers, but free people who would have effective representation or self-government—and, through skill and good fortune, they made it stick. Civil rights activists in the 1960s said they were not communists (as repeatedly alleged) or malevolent agitators, but also free people who would have freedom now—and slowly they got some. Agrarian populists, the International Workers of the World (IWW), the American Indian Movement (AIM), and others, for a variety of reasons, all suffered suppression and a deviant label that stuck for actions no more intrinsically radical than those of George Washington and Martin Luther King, Jr.

Tolstoy mused about the "movement of nations" and events unexplained by the will of rulers or the actions of individuals. Asking, "What does this signify?" he concluded, "that the force which decides the fate of peoples lies not in conquerors, nor even in armies and battles, but in something else...[namely] the activity of *all* the people who participate in the event." So, in the case of attempts at social control that may ensure order or tumble into rebellion, the "something else" that causes the difference is the social condition that makes individual and institutional lines of action dovetail with state power or veer off in another direction. Our task, accordingly, is to examine the conditions of state and society that explain social control.

THE TECHNOLOGY OF STATE POWER

The notion of "political technology" is more than a metaphor. The state fashions techniques for maintaining public order that are analogous to the methods industry uses to produce commodities. In each case, the technology includes ideas that define the task (the principles of mass production or of equal responsibility under the law) and physical implements for doing the job (machines or prison cells). The technology of state power appears in many related forms: in laws, courts, prisons, parole, welfare agencies, schools, congressional committees, licensing boards, riot commissions, and in hospitals that anguish over the fate of a Baby Jane Doe. Understood in this way, social-control agencies are linked to the broader social institutions from which they receive the authority to impose sanctions. The diverse actions of various social control agencies begin to make coherent sense when they are seen as originating from the common root of state efforts to maintain a particular kind of social order.

Michel Foucault (1979), the late French philosopher and historian, elegantly developed the idea in his book *Discipline and Punishment: The Birth of the Prison*. Foucault shows how, over a short time beginning in the late 18th century, the gruesome spectacle of public torture vanished as a technique of punishing crime for the benefit of onlookers and was replaced by the rehabilitative methods of the prison and asylum. The dramatic shift, in Europe and North America, coincided with the demise of absolute monarchies, the rise of modern democratic states, and coincident legal reform movements. In Foucault's terms, new states adopted a more subtle, perhaps insidious, technology of power, one that avoided public violence—which had turned dangerously against the kings themselves—and attempted instead to restore deviants to the moral order through institutional discipline. This technology attacked the soul rather than the body.

The idea of political technology alerts us to social control methods that change over time in response to economic and political developments. The role of punishment in society, as Foucault notes, goes far beyond an effort to reduce crime or deviance and includes "a whole series of positive and useful effects." One of these is an economic effect, as shown in historical studies that

> relate the different systems of punishment with the systems of production within which they operate: thus, in a slave economy, punitive mechanisms serve to provide an additional labour force—and to constitute a body of "civil" slaves in addition to those provided by war or trading; with feudalism, at a time when money and production were still at an early stage of development, we find a sudden increase in corporal punishments—the body being in most cases the only property accessible; the penitentiary... forced labor and the prison factory appear with the development of the mercantile economy. But the industrial system requires a free market in labour and, in the nineteenth century, the role of forced labour in the mechanisms of punishment diminishes accordingly and "corrective" detention takes its place. (Michel Foucault, *Discipline and Punishment: The Birth of the Prison*, pp. 24–25)

A neat example of this point is provided by English vagrancy laws. Vagrancy as a crime punishable by forced labor first appeared in England in 1349 when the plague, European wars, the crusades, and town migration all combined to deplete the supply of rural labor. Vigorous enforcement of the vagrancy statutes motivated or commandeered docile hands. In time, these problems were righted and vagrancy waned as a common crime. Miraculously, however, it reappears as a capital crime in the 16th century coincident with an expansion of commerce that was preyed upon by bandits and highwaymen—presumably the same rogues and vagabonds found roaming the countryside. Later, when the poor laws and incipient welfare systems came into vogue as a method for encouraging industrial labor, vagrancy reverted to a public nuisance and the laws were used to clear the streets of misdemeanor bums. These examples should not suggest any unmediated (or crude Marxist) link between deviance and the economy. The state not only mediates, but independently defines unlawful action according to its own interests in governing. The issue deserves elaboration.

Crime and the State

The English historian E.P. Thompson (1975) has written a remarkable book about the Black Act of 1723 that made poaching a crime punishable by death. The question Thompson asks himself in *Whigs and Hunters* is why in the world would the British government resort to a drastic law that proposed hanging country folk engaged in deer hunting (with faces blackened for stealth) in the forests and game preserves set aside for the aristocracy? Why, moreover, was this offense of "the blacks" soon joined by several hundred more capital crimes of a similar nature, ranging from breaking fish ponds to cutting sod for use in fireplaces? What purpose was the Black Act designed to serve?

The conflict had a clear history. Civil wars and the Commonwealth government that temporarily replaced the British monarchy in the previous century had greatly reduced royal amenities, including the hunt and exclusive use of the deer parks. Correspondingly, common rights to these preserves for agricultural purposes had grown. Fish ponds that flooded areas of sod-cutting and the deer that ate crops were nuisances to the agrarian economy. The "blacks" were no mere poachers. They hunted deer, cut trees and sod, broke dams, and committed other "offenses" in their efforts to farm the forest lands, an activity that they had come to consider as their right.

Yet these facts alone hardly explain the massive official reaction in the new law. Why did the state choose to make a dramatic example of the seemingly petty crimes of the foresters? On one hand, a new royal house (the Hanovers) had come to power in 1714 and realistically feared popular opposition such as the Blacks manifested by their defiant use of the forests. On the other hand, in the interests of consolidating its power, the government had begun to award new privileges of forest use to its own aristocrat supporters. Licenses for hunting game and patronage positions such as gamekeeper were distributed in a blatant bid for support. The government used "the deer as a screen behind which to advance their own interests."

When the Blacks resisted these politically motivated incursions by poaching, now intended and understood as an act of political defiance upheld by common rights, a true emergency was created because the Blacks won community support. "It was the displacement of authority, and not the ancient offense of deer-stealing, which constituted, in the eyes of the government, an emergency" (p. 191). The interests of agrarian society met head-on an effort to reorganize the state along lines of aristocratic privilege that was superseding the power of monarchy. The Black Act, therefore, was just one "ideological index" of a realignment of state power. Enforcement of the act, moreover, was "seized upon by Walpole [the new prime minister] as a heaven-sent opportunity to consolidate his power" (p. 201). Walpole and his supporters were creating a new technology of power; a state that would be independent of the throne and based on new bureaucratic forms and a law that put aristocratic privilege ahead of common interests, creating in the process a "forest bureaucracy" to share in the spoils and a new brand of criminal.

The previous points take advantage of circumstances in which a strong state was in the process of formation with the consolidated assistance of powerful social classes. In that sense, they may give the impression that states unfailingly develop potent mechanisms of social control—an observation that is subject to wide variation. Prior to independence, the British colonies in North America were governed by fragile local authority, menaced by sectionalism and religious controversy. As the English Restoration struggled to establish a new state and parliamentary form, the Massachusetts Bay Colony in North America faced a more elusive threat to public order—witches.

Kai Erikson's (1966) study of *Wayward Puritans* reveals that the Massachusetts Bay Colony underwent three different outbreaks of religious heresy, veritable crime waves that saw public prosecutions rise significantly, and that each was connected with political uncertainty about the colony's mandate and future. The most serious episode occurred around 1692 when political dissension, land disputes, and commercial competition began to plague the colony: "It was while the people of the colony were preoccupied with these matters that the witches decided to strike" (p. 141).

The witch trials of Salem Village began as an effort to stamp out a small cult of teenaged girls gathered around a household slave from Barbados steeped in the practice of voodoo. The hysteria spread until hundreds of citizens were accused and held awaiting trial as witches. The freewheeling accusations touched even the president of Harvard College and the legendary pilgrim, Captain John Alden. Erikson explains these events as a reflection of deeper social troubles, of unspoken threats to social order that call forth a renewed sense of solidarity and a reaffirmation of society's boundaries.

> [W]henever a community is confronted by a significant relocation of boundaries, a shift in its territorial position, it is likely to experience a change in the kinds of behavior handled by its agencies of social control. The occasion which triggers this boundary crisis may take several forms—a realignment of power within the group, for example, or the appearance of new adversaries outside it—but in any case the crisis itself will be reflected in altered patterns of deviation and perceived by the people of the group as something akin to what we now call a crime wave. These waves dramatize the issues at stake when a given boundary becomes blurred in the drift of passing events, and the encounters which follow between the new deviants and the older agents of control provide a forum, as it were, in which the issues can be articulated more clearly, a stage on which

it can be portrayed in sharper relief. (Kai T. Erikson, *Wayward Puritans: A Study in the Sociology of Deviance,* pp. 68–69)

A social order menaced by an invasion of witches may seem bizarre today. Yet modern societies continue to turn up diabolical threats to their own values and stability just when established boundaries are shifting. The Salem Witch trials have been instructively compared with the virulent anticommunism that swept the United States in the late 1940s and early 1950s—and has erupted periodically before and since. The comparison goes deeper than spooky and malevolent tactics of witch-hunting. Erikson's observation about witchcraft in the 17th century—that "no other form of crime in history has been a better index to social disruption and change" (p. 153)—applies as well to the periodic Red scares of the 20th century. The Red menace began cropping up in the United States shortly after the first Russian Revolution in 1905. Dissenters once labeled revolutionaries or anarchists now became associated with communism, even though the issues involved in their dissent were not systematically joined by the American Communist Party formed in 1919.

For nearly three decades, U.S. communism drew only occasional condemnation and seldom posed a palpable subversive threat to national security. Indeed, in 1936, Earl Browder ran for president on the Communist party ticket receiving nearly 75,000 votes. From its high point, when the Communist party had perhaps 200,000 sympathizers, it declined steadily, particularly after Stalin's purges in the Soviet Union during the 1930s. The Committee on Un-American Activities of the House of Representatives was formed in 1938, but achieved celebrity only a decade later. Ironically, the great anticommunist crusade and McCarthyism in the early 1950s came long after the movement had lost a significant following. What, then, explains the American Inquisition, the period of U.S. history which David Caute (1978) calls the "great fear" when thousands of citizens from the schools to Hollywood were labeled agents of the communist conspiracy?

Consistent with Erikson's interpretation, postwar U.S. society plunged into a political crisis compound of domestic strife and international challenge. For 16 years of depression and war the country had been ruled by the Roosevelt administration. With

Republicans and conservative Democrats on the sidelines, fundamental social reforms had been instituted from Social Security to unemployment insurance and labor legislation (Chapters 5 and 6). Under emergency conditions, the rudiments of a welfare state had been built that irked the political opposition all the more since they correctly saw themselves as unable to regain the White House during the war and its immediate aftermath. Growing domestic irritation was compounded by the postwar international scene. European states were in ruin and a newly empowered United States looked across the wreckage at the Russian bear.

By 1948, when Harry S. Truman ran for reelection, the political crisis was ripe for a cold war against the Soviet Union and any of its alleged domestic sympathizers: "bleeding hearts" like Eleanor Roosevelt who had defended the civil rights of communists before a congressional committee, appeasers like the late President Roosevelt who had been duped by Stalin, "communistically inclined" (in Joseph McCarthy's phrase) Democrats who had supported labor, internationalism, and related left-wing causes—in short, a large segment of the Democratic party. Redbaiting came into fashion in the 1946 Congressional elections and paid off handsomely with major Republican party gains. Truman knew he was in trouble, although he had two years before the next presidential election in which to mount his own campaign against the Red menace. And so he did with a flourish. To steal Republican thunder, Truman began a purge of purported communists in the federal civil service. An Attorney General's list was issued naming fancied subversive organizations. Deportations of suspect immigrants took place. Communist party stalwarts were indicted for alleged plots to overthrow the government. And the Truman Doctrine abroad pledged U.S. support for countries (no matter how repressive) engaged in a struggle with communism.

Judged by the result of Truman's reelection, the campaign worked. But it also let loose years of mean-spirited intimidation and a political technology of official suspicion (committees, lists, kangaroo hearings, investigations, loyalty oaths) that ruined thousands of lives, uncovering in the process no Red plot to overthrow the government. As Caute (1978) observes, Truman's tactical use of the cold war was crucial in sowing the seeds of McCarthyism. By 1952, with the popular election of General

Dwight D. Eisenhower to the presidency, the political crisis abated. The witch-hunting Senator Joseph McCarthy was disgraced and the communist conspiracy suddenly looked less menacing, although the climate of fear retreated only slowly and can still be reactivated today.

Three interpretive points summarize the historical evidence on the state and social control. First, there is a literal technology of state power embodied in ideas about and mechanisms for implementing social control. Second, that technology changes with economic and political development, most notably during times of social disruption or crisis. Finally, the state is a critical source of social control, but not the only one. State and society, government and church, for example, influence one another. At bottom, the process of defining and sanctioning deviance is a political process—whether in specific cases the deviance concerns political activity, crime, insanity, or some other malady. Social control is political because it involves exercising power for the social order.

CLASS, STATUS, AND SOCIAL CONTROL

So far we have dealt with the mechanisms of social control, where they come from and when they are brought to bear. The next, more practical, matter is how those mechanisms are actually employed and how their application is *socially mediated* by the influence of class and status. The previous discussion demonstrates how the zealousness or perceived demand for social control varies with periodic crises and shifting social boundaries. But social control is routinely affected by the power of social classes and status groups. Analyzed along these dimensions, social control tends to follow lines of privilege rather than any objective requirements of social order.

Class

A clear relation between criminal law and the interests of propertied classes appears in the examples cited previously; in the case of vagrancy laws, for example, with landowners in need of labor and merchants seeking protection from highwaymen. While the Black Acts were being enlarged, an equally impressive number of capital crimes against commerce and manufacture were added to the statute books. As the commercial core of the 18th-century world system, England also had the most bloodthirsty criminal code known to history. Douglas Hay's (1975) introductory essay to *Albion's Fatal Tree: Crime and Society in Eighteenth-Century England* offers two characteristic examples:

> An act of 1753 prescribing hanging for stealing shipwrecked goods was brought in on behalf of the "Merchants, Traders and Insurers of the City of London" whose profits were being diminished by the activities of wreckers; the existing laws were declared to be too gentle. In 1764 Parliament decreed that the death penalty would apply to those who broke into buildings to steal or destroy linen, or the tools to make it.... The criminal law was critically important in maintaining bonds of obedience and deference, in legitimating the status quo, in constantly recreating the structure of authority which arose from property and in turn protected its interests. (Douglas Hay, "Property, Authority and the Criminal Law," pp. 20–21 and 25)

The marvelous point of Hay's analysis, however, is that these draconian laws were only mildly and selectively enforced. The seeming paradox is explained precisely by the structure of class relations. That is, the severe criminal code defined for everyone a healthy respect for property. This was particularly important since the upper classes, still striving for independence from the king's power, would tolerate no regular police force. Moreover, the stiff penalties placed considerable discretion in the hands of local courts and their aristocratic supporters who monopolized the granting of pardons. The law, together with liberal use of pardons, engendered respect for property and a good deal of gratitude from would-be offenders in the bargain. In a round-about fashion, therefore, the class and legal systems reinforced one another.

The connections of class and crime appear in intricate and specific forms from one historical period of society to another. In the modern United States, the issue has been analyzed most completely in connection with what Edwin Sutherland (1940) called "white collar crime." The phrase emphasizes that legally defined crime is hardly confined to a shadowy underworld or desperate working class.

A long list of upperworld crimes compiled by Albert Morris in 1935 included usurious lending, stock fraud and embezzlement, bank manipulations of investment trusts and securities, manufacturers' price-fixing, graft in business and politics, employers' exploitation of unorganized labor, and many more. Today the list could be vastly expanded to include, for example, industrial dumping of toxic waste, violation of product safety laws from children's toys to nuclear reactors, computerized investment swindles, corporate manipulation of stock values and sales, fraud in government health programs and defense contracting, and multinational bribes to foreign government officials for the purchase of U.S. exports.

Sutherland's (1940) original research examined decisions by courts and commissions against the 70 largest U.S. industrial and commercial firms with respect to four types of laws: antitrust, false advertising, labor relations, and patent infringement. He found a total of 547 adverse decisions; each corporation had at least one and the average was 7.8 per firm. Revealingly, however, only 9 percent of the violations were treated as criminal matters, the rest being dismissed as misdemeanors or minor infractions. Noting this tendency to coddle corporations, Sutherland went on to examine the 547 incidents to determine whether, by the standards of social injury and legal provision of a penalty, these were true criminal acts. In virtually all cases, the two standards were met and the first, of social injury, applied in all 547. That is, in 100 percent of the cases corporations were guilty of having committed socially injurious crimes, although those crimes were punished as such in just 9 percent.

What were the corporate criminals up to that Sutherland considered socially injurious? In the false advertising category, he discovered the now-familiar practice of gross misrepresentation: cigarettes that claimed to cure throat irritation, facial creams billed as "skin food" that removed wrinkles, tea supposedly made from tender leaves for one firm but actually bought in bulk from the same source used by competitors. In the field of labor relations, corporations tried to prevent union organizing by employing private goon-squads to break up peaceful assemblies of workers with clubs and gas guns—over a four-year period, one steel corporation purchased 143 such guns while the entire Chicago police department found need of only 13. Corporate officials embezzled from their own stockholders in the form of paying themselves excessive and fraudulently calculated salaries and bonuses.

Finally, the large corporations were undermining the free-enterprise system and attempting to replace it with their own "private collectivism" through the restraint of trade. In the major trade associations, manufacturers conspired to limit production and fix prices. Companies protected themselves by applying for patents on "every possible modification of procedure, bringing [patent infringement] suits on every possible pretext.... The Good Humor Corporation engaged in patent litigation for more than a decade with the Popsicle Company and other manufacturers of ice-cream bars to determine which firm had invented this contribution to science and the arts" (Sutherland, 1956, p. 69). Today, roughly 40 years later, the same practices are routine in the business world, down to a protracted court battle over who invented and holds patent rights to the frozen pizza.

In a strongly worded conclusion, Sutherland (1956) claims "that the ideal businessman and the large corporation *are* very much like the professional thief" (p. 69). The corporations are recidivists; that is, 97 percent are repeat offenders. Illegal behavior is much more common than prosecutions suggest since few corporations are punished for these industry-wide practices. Violators do not lose status in the business community for their deeds and business holds contempt for legislators, courts, and government "snoopers." "Businessmen, being like professional thieves in these four respects, are participants in organized crime." Although Sutherland's original work was done almost 50 years ago, his results, if not his vigorous analogies, are replicated in recent research, by Marshall Clinard and Peter Yeager (1978), for example.

Class bias reflected in the desultory prosecution of white collar crime is further demonstrated by the enthusiasm with which social control agencies go after violations by labor unions. Sutherland (1945) notes that "of the [Department of Justice] actions against business firms and associations of business firms, 27 percent were criminal prosecutions; while of the actions against trade unions, 71 percent were criminal prosecutions" (p. 137). Official scorn is heaped on "welfare chiselers" but spares firms that defraud the government by billing for unnecessary or unperformed medical services under medicare or selling defective and overpriced merchandise to the Department of Defense. In recent cases, faulty computer chips were knowingly sold to the government and installed in an undetermined number of missiles. A 10-cup coffeemaker for the Air Force C–5 transport plane comes at a cost of $7,622 to the taxpayer.

Selectivity in prosecution is compounded in the rare instances when corporate crime is actually proven in courts or agencies, yet receives light to suspended sentences. A Canadian study of ordinary and corporate thieves by Laureen Snider (1982) shows that common criminals are much more likely to go to jail and to stay there for long terms.

The relationship between class and crime is more involved than the old exposés of white collar skullduggery would suggest. To say it is more complicated, however, does not mean that today's corporate outlaws appear in a more favorable light. Rather, some things have changed in the public and official attitude toward these crimes. New laws aimed at upperworld crime have been fashioned and applied with perhaps a broader deterrent effect than the ordinary criminal statutes. Moreover, the national political mood has shifted back and forth in support for prosecution of those who violate the public trust.

An insider's account of the U.S. Department of Justice by Jack Katz (1979) shows how a "social movement against white-collar crime" arose in the 1970s within the federal government. The timing was crucial since the Watergate scandal had stripped away the protective cover of normal corruption. Young prosecutors promoting their own careers exploited the general mood of indignation. Katz argues that the Justice Department is highly selective about which corporate crimes it will prosecute since they are typically complicated and "tough to make" (prove)—not least because of the elaborate legal defense that the firms can put up. But, when the government does decide to go after a particular offender, to put in all that work with smaller staffs and budgets, it pursues the case more vigorously. White collar crime is not casually or systematically ignored, although it is selectively prosecuted with the result that it is less risky an undertaking.

Among other saviors, corporations can usually count on changes in political administrations and the cooling fires of reformism. New administrations suspend the overzealousness of their predecessors. Katz, for example, predicted: "As a practical matter, the White House [after Watergate] temporarily lost its considerable ability to protect lesser political centers from moral attack. Accordingly, the movement against white-collar crime should recede as the Presidency is restored to the insulation of presumptive legitimacy" (p. 178).

Lately, a shift back to lenience has confirmed this prediction. In the early 1980s, investigations and prosecutions of industrial polluters dropped precipitously. At the same time, the Justice Department's active cases under the Foreign Corrupt Practices Act of 1978 dropped from 400 actions employing 15 full-time lawyers to 14 cases that now occupied just 3 prosecutors. The widespread crime of bribing foreign officials to purchase U.S. corporate products (such as airplanes) and services (oil drilling) was effectively shelved as the new administration turned instead to fraud involving military supplies, food stamps and drug money. The multinational fraud branch of the Justice Department was quietly eliminated.

Corporate crime is treated gingerly for a variety of reasons. Legislators and agency officials fear the political power of big business. Cases involving sophisticated financial dealings and resourceful concealment are difficult to make. Government agencies are understaffed for the demanding purpose. Highly paid corporate lawyers can defeat, stall, and trivialize even well-prepared cases. Violators can play on political sympathies, claiming that honest business is persecuted while muggers and rapists go free—despite the fact that these crimes are prosecuted and punished more vigorously. Typically, these methods succeed in limiting the number of white-collar crimes that are brought before the law and minimizing the sanctions imposed on those where guilt is fixed.

Social-control agencies in general, and those responsible for the definition and enforcement of crime in particular, reflect the broader social pattern of class interest. It is not the seriousness of crimes, weighed on some scale of social injury—the lives lost due to unsafe automobiles and toxic pollutants compared to the toll from street crime, for example—that determines their official treatment. It is rather the consequences of those crimes for a complex, and sometimes conflicting, set of class interests that mediate definitions of seriousness and prescribed treatments. The state and its social control agencies are deeply involved in the same structure of class privilege—often defending it and sometimes reforming it.

Status

The state and class interests, although basic, are by no means the only sources of social control. Diverse values carry prescriptions about social control, particularly values that distinguish cultural and status groups from one another. Conduct considered shameful or illegal by middle-aged white Yankee Protestant women may be seen as necessary, resourceful, or admirable by Latin immigrant young men trying to survive and better themselves in the urban slum.

Certain forms of crime and deviance are explained by the practices, even the normal ambitions, of status groups. Daniel Bell (1961) once described "crime as an American way of life," suggesting that successive generations of immigrants have provided, in small numbers, recruits for the rackets. The romanticized notion of organized crime is better understood as a status-group response to poverty and ambition. The infamous Italian Mafia, for example, was neither distinct nor permanent, but an effort by particular members of one status group to achieve wealth and prominence through illicit trades: especially prostitution, bootlegging, gambling.

Proof for this argument comes from the fact that Mafia business was previously run by the Jews and Irish, until success allowed them to move on to more respectable enterprises. As new immigrants, each of these status groups in succession responded to a situation in which their social mobility was impeded along conventional routes, but facilitated in illicit pursuits by urban political machines anxious to attract ethnic bloc support.

> The desires satisfied in extra-legal fashion were more than a hunger for the "forbidden fruits" of conventional morality. They also involved, in the complex and ever shifting structure of group, class, and ethnic stratification, which is the warp and woof of America's "open society," such "normal" goals as independence through a business of one's own, and such "moral" aspirations as the desire for social advancement and social prestige. For crime, in the language

of the sociologists, has a "functional" role in the society, and the urban rackets—the illicit activity organized for continuing profit, rather than individual illegal acts—is one of the queer ladders of social mobility in American life. (Daniel Bell, "Crime as an American Way of Life: A Queer Ladder of Social Mobility," p. 129)

A fair simplification is that new forms of organized crime appear as successive waves of ethnic immigrants are confronted with the norms of material success, restricted opportunities in legitimate enterprise, and shifting opportunity structures for illicit trades (such as the shift from machine politics and a tacit acceptance of gambling and prostitution for certain Italians in the 1930s to widespread recreational drug use today). The hypothesis suggests, moreover, that today's organized crime should assume a new look as Italians join their Irish and Jewish predecessors in respectability and new immigrant groups, such as Latin Americans, come along. This, too, seems consistent with the evidence of a South American connection in drug trafficking—a connection between status and crime that whets the appetite of social-control agencies.

The relationship between status groups and social control agencies is analogous in many ways to the previous revelations about social class. The intricate ways in which status mediates punishment adds symmetry to the general argument, just as it taps some engaging research on criminal sentencing. This is another area in which common sense is easily deceived. For example, conventional wisdom might assume that racial inequality in the United States would punish minority groups more severely than the majority for violations of the same law. Critics of racial justice sometimes ask rhetorically, "Why is a white youth caught stealing sent home with a warning, while a black adult is sent to prison?" There is some truth in the implied answer, but there is also much error. Race affects social control practices including criminal punishment, but it does so in special ways that reflect the social meaning of race.

A sociological classic on prison sentencing done in Texas could scarcely be criticized for choosing a legal system that was soft on blacks. Indeed, Texas juries were unstinting in penalties meted out to black and white convicted felons alike. But they made significant distinctions according to the type of crime involved. Contrary to expectations, Henry Bullock's (1961) research showed that "Juries tended to give Negro prisoners committed for murder [and rape] shorter sentences than they gave whites who were committed for the same offense. They gave Negroes committed for burglary longer sentences than they gave whites committed for this offense." What might explain this pattern? Why were blacks actually treated more leniently in some instances than whites?

The answer was that murder and rape were mainly *intra*racial crimes, burglary an *inter*racial crime. Blacks and whites tend to murder and rape within their own racial groups. Such crimes committed by blacks victimize primarily other blacks and, therefore, were not deemed as serious or deserving of severe punishment as the murder or rape of whites (by other whites). The tendency for juries to be lenient with these black offenders was interpreted as a more fundamental *devaluation* of black people. The relationship was reversed in the case of burglary where typically propertyless blacks steal from whites and draw longer prison sentences than do white burglars. This patent racism, manifested in the devaluation of black victims, has the ironic consequence of lenience for black offenders in some cases.

This provocative finding has impressed the field of race relations as a whole, just as it has been replicated in the study of social control and victimless crimes associated with drugs. Drug-related crimes have the additional advantage of showing how the social definition and perceived threat of drugs change over time, as do the methods of punishment.

For many years, the recreational use of nonprescribed drugs, with the exception of alcohol, was primarily a minority group practice: of blacks, Mexican-Americans, Indians, and such occupational groups as musicians and physicians. Given the status of most of these users, they were treated relatively unambiguously as criminal. In the late 1960s, drug use became more common among white and middle-class youth, provoking something of a crisis in the social definition of drug crime. As more white kids flagrantly committed this crime, agents of social control, faced with the unhappy choice of prosecuting their own children or ignoring their laws, conveniently chose a third course. Drug offenses were redefined in the federal Comprehensive Drug Abuse Prevention and Control Act of 1970, notably with a key distinction between the "real" drug-pusher criminals and the guileless drug-user victims. In short, one-time offenders became officially defined as victims because the status, and intertwined class, backgrounds of the drug-using population changed to coincide more with majority groups in society.

All this created an unusual situation since a fair number of drug users were still minorities and most drug dealers were white. That would suggest a contradiction with earlier patterns of enforcement and punishment that focused on minorities who were the principal users. Nevertheless, an imaginative study by Ruth Peterson and John Hagan (1984) reasoned that the new definition, so urgently arrived at, would primarily dictate enforcement patterns (interacting with racial factors in exceptional cases). This is essentially what they discovered in a study of New York prosecutions. Beginning in the early 1970s, sanctions against drug use declined sharply, while drug dealing became a more severely punished crime—meaning in this case that the majority of white dealers were punished more harshly than before. Black drug-users actually enjoyed dual qualification as victims, of racism (in the liberal climate of the time) and of mercenary dealers, and received the most lenient sentences, followed by white users. The exception to this pattern, however, was the rare black dealer who was punished even more severely than the white dealer on the premise that it was especially contemptible to victimize fellow victims.

The specific point demonstrated in all this work concerns the situationally prescribed social meaning of race; that a

> convincing explanation of differential lenience *and* severity in sentencing is to be found in race-related conceptions of offender-victim relationships, conceptions that are specific to the contexts in which they operate. (Ruth D. Peterson and John Hagan, "Changing Conceptions of Race: Towards an Account of Anomalous Findings of Sentencing Research," p. 57)

Generally, status groups are associated with patterns of the origin and treatment of socially controlled conduct.

SUMMARY

The interplay of status and social control ranges over a much broader field. Social status affects the likelihood, for example, that a person perceived as a troublemaker by his or her associates will be committed to a mental institution, and for how long a period. An absorbing subject of social control research concerns "status offenses" or rule infractions defined by *who* does what: minors who purchase alcoholic beverages or parolees who carry a firearm, for example. Status offenses often arise from social reform movements such as the 19th-century efforts that sought to protect children from criminal careers and adult punishments, although, by creating the special legal status of juvenile delinquent, they also left children assigned to that status without formal procedural guarantees in law. Suffice it to say that these issues have distinctive origins and effects, much like the parallel developments discussed in connection with the links between race and punishment and the changing definition of property crime.

Social class and status affect social control in blatant, subtle, and intricate ways. Separately and in combination they help to determine what actions are defined as criminal or otherwise deviant. These designations change over time; innocent vagrancy or hunting at one time was later punishable by death. And criminal/deviant actions change as a result of emergent class and status interests. Beyond their influence on the definition of *what* is deviant, class and status interests play key roles in determining *how* the deviant is treated; whether corporate criminals are tolerated or drug pushers rapidly become the most dangerous of public enemies, as their clients become victims. Implementing all of these changes and inconsistencies is the state which at one time fronts for class interests and at another—in an era of political crisis, reform, and official career-making— suddenly turns on corrupt practices in politics and business. We are understandably fascinated by the exceptions to common sense, the circumstances in which deer hunting becomes a hanging crime or blacks ironically get lighter sentences. Conversely, we may find tiresome yet another sensational exposé of class privilege in the very machinery designed for social justice. Yet all of these tendencies coexist and join in a pattern that changes, but is far from incomprehensible at any moment. Social control is control by the powerful; but it is also limited, replete with irony, lenient when its subjects are not valued, forgiving when it needs their loyalty, and always susceptible to challenge. Social control, in short, is politics.

PART II
THE LIMITS OF CONTROL

Social control has decided limits. People do not always follow the dictates of power, nor can they be coerced without end. On occasion they withdraw, decline cooperation, resist, rebel, or simply move en masse apart from their leaders and agents of social control. Foremost among the conditions of social order and the limits of social control are what people are willing to obey.

Social control is flouted in rebellion and in passive, nonviolent ways. The latter takes two additional forms that differ in assertiveness: noncompliance and resistance. Let us begin with noncompliance, the circumstance in which laws or expectations promulgated by social control agencies are ignored and subverted.

NONCOMPLIANCE

Instances of noncompliance are commonplace and provide handy ammunition for critics of society's hypocrisy. Standard examples include widespread use of alcohol during Prohibition, perennial gambling and prostitution, recreational drug use, income-tax cheating, abortion when and where it is illegal, evasion of the military draft or registration, and so forth. The accusation of hypocrisy, however, mistakenly assumes that some kind of moral consensus is possible at all and misreads deeper sentiments of value conflict that prompt people not to comply. Noncompliance on a broad scale does not arise from perverseness, but from rational, material, and ethical motives in their own right. Two kinds of noncompliance demonstrate the point: one arising in public opinion or societywide disaffection from the norms of particular social-control agents, and a second originating within the apparatus of social control through conflict and stalemate in official circles. In concrete cases these two overlap, but their distinction is useful for identifying origins of noncompliance.

Occasions of societywide disaffection from the state's agenda are rare but decisive. A splendid example is the way broad public support for the Vietnam War reversed itself, becoming widespread opposition within the calendar year of 1968. In January of 1968, public opinion polls showed that Vietnam hawks, favoring a stepped-up war effort, outnumbered doves, supporting peace negotiations, by two to one (56 percent to 28 percent with 16 percent having no opinion). Within just two months, however, the percentage of hawks fell by 15 points (to 41 percent) and the doves gained about as much (to 42 percent), and that trend continued: by the end of the same year, doves outnumbered hawks by nearly two to one.

Sociologist Howard Schuman (1972) asked, "Why the massive shift? What prompted the public to reverse its stand on such a basic issue in so short a time?" Two facts informed a sensitive interpretation. First, the campus-based antiwar movement had peaked earlier and did not appear to spill over to the general public. Indeed, the public disapproved of the tone and methods of student dissent. Second, the deterioration of support for the war coincided with a major (Tet) offensive of U.S. foes in Vietnam, coming at a time when the administration and military were announcing imminent victory. In short, the public rather abruptly became disenchanted with the war, got sick of hearing about U.S. casualties in an indecisive fight over vague objectives, decided it was a mistake on pragmatic (rather than the students' moral) grounds, and withdrew its support despite the continuing efforts of leaders to rally patriotic zeal.

Vietnam produced a collapse in the moral authority of the state—a temporary and circumscribed collapse, to be sure, but one that is not without precedents and antecedents. Not only did the people desert leaders, social control agencies found themselves without customary power to command and enforce purported deviance. Summons from draft boards went unheeded; prosecutions for draft evasion were contested and discredited. Ultimately the military draft was reformed and an amnesty of sorts offered to evaders. Massive civil disobedience, when it led to arrests, was treated lightly by the courts. The state had exceeded its limits of control and was forced to backtrack.

In less dramatic ways, state power and the limits of social control are continually renegotiated. One reason for this is simply that the times, circumstances, and attitudes change in ways that sap the authority of earlier definitions of deviance. Specific instances have their own causes. Taboos and social control practices surrounding homosexuality, for example, have fallen away rapidly in the last 20 years or so. This, no doubt, has to do with changing sexual mores, an expansionary period for civil rights, and the organized political power of the Gay Liberation Movement.

A second kind of noncompliance originates in conflicts within diverse interests for and agencies of social control. Systems sometimes break down under the sheer weight of competing demands over the definition and enforcement of nonconforming conduct. A lucid example is Pamela Roby's (1969) analysis of what was intended as a straightforward revision of the New York State Criminal Code on prostitution. Proposed reforms unexpectedly brought forth legions of interest groups at each stage of planning and implementation.

Initially, a state commission proposed reforming old laws in a manner that would reduce the penalties for prostitution and, in the interests of equality, make patronizing a prostitute a minor offense also. At public hearings on the proposed reform that followed, the American Social Health Association objected to reduced penalties in the interests of containing venereal disease and police demurred on arresting patrons who were usually their only witnesses against the prostitutes. When the new law was implemented, particularly with police sweeps of New York City centers of action, hotels and businesses complained about harassment of their patrons, police and politicians lauded their own clean-up campaign, the Civil Liberties Union protested over innocent women caught in the dragnet only because of their stylish dress, judges and police quarreled over the politically mandated number of arrests that crowded busy courts and jails, the Legal Aid Society objected to racial and sex bias in prostitute arrests and lax enforcement for patrons, and classy prostitutes remained indifferent since they never worked the streets where enforcement was focused. Negotiation that attempted to accommodate all those interests capable of exerting power at some stage in the process led to stalemate. In the end, the reforms were retained but enforcement lapsed.

The lesson to be drawn from New York's engagement with prostitution is that social control (and law) is a highly politicized process. Theoretical limits to the definition and sanction of deviance are drawn by wide-ranging interests and very practical limits are set by those charged with enforcement in an atmosphere of conflicting pressures. The usual result in such cases of ambiguous moral authority is a deterioration of control. Moreover, what is demonstrated here in a minor instance of vice control, applies broadly to other victimless crimes and controversial policies whether they concern the environment or social welfare.

Noncompliance with the designs of social control, therefore, may originate with the people, as in the Vietnam experience, or with the controllers themselves. These two overlap or converge. Vietnam certainly produced deep splits between Congress and the administration, just as competing social control agencies in New York responded to different organized segments of the public. The distinction is useful, however, for illuminating the diverse sources of noncompliance and, perhaps more important, its ubiquity within the boundaries of relatively conventional social groups.

Resistance

Resistance is another matter, differing from noncompliance in deliberate efforts to escape or repudiate the clutches of social control. I use the terms "escape" and "repudiate" advisedly because resistance, too, comes in many shades of passivity and activity, with the former doubtless more common.

Passive resistance to social control as a group phenomenon generally takes the form of some alternative society—religious communities such as Quakers, farming cooperatives, hippie communes, bohemian villages, and secret societies (from Freemasons to Communist party cells). It is no accident that wartime resistance movements, such as the French in World War II, employ and re-create these types of secret organizations. The underground during Nazi occupation found moral and organizational support in alternative structures such as the radical political parties, secret societies, the church, and the independent peasantry. The same is true with more contemporary underground networks of U.S. political radicals (Weathermen) and humanitarians assisting Central American refugees (sanctuary).

Although alternative societies have a long pedigree, in most historical periods they embrace a minute segment of the population. Judged by such numbers, passive resistance to social control would be rare indeed. Yet there is a much larger buffer zone between alternative and straight societies. Large numbers of relatively conventional people engage in denatured versions of radical nonconformity. David Matza (1961) made this point in a memorable discussion of the "subterranean traditions of youth." Pure forms practiced by extremist minorities include delinquency, radicalism, and bohemianism, but each is paralleled by "conventional versions of these traditions...experienced by broad segments of the youthful population" (p. 105).

> Conventional versions are reasonable facsimiles of subterranean traditions in which their most offensive features are stripped away or tempered...this is not by design, but as a result of emergent syntheses of conventional and rebellious sentiments or as a consequence of the fortuitous existence of independent traditions. A conventional version of the delinquency tradition is what has come to be called teen-age culture....A conventional version of the radical tradition may be found in the long-standing American posture of "doing good." (David Matza, "Subterranean Traditions of Youth," pp. 105 and 116–17)

Matza's point is that youthful resistance to the dominant culture comes in several forms and together they signify much more disaffection than would be indicated by open rebellion alone. Events of the last 20 years seem to confirm and extend the argument. From the late 1960s onward, a counterculture attracted a broad following to the clash between an efficient yet value-barren technocratic society and its growing youthful opposition. Theodore Roszak's (1969) book on *The Making of a Counter Culture* observes that "no analysis seems to make sense of the major political upheavals of the [1960s] decade other than that which pits a militant minority of dissenting youth against the sluggish consensus-and-coalition politics of their middle-class elders" (p. 2). Illuminating as it was, the counterculture beacon began to fade in the mid-1970s with the end of the Vietnam War (and military draft) and of a long wave of economic prosperity. The generational revolt that Roszak expected to peak about 1984 looked very different when the fateful date arrived. Yet the "emergent synthesis of conventional and rebellious traditions" (p. 116) that Matza spoke of continues today in a deeply divided world of youth and adulthood.

The very term "youth" has replaced the transitional notion of adolescence and come to signify a distinct subculture with its own values, troubles, and entertainments. The world of rock, heavy metal, punk, and new-wave music, though tightly controlled by the major recording companies (as subsidiaries of other major broadcasting and entertainment industries), is nevertheless foreign to most of adult society. Problems of discipline in the classroom may stem less from the possibility that today's youth is more incorrigible than usual, than from an increasingly competitive and uncertain occupational future. As the connection between education and available good jobs becomes murky, the instruments of social control once relied upon by the schools lose their potency. If Durkheim was right, and it seems he was, the increasing rate of teenage suicide points to a heightened sense of normlessness that is troubling to many young people.

Finally, resistance to social control takes active forms that go far beyond subcultural alternatives. Protest movements once focused on the Vietnam war, civil rights, and the environment persist, addressing new objectives such as nuclear disarmament and peace in Central America. Anti-abortion forces have grown to a sprawling social movement engaged in actions as diverse as prayer vigils and abortion clinic bombings. Today's technocratic society spawns a new kind of computerized rebellion: break-ins using personal computers to tap the secrets of U.S. defense establishments, research hospitals, and banks. Although innocent in many cases, even careerism in others, some young rebels also recognize the new vulnerability of a society increasingly dependent on information that can be freely appropriated. A one-time political activist turned software engineer explained to *The Wall Street Journal* (October 1, 1983):

> Information is becoming our most valuable commodity, and yet electronic information is being housed in a technology that makes free dispersal of it very easy. So while the establishment is pouring millions into perfecting its computer technology, it is undermining its centralizing power. I hope the establishment realizes it is being revolutionized.

Just as outlaws once enjoyed public sympathy for robbing the rate-gouging railroads or mortgage-foreclosing banks, certain indisputable crimes against powerful institutions are considered just or clever today. Donald Black (1983) draws an even broader lesson from the past: "Much of the conduct classified as crime in modern societies such as the United States is similar to...traditional modes of social control and may properly be understood as self-help" (p. 34). Black has in mind a set of defensive and rebellious acts intended to redress wrongs: robbery as a form of debt collection, assault in self-defense, homicide in response to adultery or seduction into drug addiction, vandalism (spray painting) as protest, looting as retribution for merchant exploitation, and so forth. Whatever the consensus on whether these acts are justified, a good deal of nonpredatory crime is at least intended to right wrongs. It is social control in Black's view, or certainly social control from below. In many instances, it is also active resistance to institutions that monopolize legitimate social control.

In summary, noncompliance and resistance to social control are far more extensive than normally appreciated. They appear in unexpected forms: behind common instances of public opinion about war, in lax law enforcement, youth disaffection, and a variety of justifiable or mitigated crimes. Whatever we may think about these actions, their considerable analytic importance lies in demonstrating real limits on the scope of official social control. Viewed in this light, the degree of legal and moral conformity (or value integration) in society is far less than conventional social theories claim.

Finally, noncompliance and resistance are based on more than public opinion, conflicting social control agencies, and subcultural disaffection, or any other set of restraints on social control. The limits of social control are a matter of more than imperfect coverage or incomplete value integration. There is also a positive right to dissent; a cultural and political basis precisely for questioning the legitimate limits and the moral authority of social control and its official agents. The right to dispute social control is also a value.

In 1849, Henry David Thoreau (1960) wrote,

> I think that we should be men first, and subjects afterward. It is not desirable to cultivate a respect for the law, so much as for the right. The only obligation which I have a right to assume, is to do at any time what I think is right.... How does it become a man to behave toward this American government to-day? I answer that he cannot without disgrace be associated with it. I cannot for an instant recognize that political organization as *my* government which is the

slave's government also. (Henry David Thoreau, *On the Duty of Civil Disobedience,* pp. 223–224)

Thoreau's essay later became a basic text for Gandhi's anticolonial struggle in India as well as for the civil rights and antiwar movements in the United States of the 1960s. It inspired people to claim a right that superseded the existing premises of social control. In that sense, of course, Thoreau and other writers succeed by articulating deeper cultural values.

Yet the connection between moral acts of civil disobedience and social movements of resistance is complex. Resistance movements have broader and more pragmatic causes, and may even embrace sentiments hostile to the lofty principles of civil disobedience. Thoreau's objections to slavery were not among the social forces leading to a civil war that freed the slaves. Civil disobedience helps spark rebellions and provides them with important symbols. Whether they catch fire or how hot they get depends on the social kindling. That is the final consideration.

RIGHTS AND REBELLION

Rebellions are organized, sustained, and violent struggles by groups who refuse to continue living under their present conditions. The discussion that follows uses rebellion and revolt interchangeably. Organization, persistence, and a clear purpose distinguish rebellions from riots, which are usually short and spontaneous. Unlike protests that are typically nonviolent and brief, rebellions are sustained and usually result in violent conflict, even when that is not part of the plan—for example, as a result of official retaliation. Revolutions include the characteristics of rebellion, but involve further an attempt to take state power. Rebellions, by contrast, may be local affairs and usually aspire only to the restoration of better times once known.

Rebellion issues from ordinary forms of dissent rather than from rare and monumental causes or sudden traumatic changes. The causes of rebellion lie in normal group politics. More precisely, they arise in conflicts between aggrieved groups and social control agencies that become irreconcilable within routine politics. Indeed, rebellions usually begin when dominant groups and their social control agencies—their guards, police, or armies—take some coercive action against dissident groups in an effort to finally solve a problem or transform a situation troublesome to the dominant groups themselves. Contrary to conventional thinking, rebellions seldom originate with intrepid rebels who decide to take on the established order or to make a revolution. Insurgents get such ideas only when concrete exploitative conditions in some sense force them to do battle. Nobody starts a rebellion for the romance of it all, or even to create a just society as opposed to eliminating onerous injustices.

This interpretation of rebellion is drawn from a variety of sociological studies devoted to protest movements, strikes, riots, revolutions, and, generally, to the subject of collective violence. It comes also from attempts to test popular theories about when and why social groups rebel. Some of those are based on common sense. Simplifying somewhat, these theories may be divided into three categories claiming, respectively, that rebellion is caused by: (1) the common sense of *immiseration,* the idea that desperation and rebelliousness grow apace of misery and, particularly, economic hardship; (2) the counterintuitive hypothesis of *relative deprivation,* or rising expectations; and (3) the recent synthesis of *moral and political economy* characterized in the preceding paragraph.

Immiseration or hardship interpretations are based on the seemingly obvious proposition that rebelliousness is directly correlated with mounting inequalities. People endure exploitation up to a point at which they can't take it anymore. Rebellion occurs when conditions become so bad that starvation, slavery, a way of life, or life itself is in the balance. The best that can be said about this idea is that it receives little factual support. The worst of times are often the most socially quiescent.

Second, and conversely, relative deprivation reasons that rebellion occurs when formerly miserable conditions are improving. Alexis de Tocqueville studied life under the old regime overthrown by the French Revolution and concluded that "the French found their position the more intolerable the better it became" (quoted in Davies, p. 6). The plausible idea here was that as bad conditions improve people acquire both a sense of what they have suffered and a hope that all suffering may be eliminated. Marx advanced a similar, if grimmer, prediction that the revolution will come with the "relative immiseration" of the working class—not necessarily a growing absolute poverty, but a declining share in the total wealth of society, even though that wealth may be increasing. Growing inequality would attack the higher classes, reduce many to the ranks of workers, and spread a revolutionary to the majority.

The ideas of de Tocqueville and Marx have been reformulated to fit a variety of modern forms of social protest according to the theory of relative deprivation or of rising expectations. People rebel, according to one exponent of this idea, James Davies (1962), when an intolerable gap appears between what they want and what they get: "when a prolonged period of objective economic and social development is followed by a short period of sharp reversal. People then subjectively fear that ground gained with great effort will be quite lost; their mood becomes revolutionary (p. 5)." Although, once more, the idea is intuitively appealing, it receives little research support.

The third view, itself containing several variants, is broader and more historical. It rejects the simple idea that revolt and collective violence can be explained solely or even principally by material conditions. Causes must be sought in the moral order that justifies rebellion and in the political order where protesting groups and the state interact. Protest and rebellion require the interaction of at least these two parties, each with its own motives for pursuing the conflict. David Snyder and Charles Tilly (1972), for example, find no historical connection between economic hardship and social protest. Collective violence does correlate, however, with major periods of political activity including occasions of governmental repression. Economic conditions clearly play a contributing part in rebellion, along with the structures of class and status in which they are embedded. Particularly, economic conditions mobilize groups when an alternative to hardship appears. But alone they are insufficient to explain when and how protest makes its appearance. The most promising alternatives lie in the analysis of struggles for power. To say the same thing in another way, rebellion arises in struggles over social control and represents the extreme at which conflicting values defy coexistence or negotiated compromise. At bottom, rebellions are always about claims of injustice, sharply opposing values, and political tactics—about the moral and political economy.

Some examples help clarify these points in two ways. They allow, first, an evaluation of the theories presented. Second, they make the thematic point of this discussion by showing how rebellion occurs, under specifiable conditions, as an extreme recourse for solving endemic conflicts over social control. In that sense, rebellion does not differ from noncompliance and resistance because of the issues that prompt it, but in the circumstances that prevent a simpler solution. To provide some scope for this interpretation, the following illustrations are chosen from such diverse settings as the total institution, community, and society.

Rebellion in the Institution and Community

The sociological laboratory is a useful tool for analyzing elementary relationships such as that between rebellion and social control. We may examine, for example, a setting in which social control seems so complete that revolt is impossible. If, despite all odds, rebellion does occur in that place, it probably reveals something quite essential. This is the elegant point of Gresham Sykes's (1965) book *The Society of Captives*, which argues that even in the most formidable institution of social control, the maximum-security prison, ruling groups do not enjoy total power or servile subjects.

Prisons have this in common with any society: they must maintain order and get work done, if only to complete peacefully their daily routines. To the extent that prisoners can withdraw their cooperation by refusing to work or to act peacefully, they have some power, since their custodians' success depends on their compliance. This implies that the prison must provide inmates with certain incentives to cooperate; what Sykes calls the institutional reward system: freedom from close supervision, immorality, a blind eye to such practices as the contraband trade in narcotics, gambling, and home-brewing. It is mainly by manipulating these small privileges, rather than by force, that the power of custodial rulers is peacefully maintained.

The only hitch in this delicate balance of power is that it relies on corruption from the standpoint of strict prison management—the official rules that are bent precisely to give bargaining power to the rulers and the ruled. The prison runs smoothly only by creating incentives for cooperation based on *negotiated rules,* including clear violations of official rules. Sykes insightfully labels this fact the "defects of total power" (p. 40ff). Thus, the New Jersey State Prison functioned, corrupt but peacefully efficient, until reformers came along intent on restoring the system to sound management. The result was a destructive prison riot which had all of the characteristics of rebellion—that is, duration, organization, and purpose. The rebellion, following reforms aimed at eliminating corruption, revealed

> a basic paradox: The system breeds rebellions by attempting to enforce the system's rules.... The effort of the custodians to "tighten up" the prison undermines the cohesive forces at work in the inmate population and it is these forces which play a critical part in keeping the society of the prison on an even keel. (Gresham M. Sykes, *The Society of Captives: A Study of a Maximum Security Prison,* p. 124)

To place this interpretation in a broader context, the prisoners did not rebel because they were put away and suffered the pains of imprisonment. Instead, from necessity, they developed a social order and a culture for managing their unhappy plight. They *did* rebel when their means for coping with life were threatened, when the "rights" they had struggled to secure were purloined. They rebelled because the moral economy was upset. Conversely, the "technology of state power"—of which Michel Foucault (1979) makes so much in the precise case of the prison—has its defects, its material and cultural limits beyond which control crumbles into revolt. Social control and rebellion exist in interaction, the potential, nature, and limits of each defining the other.

What is true of social order and the roots of rebellion in prison applies as well to communities and societies. Another modern sociological classic dealing with this question is Liston Pope's (1942) study of *Millhands and Preachers.* Here in the North Carolina town of Gastonia, a textile manufacturing center developed in the late 19th century in an industrious, God-fearing, and notably paternalistic setting, workers came out of the southern mountains to take places in the factories, mill-sympathizing churches, and company-provided houses, acquiring in the transition an appreciation for drudgery in their jobs and patrons' favors. "Up to 1929 the political and moral rights of the manufacturer to dominate the entire community had hardly been questioned" (p. 214). Yet on April 1, 1929, a bitter, "communist-led strike" erupted that shattered the moral order of the industrial community.

> Gastonia was catapulted from obscurity into headlines around the world. In rapid succession metropolitan newspapers told their readers of a communist uprising in the little textile town, of mass parades and the use of troops, of mob scenes and the destruction of life and property. Outbreaks of violence flared for several weeks, culminating in the death of the chief of police and the wounding of several of his officers in an armed skirmish with communists and strikers. Scores of arrests followed, and two dramatic trials focused the spotlight of publicity on a tense courtroom for additional weeks. At last seven men were convicted of murder and sentenced to prison, only to escape their sentences by flight to Russia. (Liston Pope, *Millhands and Preachers: A Study of Gastonia*, p. 3)

What happened? Pope reviews the standard explanations such as low wages and worker grievances, industrial competition, and outside agitators, but finds none of those satisfactory. What had been happening in Gastonia over a period of years was a reorganization of the community amounting to a social and cultural crisis. As prosperity in the textile industry began to decline after World War I, the companies looked for ways to reduce labor costs. Wages were cut. A stretch-out system of mechanization was adopted in the mills requiring workers to operate several machines at once and deliver more labor for less pay than previously. Lower wages, however, did not incite the strike "nor was the fact of a stretch-out of supreme importance" (p. 231). Rather, the arbitrary and impersonal methods of management were a basic cause, particularly as cost-cutting methods unwittingly attacked the tissue of community order.

Industry's social-welfare paternalism was changed from a system designed to promote loyalty to one preoccupied with labor discipline. "Established residents of the community and leading church members were dismissed under the stretch-out...and their places were taken by cheaper workers from outside" (p. 232). A community integrated around traditional factory methods and their reflection in a company town was converted to an agglomeration of individuals to whom the appeals of militant unionism made more sense as a substitute.

The deeper causes of strife were not simply economic but cultural in a broader sense. Alien methods of industrial relations had been introduced into an industrial situation which had come to depend, for unity and peace, on paternal relations, and to expect emphasis on community welfare rather than on productive efficiency alone. (Liston Pope, *Millhands and Preachers: A Study of Gastonia*, pp. 232–33)

National Rebellions

These insights about rebellion gleaned from total institutions and communities may be generalized to societies in a manner that brings together many of the themes developed in previous chapters. Riots, protests, and protracted rebellions have recently occurred in developing countries in response to austerity policies of international agencies, particularly the International Monetary Fund (IMF). These uprisings resemble in a general fashion the response of New Jersey State Prison inmates and Gastonia workers to reform measures that undermine methods of survival. Recently in Brazil, the Dominican Republic, Peru, the Philippines and a dozen other countries, social protests have occurred which the press calls "IMF riots." The IMF has required debt-ridden countries to reform their economies (and pay back the international banks) through policies that visit new hardships on the poor and, especially, the urban working class. For example, government subsidies of basic foods and petroleum have been ordered cut, wages must be held constant in the fight against inflation, government social-welfare spending should be reduced. Poverty and inequality are not new to these countries and urban workers do not riot under those ordinary hardships. The recent violent protests, killing 60 in the Dominican Republic for example, were prompted by the workers' belief that their rights to wage increases consistent with inflation and sufficient to sustain basic necessities were violated.

Revolutionary movements in the Third World arise in conditions of economic underdevelopment and social inequality: commercial agriculture that dispossesses peasants, urban migration to an overcrowded service economy, multinational exploitation of labor, and growing unemployment. Yet, again, these conditions provide the backdrop to revolutionary movements that spring more immediately from social dislocations, cultural judgments of injustice, and political depredations. The social revolution in El Salvador began in 1980 when the U.S. government and local elites instituted a series of reform measures in the agricultural and export economy. The reforms were designed to avoid "another Nicaragua" in this neighboring country. The effect of the reforms, however, was to impoverish more peasants and antagonize the right-wing coffee planters and industrialists. Moderate politicians were driven out of a coalition government, by the army and its death squads, and into a revolutionary movement. The rebels never started out to make a revolution but, on the contrary, pursued legitimate methods for achieving equality that aroused official violence.

In summary, rebellion is not the opposite of social order, not the world of social control turned upside down. Rather, it is an essential feature of the negotiated social order; a last-ditch response or defensively militant effort by exploited groups to change burdensome systems of social control. Rebellion, therefore, is a desperate extension of more common forms of noncompliance and resistance. The several theories that endeavor to explain it capture parts of the complex pattern of causation. Hardship is important in the sense of identifying objective conditions, and relative deprivation makes it clear that group perceptions of those conditions and their alternatives are keys to mobilization. A complete explanation, however, depends on understanding aggrieved groups and social-control agencies as they interact politically over conflicting moral claims. Rebellion and dissent are mistakenly considered rare. They lurk in the moral order, popular culture, and sundry forms of deviance. They limit the reach of social control and periodically make a fight over what some people believe is rightfully theirs.

CONCLUSION

Repeatedly in these pages, we have encountered protest movements that challenge the prevailing tenets of social control: urban riots aimed at police, merchants, and unemployment; farmworkers marching for unionism under the galvanizing symbols of ethnicity and religion; blacks and women organizing around the rightful claims of those relegated to the lower ranks of employment; populists who saw their rural way of life torn away by government-supported agribusiness; young people who read Thoreau and resisted going to an ill-conceived war, and older people who mourned for many of their children who did go.

In all of these cases, the agencies of social control did two things. First, they urged that people stay in their place: women in the home, blacks in the lower and unemployed ranks of labor, Mexicans in the fields, students in the classroom and the draft pool. Second, they labeled as deviant those people who challenged the established order: women's libbers, black revolutionaries, hippies—labels designed to belittle dissidents and presume a silliness or malevolence in their motives. In these familiar examples, it is the tenets of social control that look silly or mean-spirited today. Yet there are countless other instances of social control where the rebels fail or where few would doubt the legitimacy of social prohibitions and the depravity of their violators (for example, agrarian radicals, welfare and convict rights advocates, predatory criminals, traitors).

Two points emphasized in this discussion help explain the difference. First, deviance is always arbitrary in the specific sense that it relies on group support and conforms to changing social definitions. What may be understood today as legitimate dissent or tragic illness was often, even recently, considered heinous perversion (criminal insanity or pacificism in World War I). Some of today's depravities are doubtless headed for reappraisal with advances in medical and political knowledge. Second, the process in which those definitions are maintained or altered is in the broadest sense a political struggle. Neither of these statements implies moral relativism or the notion that, because it changes, the moral order is frivolous. On the contrary, because it is socially determined and changes with emergent needs, the moral order mediates our social and material existence.

These observations summarize the interplay of social control and dissent: the social consensus and struggle over tolerable conduct. But there is a more profound lesson in the conflict over social control. Laws, courts, agencies, and the instruments of control generally are designed to protect the state and the social order of class and status upon which the state rests. Yet the same instruments that support this order are available to and used by disadvantaged groups to defend their beleaguered rights. The so-called tools of the establishment are sometimes converted to undoing or transforming the social order. The civil rights movement used the streets, the vulnerabilities of political parties, and the courts. Social change happens dialectically or, more simply, through the tendency for one day's orderly solutions to be followed by the next day's changes that contradict or undermine earlier intents while serving new ones. The comfortable racism of one era, for example, becomes the political albatross and moral energizer of another. It is for this reason that social change moves fitfully in unexpected directions. E.P. Thompson's (1975) study of the Black Act concludes with an observation about law and class power that applies as well to social control and the interests of class, status, and the state. Thompson says it is not true that "law equals class power," but

> On the one hand it is true that the law did mediate existent class relations to the advantage of the rulers....On the other hand, the law mediated these class relations through legal forms that imposed, again and again, inhibitions upon the actions of the rulers...in certain limited areas, the law itself [becomes] a genuine forum within which certain kinds of class conflict were fought out. (E.P. Thompson, *Whigs and Hunters: The Origin of the Black Act*, p. 264)

If the conclusion is not simple, neither is it mysterious. Social control is power; not total power but a fair assembly of society's dominant class and status-group interests. At the same time, control is always limited: by noncompliance, resistance, rebellion, and, ultimately, by the cultural values that support them. Sometimes social control coerces with force, and, on rarer occasions, it collapses under rebellious siege or sheer desertion of the faithful. More often it tolerates and negotiates within rule-governed limits. In that case, the rules shift from authoritative dos and don'ts to strategies for struggle and change. Recognizing, finally, that all of these things may go on simultaneously across interrelated arenas of social control—where gains in civil rights may synergize antiwar efforts and both regird the defense of class privilege—we appreciate the complexity of social change but also see clearly its locus.

At bottom, therefore, societies are neither integrated nor especially orderly—except, perhaps, in their persistent struggles that transform the prevailing order, such as it is, to someone's advantage. Societies are forever changing and it is within the conflicts over the direction of change that societies reveal their structure.

SELECTED BIBLIOGRAPHY

BECKER, HOWARD S. (1975). *Outsiders: Studies in the Sociology of Deviance*. New York: Free Press.

BELL, DANIEL (1961). "Crime as an American Way of Life." In *The End of Ideology: On the Exhaustion of Political Ideas in the Fifties* (pp. 127–150). New York: Collier Books.

BLACK, DONALD (1983, February). "Crime as Social Control." *American Sociological Review, 48,* 34–45.

BLUMER, HERBERT (1962). "Society as Symbolic Interaction." In ARNOLD M. ROSE (Ed.). *Human Behavior and Social Processes: An Interactionist Approach* (pp. 179–192). Boston: Houghton Mifflin.

BULLOCK, HENRY ALLEN (1961, November-December). "Significance of the Racial Factor in the Length of Prison Sentences." *The Journal of Criminal Law, Criminology, and Police Science, 52,* 411–417.

CAUTE, DAVID (1978). *The Great Fear: The Anti-Communist Purge Under Truman and Eisenhower*. New York: Simon & Schuster.

CHAMBLISS, WILLIAM J. (1964, Summer). "A Sociological Analysis of the Law of Vagrancy." *Social Problems, 12,* 67–77.

CLINARD, MARSHALL B. & YEAGER, PETER C. (1978, August). "Corporate Crime." *Criminology, 16,* 255–272.

DAVIES, JAMES C. (1962, February). "Toward a Theory of Revolution." *American Sociological Review, 6,* 5–19.

ERIKSON, KAI T. (1966). *Wayward Puritans: A Study in the Sociology of Deviance*. New York: John Wiley & Sons.

FOUCAULT, MICHEL (1979). *Discipline and Punishment: The Birth of the Prison*. New York: Vintage Books.

HAY, DOUGLAS (1975). "Property, Authority and Criminal Law." In HAY, et al., *Albion's Fatal Tree: Crime and Society in Eighteenth-Century England* (pp. 17–63). London: Allen Lane.

KATZ, JACK (1979, Winter). "Legality and Equality: Plea Bargaining in the Prosecution of White-Collar Crime and Common Crimes." *Law and Society Review, 13,* 431–459.

——— (1980). "The Social Movement Against White-Collar Crime." In EGON BITTNER & SHELDON MESSINGER (Eds.), *Criminology Review Yearbook* (pp. 161–184). Beverly Hills, CA: Sage Publications.

KITSUSE, JOHN I. (1962, Winter). "Societal Reaction to Deviant Behavior: Problems of Theory and Method." *Social Problems, 9,* 247–256.

LEMERT, EDWIN (1967). *Human Deviance, Social Problems, and Social Control.* Englewood Cliffs, NJ: Prentice-Hall.

MATZA, DAVID (1961, November). "Subterranean Traditions of Youth." *The Annals, 338,* 102–118.

PETERSON, RUTH D. & HAGAN, JOHN (1984, February). "Changing Concepts of Race: Towards an Account of Anomalous Findings of Sentencing Research." *American Sociological Review, 49,* 56–70.

POPE, LISTON (1942). *Millhands and Preachers: A Study of Gastonia.* New Haven, CN: Yale University Press.

ROBY, PAMELA A. (1969, Summer). "Politics and Criminal Law: Revision of the New York State Penal Law on Prostitution." *Social Problems, 17,* 83–109.

ROSZAK, THEODORE (1969). *The Making of a Counter Culture: Reflections on the Technocratic Society and Its Youthful Opposition.* Garden City, NY: Anchor Books.

SCHUMAN, HOWARD (1972, November). "Two Sources of Antiwar Sentiment in America." *American Journal of Sociology, 78,* 513–536.

SNIDER, LAUREEN (1982). "Traditional and Corporate Theft: A Comparison of Sanctions." In PETER WICKMAN & TIMOTHY DAILEY (Eds.), *White-Collar and Economic Crime* (pp. 235–258). Lexington, MA: D.C. Heath.

SNYDER, DAVID & TILLY, CHARLES (1972, October). "Hardship and Collective Violence in France: 1830 to 1960." *American Sociological Review, 37,* 520–532.

SUTHERLAND, EDWIN H. (1940, February). "White Collar Criminality." *American Sociological Review, 5,* 1–12.

—— (1945, April). "Is 'White-Collar Crime' Crime?" *American Sociological Review, 10,* 132–39.

—— (1956). "Crime of Corporations." In GILBERT GEIS, *White-Collar Criminal: The Offender in Business and the Professions* (pp. 57–70). New York: Atherton Press, 1968.

SYKES, GRESHAM (1965). *The Society of Captives: A Study of a Maximum Security Prison.* New York: Atheneum Publishers.

THOMPSON, E.P. (1975). *Whigs and Hunters: The Origin of the Black Act.* New York: Pantheon Books.

THOREAU, HENRY DAVID (1960). *On the Duty of Civil Disobedience.* New York: Signet Classics. (Originally published in 1849.)

TOCQUEVILLE, ALEXIS DE (1888). *On the State of Society in France Before the Revolution of 1789.* London: John Murray.

Epilogue

Sociology is a complex craft. But so is social life, not to mention any craft that we come to know well. In this book, I have tried to clarify, but not to minimize, these complexities since they merit appreciation, reflect human inventiveness, and reveal some of what was once mysterious. We still do not know what we need, much less all that we want to know. We know even less about how to put to good use what we do know. But we know a lot and have come a long way from the cocksure common sense that Lazarsfeld was moved to rebut in defense of sociology just 40 years ago. Most important, we know better how to find out what we want to know, how to formulate why questions in ways that yield useful and theoretically critical answers.

Whether our aim is to practice or simply to appreciate the sociological craft, its classical tradition is still the best starting place. Today's social issues reenact the past in certain essentials. The questions that Marx posed about the fate of the working class and Weber's vision of status-group insurgency are as vital as ever—perhaps more so in our age of disappearing industrial jobs and politically organized minorities, women, and religious groups. Sometimes the classical answers, such as Durkheim's analysis of social regulation and suicide, are still the best we have. At other times, better answers are produced by evaluating classical formulations and learning for the first time that class and status, for example, interpenetrate and reinforce one another in unforeseen ways. The present profitably reworks experience.

We do not have to be Marxists or Weberians in order to come better equipped to today's problems. For those concerned with history and social inequality, "Marx is on our side; we are not on the side of Marx" (E.P. Thompson, 1975, p. 192).

The classical tradition, however, shades imperceptibly into a second, third, and fourth generation of modern sociological research classics. Some sociology is extraordinarily good reading: C. Wright Mills's distillation of the meaning of *White Collar* life, Liston Pope's empathetic account of the disrupted world of *Millhands and Preachers*, Herbert Gans's sensible description of *The Urban Villagers*, and so many more that inform this narrative.

Critical work goes on in the sense of research and writing that frankly explores the radical roots of social problems, whether those lie in capitalism, religion, the welfare state, or the political system. Critical sociology is also constructive sociology by virtue of its premise that people make their own history and may make it better by understanding the consequences of social choices. It connects biography and history in ways that begin to make clear what the choices are.

Since the 1960s, sociology has experienced a renaissance that is only now coming together in a reformation. The discipline has shed some of what Mills called its "grand theory," although "abstract empiricism" persists. Sociology is less parochial, more crafty. Major concepts such as class and status have departed anecdotal usage in favor of rigorous interpretive application. The role of the state has assumed its appropriate (and classical) position in social analyses. It is now clear that the world political economy affects the domestic affairs of all countries.

If the foregoing are mainly, and appropriately, intellectual accomplishments, sociology also affects public life. Although social research seldom pleases its subjects, for good and bad reasons, its central virtue is that it is a public discourse and method. If it sometimes serves special interests, and it does, sociology is still relatively open to informed criticism and better argument. Among social sciences that are increasingly captured by or written for technical experts, sociology remains a forum for examining where we are headed as a people—it is a public science and a publicly accessible means for achieving an open society. In that sense, sociology is part of our struggles and a right worth respecting.

Index

About the Author

John Walton is Professor and Head of the Department of Sociology at the University of California, Davis. For a number of years he was Professor of Sociology and Urban Affairs at Northwestern University before moving to his current post. He has served the International Sociological Association as a member of its Research Council and Director of one of its research committees and has been a visiting professor at universities in Latin America and England. His books include *Elites and Economic Development* (1977), *Labor, Class, and the International System* (1981 with Alejandro Portes), and *Reluctant Rebels: Comparative Studies of Revolution and Underdevelopment* (1984). *Reluctant Rebels* won Honorable Mention for the 1985 C. Wright Mills Award given by the Society for the Study of Social Problems and was described by the *American Historical Review* as "comparative history at its finest." In 1984 he reported on the civil war in El Salvador as a Special Correspondent for the *Sacramento Bee*.

A Note on the Type

The text of this book was set in 10/12 Baskerville using a photo-composition version of the face designed by the Englishman John Baskerville in 1757. Displaying a pronounced contrast between thicks and thins, it has more refined, bracketed serifs and a stronger vertical stress than the Old Style faces that preceded it. It is one of the forerunners of the Modern group of faces. Baskerville is a readable and beautifully proportioned typeface.

Composed by Publication Services, Champaign, Illinois.

Printed and bound by Malloy Lithographing, Inc., Ann Arbor, Michigan.